DAFFODIL

Eileen Veronica Richmond

authorHOUSE®

AuthorHouse™ UK
1663 Liberty Drive
Bloomington, IN 47403 USA
www.authorhouse.co.uk
Phone: 0800.197.4150

© 2015 Eileen Veronica Richmond. All rights reserved.

No part of this book may be reproduced, stored in a retrieval system, or transmitted by any means without the written permission of the author.

Published by AuthorHouse 02/26/2015

ISBN: 978-1-5049-3643-9 (sc)
ISBN: 978-1-5049-3644-6 (hc)
ISBN: 978-1-5049-3645-3 (e)

Print information available on the last page.

Any people depicted in stock imagery provided by Thinkstock are models, and such images are being used for illustrative purposes only.
Certain stock imagery © Thinkstock.

This book is printed on acid-free paper.

Because of the dynamic nature of the Internet, any web addresses or links contained in this book may have changed since publication and may no longer be valid. The views expressed in this work are solely those of the author and do not necessarily reflect the views of the publisher, and the publisher hereby disclaims any responsibility for them.

Contents

Message To The Reader xi
Dedication xiii
Acknowledgements xv

Daffodil 1
Shirley Mac'laine 13
Cheltham Races 15
Childhood 20
My Father 23
My Mother 26
Adoption 28
Saturdays 30
Bernard Badger 32
Early Recall 35
Memories 37
Angels 41
School 46
More Memories 49
The Early Days 51
Anita 58
Ibiza 61
Harry Edwards 71
The Crux 74
Despair 79
Alan Bellinger 82
Joyce Bellinger 85
Princess Dianne 87
Jill Dando 89

Decision	90
Ken	94
Rock Bottom	96
Stephen Turoff	105
Paul Parker	110
My Little Red Car	113
Tony	115
Forget-me-nots	118
Joan	120
Meditation	127
The Seven Chakra Colours	130
Katie	134
The Ones Who Have Passed Over	138
Mary	139
Past Life	144
Past Lives	147
Birth	153
Christopher	157
Eternal Life	159
Bessie	161
Harry	165
Mind over Matter	170
Molly	178
Questions Asked	192
Disasters	196
Karma and Rebirth	200
Peggy	207
Angel in Blue Jeans	210
Julia Winfield	214
Red Meat	220
Religion	222
Timing	225
Schizophrenia	227
Precious Lives	232
If Life Is a Game,	237
Holiday	238
Never Give Up	242
Martin Luther King Jr	244

The Akashic Records	248
Past Life	251
More Past Lives	255
Answered Prayer	258
Finding Dianne	260
Jade Goody	262
Near-Death Experience	264
What Happens at the Point of Death?	269
Miracles	273
The Right Time	275
Angel Poem	278
Live in the Moment	281
Harry	283
How to Become a Healer	286
The Pendulum / Dowser	290
More about the Angels	293
Christmas Day	296
My Peggy	300
Bram	304
Plants	307
Knowing	310
Miracles	311
Joanne	314
Finding God	316
The Beginning	318
Second Version	321
The Planet	326
Cross Breeding	331
A New Beginning	332
We Can All Take Part	336
Marlene	340
To Make It Clear	342
The Original Ten Commitments	344
God Space	347
Changes	349
Family	354
Vanity	356
William Roache	358

A Visitor	361
Revelation	363
Useful Knowledge	366
The Adrenal Glands	371
The Interview with God	373
Friends	375
Past Life	379
Drugs and Alcohol	384
The Saviours	386
Jealousy	388
Fear	392
Forgiveness	394
Love	396
Happiness	398
Racism	400
The Titanic	402
In the Early Hours	405
Tina Nash	408
19 May 2012	412
23rd June 2012	426
Important Synopsis	431
Evil	440
Euthanasia	441
Casey Watson	444
The London	446
Full Circle	448
April Jones	455
Jimmy Savile	457
Angel Message	460
Slaughter of the Innocent	471
The Beatles	473
Threat to Our World	475
More Past Lives	479
The Secret	485
Past Life	493
Beryl Bressinger	500
Eileen Cooper	503
Christine	506

The Change	509
Refined White Sugar	511
Cake Recipe	517
Diets	520
Microwave Ovens	523
Heat Wave	525
Inhumane	528
Herbs versus Medication	531
Sir Bob Geldof	536
Malala Yousafzi	538
Nelson Mandela	541
The Syrian Conflict	543
The Trauma of Life	546
Devastation	548
Shame	558
More Animal Slaughter	560
Amanda Holden	563
Barbara Thompson	565
Letter to Barbara	567
Past Memory	576
Heidi Baker	578
Stephen Sutton	582
Introducing the Violet Flame	583
Results	588
June 2014	589
God Help Us	593
My Payer Each Night	597
Come, Little Children	599
Afterword	603
Recommended Books	605

Message To The Reader

Thank you for choosing my book; albeit, you were meant to read it.

This is the first book I have written, and it will probably be my last.

When I started to write the book in 2006, I didn't know where it was going to lead me. I am a complete novice.

Not only have I written the book, but I have created my own editing and my own proof reading, grammar etc.

I ask you the reader to take into consideration what a hard challenge this has been for me.

As you begin reading through the book you may find some of its content repetitive at times. However, this was the only way I knew how to inform the reader of its great importance and understanding - that I pass the messages on.

Also they may be a few text errors along the way.

I ask for your patience and understanding.

I hope you enjoy my book; and that you find it not only helpful, but inspiring too.

Yours truly.

Eileen Veronica Richmond.

Dedication

I wish to dedicate this book to Alan Bellinger, for all the hard work he has achieved in his lifetime. He was eighty-four in 1997, when I first met him. He spent a lifetime dedicated to helping and healing others for little reward. I feel honored and privileged to have known this man – my guide, my teacher.

To my wonderful and caring husband, Harry, my rock.
To my four wonderful sons, Wayne, Darren, Richard, and Michael, who have brought such love and joy into my life.
To the magnificent seven, my wonderful grandchildren: Jason, Christopher, Jordan, Ryan, Kieran, Emily, and Katie.
To Joanne, my dear daughter-in-law. To Joan, who no longer is; may we always remain friends.
To Maria, my future daughter-in-law. And to Joanne 2, Wayne's new partner, whom I have come to know and love.

For Barbara Thompson and Wendy Early, my true friends, who at times saved my sanity over the years.

To Dr Winfield and Mr Getty, who worked for the Royal Hallamshire Hospital in Sheffield. They both did their best, and now they are retired.

To the spirit world.

To my guides and angels for their wisdom and guidance. To my mother and father in heaven. To my grandmother Elizabeth Molloy, whom I never knew but who has protected me throughout my life. Also to my grandfather Edward Molloy, whom I idolized.

Before I decided to write this book, I could never make my mind up about whether God existed. I was brought up in a strict Catholic family. Although I believed in the angels, I also believed in Jesus of Nazareth at that time. I thought Jesus was the greatest medium, psychic, prophet, and visionary But **God I wasn't sure about?**

Acknowledgements

To Alan Bellinger. Without him, they may never have been a book.
To Richard, my son, for all his hard work and patience in helping me with my computer problems.

To all the wonderful people I've met along the way: Barbara Thompson, my best friend; Julia Winfield; Paul Parker; both mediums; Stephen Toroff; Wendy Early; and Marlene Thewlis. Sandra & Martin our new neighbors.

Many thanks to all the authors of all the books that I have read, which have guided me and prepared me for my spiritual journey

We are each on a journey through life.
But what many of us don't contemplate is.
That while the journey may end for the body.
Our soul endures through birth, life death
And beyond in an endless cycle.

The Buddha.

Daffodil

In 1983 my father suffered a stroke. The last time I had seen my father, I had gone to collect my mother for the annual Christmas dinner. I remember that I'd wished I'd brought Dad a few cans of beer and some chocolates. Dad was sixty-nine. He was taken to the Northern General Hospital in Sheffield after suffering a stroke. I went along to see him in the hospital along with my husband, Harry, and my mother.

I noticed my father was very agitated as he lay in his hospital bed. He kept pointing to his throat. We called for the nurse, but she was like a headless chicken running around the ward, wondering what to do next. It didn't give me and Mum much confidence.

I discovered about a year later, from Bill Campbell, a medium, that the reason my dad suffered a second stroke was because the nurse tried to give him some tablets with not much water to drink! Dad started to choke on them, causing him to panic, and it brought on another stroke. My father also said, "The nurses did their best."

My father deteriorated over the next few weeks. He later died on 19 January 1984. It was a great shock to me. I could never accept the death of my father. I was devastated and heartbroken. I cried for weeks on end. That's when I started to question my own mortality. His death was to change my life forever.

When I used to go see Dad in hospital, I would go straight from work after my shift. One particular day, Mum and I were walking towards his room. His door was opened wide, and we both saw that my dad was almost sitting up and looking into the far corner of the room, with one of his arms stretched out. It was as if he was speaking to someone.

When we entered the room, Dad wasn't aware of us. I remember looking at the expression on his face. He looked so serene, so peaceful. It was as if he had seen an angel. Dad saw something that we couldn't see.

The last time I saw my father in the hospital, I knew he was dying. I remember showing the sister who was on duty that night a photograph of my dad, the way he used to look. He had deteriorated so much that he was unrecognizable. She could see that I was in a bit of a state and tried to comfort me. The sister then left the room and later returned with a large, folded, thick white towel. She placed it in both my arms, never saying a word. The sister then left the room. I looked down at this large, thick towel and thought, *what am I supposed to do with this?*

Then it dawned on me. I'm sure she wanted me to smother my dad, to help him on his way, because she knew he was dying anyway. They usually put the dying patients at the end of the ward in a single room. I think they like to hurry death along in hospital, especially when they are waiting for hospital beds. The patients were going to die anyway. What else could it have been for? She made it so obvious.

By this time Dad couldn't communicate; all he did was sleep. I thought Dad wasn't aware that anyone was in the hospital room with him. I wanted desperately to tell him I loved him. I said to him, "Dad, if you can hear me, squeeze my hand. Once for 'I', two for 'I love', three for 'I love you.'" To my great relief, he reciprocated. Even though he had suffered two strokes and appeared unconscious most of the time, we could communicate in this way.

People who suffer with strokes and can't speak may be able to communicate in this way. It's so important to try to communicate, to let them know you love them. If they are dying, it helps the transition over into the next world when they hear the word "love". Love is the greatest thing we take with us when we go home.

I was exhausted, and I said goodbye to my father. I knew it would be for the last time. Later, Mum and my sister arrived. As I was driving home from the hospital, thinking all the time about Dad, I was unaware of the amount of traffic that had built up behind me. When I looked

Daffodil

through my rear window, there was a long line of slow traffic – it was all down to me!

I soon pulled myself together. Then as I approached a set of traffic lights, I pulled to a stop.

I remember looking to my left, and I saw through the passenger-seat window the spirit body of my father standing on the pavement. He looked just the same. He bobbed his head down to his chest as he held his jacket closed. It was as though he was still alive and getting into the passenger seat, but he appeared transparent. I shook my head and thought it was my imagination.

As soon as the lights changed, I pulled away thinking, *Well, it's been a long day.* I put it down to exhaustion.

As soon as I arrived home, I ran upstairs, climbed onto the bed, and cried, still clutching his photograph in my hand. I knew straightaway that Dad had passed away after I saw him stand at the traffic lights. A few minutes later, my sister rang to say that Dad had died.

I know now that my dad was hanging onto life to make sure that I arrived home safely. It wasn't my imagination; I did see dad.

When I saw him in his coffin, I thought, *that's not my dad.* They had darkened his hair, and he had rouge on his cheeks to make him look healthy! At the time I didn't know whether to laugh or cry. He was just a shell, a husk. I stared and stared at him. *Where have you gone, Dad? Where are you?*

Later that week, I had a dream about my father, which I later found out was in fact an out-of-body experience, or OBE. When you go to bed at night, at the point when you are asleep, your spirit body hovers inches above your physical body. Your physical body and your spirit body are held together with a silver cord whilst you sleep; it is the same cord that detaches from the body at the point of death, releasing you from this world to the next: heaven.

Sometimes the spirit body can travel anywhere whilst the cord is still attached, perhaps to other countries, other dimensions, or space. There is no limit. Another name for it is astral travel.

Have you ever had a dream were you feel yourself flying, or you have a really strong dream where you feel it really did happen? Then you had a feeling that you had to get back, and you were suddenly awake? You remember everything so vividly, every little detail. That memory will stay with you forever.

In my OBE, I saw my father in familiar surroundings, like an old public house. He was sat at the side of my mother having a drink. I noticed my mother looked younger; her hair was darker, and she was wearing her trench coat. She had quite a serious look on her face as I glanced at her.

I remember feeling confused and thinking, *what are you doing here?* My mother was still living at the time. As I turned, I saw an old friend of ours who was still alive and who stood at the fireplace having a drink. I then turned back towards my father.

He was wearing his usual clothes: trilby hat, jacket, tie, and checked trousers. My father always dressed smart in life. I remember other people being around. It was a typical pub scene, and the atmosphere was just like the old days.

I rushed towards my father, in shock at seeing him. I knelt down in front of him, and he turned to face me. I put my hand on his lap. "But it can t be you, Dad. You were so poorly" As I said this, I moved to stroke his cheek with my other hand. My hand went straight through his cheek!
He replied, "They are working on me, lass. They are working on me."

I later found out that the spirit realm puts you in these scenarios, even with the souls that are still living, so that you can have this experience with loved ones who have passed on.

The spirit world arranged a familiar scenario so that we could have this last experience with our loved ones, just to comfort us one last time. This also helps the ones who have died. They don't want to see you grieving, especially when they are so happy in their new lives.

That morning when I awoke, I felt so happy. I kept going over what I thought was a dream. What did my father mean, they were working on him? In the years to come, I was to find out that whatever we die from, or whatever we suffered from whilst living on earth; we are sent to a resting place till we are restored to our perfect selves, whether it be a mental or physical issue. Whatever caused our deaths, we will be restored. We will be made new, as God states in the Bible.

People who have lost limbs. People who were blind. The mentally handicapped. We are there till we come to terms with the fact that we are not truly dead! This can be a real shock for people who have just passed over, especially for skeptics.

Although it is not life as we knew it, it is a far better one.
Our body is a vehicle for this lifetime on earth; it fades and dies, and that's when we go to our real homes, back to the real life, back to our heavenly Father, God.

Have you ever asked yourself, "Why am I here? What is life all about?" At some point in our lives, we will ask this question. This planet we call Earth, which we live on – some say it's like a school where we all come down to learn lessons, and in a way, it is. But God says we have no lessons to learn, because we already have all the answers. We have all the knowledge; it's simply that our memory is taken away at birth, and for good reason, which you will understand as you read on.

The reason that you are here is to create yourself all over again by the choices that you make. Whatever you think, you will create, and then you will make a choice. This is how you will build your character, by the choices that you will make in this new life.

For example, by asking yourself, "Is this the person I want to be? Is this who I am?" you make the choice, and in this way you create yourself and find out who you truly are. When you make the right choices, you will have remembered who you are; this is how your soul will begin to evolve once again. All the lives that you have lived before are stored in the great library in heaven. The Akashic Records, which I will explain further in the book.

When we are born again, we can select the people, places, and events; the condition and circumstances; and nationality. The most important aspect of life is to find out who we truly are so that we find our way back home to God. It's like a game, but this game is not an easy one. It comes with adversity, strife, struggle, upheavals. We can all be winners in this game of life.

We also choose to be born. We are here so that our soul can progress and evolve in this lifetime by finding out who we are. That's why our memory is taken away after birth and we are given free will when we enter this new lifetime.

We also choose our own parents. I can hear you all, as you read this sentence. Some of you will think, "Why would I choose my parents, or my siblings?" The answer is because it's just what you needed for this new life. It all goes best towards your soul development in this new life. You're given the right props to work with on stage, the right ingredients. Of course, you knew all this before you were born, but like I said, your memory is taken away for a good reason.

At the beginning of our lives, as we grow with or without family, it moulds us into the people we are today as adults. We have chosen the most appropriate scenarios for this lifetime, for our soul's purpose. Sometimes we come down in group souls. We will attract the souls needed throughout our lives for this new lifetime, in order to help us with our journey. We also help them with their lives. We may be born into the same family time and time, all evolving together.

Take the handicapped child, for instance. That child may have been born that way for the sole purpose of the parents, so that the parents can evolve. The handicapped child has come down to help them evolve, and to learn such things as love, compassion, patience, and endurance. But most of all, the parents need to learn unconditional love for their child and also for each other. This can be a hard lesson for the parents involved.

This applies even to children who have adopted parents, orphans, foster children, children who fend for themselves, and Children who lose their parents in unforeseen circumstances. It's all part of their story, their journey. It's all meant to be. You yourself chose these circumstances and scenarios for the learning experience, in order for your soul to progress.

Daffodil

We all have to get through life no matter how we start off, whether it is on our own or with loving parents. Our lives are mapped out before we are born. That is why we have all been given a guardian angel to help us through our lives. God knew that life would be difficult at some stages; all we have to do is ask for help.

We choose our parents for our own personal development in whatever scenario we need to evolve in this lifetime. Sometimes we get it right, and sometimes we get it wrong, but no matter what we will keep coming back to earth till we get it right, going through the same scenarios and the same unresolved issues we had in our past lives. We never stop learning, just like the world will never stop turning. Life is a cycle.

We have all had many lives. The great medium and psychic Edger Cayce once said, "Reincarnation is a fact of life, whether you like it or not." Life is not always easy, and sometimes the scenarios we have given to ourselves can be harsh.

God didn't intend for you to suffer. The souls that are suffering right now on this earth are evolving souls, living out every experience there is. In this way the soul becomes more pure, reaching higher levels. Its purpose is to reach nirvana, the highest level.

The souls that seem to glide through life with very little challenges or problems are at different levels from the souls that have chosen difficult lives.

Every one of us on this planet is at different levels. That's why some people find an affinity with others on the same level. Then there are others that you don't get along with. Sometimes when this happens, it could be that there are lessons for you both to learn. Also, the people we tend not to like can turn out to be our greatest teachers.

Life is a roller coaster, and we may have to suffer along the journey to get there. No matter what adversity life throws at us, we have to get through it one way or another. An easy option for some is to commit suicide, but this is not an option. People who commit suicide have to keep coming back till they find out who they truly are and who they want to be. We are all on the same journey, and there is no easy way out.

It is not the same for people who are in chronic pain on a daily basis, with chronic diseases. When there is no hope left, when all that person feels is chronic pain twenty-four hours a day, and there is absolutely no hope left and only the promise of a slow painful death, then this becomes a whole new set of circumstances.

This is when assisted suicide should be granted – in other words, euthanasia. Especially when the person has a loving family who understands the predicament and wants to help the loved one make the transition easier. God never meant for you to suffer, and neither can he intervene. God can only observe, because to intervene would take away your contract for this life, your blueprint. It is always your choice.

How can anyone stand by and watch a loved one suffering all the time; knowing that there is no hope? Life is a cycle just like the seasons: we die so that we can be born again, and we are born so we can die again. The soul goes on forever evolving, and it keeps coming back time and time again in a different body, till hopefully it will reach perfection.

If God took away man's suffering on a global scale, the world would not exist. We are all connected. It doesn't matter how academic you are, how rich or how poor, what race you belong to, or what religion you follow. We are all the same, and we come from the one source.

God does not discriminate. After all, we are all part of God, the whole. Why would God prefer one person over another, just because his skin is a different colour, when God created the colour of skin in the first place? Why would God prefer one religion to another, when we all come from the same source, the same God?

It is man who made these rules and myths, who invented religion and racism born out of fear. These fears were passed down from generation to generation. God loves us all unconditionally. Till man learns to live in harmony as God intended, nothing will change. It's up to us! Love is the most important lesson we can learn on earth. It's about how we treat others and the choices we make whilst living on earth.

When we die and pass over into the spirit world, we are given a review on the life we have just left behind.

Daffodil

There is no God who sits in judgment, sending some souls to hell and some to heaven. Man was responsible for this lie, and for the belief that we have to fear God.

We will see the good things we did in our lives, as well as the bad things. For every thought we had, good, or bad, we are our own judges. There is no hell, only what we make it in our thoughts. Sometimes we can be quite hard on ourselves for the life we have chosen for the next time round.

This doesn't mean to say that evil does not exist, because we all know it does, especially on this planet. One night I went to bed as usual. Harry, my husband, was asleep beside me. I awoke at about 2.00 AM. All of a sudden I felt a presence in the room. I had this awful dread in the pit of my stomach; whatever it was felt evil. I could see in my mind's eye this spirit come through the wall on a two wheeler bike in my bedroom! I know this sounds crazy, but it's true.

When I opened my eyes, to my horror this spirit stood at the side of my bed looking at me. It was male and appeared thin and small in stature. It wore what looked like to be a long, heavy, doubled-breasted overcoat. It had unkempt greasy hair, and it was so ugly that it was drooling down one side of its mouth.

It reminded me of one of those characters from the Michael Jackson video "Thriller". I froze. It moved its horrible face closer to mine, to within an inch. After shaking its head slowly from side to side, it said to me, "You and your God! You and your God!" It kept repeating over and over again.

I was dumbstruck! I tried to grab Harry's attention, but I couldn't move. No words would come out of my mouth as I tried to speak. All I could think about was what Loretta Cusworth, my reflexology tutor, had taught us in class. If ever we came across anything evil, we were to stay calm, acknowledge the spirit, and tell it to go towards the white light.

Not all spirits are evil; some are simply stuck between the two worlds. Perhaps they do not want to leave loved ones behind, or there may be some unresolved issues that were left behind when they died. Some dead spirits need help to move into the light. There are people who work with spirits called Earth Rescuers. These people do this all the time, moving spirits to the next dimension. They also help children that might have become lost.

In my mind I kept shouting and repeating, "God will protect us, Harry. God will protect us!" Finally it vanished as quickly as it appeared. I turned over in bed, my first thought was, *What the Effing hell was that!!*

The next day I went over what had happened the night before. I found it very disturbing. What did it all mean? Why me? Was I been tested by the spirit world?

I had my own experience of rescuing a spirit once, but it wasn't where we lived now. It happened in our old house, where we had lived for twenty-two years.

I must have travelled there in my sleep. I remember Harry and I were in bed, but I could hear movement on the landing. I said to Harry, "Can you hear that?" He nodded his head, startled. I walked towards the landing. As I opened the door to the landing, this little man walked straight towards the box room. As he passed me, I caught hold of his wrist, and he looked terrified. I admit I was quite startled myself, but at the same time it was funny. I think it was a dwarf, somehow I felt sorry for this little person.

He looked lost. I got back into bed, I didn't feel afraid. I said a little prayer, asked the angels to take care of him, and sent him towards the light. Afterwards there was a sense of peace; he made it home.

Some people are more sensitive than others, more open intuitive with the spirit world. There is evil, and there is good. The lower realms try to interfere with the good all the time. If they know of a person that is working towards the light for the good of mankind, then they will do their best to interfere. Therefore always ask for protection from your guardian angel.

Daffodil

Evil spirits like to hang around alcoholics, people suffering with depression, and drug users. They feed on the fear and energy of people. The more negative the situation, the better it is for them.

Before asking for help for a lost spirit, ask the spirit guides and the angels for God's protection. I find that this always works for me. It should always be done before you proceed. When you've completed your rescue, send them on their way with the help of the angels to go towards the light. Then thank the angels and the spirit world, and ask again for the spirit's protection, just to make sure.

Whenever I have had that awful sense of fear that something is about to happen, it's as if I get a warning from the spirit world first, before it takes place. When I feel it coming on, I concentrate on something else entirely different. My guardian angels prevent it from happening, thank goodness. All you have to do is change your thoughts immediately. Your mind is very powerful; it will believe what you tell it.

When I first started healing with Reiki, some frightening and unexplained things would happen. I was once in bed one early morning, and it was just starting to come light. Harry had just left for work. I was half asleep. Suddenly I had this awful dread that something was about to happen. I felt the top sheet underneath the duvet begin to slide down the bed. I felt quite panic-stricken, so I kept repeating the Lord's Prayer. It's not as if I was religious at the time. I didn't know what else to do, but it worked. This was my soul remembering.

When things like this happen, it's as if you are aware of everything around you, but you can't move. It's as if your body becomes temporarily paralysed in that moment in time. When I finally got up that morning, the sheet was in a heap at the bottom of the bed – a reminder that it wasn't a dream and did really happen.

After these awful experiences, I wanted to know why. I got in touch with Alan Bellinger, a healer whom I will introduce you to later in the book. After speaking with Alan about it, he put me in touch with Eileen Gowen. A lady from the spiritual church in the Sheffield city centre that specialises with this kind of problem. She had two spirit nuns as her guides who dealt with matters like this. I spoke to her on the phone for about an hour one day. She told me that she would speak with her nun guides that night and ask for their help.

The next night I was just about to get into bed. I was sat on the edge of the bed, and suddenly in my mind's eye I saw a picture of two nuns. They were wearing big starched white hats, walking along in what looked like some church grounds, they were both chatting to one another with their hands tucked underneath the yoke of their habits.

As I was looking at this scene, it was like watching a movie in black and white. Then I noticed steel bars across the picture between the nuns and myself. It dawned on me that the steel bars represented protection! Ever since then, I have had no problems.

The secret is not to allow it into your thoughts. Changing your thoughts immediately will prevent it from happening. I've used this method several times now, and it always works.

Shirley Mac'laine

Shirley Mac'laine is an American film star. She stared in many films such as *Around the World in Eighty Days, Two Mules for Sister Mary,* and *Artists and Models,* to mention a few. When I was eleven or twelve, I remember being at home and walking by the TV. I happened to see her face on the screen, and I was immediately drawn to her. I sat down to watch the film.

There was just something about her, something familiar. I felt as if I knew her, I took to her straightaway. My thoughts were, *who are you? Why do I feel so drawn to you?* She made me smile to myself. She fascinated me.

After that, whenever she was to appear in a film on TV, I would drop everything I was doing. The feelings towards her continued. At the time I didn't know why.

Then after the death of my father, I was researching evidence about the survival of the soul and the meaning of life. I happened to come across a book in our local library called *Out on a Limb,* written in 1983 by Shirley Mac'laine. The book was about her spiritual journey. I know now that the angels led me to this book. It was no coincidence; it was simply what I needed at the time. Later the book was made into a feature film.

After reading Shirley's book, I felt inspired to find out more and to do more research on spiritualism. I remember at the time that when her book was published in Hollywood, she was ridiculed for her beliefs, especially from some of her so-called friends. The media had a field day.

Nevertheless, Shirley stuck to her guns. She always has done so. I think it was very brave of her. At the time, little was known about the survival of the soul. It was hardly heard of. She knew she was risking her career – hence the title. This was why I'd felt a connection with Shirley all those years ago. We were more or less connected in a spiritual way. We were trying to help mankind; we were both on a mission to make the world aware.

Well, I for one believed in Shirley. It was one of the first books that I had read on this subject, and it set me on my journey to find proof that the soul does survive.

I suppose in away it planted the seed. I must have read hundreds of books over the last thirty years. I'm sure if I ever meet Shirley face to face; there would be some recognition on her part – a knowing, without words been spoken. I give thanks to this courageous woman. Perhaps we were in the same class in heaven, or we are on the same spiritual level. All I know is something connected me that day in a spiritual way.

Cheltham Races

One morning I was in the kitchen making my breakfast: tea and toast, as usual. I had already put the TV on in the lounge and was listening to *Good Morning with Richard and Judy*. I was still in the kitchen when suddenly the channel switched over to the racing channel by itself. As I walked back into the lounge, it switched itself back to the *Good Morning program*.

Strange, I thought. *What could that be?* At the time we didn't have Sky TV. I tried all the five channels on TV, but none of them had racing channel on. After a while I thought, *is a spirit trying to communicate with me?*

This is what happens sometimes, when a spirit is trying to grab your attention. Sometimes car keys go missing, only to turn up later in a place where you know you have already looked. It also happens a lot with electrics and light bulbs, and with things being moved around. As I thought about it, I asked myself, *why the racing channel?*

Then it dawned on me. It had to be my father, because he loved racing. It was his hobby to place a bet on the horse race. But why? Did he know I had decided to write the book, and was he coming to give me some encouragement? It gave me an idea for the book. It was ironic that the Cheltham races started in the afternoon on TV that very day. (I say ironic because there's no such thing as coincidence.)

Later that week, I was to have another out-of-body experience. It had been twenty-two years since I'd last seen my father on this earth. In this OBE I was in St Catherine's Church in Sheffield. I stood in the very spot where I had been married, and where my children were all christened. I was also confirmed there and spent many Sundays as a child going to Mass and confession.

Then I could see my father walking towards me down the aisle of the church. I couldn't believe what I was seeing! He looked about in his mid-thirties and had on a light grey herringbone suit, with a waist coat and a shirt buttoned up to the neck with a collar stud. He was also wearing a cap.

We reached out our arms and embraced one another, holding each other tight. There was a chill of cold air around him. I was so happy he felt solid. I stood back, still holding both his shoulders. I looked at his clothes and down to his shoes, I said to my father, "Let me take this back with me." I was looking at every little detail of his attire so that I wouldn't forget. I must remember. I remember looking down at his shoes, all neatly laced up. His whole being seemed to shimmer on the outside.

The feeling I had was as if I was being congratulated, as if I had achieved something very special in my life. It was something of a spiritual nature. The spirit world had arranged the meeting with my father as a reward. It definitely felt that I was being rewarded.

I was aware of two other beings also with my father. One looked like my grandfather, and the other one looked like my Uncle Eddy. It was as if they were escorting Dad. But I didn't really take much notice of them – my father absorbed all my attention.

When I opened my eyes, it was about three in the morning. I was bouncing with such energy and zest, such happiness – something I hadn't felt in a long, long time. I wanted to tell Harry what I had just experienced, but he was a skeptic, I didn't think he would have appreciated it that early in the morning.

How I wished I could share the wonderful things that happened to me. Sometimes it was as if he was completely shut off from what I was saying to him. He always gave me that polite nod, hoping not offend me.

Then sometimes I thought it must be hard for him, too, if he couldn't share with me what I had come to believe. Perhaps rather than say what he really thought, he'd rather not say anything. I knew that he wouldn't want to hurt me.

Daffodil

Years ago at the beginning of my research, we were discussing the situation, at the end of our conversation he shouted, "I'm sorry, but I think it's a load of bullshit." I suppose a lot of other people may think the same. I've tried so hard in the past to draw him into conversations about it, asking for him to give me some kind of explanation or logical reasons that these things happen, but to no avail.

Anyway, getting back to my father. All that day I kept thinking of my dad. What did it all mean? I didn't remember my father ever wearing a cap – and how come he looked so young? Then I suddenly remembered an old black-and-white photograph where my father was wearing a light suit with a cap. He looked about to be in his mid-thirties, and the photograph was taken at the races!

Did this have a connection with what had happened with the channels changing on the TV? Was this why I had to remember in detail what my father was wearing? It wasn't just a dream – it was real! Was my father trying to communicate with me? Yes!

When we die, at some point we will want to come back and visit our loved ones. We can come back at any age we want to be, and we can wear familiar clothes that we once wore on earth. I saw my mother one evening. I had just climbed into bed; I was in a sitting position, so I was fully awake. At the time I remember thinking about my hospital appointment for the next day; I was quite concerned about it.

A little later Harry walked into the bedroom. As he walked around the foot of the bed. I suddenly saw my mother. She was sat on the corner of the bed in a black dress with a square neckline, which I recognised. Her hair was auburn, short, and brushed back in the same casual style she used to have when she was alive. She looked much younger. We stared at each other, she told me that I was going to be all right, and not worry.

When Harry reached his side of the bed, I saw my mum look up into his face, but he walked straight through her transparent body. She then disappeared.

I remember staring at this scene as if it was perfectly normal. I never spoke of it at the time, not even to Harry. I kept it to myself. After all, people would think I was crazy. When this took place, I remember feeling so calm, not one bit scared. Incidentally, all was well with the hospital results.

***

We have seven wonderful grandchildren, and I like to call them the magnificent seven. At the time of writing, Jason is sixteen, Christopher is almost thirteen, Jordan is twelve, Ryan is nine, Kieran is seven, Emily is nine, and Katie is five. All have been blessed with good health, and they're developing into wonderful characters, bringing happiness into our lives. Every night I ask for God and the angels for good health and to protect them all.

About a year later after Mum had died, something unusual happened one Friday night, when Emily and Katie stayed over. I was looking after both of them; I wasn't feeling at all well. I was stiff and sore with arthritis, and I was using my crutches at the time.

I had put Katie, who was eighteen months at the time, to bed at about eight thirty. Once or twice Katie had woken up from dreaming and was restless, which wasn't unusual for her.

When I went into the bedroom later to check on her. She had fallen asleep with her body across the bed with her head pointing towards the wall, instead of lying straight in bed. I remember thinking that it looked like she had had a battle with the covers; her top sheet and duvet were askew. She was in the bottom bunk bed, I thought, *Rather than disturb her, when I'm ready for bed; I'll move her back properly and remake her bed.* I gently covered her with the top sheet and quietly closed the door.

About an hour later I was just about to put Emily to bed. As I opened the bedroom door, to my amazement Katie was on her side with her head on the pillow. She had her dolly nestled under her chin, and the top sheet and the duvet had been remade. It was so neatly done that the duvet was laid corner to corner and tucked below Katie's ear. Anybody who has ever owned bunk beds knows how difficult it is making these beds, especially when trying to make a neat job of it. I feel sure my mother had something to do with it, knowing how unwell I was feeling at the time. She would have pulled out all the stops to help me. I was grateful, and I said so. It was either Mum or the angels.

As I leaned against the door, a voice in my head kept saying, "Just accept it." A calmness came over me.

Childhood

My name is Eileen Veronica Richmond, née Molloy. I was born in Sheffield on 15 October 1947. That makes me a Libra. "The scales of justice" – oh so true to my personality. I hate any injustice. I was brought up in a Catholic environment, and I attended Catholic schools.

They say that school is supposed to be one of the best times of your life, but I am afraid it wasn't for me. All I remember is humiliation, fear, and sometimes physical abuse. Looking back now over the years, it had a lot to do with the way I was brought up.

From a very early age, all I can remember is fear. My parents were always verbally abusive to each other, their relationship was very volatile. More often than not, it would come to blows. I also feared my sister Mary. One night my mother and father had returned home from the pub, and they were having an argument – nothing unusual. All I could hear was my father's voice shouting, which always frightened me.

When this happened, my mother would encourage me to come downstairs, whether I was asleep or not.
She would sit me on her knee, and I would act like a shield between my mother and father, preventing him from striking her. This always frightened me, as my father came closer towards us again and again, shouting at my mother. He took a look at me on one of these occasions and said, "You're going to damage her one of these days." It's something I've never forgotten. I was only about two years old at the time.

On the odd occasion I would see my mother and father kiss and make up, it would instantly make me feel happy and secure.

Daffodil

When I look back, my parents were constantly at each other's throats, even throwing pots and pans. They constantly shouted at each other. Many Christmas dinners were spoilt by these events. The only time there was any peace in the home was when they were apart, at work or in the pub.

When you are a little child, you think this is normal behaviour, but I was always scared.

When I was thirteen or fourteen, my parents decided to divorce. When I first found out, it was such a big relief. I couldn't understand why they had left it so long. Now, that's not normal thinking, is it? Especially for a child. Any normal child would be heartbroken at the fact that their mum and dad were going to break up.

But it never happened. They got back together again, and my heart sank. The arguments continued. I soon went to live with my sister Mary. That was one of the many reasons why I wanted to get married, instead of following my dream to become a professional dancer one day. Obviously it wasn't meant to be. Oh well, maybe in the next life hey.

Sometimes life doesn't always pan out like we want it to. The reason is because we have lessons to learn, and that's why we chose this life: we chose our own stories. It's no good blaming anyone if you are living a difficult life and you seem to have more than your fare share of adversity.

Later in the book I will show you how to change your life for the better. Your life was meant to be the way it is right now, but no matter what your life entails, you are meant to be happy. It is your birthright. Your life is not always about you. It's also about the people that you live with, your family, and the people you will encounter in your life.

When we are small children, we look up to our parents to teach us the right way. We are conditioned by what our parents say and do, and we are very impressionable at this age. We think our parents know best, and that's how it should be – but this is not always the case.

Because of these outbursts between my mother and father, I always tried to make sure my children never witnessed Harry and me arguing or using threatening behaviour. I didn't want them to feel like I had felt as a child – the insecurity, but mostly the fear. I wanted my children to feel loved and secure. I tried to do my best as a young mother. There was never enough money, but we managed. But when it came to that special word 'they call love', then we were millionaires.

When I was growing up as a child, at school I would be very fearful of the other children, especially if they used threatening behaviour towards me. I took on this tough persona, making out like I wasn't frightened of anyone or anything, but deep inside I would tremble.

When anyone picked on me at school, my legs would turn to jelly, and I would go very pale and feel sick. The trick was, I wouldn't let anyone see this. Everyone thought that I was this tough kid who was scared of nothing. Later I was labeled a bully. I never looked for trouble, but I stood my ground if it came looking for me. I hated violence of any kind.

That's another reason why my school work suffered: I simply didn't want to be there. I know there are many children out there going through exactly what I went through. In fact things have worsened due to gang crime and children carrying knives. The underlying cause is fear every time. I feel sorry for the kids today. I think it has become much tougher in today's society. The children hear such horror stories, and that's before some of them have even started school. It's an extra burden for the parents to be worrying about their children.

I've always send out a prayer to the angels to protect my grandchildren at school. You can do this too, if you are a parent or grandparent; it applies to everyone in any worrying circumstance. That's why the angels are here: to help us through this life. They know that life is not an easy journey. Remember that all you have to do is ask your guardian angel.

My Father

My father was a small man who stood five foot five inches. To look at him, he could appear quite disarming. He had a cuteness about his demeanour, but what a tyrant, what a temper, and what an angry, frustrated man he was. Although he never physically abused me, I was frightened of him. I felt I had to creep round the house so as not to disturb him. It felt like walking on egg shells all the time. That's how it was with my dad: we kept out of his way.

I never remember my father showing me any love or affection, or playing with me. But in the fifties I don't think many fathers did. Harry's father was the same in those days. Some of the fathers seemed to like to put on this tough persona like they were all gangsters, just like in the popular movies at the time. They tried to portray their idols; such has James Cagney, Humphrey Bogart, and Edward G. Robinson. It was the trend at the time. It also wasn't unusual if a man struck his wife.

When I was five, I remember my mother saying to me one night when they came back from the pub, "Go and sit on your dad's knee." She wanted me to show him some affection – but how could I? He never showed me any love. It felt unnatural. Reluctantly I did has she asked.

Dad turned and looked at me. He said, "Your mum told you to do that, didn't she?"

That's one thing I have noticed about my four sons. Three of them have children, and sometimes I have sat back and watched their dads playing with them, being affectionate, having patience, and joining in the fun. I feel very proud of them all.

Michael, my youngest son, has three wonderful boys: Jordan, Ryan, and Kieran. The sad thing is, Michael is now divorced, through no fault of his own. Yes, I'm his mother, and so of course I would say that, but it's the truth. He is a wonderful father and copes with his children extremely well under the circumstances.

I think you lose that special connection with relationships between grandparent and grandchild, when parents divorce. I often wonder if the grandchildren feel the same. Because of the divorce, we don't get to see the grandchildren as often as we would if the parents were still together. Somehow everyone loses out. It doesn't help that the fact Michael lives and works in Manchester. I think it's a very sad situation, but then, that's life. I hope my grandchildren will always stay close to us, and that they remember the happy times we had when they were small. We will always be there for them.

Michael always believed in the importance of the family unit. He loved family gatherings and parties, and he was always eager to join in the fun whenever the occasion arose. But sadly, his marriage wasn't meant to be.

Nevertheless, he should be very proud of himself. I'm sure that when the children grow up and look back on their lives, they will appreciate what a good father Michael was, and still is to this day.

Despite my eldest son's Wayne's divorce, he has always shown great loyalty to his two sons, Jason and Christopher, always looking out for their best interests at heart.

Darren and Joanne are both loving and caring parents to their daughters, Emily and Katie. I've had nothing to worry about in that sense. They all have stability in their lives, which is important in children's lives.

Richard and Maria wanted children in the beginning, but it didn't happen. They both worked full-time. I suppose you get used to a certain lifestyle, and then time passes you by and it's too late. Still, it's the life they both chose before they were born. Then sometimes I would wonder whether they were meant to adopt.

There are lots of little children out there who desperately need a home, who need someone to love and care for them. The amount of children waiting to be fostered or adopted is heartbreaking.

My Mother

From a very early age, I adored my mother. She showed me love and affection. She seemed to make up where my father was lacking. I remember as a child, when Mum came home from work, I would be so excited to see her. I would either hide under the table, or I would run to the door to greet her.

I couldn't wait for Mum to sit down so that I could sit on her knee for a cuddle. "Nurse me five minutes, Mum!"

"Oh come on, then, just for five minutes," she'd say. I would bury my face into her neck and smell her perfume. At that age, in my mind my mother could do no wrong.

My mother, Irene Molloy, was taller than my father. She was a smart, attractive woman with good posture that always seemed to make her look younger than she was, especially as she grew older. I was very proud of Mum.

As I grew older, my mum told me that at the age of fifteen, she learnt that she was adopted. One day when she came home from school, her parents wanted her to sign an insurance policy that they wanted to surrender. Mum wanted to know what it was all about, and that was how she came to find out that she was adopted. This was to have a profound effect on her as she grew older, especially in her later years.

My mother was only a teenager when she received this devastating news. Can you imagine going through all the traumas of what puberty can bring, and receiving the news during that time? She ran out of the house crying.

Daffodil

My mum used to talk about her adoptive parents with great affection. They loved her, and she could be quite spoilt at times. Nevertheless, the news devastated her and broke her heart. It's a terrible burden for children to carry: the fact that they were abandoned when they were just a baby.

I asked her once if she would ever consider finding out whom her real parents were. After all, I wanted to know who my real grandparents were. I could see she was deeply hurt as soon as I mentioned the subject. She replied if they wanted to know where she was, they would have come looking for her long ago, she just left it at that.

Adoption

Parents who choose to adopt are put with the children they are supposed to be with. This was all prearranged by parents and the adoptive children before birth. There are no mistakes. Adoptive parents may think they are making the wrong decision by adopting, but it was all planned prior to their births.

If only my mother had known this. I wonder whether it would have made any difference to her. I suppose she wasn't meant to know; it was all part of her journey. It's just that when I saw that sadness in her eyes, I wanted to make it better. If I had had the spiritual knowledge then, when she was alive, I could have passed it on to her, and she might have found it easier to bear.

Yet my mother had a happy childhood. She was a champion swimmer at school. It was only as she got older that she thought more about being adopted. The feeling of being abandoned or unwanted is a terrible burden for anyone to carry. I think it made her bitter at times. But then, we don't know of the mother's circumstances at the time. Mum once said to me, "I came into this world alone, I will go out of this world alone."
"But Mum we all will,"

It breaks my heart for any mother to give up her baby, and we should never judge. This was part of my mother's journey for whatever reason.

I'm sure that now that Mum has passed over, she will have all the answers why this had to take place. Eventually when we all pass over; we will be given all the answers to whatever adversities, trouble, and strife we had to endure. It will all make sense one day, and we will see the bigger picture.

Daffodil

To all the children and grownups out there who are adopted and are reading this, rest assured that all was meant to be, even if you are searching for your biological parents. Just know in your heart and soul that someday you will meet up with your biological parents, when you pass over into the next world. There will be an understanding.

My mum was the strong one in our family. She seemed to take on the role of both mother and father. She had worked ever since I could remember; in those days it was necessary. But we were always broke, because the money seemed to go to booze, gambling, and debt, even though both my parents worked full-time. We probably should have been well off. If there's one thing my mother taught me, it was never to get into debt. There was always someone banging on the door wanting money, and we had to hide behind the sofa.

Mum would get into debt, and Dad would spend his time in the betting office or in the pub. My sister Mary had to hide any post that came through the door; just in case it was a red letter. Dad made the mistake of giving Mum the money to pay the bills. She rarely paid, and eventually Dad would find out. This would cause a fight with pots and pans flying everywhere.

I remember once going out with my mum to look for employment when she was out of work, which was very rare. As we walked along the back streets of the working industry, she suddenly looked at me and said, "Eileen, keep your eyes peeled for any coppers you might find on the street." I remember thinking to myself, *Oh no; things aren't that bad, are they?* It upset me and made me feel insecure.

I know times were different then, but it never stopped me loving her. I hated poverty, and there was a lot of it in those days. In the olden days, Mum used to say, "If you are poor, society looks down on you, as if it is your fault for being in that position."

My mother tried her hand at everything, from being a bus conductress to driving a forklift truck, to being a nurse. What she didn't know, she would learn quickly. Nothing would faze her as long as she was employed.

Saturdays

Daffodil Day

Every Saturday my mum would give me sixpence pocket money. On Saturday afternoons I would run all the way from Grimesthorpe Road (where I lived) to Spital Hill, through the Wicker Arches in Sheffield, and then all the way into town to Dixon Lane where the market stood. This was about a two-mile round trip.

Life seemed a lot safer in those days for an eight-year-old. I did this trip every Saturday just so that I could buy Mum a bunch of daffodils.

The daffodils would cost me three-pence, or 3d in old pennies. This left me with some money left over for sweets. After buying them, I would run all the way back home to give her the daffodils. But more often than not, Mum and Dad would be in the pub, so I would have to run all the way down to the pub so that I could see her face light up when I gave them to her. It was worth it. I craved her affection, and she always acted surprised. It gave me as much joy as it did her. I did this week after week, and it became a ritual.

That's why daffodils mean so much to me. I often go over that memory in my mind, when I think of her. It made me so happy as a child to see that look of appreciation on her face.

When my mother died, I was told by a medium that my mum was bringing me the biggest bunch of daffodils so that I would know it was her. I always think of Mum whenever I see daffodils. It is also the colour of the soul, the third chakra. It represents happiness.

It was one of the happiest memories of my childhood – hence the title of the book.

I can still see the old market street when I think about those days: all the fruit and vegetables on display, with lots of different flowers in abundance.

But it was always the bunches of daffodils that drew my attention, and the smell of them. I would spend my time looking for the perfect bunch.

Bernard Badger

Six months after the death of my father, my mother met a man called Bernard Badger. Bernard had served in the paratroopers in the Second World War. He became very fond of Mum, who was still a very attractive woman. They soon built a relationship and eventually married.

As the years passed, I knew Mum wasn't happy, and neither was Bernard. I think they were too set in their ways. I always got along with Bernard; I grew very fond of him. He seemed to fill a gap in my life: he was more like a father figure he looked after Mum well. They would go on lots of holidays together. Mum had never had it so good … but I knew she wasn't happy.

Bernard and I had many conversations over the years that I knew him. He was very polite and attentive to what I had to say. I thought he was a real gentleman.

Years later I received a phone call from one of mum's neighbours, Muriel. In a stuttering voice she said that Bernard had suddenly collapsed in the greenhouse and had died. I was in shock. To suddenly lose him like that was hard. I'd grown to love and respect Bernard.

I had seen Bernard two days earlier before he died. I remember having this strange feeling as I said my goodbyes that day. Bernard had been directly behind me as I was leaving by the kitchen door, suddenly I wanted to turn around and hug him for some reason, but I didn't. It left me with a strange feeling.

Both Harry and I went straight to see my mum. The funeral directors had come to collect Bernard's body when we got there. When we entered

Daffodil

the living room, Bernard was laid out on the sofa with his face covered up. I asked if I could see him one last time. I noticed a bruising on the side of his forehead; it must have been caused by the fall. I kissed him. I was surprised how upset I was, and I couldn't stop sobbing. I looked at my mother. Although she looked shocked, she never shed a tear.

Although I often gave him the odd peck on the cheek, I never told him how much he meant to me. But I know that he knows now.

That night I stayed with Mum, we slept in the same bed. I had taken up Bernard's space next to mum. At about 4.00 AM I couldn't sleep, and I kept thinking about Bernard and the shock of it all. I laid there thinking all sorts of things. How was Mum going to cope? She had become so reliant on Bernard. Mum was asleep, so I went downstairs to make myself a cup of coffee.

I approached the living room, I didn't bother switching on the lights because the curtains were opened; and the street lights seemed to light up the whole room. As I walked towards the window, I looked at the photographs lined up on the windowsill. I remember sighing and whispering, "Ho, Bernard, where are you?"

All of a sudden I heard Bernard say, "I've never left, lass. I'm still here. Come on, get yourself off to bed. You'll be shattered in the morning." I wasn't a bit frightened, I accepted it with calmness.

Early that morning when I awoke, in my mind's eye I could see Bernard stood at the foot of the bed wearing a crisp white shirt over the top of his trousers, as if he was about to button his shirt. He looked over at me and then at my mother. "Well! I'm glad you're with your mother and that she's not on her own." Then he disappeared.

About eighteen days before Bernard had collapsed and died of a heart attack, his brother Alec had also collapsed and died of a heart attack in a garden! This had a profound effect on Bernard, because they were both very close brothers.

I remember Mum saying to me one day, "Bernard asked me if I believed in the afterlife just after Alec had died. 'Of course I do,' I told him."

I think Bernard had an experience with his brother, like I did with my father after his death. Bernard would never have said this to my mother under normal circumstances; he would have kept to himself. He was a very proud man. I wonder whether Bernard was also a sceptic.

Sometimes the deceased one will try his best to communicate with loved ones and family, especially if the loved ones are inconsolable and the whole experience has been very traumatic for them.

Loved ones may have a dream, or if they're lucky, an OBE. This is all engineered by the spirit world, depending on the circumstances. Somehow they pull it all together. It never ceases to amaze me how hard they work at it.

They will be put in a familiar scenario, like a family party or some sort of gathering. At some point the loved ones will have contact with the deceased. If you have one, I guarantee the next day you will feel so happy. The experience will stay with you for life. It may even change your views, if you were a skeptic. I'm sure you will feel inspired.

The veil can become very thin between the two worlds at times, so that you can be given glimpses of the other side.

Early Recall

We all have early recall as babies and infants. My earliest recall was when I must have been lying in a pram with the hood pulled up. I looked straight ahead and remembered it looked as if I was looking at the shape of a horseshoe. When I think about it now, the hood on the pram would give this appearance for a baby lying on its back and looking upwards.

I remember looking at a yellow brick painted wall. All of sudden I was filled with dread and fear. I thought, *Oh! I don't like this! I don't want to be here!* But as I began to protest, what came out of my mouth was a baby's cry. Although I felt like a newborn baby, my mind was adult. It was as if I was outside the pram. This was my higher self; my soul was speaking to me.

When I was a child, we lived in a two bedroom terraced house with an attic. In the kitchen the walls were brick and were painted different colours over the years. That was my first memory of being here. My soul remembered that I didn't like being here, but I had no option.

On one occasion my father lifted me up onto a shop counter. This lady put some items of clothing by the side of me, and I remember looking down at this lovely, soft material. It was cream with little tiny pink roses on it. There were two of them, what appeared to look little underneath slips.

The next thing I knew, I was being taken to my Aunt Biddy's. I remember being put to bed. Then it hit me that my mother wasn't around, I screamed the house down. I knew something was terribly wrong. I remember my aunt giving me a stern look, as if to say, "You will do as you are told. You will behave!

"The look was enough.

I found out later that I was only eighteen months old when this took place. Apparently for whatever reason, my mother had left my dad for someone else. She had taken my sister with her. It soon ended, and Mum and Dad were back together again – only to continue the rows and abuse all over again. It never ceased.

Memories

I only remember my grandfather on my father's side, Edward Molloy. My grandmother had died in the same year I was born, 1947. When my grandchildren were born; I started to think of my grandmother a lot, especially when I was nursing my babies in my arms. A grandmother's love for her grandchildren is so special. I started to wish for that lost love, to have been held in my grandmother's arms. But I am comforted that she is always around me and still is to this day.

My mum told me that my grandfather never stopped talking about me with great affection, especially down at the local pub. By the time he had finished, he would be getting on everyone's nerves. I became very close to my grandfather. He was a tall, handsome man with white and silver hair.

I used to stare at him sometimes as he sat on a stool in front of the coal fire. Sometimes he would toast some bread on a large meat fork. He'd just sit there warming his hands in front of the fire after having come back from the pub on a cold winter's night. I'd stare at him and think how handsome he was, as the glow from the fire shone on his face.

I remember it vividly: My father was working the night shift. Mum, my sister, and I were sleeping together in one bed. There was a knock at the door in the middle of the night. It was as if my mum was expecting it. We received the bad news that Grandfather had passed away in hospital. I'm not sure, but I think it was pneumonia.

I heard my mother telling my sister that Grandfather had died, and she comforted her. It was as if Mum thought I was too young to understand what had happened. It felt like my heart had been ripped out. I was three years old, and I loved my grandfather.

***

Dad once said to me, "Isn't it awful, Eileen, when you see people with their arms and legs missing?" I had overheard Mum and Dad speaking of a mutual friend that suffered from diabetes. Unfortunately the chap had lost his leg.

"Yes," I replied. "You would think that God would have made us so that if we lost a limb, it would grow back again, like the salamander. If it loses any of its limbs, it has the ability to regenerate. It doesn't seem fair."

Sometimes as a child, when Mum and Dad went to the pub, after about an hour I would follow them. I didn't want to be on my own or with my sister. I can remember spending what seemed like hours outside the pub, waiting for them to come home.

Every now and then, I would pop my head round the pub door to look for them. I'd get the odd bottle of pop, or a bag of crisps. I remember the thick, heavy cigarette smoke, every time I opened the door. It was so thick I could see it floating in waves in the air. How could anyone breathe!

There was no ventilation for the smoke to escape. And eventually the Government had to make it compulsory. That's how it was in those days: many kids would hang around public houses, waiting for their parents and hoping for a bottle of pop and some crisps. When I look back, I was very lucky. It could have been a dangerous place to be, compared to what happens to children today. I should have been at home tucked up in my bed.

I remember Mum and Dad coming back from the pub, and I would sneak down stairs. Mum would always let me stay up. I never remember my sister being around on these occasions. I have very little memory of my sister being around at all, come to think of it. Mary was six years older than me.

In the late 1950s there was a program on TV in black and white called *War in the Air*. I was allowed to stay up on these occasions. It would seem quite cosy, and I felt safe. Mum would make some tea and

Daffodil

sandwiches and turn off the light, and we would gather round the fire waiting for the programme to begin. The program always began with aero planes flying across the TV screen. This went on for a couple of weekends. I was about four or five years old at the time.

Then on the next occasion we settled into our usual routine, waiting for the program to begin. To my horror, as I watched the screen, I couldn't believe what I was seeing. All of a sudden this great big, mechanical shovel was shoveling a pile of dead bodies into a big hole in the ground!

This was a documentary film from the Holocaust, at Auschwitz, just after World War Two. I remember looking at this one woman in the pile of bodies. She had no clothes on, and she was about twenty-five. She seemed to be so stiff, and her legs and arms never moved. I was transfixed in that moment in time. That has stayed with me to this very day. The giant shovel pushed all the bodies into the hole.

I must have had a look of horror on my face as Dad looked at me. I remember him shouting at my mother in the kitchen, "Irene! She shouldn't be up watching this sort of thing at her age."

Mum replied, "Oh, you can't hide things that went on during the war. She will find out sooner or later!"

How irresponsible was that of my mum, to expose a little child to such horror? It's no good thinking, "She's just a child. She doesn't understand." Little children *do* understand! This had a terrible effect on me. I had never seen dead bodies before, especially the horrors that occurred in the concentration camps in World War Two. In years to come, I could never watch anything to do with the war; it always disturbed me, especially when it showed children in the concentration camps. I could never watch *Schindler's List* as an adult.

Today, parents let their children watch anything at an early age, whether it's horror, violence, or sex. They grow up desensitised they think that it must be normal. It gives them the potential for having the wrong mindset.

I once attended a funeral, a cremation from work. Elsie Woods died aged fifty-eight. She was a dear friend who had suddenly died from a brain haemorrhage. It came as a great shock to all of the staff at work. Elsie was a lovely woman I used to work with at C&A.

When the funeral was over, we all made our way back to our cars. I felt compelled to turn around. As I did, I was reminded yet again of the concentration camps. There was smoke coming out of the crematorium chimney. It looked like a scene from that era, and it made me shudder as I walked back to my car.

Angels

Angels are God's gift to all of humanity. They are there to help us throughout our lives, especially when life becomes difficult. Not a lot of people are aware of this. Perhaps it's because they were never informed from their parents, or it may depend what religion they were brought up in. God gave everyone on this earth a guardian angel to watch over us from the day we were born. All you have to do is acknowledge your angel and then ask for help.

I truly believe in angels. I have read many books on this subject, as well as some very interesting true stories. But there was one book written by Gary Quinn that stood out. I highly recommend it. As I read the book, it gave me instructions on how to invoke the seven angels to help you in your life.

1. The angel of vision
2. The angel of wisdom
3. The angel of purity
4. The angel of love
5. The angel of strength
6. The angel of peace
7. The angel of victory

I thought, *I've nothing to lose. I'll give it a try.* One night after finishing the book I put it into practice. I climbed into bed and made myself comfortable. At the time I thought, *I will concentrate on the first two angels.* I started with the instructions to invoke the angel of vision. Spontaneously in my mind's eye, to my amazement I could see this beautiful being. It could only be described as an angel.

The angel was wearing robes. He looked about thirty years old, and he had the most beautiful, translucent complexion I had ever seen – a true vision of beauty. He had the typical white, soft, curly hair that angels have. The question came straight away. The angel said to me, "Where do you want to be in six months' time?"

Without thinking I replied, "I want to be strong, up and out of my wheelchair, and walking about my home with strength and confidence." I had recently fallen over our dog, Bessie. Unfortunately I had broken my right hip.

The next thing I saw was another angel in identical robes. He stood facing me. He had such piercing blue eyes, but he looked quite old and wrinkly. He must have been the angel of wisdom.

I remember one evening; Harry went to bed first at about eleven thirty, followed by Christopher, my grandson. That left me to switch everything off, which I normally didn't do. It was always Harry who was the last to bed.

As I started to walk through the hall towards the bedroom, the light was shining from Christopher's room and flooding the hallway. All of a sudden Christopher closed his door, which left me in darkness for a split second I slid my hand across the wall towards the light switch, but unbeknown to me, Bessie was asleep at my feet. I came crashing down on the floor and landed on my side, screaming in agony.

Christopher was first on the scene. I told Christopher to place his hands on my hip and to ask the angels for help and healing. He did it straight away without question.

Harry wanted to send for the ambulance, but I wouldn't let him. I said that perhaps I had just jarred my hip, and that I would be alright. As I lay there, my body started to shake. I had a gut feeling and knew that it was something more serious. All the time Christopher was watching me with panic in his eyes, so I started to control my breathing, and soon the shaking subsided.

Daffodil

"If I can sit up without any pain, then I can't have done much damage," I said. I started to sit up with the help of my husband with no problem at all. We all sighed with relief and thought that I couldn't have broken my hip.

Harry slid me along the wooden floor on a rug, still in the seated position into the bedroom. Then he lifted me on to the bed. I managed to get through the night without much disturbance.

The next day when I got up, I was in pain, but it was nothing I couldn't handle. I even managed to get in and out of the bath. I got into my wheelchair that day with a promise that I would go to the hospital the next day.

I already had an appointment scheduled with my consultant, Dr Winfield. They had started me on a special drug treatment for rheumatoid arthritis, and if Harry had sent for the ambulance that night, I would have missed my treatment.

It was important that I have this treatment first. Looking back now, I realise that it was very foolish of me. After all that, the treatment for the RA failed to work, anyway.

At my appointment I told Dr Winfield what had happened. He sent me for an X-ray, which confirmed that yes, I had broken my hip. I would need an operation straightaway to try to save the hip, and to avoid having to replace it. I was devastated.

Dr Winfield left the room for a while, leaving me on my own. I remember crying and being very angry. I shook my fist towards the spirit world and screamed, "Why, why!

Why?" This was a build-up to all that I had been through the last six years. I'd had numerous operations to try and save my right leg.

I was having operations to correct other operations, due to medical negligence. Over the last nine years, I had spent all my time trying to help others heal with reflexology and Reiki treatments. I lead a spiritual life trying to help others, as well as putting up with excruciating pain over the last seventeen years due to rheumatoid arthritis. Then I started going gradually blind through the steroid treatments I was taking to alleviate the RA, causing cataracts. I needed yet another operation. I couldn't take anymore and had had enough. This was the last straw!

If there was a God, then where was he when I needed him? Where were the spirit guides? Where were the angels, if all that I had read and studied was supposed to be true?

The next day I was operated on to try to save the hip with screws. It was to no avail. I had to wait another five months, leaving me in my wheelchair. I eventually had my hip replacement, which was successful thanks to a Dr Buckley, an orthopaedic surgeon at Northern General Hospital in Sheffield.

Now, as I called upon the angels, here I was telling the angel of vision what I wanted in six months' time: to be up and out of my wheelchair, walking around my home with strength and confidence.

It is almost six months since my operation and almost a year since I asked the angel of vision what I wanted. I am glad to say that I am up and out of my wheelchair; I'm feeling much better with the strength and the confidence to walk around my home. I have a long way to go as regards to my health, but there is no denying the angel of vision answered my prayers that night.

One of the instructions in another angel book I read was to ask, "Who am I, and where do I come from?" One night I sat on the edge of my bed, I asked my guardian angel. As it became light the next morning, I was aware that there was something in the corner of the room, but this time it didn't feel evil. It felt spiritual, I could see this figure of a man It was gigantic it touched the ceiling.

He had his back to me from the waist up. I could see his profile: he was very bronze, with thick black hair. He reminded me of a gypsy that one would see at the fairground in the olden days. It was as if he was showing off his physique. He was so beautiful. He looked like a giant archangel.

Daffodil

The next thing I knew, I felt like a little child as I stood in front of this being. All the time I was aware of my surroundings. I was in my bedroom and stood at the side of my bed. I felt about three to four years old. Then the angel looked down at me and gently put two fingers under my chin to tilt my head up. He said, "You are a child from the concentration camps!"

Is this why he appeared the way he did? He was a Jewish gypsy, and he was very proud to be. Not all angels have wings.

School

My first day at school, I remember being petrified, but most kids were in those days. I always remember the first teacher we had, but not her name. She said to all the children in class one morning, "Now, boys and girls don't forget that you all have a guardian angel who is watching over you all the time." I didn't understand at the time, but I liked the sound of having my own guardian angel!

The school was run by a mixture of teachers, some male and some female, and two or three nuns. I remember Sister Veronica and Sister Gonzales. But there was one particular female teacher, a typical spinster named Miss Smith. I remember she was very thin and wore glasses. She was very strict, and all the kids were frightened of her, I included.

One particular day, I had to go stand by her desk at her side to do some maths. I remember feeling very nervous at the time. The next thing I knew, I must have answered a question incorrectly. She picked up a pencil and started to tap it hard into my right temple, shouting at the top of her head; repeatedly "you noodle" I was mortified, it felt quite painful. I was five years old. What a great start to my education!

I remember shouting in my head, *why do people have to shout at one another? I hate it!* Of course it was my parents always shouting at one another that brought on my dislike. My first day at school was like jumping out of the frying pan and into the fire. From that day forward I became very frightened of school, I kept my head down.

When I moved up into junior school, there was a nun called Sister Veronica. She was the only teacher who was gentle and kind to me. She was soft-spoken and taught me how to sew.

Daffodil

Then there was another nun – I can't remember her name, or maybe I have just blocked it from my memory. I had to stand by her side to do some reading. As she started to trace her finger along the wording, I stumbled on a word and found that I couldn't carry on. Even though I knew the word, my throat froze. The nun's response was to wrap her hand over the back of mine, curl my knuckles in her hand, and knock them hard on the table several times till it hurt. Well, that did it! I thought *this isn't right. Every time I get things wrong, I am going to be punished!* From that day on, I kept a low profile. When I look back on those days, I was frightened of my own shadow. Fear ruled my life.

I remember days when I didn't go to school. My mum and dad went to work. I would stay away from school through pure fear. I wouldn't stay in the house on my own, though; I always felt as if I was been watched.

There were some steps across the road that led to a neighbour's house, with high walls on either side of the steps so that I couldn't be seen. I would spend my days there in all weather, even when it was raining, till school turned out. Soon the authorities found out, and soon put a stop to it. Things never seemed to get any better. I was too afraid to ask the teachers a question or raise my hand, even though I might know the answer. In the end I left school with the basics. I had no qualifications. I was also near-sighted but wouldn't wear glasses for fear of being picked on.

There were many times I wished things could have been different. It's so important that children have a good education and a good start, especially when they start school for the first time. It can have such an impact on their lives. It's nice to think that my children had a better start than I did. They enjoyed their school days, except for my son Wayne. He was more like me that way – a bit of a loner. He never settled into secondary school when we moved house. He left school with little qualifications. Yet Wayne now runs his own business.

Wayne is now forty-six. I'm so proud of him for what he has achieved. It's the same with my other three sons: they, too, have managed to hold jobs down since leaving school. They've all been good providers for their families.

It's important to note that a good education and being academic does not qualify you for having a good soul. You don't need qualifications to have a good soul – only a good heart! My kids certainly have good hearts. I'm so grateful for having them in my life, and I'm proud of them all. Thank you, God, for lending me your precious children.

More Memories

Because Harry and I married very young, we liked the same type of music with our children. Music played constantly in our house, and there was always a nice atmosphere: laughter, dancing, and singing. I guess that's what happens when you marry young. You all grow up together. We were only kids ourselves.

One day when Dad called unexpectedly, the music was blaring out as usual. He noted, "There's plenty of love radiating from this house. You can feel it when you walk in."

I know now what he meant. He used to say, "You two will still be young, when the kids have grown up. You'll still have your lives ahead of you."

Over the years I suppose my father was teaching me spiritually without being aware of it, and neither was I.

I was supposed to go to church every Sunday at an early age, and sometimes to Holy Communion. This meant having no breakfast. Sometimes we would have to go to communion before going to school, and yet again we'd have no breakfast.

Sometimes I would feel quite faint. My knees would hurt because we would have to kneel and pray for what seemed like forever on those dark rainy mornings in the winter, with no heating in the church. I used to think, *if there is a God, he wouldn't want me to feel like this*. It didn't seem right. I always thought that if I believed in God, then that was between me and God alone. It was a very private matter.

I brought my children up in that manner. I never forced religion onto them. If they wanted to know more, they were free to do so. I didn't believe in all this going to church, kneeling down, and doing all the rituals that went with it – going to confession to be forgiven for our sins, saying ten Hail Mary's and ten Our Fathers to be forgiven – so that whatever sin we had committed, we could do it all again the very next day! It seemed ludicrous.

Then one day in church, I saw a priest wearing a deep purple robe. I couldn't take my eyes off this colour; it was the first time I'd ever seen it. I made my mind up there and then that this would be my favorite colour of all time. Little did I know that it is one of the highest colours in the spiritual realm.

My father had very strict views on Catholic religion. He went to mass every Sunday; if he missed morning mass, he would attend the evening session. If we hadn't attended mass, my mother included, he would turn around just before he left for church and say, "Well I suppose I will have to pray for all your souls."

Mum would reply, "You don't need to bleedin' bother. It will take you all day to pray for your own." We couldn't help but laugh. He wanted me to be the same, but my heart wasn't in it.

Why did I feel this way? Was I a bad person, or was I remembering who I truly was? I remember one particular time, my father shouted, "Eileen! Have you been to church today?"

"No, Dad."

My dad shouted at the top of his voice. "Why?" I came up with some meager excuse. "Well what sort of God do you believe in, then? Get out in bleedin' yard and worship the sun." He promised fear and damnation, and that I would go to hell! I looked up at my father's face, trying to look serious and holy, but I had to turn my face away to suppress my laughter. I'm sure my father caught me out of the corner of his eye, which brought a smile to his face.

Despite my father's anger, at times he did have a good sense of humour. I remember onetime, Mum was cooking bacon sausage and eggs for Dad's breakfast. It would be burnt to a cinder more often than not. She would place the meal in front of him. Dad would take one look at the burnt sausages and say with much sarcasm, "She's the only person I know that can go bleedin' shopping and cook at the same time." This always made me and mum laugh.

The Early Days

I met Harry my husband when I was fourteen. We met in a café called Why Worry. It was in Attercliffe, in Sheffield. He was stood with a crowd of friends; I was with my best friend at the time Kathleen Creaghan. We were wearing the latest fashion, with starched underneath skirts that made our dresses stick out for miles, but it didn't half make our legs chafe when we walked, with the amount of starch that went into them. We wore our hair in the latest style, the bouffant. We thought we looked sensational.

Harry was sixteen. He looked so smart wearing an Italian suit, white shirt, and tie. His hair was combed back at the sides, with the top all tousled and sprayed with sugar and water, home-made hair spray.

He walked over to me and asked if he could sit down. We started chatting. When we said our goodbyes, he looked into my eyes and said, "You have the most beautiful blue eyes. Can I see you again?"

Well, that was it! We married in December 1963. I was sixteen and pregnant, and Harry was eighteen. Wayne, my first born, arrived in 19/7/64. I was to bear another son, Darren, on 15/4/66, and then twin boys, Richard and Michael, on 29/6/68.

It was two weeks before I gave birth, after I was told I was having twins! We couldn't believe it we were both in a daze. We were so young – how were we going to cope with four little children? But somehow you do, we just got on with it.

Looking back now, I feel totally blessed that I gave birth to four healthy children. It was hard work, but I wouldn't have changed a thing. Mum used to say to me, "You shouldn't be married and tied down with four kids at your age. You should be out enjoying yourself with your friends." She was right, of course, but you know what teenagers can be like. They think they know everything at that age.

Then sometimes she would say, "Well, I suppose I don't have to worry about you getting in with the wrong crowd and dabbling in drugs. It could be a blessing in disguise." I didn't miss that part of my life. Harry and I were always out dancing with our friends whenever the opportunity arose. The drug scene never interested us; I was too obsessed with keeping my body fit.

Mum may have been right in some ways. But it was my choice; I know I made the right one.

The life I had chosen for myself was a better life than I had when I was living at home. No disrespect to my parents, but that was simply the way it was.

Harry once took me to Scarborough. I was about fifteen at the time. We were walking along the sea front, and we came upon one of those fortune tellers. Harry said, "Go on, I dare you," and he shoved me inside the doorway. I went in, and it cost two shillings.

The fortune teller told me that we would marry, would have children, and would have twins. Also, he said we would be happy. We ran away laughing, but it all came true!

We have had our ups and downs, like most marriages do. We were only kids when we married.

Almost forty-three years later, we are still going strong with seven wonderful grandchildren. I feel blessed.

Harry always worked hard to provide a home for us, working long hours. Sometimes he would work twelve hours a day, seven days a week. It was very hard bringing up four children. There never seemed to be enough money to go around.

Sometimes we didn't even have a shilling for the gas meter, but we always pulled through. Most of all, we could laugh about it. Something

Daffodil

always turned up. There's no shame in being poor, we did the best we could. The kids never went without, although we wished we could have given them more at the time.

I used to buy items from a shop on the weekly, mostly children's clothes. I never missed a payment. If there was one thing my mother had taught me, it was never to be like her when it came to money. I couldn't get a job while the children were so young.

At twenty-one years old, I had four children all under school age. Life wasn't easy in those days; family allowance was paid on a Tuesday. We hoped we would manage till payday, and we always did. I don't think much has changed today with young families.

It wasn't like it is today; with all the benefits you are allowed. There's got to be something wrong with the benefit system, when they actually pay you more benefits for the more children you have. But I don't want to dwell on this topic.

One particular day, after a bad night coping with the twins' colic problems, Harry had been working the night shift. I walked into the bedroom and disturbed him. "I can't cope anymore, Harry!" I was shaking and crying at the same time. I'd never felt like this before. What was happening to me! Was I having a nervous breakdown? It wasn't like me, it was frightening. After a good cry, I knew I had to pull myself together. I had to be strong for my kids. I don't know how, but I found the strength.

When I look back at that time; it makes me wonder whether it was postnatal depression, which was unheard of in those days. Nevertheless, I knew that only I could bring myself out of it, and I did. I made the right choice when I could have easily gone under.

Harry was always so patient with me when times got tough. He would talk me through it all. I would calm down eventually, and my strength would be restored once again.

I learned to drive because it made it much easier with the kids; we always had a holiday. Dad used to say later in his life, "Isn't life wonderful, Eileen?"

I used to look at him whilst frowning and think, *Is it?* I found life hard most times.

I found that if I could engage my father in a conversation, he'd seem to calm right down, as if he lost his anger and frustration. That was how I became closer to my dad in his later years. Dad always seemed uptight, like a coiled spring ready to pounce at anytime, ready for confrontation. It scared me a little. Sometimes I would find him in one of his moods, I would start the conversation. Soon I would see that calmness wash over him.

He would say sometimes when he'd had a drink, "I'm nothing but a failure. What have I done with my life?" I could see the regret and disappointment in his eyes; he'd look so sad and despondent. I never knew what to say to him.

I would laugh and say, "You! How could you be? You have two beautiful daughters!"

This answer always seemed to pacify him. It was to become a regular thing. I think he simply wanted to hear me say those words to him, so that he would feel better. It's saddens me.

My dad wasn't a failure. He was my dad, after all, deep down I loved him despite his outrageous behaviour at times. All the shouting and raging he did, all the anger inside him – I believe it came from his childhood. Dad didn't have it easy as a child.

When I saw the medium Paul Parker, my dad came through; he spoke of his childhood difficulties. He was unhappy as a child, my grandfather was always trying to toughen him up, to make him do things he didn't want to do. He didn't have it easy growing up as a child with his parents. Paul Parker said that my father came through as a lovely, gentle, spiritual man. Deep down I knew he was.

When my children were old enough, I tried my hand at different jobs. I finished up working for the C&A Department store in Sheffield in 1974 at age twenty-seven, as a sales assistant.

It was a good firm to work for and a very well-paid job, but some of the staff were very unpleasant. If you were pretty and had a nice figure,

Daffodil

it didn't always go down very well, especially with some of the older ones. I was always in trouble for some petty crime, like talking or chewing when I was not supposed to, or calling everybody by first names instead of Miss, or Mrs.

Although I only worked part time, certain members of staff could make my life hell. I remember days going to work happy and content, but I'd come home in tears. I used to ask myself, *is it all worth it?* I was always getting singled out. Despite it all, the pay was good; I stuck it out for almost twenty years.

Little did I know over the years working for the C&A, all the stress of working in that environment for a long time took its toll on my health? I was never relaxed at work, and there was always tension in the air. One day I was serving customers on the desk, and suddenly I wanted to drop everything and run out of the shop. That's how bad it got.

As I said before, it was a good firm to work for. It was down to certain management and staff at the time.
I know this sort of thing goes on all the time in the workplace, but the reason I mention this is because stress on the body over a long period of time can be detrimental, especially on the immune system.
It can cause all kinds of illnesses, both mental and physical problems. I am sure this fact contributed to my illness. It is so important that we are happy in the workplace.
I loved working with clothes and the new fashions trends that were coming in all the time. I loved being dressed up with my makeup and hair done. It was a pleasure to work in those days. The trouble was, I spent all my wages on clothes for myself and the family. We had some great bargains over the years, especially with a 20 per cent discount.

If you are working in an unhappy environment that is making you ill, my advice is to get out! Find a job you are happy in! If you don't, it will take its toll on your well-being. Be happy in your surroundings.

I was talking to a retired man the other day. He said that he had worked behind a desk for thirty-one years. He used to dread going to work every day. He had recently found a little part-time job, a manual job. He said that he was enjoying himself for the first time in his life, he was happy and relaxed. He felt so much healthier.

Constant stress on the body takes its toll, It's got to come out somewhere, because we are human, not machines. That's why people have nervous breakdowns, by letting stress build up.

For the person to have a healthy body, the mind, body, and soul have to work in unison, as a whole working in harmony. The correct term is homeostasis. That's why meditation on a daily basis is so important. Even if everyone did only ten minutes a day, the national health would save millions of pounds a year.

Oh, how I'd wished I'd known all those years ago what to do. But that wasn't my life's path. I had to experience first all that I have written before I could write the book, so that I could help others. Phew, what a journey it's been!

Now, I have a confession to make. I stole from my employer C&A, the company who paid me a good salary, provided me with two uniforms every year, and gave Christmas bonuses, not to mention a 20 per cent discount every year. Yes, you read right. How could I? But before you judge me, read on.

When I was searching for the truth about the meaning of life, when I thought about taking on the task of writing a book, I knew I would have to be totally honest – not just with the reader but also with myself. I would have to confess. I had to come clean. Why did I do it? I didn't need to. I was in a well-paid job.

I was an opportunist, so whenever the opportunity arose, I would steal the odd garment now and then.

Eventually the guilt kicked in and started to eat away at me. I had a permanent worried look on my face,

Friends would say, "Are you all right, Eileen? You look worried."

Of course I couldn't confess to anyone, not even Harry. I'd lose everything – my job, my dependence, and respect from my friends and family. What a complete idiot I'd been. There was no excuse at all.

I couldn't eat, sleep, or relax; it was taking control of me. There was just no justification as to why I did this. I got no joy out of wearing the garments or a buzz from it, like most shoplifters say they experience. It didn't make any sense.

Then one Saturday afternoon, I came home from work and went to bed to try to catch up on some sleep, but to no avail. I was beating myself up in my mind all the time. It suddenly occurred to me that I had to gain control of my life. Only I could bring a stop to this.

From that day on, it never happened again. I felt free and happy again. Once I had taken control of my life, it was that easy. I tried to make amends by working twice as hard. All I could think about was how fortunate it was that I was never found out. My psychic mind tells me that some of my colleagues were suspicious.

Many times I felt a presence around me when I was about to steal something; it was as if I was being watched from above. At that time I hadn't discovered my spiritual journey. Many times I would hear a voice in my head warning me, but I would ignore it and think it was my imagination.

I'm very ashamed that this happened to me. I hope my family will forgive me when they read this. Now that I have confessed, I know God will forgive me.

Did this happen yet again so that I could warn others if they are stealing, or even contemplating stealing? Don't do it! Nothing goes unnoticed. Even if you think you've gotten away with it, you are being watched from above.

By confessing and saying sorry to God of this sin, my soul will be purified. After all, it is written in the Ten Commandments, "Thou shall not steal." In fact they are really the Ten Commitments, which I write more about towards the end of the book.

This is why I had to confess. I didn't have to, for no one ever found out about me and my misdemeanour. But it would be a blemish on my soul if I hadn't confessed. I don't want to take that home with me when I pass over. To anyone out there who is stealing for whatever reason, or even contemplating doing so, please think very carefully. There will be consequences- karma.

Anita

One of my memories of working for the C&A was a lady named Anita. She worked full-time and had worked for the C&A for quite some time. We didn't always get on well. She could make my life hell if she felt inclined. But she wasn't just like that with me – she was like that with other members of staff. It wasn't the fact that I disliked her – far from it. Anita was a very attractive woman, her looks being a cross between Marty Cain the Sheffield comedian and Sophia Loren the film star.

As the years passed on and I got to know Anita, I could tell she was a very unhappy woman, especially when she lost her husband, Jim, at the age forty-one to a heart attack. Jim was at home at the time, Anita was at work.

Jim had sat in his armchair at home, and suddenly he turned to his eldest son. He held out his hand, towards him "I'm going, son, I'm going." He died there and then in his armchair. I think to myself, *what a pleasant way to die, especially if it is your time.*

Anita became very insecure over the coming years. She worried about getting older, losing her looks, and not meeting the right man. I began to tolerate Anita more. I put up with the bad days, when I had to work with her. If she was in one of her moods, it would affect everyone who worked with her. Looking back now, it is easy to see that Anita was suffering from depression.

In 1992 just before I had to retire due to ill health, Anita and I became much closer. I remember Anita asking me if I would like to go see a clairvoyant. I didn't really want to at the time, because I had started

Daffodil

with my illness. I didn't want to receive more bad news, but I went along with it anyway, for her sake.

I remember the clairvoyant saying to Anita that she saw her wearing a fur coat and getting onto a plane in the middle of winter with snow on the ground. Anita was coming up for retirement; she was about fifty-eight at the time. All she would talk about was her new flat, what she was going to do to it, whether she was going to meet Mr. Right and be happy. She mentioned all the things she would do when she retired.

Anita was a smoker, and sadly she died of lung cancer before she retired. I remember going to see her in hospital before she died. There was snow on the ground. It made me think of what the clairvoyant had told her. Was she getting on the plane to the next dimension? Did the clairvoyant see her death approaching?

The day of Anita's funeral, I remember being in the chapel. It was packed with work colleagues, friends, and family. I stared at the coffin on the platform. All of a sudden I saw Anita standing at the side of her coffin. She looked radiant. She was wearing a black pencil skirt just below the knee, with a peach twin set and a string of pearls round her neck. Her hair was an auburn colour that came to her neck. She looked beautiful, radiant, and healthy.

The thing that struck me most of all was her energy. She was so happy. She had the biggest smile on her face. It was as if she couldn't believe all the people that had attended her funeral. I had a feeling she thought that people didn't care much for her, and that she wasn't loved.

Then she looked at me and smiled. She spoke to me, "I hope you are not chewing, Mrs. Richmond!" As I write this memory, I can see her as plain as day, but at the time I thought it must be my imagination. Thanks for that, Anita.

Was it her way of saying, "Sorry. I know I wasn't always kind to you"?
After Anita died, I couldn't help thinking how unfair it all was. She had nearly reached retirement, and had made plans for the future. But that's life. We should never take life for granted, because we never know what's around the corner.

As the years passed by and my illness progressed, I remember lying across my bed one day in terrible pain. In my mind's eye I saw Anita sitting at the top corner of my bed, next to my pillow. She had her arms folded and was sobbing softly, as if not to disturb me. She knew I was in pain; she could feel it. I felt comforted by her presence.

Ibiza

In 1989 Harry and I went on holiday for two weeks to Ibiza, just the two of us. The children were off our hands, we were enjoying life. We sat outside a bar on our last night in Ibiza. We were flying home the next day. I remember feeling quite shivery, and I could feel a lump in the back of my throat when I tried to swallow. I thought perhaps I was coming down with a bad cold.

The next day I seemed to be all right. We got home, and on Saturday night we went out with our friends. The following Sunday morning, when I got out of bed, my body felt so stiff, as if I had overdone it with the exercise.

As the day went on, my left upper arm felt as if someone had stabbed me with a knife and was twisting it round and round. I was in agony; I didn't know what to do. I didn't keep any medications in the house. In those days, I wouldn't even take an aspirin for a headache. The only thing I had in the house was red wine. I was so desperate that I drank it from the bottle, but to no avail. I couldn't get any relief.

Harry took one look at me and sent for the doctor, who arrived late Sunday afternoon. He examined me but seemed more interested in my suntan. He gave me painkillers and said if I was no better, I should attend surgery later that week, which I did. I felt so lethargic, all my joints ached, and I couldn't even lift my arms.

Six months later, it was discovered that I had Rheumatoid Arthritis. I'd never even heard of it; I thought arthritis only affected old people. I had never been ill in my life, apart from a cold or flu now and then.

I was forty-one I had always taken care of myself after having had four children. I couldn't believe it was happening to me, I was devastated.

I was given some drugs, by a consultant at the hospital. He told me to come back in three months time. The next thing was to try and read all the books and information I could get my hands on to help myself. There were books that said I could cure it through fasting, detox, or strange diets. I spent pounds on pills, potions, and homeopathy, all to no avail; although I do believe that some diets helped a little.

This was in the early stages. As the years went on, the pain worsened. I was told that there were varying degrees of RA. I had the worst form of the disease, and it was very aggressive. It was ruining my life. I had difficulty working, and later I developed osteoporosis, too.

At the beginning of the illness, I would experience remissions now and then, which gave me hope it would never return. But it wasn't to be. It's been twenty years since I had a remission. Still I live in hope that one day they may find a miracle cure for me. Especially when I hear of a miracles happening, like the man who had his eyesight returned to him after ten years, which I've wrote about in the book. I never give up hope, and you should never give up, either.

In the end, I had to give up my job by August 1993. That morning I was so bad that I couldn't even get out of bed. How could I possibly hold on to my job? I was devastated. I'd lost my independence. Meanwhile, the disease worsened. I had to do something. I couldn't go on like this, and it was affecting all our lives, although I had love and support from Harry, and the children.

One night I went to bed in excruciating pain. I cried out to God to help me. I became so desperate. "If there is a God out there! Then please show me the way. Tell me what to do. Please help me." I cried myself to sleep. During the night the pain woke me up once the drugs had worn off.

Then it was like a voice in my head, a female voice (was this my higher self?) saying, "Eileen, take the pain out of the body, away from the body."

I thought, *but how?* It was as if I had to separate my body from the pain by putting it on the outside.

Then I started to visualize. I saw all the pain around my body as red inflammation. I started to concentrate on my breathing. I imagined that as I was breathing out, I was breathing out all the inflammation, all the negativity I felt.

Then as I started to breathe in, I visualised the colour blue, and it was cool and soothing to my body. Blue is the colour for healing, although I didn't know it at the time. It began to ease the pain and stress of it all. Eventually I had the best night's sleep in a long time!

If you can visualize whilst trying to heal yourself, then that's all the better. It's a great asset, and your body will believe what you tell it, just by a simple thought. When I have had an appointment for the next morning, and I haven't had an alarm clock to wake me, I've said to myself, "I must be up for a certain time." I have always awoken just before, or on the hour.

For all the pain sufferers out there who are in need of pain relief, breathe in the blue, and breathe out red. It is a good idea to breathe out all of the negativity as well. That's all it takes. Use your thoughts and imagination. If it doesn't work the first time, keep practicing and don't give up. Never give up!

Colours can be used in all sorts of healing. Our chakras are made up of colours. There are many reference books available which discuss the powerful healing effects of colour. There have been many tests carried out on people using colours. One of the tests patients were subjected to was the colour violet, for instance. Several of them had drops in their pulse rate. There is also a method with crystal therapy for healing the body; it can accelerate the healing power in the body.

I started to read books on meditation and mind over matter. I soon became interested in all the alternative therapies. One particular therapy I became interested in was reflexology. I found it very soothing and therapeutic. It took all my stress away, and I was sleeping so much better. I was so impressed that I took a foundation course with the International Institute of Reflexology in South Yorkshire. It was an accredited course, and it wasn't easy.

Then I started to have doubts. I had no idea what it all entailed. First of all, we had to study anatomy and physiology. Had I bitten off more than I could chew? What had I gotten myself into? Panic struck, but it was too late. I'd got to go ahead with it now because I had paid the eight-hundred-pound fee. However, it was the best thing I had ever done in my life! It was so rewarding, I passed all my exams and became a fully trained reflexologist.

I always remember our tutor saying to us all on the first day in class, "My name is Loretta Cusworth, and I would like to welcome you all. By the way, you know we have all been here before." Loretta got some strange looks from the class, except me. Straight away I knew I was going to get along with this woman. She also mentioned that all dolphins eventually would become extinct, and that we would all be needed in 2012. What did she mean?

Years later, I realised what Loretta meant. In the near future I would be writing a book to help humanity, and all my research and experience would end up in a book. The world was going to change dramatically after 2012. The world was going to need all the help it could get and we should expect great changes to take place.

I also met Wendy Early in class, and we paired up whilst learning reflexology. When it came for me to work on Wendy's feet, I had the strangest feeling come over me. I was looking at her without her noticing me. It was like that déjà vu feeling, as if I had done this before.

We became good friends, mainly through illness – me with my RA, and Wendy with myalgic encephalopathy. We helped each other with reflexology and Reiki treatments on a weekly basis from 1998 to 2008. I owe a great deal to Wendy. She has also counseled me, too, especially when the pain was unbearable. She is a true saint if ever there was one. I trust Wendy with my life. I feel that I have known Wendy in another life, perhaps. We share a very strong bond with each other, despite the age gap. Wendy now works in hospices giving reflexology treatments to dying patients.

When my studies were coming to a close, we were given the opportunity to learn Reiki in the first and second degree. Reiki is a

Daffodil

form of Japanese healing and is the Japanese word for "universal life force energy"; another word for this energy is chi, and in Chinese it means "life force energy". We all have this and are born with it. It is our birthright to connect with this.

Once you have been attuned in the initiation process, anyone can lay her hands on another person to help accelerate the healing process by transferring magnetic energy. It works on the energy centers also known has the chakras. The patient will draw enough universal life force energy to the areas of the body that need it. The person giving the Reiki treatment also receives treatment at the same time.

The energy enters at the crown the seventh chakra, which is situated on the top of the head. The energy then passes through other energy centers to the throat, heart, solar plexus, and groin area, and then through the arms and hands to the patient's body. This is where the chi is activated. Sometimes the chi can become blocked, just like in reflexology. Reiki and reflexology helps clear theses areas, bringing life force and a feeling of well-being back into the body.

In 1997 while studying to become a reflexologist I noticed that my hands had improved. By keeping my hands manipulated, I had good movement in them, although the damage to my wrists was obvious. By this time I was limping quite noticeably, and the pain in my right ankle was horrendous.

I had to find someone to help me. I rang up the National Federation of Healers and made an appointment with Mr. Alan Bellinger. This man was to change my life forever.

Alan lives in a beautiful house that sits deep in the Valley of Hope in Hathersage, Derbyshire, with beautiful countryside surroundings. I remember thinking what a beautiful setting, and how appropriate it was to call it Hope Valley.

Harry drove me to Alan's home for the first time. I knew he'd be straight off and wouldn't want to come in with me. "I'm off, then," he said. "I'll have a walk round the village to pass the time. See you in about an hour, love."

Alan opened the door with a cheerful welcome. He was of slight build with fair hair and blue eyes. He was quite sprightly on his feet for a man of eighty-four; he seemed to have bounds of energy – a lot more than me. Alan introduced me to his wife, Joyce. She looked like a rather elegant lady, with her hair swept up in a chignon.

After we had spoken, Joyce left the room. Alan told me to sit on a stool that was in the centre of the room. Alan left the room for a couple of minutes. As I sat there looking around at the beautiful surroundings the furnishings and portraits, the strangest feeling came over me. I felt so warm so peaceful; it was as if I had come home, like this was the beginning of the rest of my life, a new chapter was about to unfold.

When Alan came back into the room, he said, "Well then, Eileen, how can I help?" I gave him a rundown of my problems, but mainly it was my right ankle that was giving me so such pain. He said he would do his best, but he couldn't promise me anything. As Alan proceeded, I soon became very calm, but to my disappointment I didn't feel any different. Alan didn't even charge me any money.

I felt obliged to make another appointment the following week. On the next appointment, once again nothing happened. I was so disappointed. As Alan was healing me, he said, "You know, people who commit suicide just have to come back to do it all again."

I thought *what a strange thing to say.*

Alan offered to help me with my coat, but he must have seen the disappointed look on my face; I'm not good at hiding my feelings. As we said goodbye, Alan gave me a quizzical look. It was as if he must have read my mind: the healing wasn't working. After nodding his head, he gave me a wink and said, "Oh, but it will. It will." He was so confident and sure of himself.

The next appointment with Alan was in June 1997 on a lovely sunny Friday afternoon. We arrived at 3.00 PM, and this time Alan made a point of introducing himself to Harry before my husband sped off to the village. After entering the house, we had our usual chat before starting. I sat on the stool waiting for Alan to proceed, hoping with all my heart that something would happen. I was getting desperate.

Daffodil

Alan started the session. He placed his hands on the top of my head, which represents the seventh crown chakra. I will explain about the chakras later in the book. Then as he reached the area round my throat, I felt as if I was swaying and not in control of my body. My head started to drop to my chest. Alan must have thought I was going to fall, he whispered in my ear to move over to the sofa. I didn't want to move. It felt so relaxing, I didn't want to come out of it, yet I was aware of my surroundings and what was happening in the room. With my eyes half closed, I drifted over to the sofa. I was thinking; *Please don't let this feeling stop.*

The next thing I knew, I was not in this world! It felt as if I was in another world, some kind of other dimension. I found myself in a little, old chapel, sitting amongst other beings. I could feel this tremendous, unconditional love all around me, it filled my body.

Then all of a sudden it was as if, from a distance, I could see this man stood on the church rostrum. He had an open book in his hand and was pointing a finger towards me, giving me instructions. As I looked down the church aisle, on either side there were angels singing on my behalf. It was all for me! I found this very touching.

The feeling I had was as if I had been chosen to perform some kind of task, something very special. But I wasn't told with words; I was told by telepathy, an understanding without words spoken. I felt unworthy of such a task, and I started to protest that I was an ordinary person. I kept saying in disbelief, "Me? But I'm nobody. I'm not good enough to do this. I can't do it!"

Then all of a sudden I lowered my head and had a feeling that said, "Don't you realise where you are?" I knew I was in the presence of something beyond my comprehension, and it was so powerful. I knew it was divine. Then it was as if I suddenly remembered. I feel very honored and privileged. But most of all, I felt very humble in front of these beings. Yet again I felt this tremendous, unconditional love. I felt like an innocent child in this experience.

I had no memory of the task in hand. It was as if that was for me to find out, and that was my life's journey. It was why I was born. I only had this feeling of being chosen, whether or not I liked it. It was a kind of knowing, to do this task before I die. It became my mission. I was in total shock.

Then I was aware of my surroundings, I decided to test my right ankle. I got up to walk across the room so that I could sit in the armchair on the right far side. Alan stood in front of the fireplace, looking in the opposite direction towards the sofa. I realised, *I'm out of my body!* It was as if I'd left my physical body behind, still on the sofa! I was aware of everything in the room. As I looked at my surroundings, I checked the sofa.

I saw a man with his back to me, and he was talking to me on the sofa. I sat in the chair on the opposite side of the room in my spirit body – or should I say out of my body! I sat and watched this man. I saw his every detail. He wore a dark navy pinstripe suit. I saw his curled-up right hand by his side. In his left arm he held a book. Could this be the same man I saw in the chapel, on the rostrum?

His hair was thick and silvery white, and it rested over the back of his collar. I felt he was some sort of doctor or guide. I stood up, facing Alan and banging on my chest with my fist, shouting, "Alan, I'm here! I'm here!" He didn't see me or hear me; he was looking over towards the sofa at my physical body. I could see everything around me, but why couldn't Alan see me or hear me? What was happening to me? This was not a dream.

I remember thinking, *so this is how it is. No one will ever believe me!*

Then I look upwards, and I saw a spirit body floating above my head; it was male. I only saw it from the waist up. He was wearing a white shirt, and he had silver white hair. He looked to be in his late sixties. He repeatedly told me, "It's going to be all right, it's going to be fine." Again, everything was telepathic.

This took place in broad daylight, in the middle of Alan's living room on a lovely, sunny Friday afternoon in June 1997. It is a day I can never forget.

Soon I was aware that I was back in my body. I was sat on the sofa, and I opened my eyes. My cheeks were wet with tears. I was overwhelmed

Daffodil

and so happy that I couldn't speak. I felt in a daze. It felt like I was in shock, but in a nice way, trying to comprehend what had just taken place. Life would never be the same again.

Alan sat on a stool in front of me, and he said, "Eileen, tell me what happened." There was excitement in his voice; I could see he was also shocked at what had just happened. I didn't know where to begin. I just kept staring at Alan and moving my head slowly from side to side. Still in a daze, I started by saying to Alan, "It must be wonderful to be able help people heal."

By this time Joyce, had entered the room to see what all the commotion was about. Alan answered by saying, "Yes, it is, but we would like some recognition for it."

Automatically I said, "I will give you recognition." Where did that come from? Who did I think I was? How dare I come out with such a statement? All I know was it felt right at the time.

Alan said that while I was out of it, he had been watching me. I was either laughing or crying, and sometimes my face would change into a young girl's, like some kind of metamorphism kept taking place. I remember feeling like an innocent child once again.

I wanted to tell Alan in every detail what had just happened to me, but I was so astounded by it all that I didn't know where to begin. Then it was like someone was saying to me, "Now is not the time." This was my higher self speaking to me, although I didn't know this at the time. I kept it quiet.

It wasn't till later in 2006, when I started writing my book, that I gave all the details to Alan.

On the way home on that special day from Alan's, Harry asked me how I felt. I was still reeling from what had just happened. I thought *how am I going to explain this to Harry?* All I knew was what had happened was real. My life would never be the same.

As Harry and I were driving home, we pulled up at a pelican crossing in a busy area. I watched all these people crossing the road; I was looking at their faces one by one. Suddenly I wanted to get out of the car and shout to all the people, "This isn't all there is! I know, because I have just witnessed it! I have seen it with my own eyes!"

I started to tell Harry in a round-about way what had taken place at Alan's house. I could see that he was struggling, trying to come to terms with what I was saying to him. He listened to me as he always did, but it made no impact on him whatsoever. However, it had on me, and that was all that mattered!

Oh how I wished Harry would believe in me. I wanted to cry with great frustration. To have something so overwhelming happen to me, and for no one to believe me, had to be a crime. Sometimes when I tell Harry things that happen to me, it's as if he is only half listening. He's always looking for the logical reason. But this was so special, so how could he not believe me?

Nevertheless, I knew what I had just witnessed. I felt elated and was on cloud nine for weeks. I was hardly able to contain myself. I wanted to tell the world! I have to tell the world.
When something of this great magnitude happens to you, there's no going back. You don't go back to your old life. Things are never the same, your life changes forever.
But why had this happened to me? What did it all mean? I was just an ordinary, down-to-earth person.

Harry Edwards

Whilst visiting Alan's, he asked me if I knew a Harry Edwards. I had never heard of Harry Edwards, but by this time I had become very interested in my research into spiritualism.

Alan gave me some information on books and tapes that I could acquire from the Harry Edwards Healing Sanctuary, in Guildford, Surrey. I soon sent for the information and I ordered a couple of his books. When they arrived, I couldn't wait to start reading them.

As I started to flip through the first few pages of the book, there was a photo of the author, Harry Edwards. This was the very same man I'd seen at Alan Bellinger's, floating above my head! The same man who told me I was going to be all right! I couldn't believe it! I did my research and read all I could on Harry Edwards. Harry I even went down to Surrey to visit his healing sanctuary.

Synopsis: - Harry Edwards. Was a modern-day Jesus Christ, doing God's work? His life's journey his soul's purpose was to come down to earth to help mankind with the wonderful healing gift that he had been granted from the spirit world. For over forty years, he brought relief to countless thousands of people from all over the world, suffering from every known physical and mental sickness. He publicly demonstrated his wonderful gift of healing in every major city and town throughout Britain, in many countries abroad, performing what the press often termed "miracles of healing". What a wonderful man.

Alan and Joyce witnessed many of the healings right before their eyes: curvature of the spine, club foot, and severe arthritic conditions. How can you witness such a wonderful thing and not have it change your life or make you think? How can people simply sit there and accept what's going on in front of them? I wanted to find out more. I had to search for the truth. What was behind it, how could this be possible?

These two lovely people, Alan and Joyce Bellinger, have opened up their home to the public to whoever needed healing. They have devoted most of their lives to helping and healing others for little reward, other than seeing people healed. I think it is something to be proud of. I feel very honored and privileged to have known these two people, even if only for a brief moment with Joyce, who later died of a heart condition.

On the day Joyce died, Alan told me he had brought her breakfast in bed that morning. She asked him to stay awhile; she just wanted to talk. Joyce patted the bed for him to come and sit down. She said she felt peaceful at the time. After a few minutes of idle chatter, Alan started to do his neck and eye exercise. He always kept himself fit on a daily basis.

Joyce remarked that at his age, didn't he think it was about time he started slowing down a bit? "Of course not," Alan replied. "I've done it all my life. One day I will be the fittest corpse in the mortuary."

Joyce started to laugh, as she gasped, then she was gone! Despite Alan's attempt to resuscitate her. Joyce passed over peacefully. I am pleased that they were together at the end. Joyce suffered with heart problems all her life. One might say, "Well, if that was the case, why hadn't Alan and Harry Edwards, who were both healers, done something about Joyce's heart condition?"

At some point in Joyce's life, she had been to visit Steven Toorof, where he performed psychic surgery on Joyce's heart. The only evidence visible afterwards was a two-inch red line across Joyce's chest near the heart. Maybe this added more years to Joyce's life.

The only thing certain is that Joyce died at the correct time. When it's our time to die, no one can intervene. There will always be a right time to be born and a right time to die. This was how it was supposed to be. I've no doubt that Alan and Harry Edwards did try at some point to help Joyce with her heart condition.

It's like I explained earlier, regarding why some people are healed and some are not. You can only ask for the client to be healed for her highest good. If the healing doesn't take place, then there is a good reason. It would interfere with their blueprint for the life being lived now. This has to do with the spirit, the soul. You must remember that you are not being punished. You will find out the reason why sooner or later, it will all make sense one day.

Alan used to tell me that as a boy, when he was bored, he used to leave his body at random. He thought that everybody could do the same thing; he thought it was normal.

The Crux

Have you ever noticed that sometimes life feels good and everything is going so well, and then your world can turn upside-down in a split second?

You have fallen victim to a devastating situation and find yourself in crisis. Suddenly you've lost your job. You find out you have cancer. Your spouse has been having an affair with your best friend. Your son has been murdered by a gang. Anything can happen in a split second to change your whole life. Life can be so fickle.

You feel the world collapsing around you and say, "How am I going to cope? What am I going to do if I have no job? We are going to lose our house. Why is this happening to me?" The first thing you will say to yourself is, "Why me? Why has this happened to me?"

You may think you have done something wrong and that God is punishing you.
Sometimes I ask myself, "Why does God always get the blame when everything goes wrong?" First, God does not punish. Why would God want to punish his own children? He would only be punishing himself. This is the first thing you have to believe and accept: God loves you unconditionally.

Take another look at the situation. Ask yourself why this has happened. Your life was meant to change; this is what is supposed to happen. You may not think it at the time, but no matter how horrendous your situation, it's what you wanted to do before you were born.

Daffodil

Some souls would rather not know what is going to happen to them before they are born. It will depend on the soul's spiritual level. For every soul that is living on this planet, there is a reason why it is here. Your story, your scenario, is about to unfold by this crisis that has just changed your life.

There are no mistakes. Even if a soul is murdered, it gave permission to the soul that committed the atrocity before they were both born into their present lives. The victim and the murderer are both ends of the spectrum, the good and the bad.

Any parent who has lost a loved one in this devastating scenario will find this revelation absurd or unbelievable, and who could blame them? This astonishing information was revealed to me while I was writing this book. I must admit that it was hard for me to digest. All I know is, I'm been guided by the spirit realms as I write this book. The more I thought about it, the more sense it made.

You ask yourself, "Why would anyone choose an horrendous scenario?" At the time prior to reincarnation, these two souls knew that for whatever reason, they both chose to experience this on earth. **They already know; it is only an illusion**. None of it is real. It is only a lesson. The only thing that is fact, and is real, will be the **choices they make.** How will they deal with a situation as bad as this?

If we are all down here living in different scenarios, then we must be all actors. We act for God because God gave us free will. He cannot intervene; He can only live through us and watch the choices we make. It will be up to us. If we make the right choices, we will keep forever progressing with our souls.

So you see none of this is real. The life we are living on earth is not real reality, as we've been brought up to believe. We live in a world of illusion, a world where we come to learn. We have been conditioned by our parents that we only have the five senses: see, hear, smell, taste, and touch. Nothing is taught of the soul and the six senses. We are also spiritual beings as well as human beings.

Most people fear death when there is absolutely nothing to fear. There has to be a beginning and an end to everything. I myself do not fear death because I know what awaits us at the point of death. We have so much to look forward to.

I know it is hard to believe that the life we live is an illusion, because we are all conditioned not to think otherwise. But wouldn't you rather believe this when looking at the state the world is in – and it's getting worse. Only real reality belongs to the next world, heaven, where real life goes on and on, eternally.

Look at life in a different way. People protest against God. If there is a God, why would God have allowed wars to happen, or human suffering? The Holocaust. The despots. Continued starvation and suffering across the globe.

Wouldn't the mother who lost her son to a gang killing, prefer to think that this wasn't for real, that it was just a learning experience for the people involved in this scenario? The mother never really loses her son. Only in this world of illusion do atrocities take place. She will see him in the next world, the real world called heaven, or whatever you wish to call it. Earth is not our real home.

If only the ones who commit suicide were aware of that; then suicide may never occur. Ask yourself why God gave you life. Would you prefer to think that all the adversities, life's ups and downs that make your life so difficult, were true reality? We put ourselves in situations like this, but God always gets the blame.

A son is murdered, stabbed to death. The mother is devastated. How will she ever get over her dearest son being murdered in such an horrendous way? She won't. She'll think about it every waking moment. It has destroyed her life and those around her. What can she do? She doesn't want to live anymore, but she knows she has to for the sake of the rest of the family, who have also been hit by this terrible tragedy. Where is she going to find the courage and strength to carry on? Deep in her soul lies the answer: because she is a part of God. None of us realise how powerful we are.

Daffodil

This is when your soul starts to take over the situation. Weeks and months pass by maybe even years. You keep asking yourself the same questions over and over again. "Why has this happened to me? Is God punishing me?"

Are you going to find that inner strength, the tool that God gave you, the power to rise above it all? How can you stop this happening to another mother? You don't want anyone to suffer the way you have. No mother should have to go through that.

Have you noticed that mothers who have lost sons to gang violence often set up campaigns to stop all this from happening again? They try to get gangs and knives off the streets; they try to do something positive about it, to make a difference so that their sons' deaths won't be in vain and become just another statistic. It has to end.

To all of the mothers: be assured that your sons are alive and well in heaven. They do not want to see their mothers grieving all the time. It's no good for anyone. Not only are you holding yourself back from moving on, but you also hold your sons back from moving on. Your sons will never leave you until you stop your grieving. They will always be there to visit you, especially when you need them. You only have to think of a loved one who has passed over, and he or she will come to you straightaway, especially when you become ill.

A mother will never get over this terrible tragedy, but she can make her life easier by changing her thoughts try to think of all the happy times you shared together. Celebrate his life. Give thanks to God for letting you borrow his child, even though it was only for a short time. Know in your heart that you will be with him again. You will understand why all that took place and had to be. Trust and always have faith.

When your son looks down on you from heaven and sees that you aren't grieving as much and are taking control of your life once again, it will fill him with happiness. He will be able to move on with his new life in heaven, knowing deep in his heart that you will meet again someday.

Your son would wish to give you this information: now that he has passed over, life does not end. His life on earth was only a learning experience. No matter how gruesome the ending of his life, he is still your son and you are still his mother. Remember that you all came down to experience the trauma of this life.

It always brings to mind the Mizan family, who lost a son in this way. His name was Jimmy Mizan, and the media was interviewing them outside their home one day. They were bewildered why Margaret, the mother, didn't feel hatred for the young boy who had committed this terrible crime. She forgave him. When asked why, she replied, "Because hatred would destroy my family. That's the trouble with this world. There's not enough love!"

How brave this woman is. She is obviously a very wise soul.

We think that we own our children, especially the mother who gave birth to her child. Yes, they are our flesh and blood, but we do not own them. We only gave life to a soul who wanted to experience what it's like to be human.

Children are God's gift to us for a short while. We raise our children in the best way we can, because they don't come with instructions. We are there to teach them how to act and think, and we give them as much love and care as is possible, so that they have love and respect for others. We teach them what is best for their future, and then one day they fly away from the nest.

All the while, God will be observing. He will not be judging, but perhaps he is hoping we've made the right choices for our children.

Despair

In your hour of despair, when you think your world has ended, it is then that you should ask for guidance. Turn to the light, your God, your Father, your Guardian Angel. Slowly but gradually, the reasons will start to unfold.

You will be given tests along the way that will put doubt into your mind. You will be given answers, and the truth is that you are being helped by the spiritual realms. It is then that you make the choice to follow your heart. Whether you believe in God, know that he is always with you in the face of adversity. Give God a chance and let him help you. Trust and follow your spiritual journey so that you find your way back home, to God. One day you will see the bigger picture, the reason why your life had to be this way. All will be revealed. I promise you will understand all of this when you pass over, because your soul already has all the answers, and it will remember.

My crisis happened twenty years ago at the age of forty-one. It's only since 1997 that my life and my crisis started to make any sense. As the months and years move on, I've become spiritually stronger, because I can see the bigger picture unfolding little by little.

Every now and then, something will happen in my life to cast doubt. There's unbelievable timing when things go wrong, but my faith never falters. I realise my strengths and weaknesses. Although my physical body is weak, I know I'm strong spiritually and that everything is unfolding the way it should.

You have to surrender to the universe, to God, to the divine, to the higher intelligence. It's no good fighting for what you once had, as I tried to do. That life has gone.

I wanted so desperately the life I used to have, and I fought for it every day. I would never accept that this was happening to me. I suppose it's only human to think in this way. After all that I have learnt about the spiritual reason that I am here, my soul's contract, I wouldn't change a thing. I know now that life is eternal; we are only here for a short while, which can seem forever. One thing I do know is that there are no accidents, mistakes, coincidences, or chance meetings. Everyone we meet, we draw them to us.

On one of these occasions whilst in hospital, in my ward was a woman with severe rheumatoid arthritis. She looked to be in her early thirties and had to use one of those electric wheelchairs. Sometimes I would watch her from a distance when she wasn't looking. I could see it was a great struggle for her, and she was so young. I tried to have a little chat with her one day, and she seemed very insular. On one occasion, I could sense that she was unhappy and perhaps bitter about being in her condition. Who wouldn't be? I tried talking to her one day. She was polite enough, but it was all pretence. I could tell she would sooner be on her own.

On the morning I left hospital, I went over to say goodbye. I also gave her a two-inch, ceramic angel that I used to carry around with me, especially if I was going into hospital. While we were chatting I spontaneously said to her, "You know, you chose to be like this."

"Huh! I don't know about that!" she said. I could tell she was annoyed with me.

I thought, *oh my God, why did I just say that!*

At the time I didn't really understand why I had said it; the words just came out before I could stop myself. It wasn't till years later that it all made sense. This has happened to me before: words have come out of my mouth, and sometimes I don't recognise my own voice.

I often wonder what happened to her, and I wonder if she remembers me. All I can hope for is that she found her spirituality, her path. Maybe one day she will have a divine experience like I had.

Daffodil

At least I will have planted the seed. I don't think she'll forget me, because what I had said at the time annoyed her, but it may lead her to other things. She may come across a book that has fallen off the shelf. This book may contain just enough materiel needed for her spiritual journey to begin – another synchronicity added to her journey, so to speak.

Alan Bellinger

Alan is now aged ninety-four and is still going strong. He is still giving healing to all who ask for it. When he's not performing hands-on healing, he sits in his chair in the evening sending absent healing to those unable to attend. Absent healing is when the healer concentrates on the person needing the healing but is unable to attend. It doesn't matter how far away the person is, whether he is in this country or abroad. The healing will reach him through the power of thought. It is a universal law. Sometimes Alan can heal as many as forty clients every evening before he retires to bed. What a wonderful remarkable man he is.

The only qualification needed for absent healing is a good heart and the sincerity to want to help others. Why don't you give it a try? Go on, experiment with someone you know who is ill. You don't even have to tell the person about it, but keep a journal of your efforts. It may take just one absent healing, or it may require several sessions. It applies to mental illness as well as physical illness.

Alan and I made arrangements to discuss the book I was writing. I had already sent him a copy of a few pages I had written so far. I needed Alan's opinion, and I wanted him to be brutally honest with me. After all, I had never taken on a task like this before. I remembered feeling like a little child handing my school work over to the teacher. I felt very anxious.

To my delight Alan was most encouraging. Although I had made quite a few spelling mistakes, it wasn't important. This was why I had asked myself time and again whether this was what the spirit world wanted me to do. Why hadn't they given me the academic skills as well? Then I realised that it was all part of my struggle, my journey. I had to do it by myself.

Daffodil

I must admit I'm at my happiest when I'm writing; Alan has given me the confidence to solider on.

Whilst there, Alan asked me if I would care to do some healing on him. I tried, but I don't know whether it worked. I was still learning. I was surprised that I could stand for so long whilst healing Alan.
Obviously the spirit world was helping me.
Alan showed me a cutting from an old newspaper called *The Grapevine*. It was published in North Derbyshire in 1991, and the editor was Ian Macgill. On the front page there's a large photograph of Alan with both his hands raised to the camera. The headlines states, "Healer and the Miracle Babies." It featured a story of Alan, then aged seventy-eight, and how he had helped to give healing to women who were told that they couldn't have children by their doctors, or they were finding it hard to conceive after trying for years.

Up unto 1991, Alan was responsible for bringing healing to these women. The result was that fifty-five babies were born into this world! Alan was told that many of these women had been told by their doctors that they couldn't have children. Alan's healing soon put a stop to that. Alan stated at the time that there may have been sixty-one babies born, but six of the women failed to report back.

In all, Alan had treated seventy-four women for fertility problems. The most incredible story was that of a woman aged thirty-four who was a midwife and lived in Stoke on Trent. She wished to remain anonymous at the time. The doctors had discovered the woman had no fallopian tubes. It would be impossible for her to conceive! Soon after receiving healing treatment from Alan, the woman became pregnant, and she now has three children!

There were several stories about Alan. He had cured cats, dogs, horses, and even a prize-winning Frisian cow called Fleur. Apparently Fleur was losing her calves before giving birth. She was treated in a barn by Alan after the rest of the herd had been brought in for milking. After the short time that Alan had been treating her over the pelvic area, she suddenly let her milk release all over Alan's shoes. Fleur was better, however, and she went on to have some more prize-winning calves.

The Grapevine also mentioned Sheffield's own artist, Joe Scarborough. Alan had cured him of irritable bowel syndrome after only one treatment. Joe said at the time, "For somebody as down to earth as me, it's unexplainable. I can only describe what happened as a laying on of hands. It was unbelievably relaxing; I was as right as nine-pence after that!"

Alan has led a very interesting life. He was the manager for Barclays Bank in Fitzalan Square, in Sheffield, from 1965–1973 until he retired. He had been in banking all his life, working at various Barclay Banks all over the country. He wrote his own biography, *Voices in the Dark*. As a child he contracted tuberculosis when he was five years old, and he survived. His mother discovered that Alan must have been special at an early age, and that he had the ability to heal. He cured his mother of an acute appendicitis. The doctor had told her that she needed an operation straightaway. She was a Christian scientist and didn't believe in doctors and medication, only in natural herbal remedies. She told Alan to put his hands on her tummy and to stroke her over the site of her appendix. She soon got better!

It's ironic that Alan was once told that he lived a past life as a top gynaecologist in Edinburgh, Scotland, around 1800. He was quite famous in his field. He was the first doctor to use chloroform as a pain relief for women who were about to give birth.

Alan is now ninety-four, and the last count of babies that have been born to mothers who have received healing from Alan has reached a staggering 120! Alan has certainly been blessed with good health in this lifetime. I suppose he had to be, for what lay ahead in this lifetime, his spiritual contract. He puts his longevity down to a good diet and herbal remedies.

Joyce Bellinger

Alan's wife, Joyce, was also a healer, and she stumbled on it quite by accident. Alan asked her one day if she could see people when she closed her eyes, like Mr. Webster could. Webster was a medium and healer. To Alan's surprise, Joyce replied that she could continue to see people when she had closed her eyes. She had assumed that it was normal and had never mentioned it to anyone before.

Can you? Do you perhaps see faces, or maybe scenes of different places? Or is it a bit like watching a movie?

Apparently Joyce saw people in colours, and the aura that surrounds the body. The colour of the aura represents the person's health condition at the time. For instance, a person who was suffering from an illness may show various colours over the problem area, usually a muddy grey colour, red, or black.

Joyce could also see the patients' deceased loved ones, who would come through in spirit form. Whilst the healing was taking place. She would draw a portrait of them to the delight of the patient. She was a very talented lady in her own right. Joyce has drawn many magnificent portraits over the years.

I sometimes wish I had the opportunity to have known Joyce more, but I only met her briefly. I remember once when Alan was healing me. Joyce came into the room and came across to where I was sitting. She put two fingers at the top of my spine and then slowly moved them down my back. It felt very cold. Then she turned towards Alan and said, "There is no black." She left the room whilst Alan continued with the healing. At the time I didn't know what it meant. When a healing is completed, the colour seen is usually a gold colour or blue. Black meant the worst, but it was not untreatable.

It was nice to learn that both Alan and Joyce were together at the end, when Joyce departed from this life. Nevertheless, it must have been a terrible shock for Alan to see his wife slip away in front of him like that. Although he did his best to resuscitate Joyce, it wouldn't have made any difference. It was Joyce's time.

Alan and Joyce have two sons, Robert and John. Both children share the same capability to heal.

Princess Dianne

In August 1997 I had an out-of-body experience about Princess Diana. This scenario was me and Diana. We were walking around together what seemed like a maze, only it was built of brick columns. We kept trying to hide in between these columns, away from the media. We were chatting away. Her energy told me she was most upset with the paparazzi, who were flashing their cameras at us all the time.

Every now and then there would be a flash from a camera, and then I would beckon Dianna to follow me quickly, away from the photographers. It was never ending, and this happened quite a few times. We would keep moving on, I would keep beckoning her to follow me, and we would keep hiding around the brick columns. As I looked at her face, I could tell she was fed up with it all and was quite depressed. That was it, and my OBE ended.

The next day I forgot all about the OBE. I was vacuuming the carpet, and I also had the news on the TV. I noticed Princess Diana was on the news, and I switched off the Hoover to listen.

She was holding a black baby in her arms at the time, and suddenly I remembered the connection with her the night before. I thought, *Yes, I was with you last night! What was all that about?*

Four days later, Diana was to die in that horrible car crash in Paris. The world was devastated, and so was I. I kept going over and over the OBE I'd had. When Diana died, it was like losing one of my own family members.

Diana was on a mission when she came to this world: to teach mankind the importance of love and how we should help one another. She certainly tried to turn the world's attitude. We are all the same, and we come from the same source, no matter our race. We are all one we need to be loved. There is no need for war. There is no need to have mine fields and weapons of mass destruction.

We should be spending all of our resources on third-world countries. No one should go hungry; everyone should have access to fresh water, food, and shelter. As long as there is war, corruption, and greed, there can be no progress in our world.

I also believe that Prince Charles had his part to play. Before he and Diana came to this world, they both wanted to help mankind. Their future was planned before they were born.

Jill Dando

It was the same with Jill Dando, the TV presenter. She appeared to me after she was brutally murdered. She was shot on her front door steps in cold blood as she was unlocking the front door.

A few days later, I closed my eyes. I suddenly saw a picture of her from the waist up. She was looking down on me from a balcony. She wore a yellow suit jacket with a white blouse, with the collar over the lapels. She had a great big bunch of flowers in her hands.

But most of all, what was upsetting was the energy I felt from her. She was crying and was absolutely heartbroken. It was as if she could not accept what had happened to her. She said to me, "It wasn't meant to happen like this. I had a future. I was to be married. It's so unfair." That was all I saw and felt.

Jill was to be married to Alan Farthing, a gynaecologist. Obviously Jill was desperate to cling on to her life. She hadn't moved on yet. Sometimes this happens, especially in circumstances like this; she was so desperate to get her life back. The spirit has to realise that the body does not exist anymore; that it's dropped away from the body. Sudden death can become such a shock to the newly deceased soul, which can hang around for years. All I could do for Jill was to help her soul turn to the light. I asked God and the angels to bring her home.

I always remember Jill Dando for her taste in clothes; she always looked smart. She always looked great whenever she appeared on TV, and she reminded me of Princes Diana.

Decision

As the RA continued to progress, my right ankle was collapsing more and more, and the pain was becoming unbearable. It collapsed further, so much so that it trapped my main tibia nerve, causing excruciating pain. I had to wait six weeks before the nerve was released.

I went back to see my consultant, Dr Winfield, at the Royal Hallamshire Hospital in Sheffield. We discussed the problem with my right ankle. He came to the conclusion that the only answer was to have my ankle fused. I was put on the waiting list.

On my next visit to Dr Winfield, he gave me the opportunity to see if I would prefer to have an ankle replacement, which was now being used to give patients more mobility. It was a new procedure that hadn't been out long, but it had been proven to be quite successful. This meant that I would be able to bend my ankle instead of having a limp for the rest of my life.

Obviously I jumped at the chance. The only problem was that my ankle had deteriorated so much that it was too late to go on the waiting list. I couldn't wait any longer. That meant only one thing: I would have to go private.

Dr Winfield referred me privately to a consultant an orthopaedic surgeon at the Claremont Hospital in Sheffield. I prefer not to mention his name for obvious reasons that will arise as the story develops.

First of all, my thoughts were, *how am I going to raise the money?* I had already given work up, and the cost was four thousand pounds. I managed to get a loan from my bank manger.

Daffodil

My operation took place at the Claremont Hospital in 1999. Hours after the operation, the doctor came to see me. He told me the operation had gone well, but he was disappointed in the condition of my bones. My bones were very soft, which was caused by the disease and the steroids. "What chance do I have of it being successful?" I asked.

"Fifty per cent," he told me.

My heart sank, and I was so disappointed. I tried to keep optimistic and was determined that it would be successful, but the ankle replacement gradually started to fail.

The rest is history. People say to me today, "Why didn't you sue him for negligence?" My case was hard to prove, because as things started to go wrong, it was as if I was been passed on to his colleagues one by one. There would be no one person to blame. Nevertheless, if I had known what I know now, I could have probably sued this doctor. You don't build a house without making sure the foundation is stable first! It's common sense. I was not given a bone density test to check the strength of my bones. That's what I couldn't forgive him for. He should have taken full responsibility for me at the time, before passing me on to the NHS. After all, I had paid privately. Why wasn't I given a bone density scan before the operation, and given the option about whether it was safe to go ahead? At the time I was going through all the pain and stress of it all, and I didn't have the strength to pursue it. I couldn't prove it, and I thought I would lose the case, anyway. I couldn't afford to lose any more money. I still had to pay for the bank loan each month, and that was like rubbing salt in the wound. What a complete waste of money.

But the last straw was when I went to see the doctor on 1/5/02. Nothing could have prepared me for the news I was about to receive that day. I will always remember it, because it was my granddaughter Katie's first birthday party, and we were all invited. During my previous appointment with the doctor, he had told me that he wanted to get a second opinion. I asked why and watched him sit in his chair with his arms folded. He threw his head back and laughed. "You know, like they do on the *Who Wants to Be a Millionaire?* Programme."

I remember looking at him and thinking how flippant he was. How could he sit there and make a joke out of a serious situation such as this?

On 1/5/02 the doctor introduced me to his colleague, Dr Royston, who had only just received his qualification to become an orthopaedic consultant. He thought he was the Gordon Ramsay of orthopaedics, with the F-word. I sat there nervously, my heart pounding. I could feel my stomach tighten as I wondered what devastating news I was about to receive.

Dr Royston looked through my notes. After a while he looked at me and said that after careful study of my notes and X-rays, the best alternative would be to have my leg amputated! There was nothing else that could be done. There were no more options for me.

I looked straight at my doctor, but he avoided my gaze. *Oh my God, did I hear right just then? Did he just say…?* I was in total shock. I started to shake inside, and I couldn't think straight. Tears welled up inside of me, and I started to cry.

I soon tried to compose myself. I kept trying to listening to what Dr Royston was saying to me. The information went over the top of my head. I sat there dumfounded, and my heart sank.

There were no words of comfort from either doctor; it was cold and professional. My doctor was still avoiding my glances. They made an appointment for me. Dr Royston came to shake my hand. I don't know why, but I held my hand out towards my doctor, too. He nervously took my hand, and I could see he was embarrassed because his face flushed. Then that was it, and they both left the room.

A nurse brought me a cup of tea, and she could see I was in a bit of a state. She asked me if I had anyone with me. I didn't that day. I don't know how I drove home. Tears kept streaming down my face. I simply had to get home to my husband. As I pulled onto the drive, I was so relieved to see Harry's car. He came out to meet me at the door, and he could see I wasn't myself.

"Just get me a whiskey, love!" I said, still in shock.

"What's wrong?" he asked.

I couldn't speak at first, but finally I told him. We were both in the kitchen. Harry was making a cup of tea and trying to stay calm. He knew it must be something bad, with the state I was in. "They say they

Daffodil

can't do anything for me anymore. The best thing for me is to have my leg amputated." Tears streamed down my face, and I felt panic stricken.

After a while I pulled myself together. Then it occurred to me: *I don't have to go through with this.* We threw our arms around each other. "No!" I said to Harry. "I'm not going through with it."

Harry said, "It's up to you, love. You know best. I'll go along with whatever you decide."

I don't know how I got to Katie's birthday that day, but I did put on a brave face. All the time I thought, *I'm in control. I don't have to go through with this.* Those thoughts kept me going ... but only for another three months. When you're not in control of your life, your body is a frightening thing. I'd never been in a position like this before.

Finally I couldn't take any more pain. It made life miserable. I made arrangements to have my leg amputated that same year. When you lose a limb; it's like part of you has died. I felt bereft. Fortunately the operation was a success. I was soon back on my feet – or should I say foot. At least I was out of my wheelchair, and the pain I was in had gone. I soon got used to the prosthesis.

What hurts more is the way I was treated by my doctor. I wish he had taken me to one side and said, "Eileen, I am so sorry about the way things have turned out. I did my best." But he never did. He didn't even give a warning about having my leg amputated. I must have had ten operations over two years trying to put my leg right. Surely I deserved a little compassion.

Well, it's just unfortunate that another operation went wrong. Next!

Ken

About a month after my operation. I had a phone call from a friend of mine. He said that my old neighbour, Ken Whittington, who used to live next door to me, had died after suffering a stroke.

I had known Ken for twenty-two years. We became good friends, and Ken was always singing to me. I'd be at the sink washing the pots, and all of a sudden Ken's head would pop up through the window in front of me, making jump and laugh at the same time. He would be singing one of his favourite operatic songs at the top of his lungs.

Ken taught me all about gardening. We shared many happy times together. Ken was a spiritual man who believed in the afterlife.

On the day of his funeral, I had to use my wheelchair. I was still being fitted for a new prosthesis. My son Wayne took me to the church. We thought it best to stay at the back of the church. I was seated in my wheelchair so that I was looking straight down the centre aisle.

As the service began, I remember looking at the people sitting on either side of the aisle. Then all of a sudden, I could see Ken shuffling his feet up the main aisle, with his hands clasped behind his back. He was carefully looking at everyone on both sides. It was as if he didn't want to scare anyone. He used to shuffle his feet when he walked down his garden path at home. He appeared transparent, just like my father did on the night he died. Ken's appearance was an exact replica of his original body. I was mesmerized by his actions. I thought to myself how wonderful it was that I could see all of this. I wondered if anyone else was witnessing what I was seeing.

The congregation began to sing an old hymn I had never heard before, "The Old Rugged Cross". I remembered thinking to myself, *what a horrible song. Fancy singing that at a funeral.* It reminded me of something from an old western movie. *Typical,* I thought. Ken obviously liked it. When I returned home, I was telling Harry about the hymn and how awful I thought it was. I remember making such a fuss about it.

About a year later, I visited the local spiritual church. One of the mediums there asked me if I had lost someone, but not a family member. I couldn't think of anyone at that moment. Then she said to me, "If I was to say to you 'The Old Rugged Cross' would that ring a bell?"

I was astounded! What a wonderful way to come back to me, to prove his survival. Thanks, Ken.

Rock Bottom

In December 2001 I fell into a deep depression. This was before I had my leg amputated, and I wanted my life back. I wanted to be happy most of all. I sank to the depths of despair.

No one could help me. I knew in the back of my mind that one day I could lose my leg. It wasn't just that; there was also no cure for my RA. I was in constant pain, and the drugs I took just weren't working. Dr Winfield tried all different kinds of medication on me, even the most expensive drugs on the market. They simply didn't work for me. On top of that, some of the drugs had really bad side effects. I was reluctant to take some of the drugs because of this, but as my health deteriorated I had to try something, and I became desperate. I was willing to try anything to alleviate the pain and to help give me some normalcy, but to no avail.

I started to have thoughts of suicide. I didn't want to live like this anymore, it was pure torture. I couldn't get the thought out of my head. I would watch TV at night, but I wasn't really watching. I would plan it all in my head. I would do the same in the morning when I awoke, lying there and not wanting to get out of bed. Nothing could sway me. Not even that precious day when I was out of my body at Alan Bellinger's house. Enough was enough. I had reached rock bottom, and I didn't want to be here. If I couldn't be me, then I wanted out. I was no use to myself or my family, and I knew that someday I would become a burden to all of them.

I kept remembering what Alan said to me one day. That people who commit suicide have to come back and to do it all again. Did he see this coming, and that was why he'd told me it that day? Nevertheless, it made no difference as things got worse. I hid it from everyone.

On a morning in January 2002, I tried to take my life. By rights I shouldn't be here. I took one hundred tablets of 30 mg Dihydrocodeine at nine in the morning. All I can remember is that I was drifting in and out of consciousness all day. I could hear voices all around me – whispers and noises in my ears. There was a feeling of concern all around me. I had planned to take the tablets early in the morning, knowing that I wouldn't be found till around four in the afternoon. That would give the tablets time to work. When things weren't going as planned, I crawled into the bathroom on my hands and knees for several paracetamol. I was still semi-conscious at 4.00 PM. Why was it not working?

When Harry came home, he thought I was simply having another bad day, and that was why I was still in bed. I had to tell him what had happened. His reaction was one of anger. He phoned the doctors, and they sent an ambulance. I threw up immediately in the ambulance, over and over again. That's what probably saved my life. But it had been all that time, over six hours. I still don't know how I lasted. I should have been unconscious, if not dead.

The consultant came to see me the next day. He was reading my notes in front of me. He seemed very kind and considerate towards me. It was as if he understood the reasons that I would try to take my life, trying to cope with such a difficult disease. He looked at me and shook his head. "Well, lady, you definitely intended to take your life. There's no doubt about that."

I know that day the spirit world had other plans for me. The angels intervened because it wasn't my time. I had things to do. When it was all over, obviously it hadn't worked. It was like taking off a big, heavy overcoat. I felt this tremendous relief disappear at once – not that it hadn't worked, but that the depressing thoughts had disappeared from my head. I remember thinking, *well, that didn't work. I've just got to get on with it.* The depression lifted, and it was like a miracle.

Prior to all this, I had never understood how people could commit suicide, or why people became so depressed. I enjoyed my life so much. I didn't have patience for people like that. I suppose looking back; I had an arrogant attitude because I'd never experienced this emotion in my own life. I'd wanted to say to these unfortunate people, "Oh come on, pull yourself together!" Little did I know? Where were my compassion and my understanding?

I didn't know what it was like to experience rock bottom. It's not a very nice place to be. In fact, my experience was like being in the depths of hell. I felt the negativity feeding off my energy. The more I let it, the worse it became.

I believe that deep down, I knew that I had to experience this in order to know what it's like to reach rock bottom. This was one of my lessons – karma. This wasn't me, and it wasn't my personality. I loved life. I had a wonderful husband and family. How could I do this to them? I desperately wanted my life back. I wanted to be happy again, and most of all I wanted to dance.

I know it happened for a reason. It was part of my journey to experience it, so that I could help others by writing about it. It certainly wasn't a cry for help, for nobody could help me.

I knew that I wouldn't get any better. As much as I tried to keep a positive attitude, there was no cure. The doctor's couldn't do anything for me. I was sick of the pain day in and day out. I wanted my life back.

When I was a child, I loved to dance. That was my dream. I wanted to be famous for my dancing. All my life I have loved to dance. It was as if I became the real me when I danced. I felt free, my sprit soared, and I became the music. To never to have that sensation again felt like a part of me had died, too.

When I was a child, I used to watch all the musicals at the pictures, at the Coliseum Cinema on Spital Hill, in Sheffield. I was very young at the time. I would go on my own to watch the films, such as Doris Day in *Calamity Jane*, or *Singing in the Rain* with Jean Kelly, or *The King and I* with Deborah Kerr. I'd be in my element. When the film had finished, I would run all the way home feeling so happy. Once home, I would jump up and down all over the furniture, running everywhere, singing and dancing and acting out the musicals. I knew every word by heart. Life was magical, then. I would dream that one day I would be just like Doris Day.

No matter how low you become, you have to find that something in you, that spark of life. No matter what adversity life has thrown at you, in this lifetime, if you don't come to terms with it in this lifetime, you will have to do it all again in another life. There's no escape; it's part of your soul's contract, a universal law.

The ironic thing is that the man who lived in our bungalow before us committed suicide. We moved into our bungalow in July 2000 – after it was becoming more difficult for me to climb the stairs.

I remember when we were looking for a bungalow; we had seen several, but the one we wanted fell through. We passed this three-bedroom bungalow on the same estate. When the first place fell through, we decided to try for the three-bedroom bungalow. I remember looking at it once as we passed by and wondering whether we could possibly afford it.

Unbeknown to me, my husband had also inquired about it. I remember seeing this man watering the border of flowers around the property. He was wearing a white shirt tucked into a pair of jeans, with the sleeves rolled up.

We decided to have a look at the bungalow, and so we booked a viewing. On the day we entered the bungalow for the first time, I remember feeling shocked. It hadn't been lived in for about two years, and it was in a bit of a state, to say the least. I' fully expected to see the vendors or a house that was lived in.

Although the bungalow needed a lot of TLC, we fell in love with it mainly because of the views from the double windows in the living room looking down. We could see across the fields, where the sheep were grazing, it sold it to us. We just had to have it. I had forgotten all about the man I saw watering the flowers at the time.

It wasn't till we moved in, that I began to sense things. When Harry went to the local for a drink one night, I decided to have an early night.

We have a beautiful dog called Bessie; she is a collie and sheepdog mix. We rescued her from the dog rescue centre, when she was about six weeks old. Words cannot express the loyalty and unconditional love this dog has given to me over the years. She is my best friend.

One night when I went to bed, as I was laid in bed, I shouted to Bessie to come and lay at the side of the bed with me, as she usually did. This particular night she wasn't having any of it; I called to her several times, but she wouldn't move.

Bessie only did this at certain times, when I was on my own or when I had gone to bed. But when Harry came back from the local, she would be back to her normal self. This happened a few times.

Several of my neighbours had told me about the couple who had occupied our bungalow prior to us. Apparently the couple had separated, and the husband had booked himself into a hotel in Sheffield city centre he committed suicide.

Then I began to feel a presence in the house sometimes, as if someone was watching me. It was always when I was on my own. It didn't frighten me; it was as if this spirit was saying to me, "This is my home. What are you doing here?" This went on for a few weeks.

Then one night I was in bed with Harry, half asleep. I could feel Harry's head nuzzled between my breasts. I thought, "Oh no, not now, love." As I brought my hands up to hold his head, I immediately knew that it wasn't Harry's head! It completely freaked me out. I looked over, and Harry had his back towards me! As soon as I touched its head and realised it wasn't Harry's, it vanished.

Then I remembered the man watering the flowers. It was the same man I'd seen that day!

After that I read a book about spirits that stay behind after dying. After a time, they can remain stuck on earth after death. They didn't know how to move on, and they'd hang around the home in which they used to live. Sometimes the new owners can hear noises or bumps in the night, and they start to wonder whether the house is haunted.

Daffodil

This is only the poor spirit trying to grasp your attention. More often than not, theses spirits are scared and frightened too. Don't be frightened. You will be able to tell if the spirit is evil by the way you feel. If it means to frighten you, you will have an awful dread in the pit of your stomach; that spirit is not a very nice one.

Normally it is a spirit that's lost its way home.

I carried out my own transition for the spirit to go towards the light. It's easy to do, and you can do it too. First, ask your guardian angel to protect you. You can use any imaginary scenario you have in mind; like your guardian angel's wings wrapped around you and protecting you. Then ask for the lost spirit's guardian angel to take this lost soul home. You can offer a little prayer to help him on its way; this always helps. Make up your own prayer if you wish; speak from the heart. Or you can choose one. You just have to be sincere, genuine, and clear about your intention. In your mind's eye; try to imagine this happening.

If you're lucky, the spirit world may even show you the spirit passing over. It just depends on what spiritual level you are at; and whether it's the right time for you to accept. Don't be disappointed if you don't see anything. Just trust and have faith. Usually you will sense a calm, relaxed feeling of peacefulness afterwards.

If for any reason you come across a spirit that is evil; you just might be able to save its soul if you can persuade it to turn to the light; to God and its guardian angel. Don't be afraid stay strong. Ask for Archangel Michael for help if you are in any doubt. He will protect you.

Every time I helped a soul to pass over; the atmosphere would change to a peace and calm. That was when I knew that it was successful. Everything seemed normal after that. Bessie was more settled and back to normal.

All animals sense spirits. Dogs seem to know when their owners will be arriving home about fifteen minutes before they actually arrive. Every Friday night, three of my sons used to come over to collect their father for a game of snooker. Bessie would go through the motions of sitting at the door every Friday night well before they arrived. From my own experience with dogs, I know they are psychic.

All animals have a soul. Some animals are more advanced than others; like in human beings. Some animals have come to earth to help their owners and act as spirit guides and teachers. Some people think that all animals are a lower form of life; when in actual fact they have more integrity than man.

After my father had died, my previous dog, Maxie, would start to walk around the sofa in circles every night around eight thirty. At the time I wasn't into the spiritual side of my life but it made me think. Could it be the spirit of my dead father that was disturbing her?

I made a point of watching her reaction at eight thirty every night. This seemed to go on for weeks; till we all forgot about it. Of course I know now that it was my dad keeping an eye on us all; just paying us all a visit; to tell us that he was just fine and that he loves us.

Years after the death of my father, my second grandchild, Christopher. Used to stay overnight with his older brother Jason, on Fridays. Harry would go off to the pub. The three of us would settle down for the night huddled on the sofa together watching TV. Oh how I miss those times. Our sofa was positioned so that whoever was sitting at the right-hand side of the sofa could see down the hallway. On many occasions Christopher would comment that there was a man in the hall while we were watching TV. This happened a few times.

I didn't take much notice at first, but one night I said to Christopher, "Okay then what does this man look like?" He said that he looked a bit like Granddad and that he was wearing a cap.

I only remember my father wearing a trilby hat. Mum said he would wear a cap when he was in his youth. Hence the explanation that spirits can return in whatever attire and at any age they want to be, so that loved ones can easily recognise them.

***

After moving into the bungalow, I was well into to my spiritual side. It seemed to take off. I was reading one book after another. I couldn't get enough, but I didn't have anyone with whom I could discuss with. Most of my friends weren't into this sort of thing; except for my dear friends; Barbara Thompson and Wendy Early.

Daffodil

I met Wendy at my reflexology classes. I'm certain I have known Wendy before in another life; we are definitely connected in some way. It's the same with Barbara, with whom I used to work at C&A in Sheffield. She also retired early through illness. That's when our true friendship took off. Although we don't see each other anymore, we have kept in contact since 1993, mostly by letter.

I feel very connected to Barbara in a spiritual way. I know she feels the same, and she is such a special person. One day when we were working together, she shook her head slowly from side to side; she said that she saw something special in me, though she couldn't explain it at the time. She stated that one day I would become famous; if not in this world, it would certainly be in the next. I remembered feeling embarrassed as she spoke to me. I used to blush so easily. Did she see that I was going to write a book to help mankind? Did she see into my future that I was going to find my spiritual path all those years ago?

Barbara is a very spiritual person. She is at one with all nature, animals, and the elements. I remember years ago when there have been times I felt so ill; If started thinking about Barbara. The very next day there would be a letter, or sometimes there would be a phone call. It was as if we picked up on each other telepathically. I would always feel much better after contact with her. It felt like I had received some sort of healing that I couldn't explain.

Eventually about two years later, new neighbours moved into the bungalow opposite ours. They came over and introduced themselves: Marlene and Stuart Thewlis.

We got to know each other very well. Eventually I found out that Marlene was into the same things as I was. She also was a Reiki healer and was into her spiritual side. Wow, I couldn't believe my luck! Although her husband was sceptic like Harry, it didn't matter. We had so much in common. It was such a refreshing change for me: that someone else thought as I did; we could share our experiences together. It's been a learning curve for both of us. We have learnt so many things from one another.

Marlene introduced me to the spiritual church. The first time I walked into the tiny spiritual church at Wombwell in Barnsley, I felt a lovely, warm atmosphere. It felt so right. I remember thinking, *if my dad could see me now!*

I went to the church on a few occasions, but I wasn't sure whether it was for me. Although I have experienced accurate clairvoyance from the mediums on the rostrums; I'm not sure I'm into all that singing and praying.

Perhaps it reminds me too much of my own experiences in church as a child. But on the whole, the people are friendly and made me feel welcome. It was a nice experience all round.

Stephen Turoff

In my research for healing, I came across a man called Stephen Turoff. I read his amazing book *Seven Steps to Eternity,* which I highly recommend. Stephen is a psychic surgeon he was born in 1947.

He has his own clinic in Chelmsford, The Danbury Healing Clinic. He often travels all over the world; he's known as the psychic surgeon, giving healing to everyone who is in need.

I gave Alan Bellinger a call to see if he had heard of him. He said that he and Joyce had paid him a visit many years ago.

I booked an appointment to see him. It was quite a long way, almost a three-hundred-mile round trip, but I was desperate to see him. I didn't want my other leg to deteriorate further. We set off. When we arrived at the clinic, from the outside it just looked like a little hut. It was situated in the grounds of the Miami Hotel in Chelmsford.

Harry decided to have a coffee in the hotel and waited for me there. I entered the clinic and gave my name to the receptionist. I was shown into a small, packed waiting room. The room had people from all walks of life. I thought *it's going to be a long day.* However I noticed that most people were coming and going within about fifteen minutes of each other if that.

As I sat in the waiting room, I noticed that the walls were full of photographs of Stephen treating his patients. I also noticed that what they all had in common; was a white light on every photograph that had been taken.

The white light was just above Stephen's head on all of the photographs. It was about two feet wide and beaming straight onto the patient's body; in all of the areas on which he was concentrating. It was amazing.

There was also a photograph of the little hut taken outside; with a beaming white light shining on the centre of its roof. The photographs were sent to Stephen from relatives of the patients, taken at the time of treatment. It was proof that this healing was coming from a divine source – God.

In the centre of the room next to the wall was a large shrine of Sathya Sai Baba; the great spiritual healer from India commonly known as the miracle man. Also, there was a picture of Mother Meera, another spiritual healer born in India who now lives in Germany after marrying a German.

She spoke of the healing light that it is everywhere, and she said that we all can activate this light. She heals in total silence. Her healing consists of a ritual; by touching people's heads and looking into their eyes.

During this process she reportedly "unties knots" in the subtle system and permeates it with light. She does not charge for this healing;

And neither will she do lectures. She says this was her calling for all mankind.

When it was my turn, the receptionist showed me into a room with a treatment bed. She asked me to loosen any tight clothing around my waist. When she left the room, I looked around. On a small table by my side were what looked to be an assortment of operating utensils? Ouch!

Then Stephen Turoff walked into the room. He seemed to have a strong presence about him, and he was quite tall with a sturdy build. I started to tell him of my concerns, and that I had already lost my other leg, but it was as if he was only half listening – as if he was listening to someone else.

He immediately laid his hands on my upper stomach near the small bowel on my left side. All of a sudden I felt this tremendous heat radiating from both his hands. I looked at his face in disbelief: where all this heat came from, his face was blood red. This seemed to last for

Daffodil

a few minutes. Then he took one of the instruments and proceeded to make an incision in my left side. I could feel something draw across my left-hand side. It felt just like a cut!

When he finished, he told me that someone from the spirit world would visit me in a couple of days to take the stitches out, and that I would feel a slight tug on my left side. I thought, *Oh come on, you can't be serious!* I wanted to laugh. He then said that the healing would stay with me for a couple of days. He left the room. I laid there still overwhelmed by all this heat. I keep thinking to myself, *there's a lot we don't know, a lot we don't understand.*

I headed straight for Harry at the hotel, and I told him what had just happened. Somehow I felt different. I was absolutely gob-smacked, and I sat there in a daze, trying to drink my coffee. "Harry do I look any different? I feel different. Something's happened in there. It's weird."

"What have you got on your forehead?" Harry asked. I remembered Stephen drawing something on my forehead, just after the healing. He said that the healing would stay with me for a couple of days.

Apparently it was a powdery substance like gray ash, and it was used in healing. It's called vebuti. It is said that Sia Baba, the great Indian healer, used to manifest this vebuti, which poured from his hands and appeared on photographs and pictures taken of him.

The next day, I sat at home on the sofa, having my breakfast. I happened to look across the room. On the coffee table was a slight dusting of this same ash, the vebuti, all over the table. I felt comforted, as if I was still being healed. Stephen had said the healing would carry on for a couple of days, and the ash was proof!

I was sick the next day. I remembered thinking that it had to do with the healing, as if I was purging my body and was being cleansed. Later the next day, I laid across my bed and did a Reiki treatment on myself. All of a sudden I was caught unaware, and I felt a sharp tug on my left-hand side! I had forgotten what Stephen had said. I have to admit, I felt more than a little sceptic when Stephen had told me that this would happen. I knew the heat I had felt was real, as well as the tug at my side because I had felt it and had proof. Still, it was hard to accept. I had never come across a psychic surgeon before.

Several months passed. I was so impressed and wanted to see Stephen again. Harry waited for me in the hotel again.

When Stephen walked in the room, he came straight to my upper bowel again! It was as if he was operating on me. I could feel some discomfort and made him aware of it. He simply laughed and finished whatever he was supposed to be doing. Yet again I felt the heat from his hands, but this time the heat wasn't as intense.

When I had given birth to my first child, Wayne, at the age of sixteen, my bowls were never the same. I suffered chronic constipation for years, for most of my life into my mid-fifties. When I started with rheumatoid arthritis, the problem seemed to worsen because of the medication I had to take. I often bled, which I was used to. I had a couple of colonoscopies in the past ten years. They found that part of my bowel was inflamed. The possible cause was the medication. I still continued with the constipation.

When I had the experience treatment with the psychic surgeon, Stephen Turoff, it started to get better. It was a slow process over weeks and months. But then, I suppose it would have to be, after all the years that I had suffered with it. For the last two years. I can honestly say that I have a normal, regular bowel with no signs of any blood.

Whatever happened that day in Stephen's treatment room was meant to happen. Obviously I needed immediate treatment on my bowel. Although Stephen didn't cure the RA, as I have explained there are always reasons why. Some healings take place and some don't. Why one person is healed and another is not has to do with their contracts before birth, their blueprints for this life. To interfere with this would be a setback and would interfere with their souls' progression.

I learnt that Stephen's spirit guide was an Austrian doctor named Doctor Khan. When Stephen was about to treat any of his patients, Dr Khan would speak to Stephen, telling him what was wrong with the patient and how best to treat the person. This was even before Stephen entered the patient's room. That was why Stephen knew to come straight to my upper bowel when he walked into the room that day. It's a good thing I went to see Stephen – if not, it could have developed into something more serious.

Search for the truth, and it will set you free.

Paul Parker

I went to see a medium called Paul Parker, who specialised in past lives. Marlene had been to see him first; she was very impressed by his accuracy, so I booked an appointment.

In 1980 I found out I was pregnant, as I have said earlier; our marriage had its ups and downs. I had fallen head over heels in love with a man to whom my father had introduced me to on my thirty-second birthday. My husband and I soon separated. I was living at home with my four sons.

The first time I met Peter, it was his voice. It sounded like a familiar echo from the past. It was as if I recognised his voice first, before I saw his face. It was a really weird feeling I couldn't explain. It's like when you visit a place for the first time, and you have this feeling you been there before.

The affair had broken down, and I was on my own. I had told my husband from the start about the affair. It wasn't his fault; it was simply one of those things that happened in life. We all went through a terrible time. I would have never have left my children; where I go they go with me. They were my life and still are to this very day. I feel so fortunate that God gave them to me.

Money cannot buy the love and joy that a child brings into your life. Our children are only loaned to us from God; we do not own them. My children don't always know the joy that they have brought into my life. I have such fond memories of them; when they were babies growing up. There are things I'll never forget. Although life was a struggle when we were young, when I look back on my life now, I wouldn't have changed a thing.

Daffodil

What was I going to do after the affair? I was three months pregnant. I had to come to a decision. I finally had a termination. At the time I had no regrets. I couldn't afford to give up my job; I had four children to bring up. We had to get back to a near normal life.

At the time, I didn't know any better; I didn't know then what I know now. Months passed by. Eventually Harry and I got back together again. It had taken me years to get over Peter. Why had he had such a big impact on my life?

For years I had no regrets for terminating the baby. I kept telling myself over and over that I had done the most sensible thing at the time; that it was the best for all of us. It was only when I started my spiritual journey that my thoughts started to change. How different I feel now. There were mothers out there who had lost babies through miscarriages. Then there were women like me who chose a termination for whatever reason.

That baby will continue to grow up in the spirit world. When our time comes, we will meet up with these babies, who have grown up. There will be an understanding that there is no sin. The spirit world understands this. You cannot ever kill the spirit – it's only the physical body that dies.

When I was having the reading, Paul asked me if I had a daughter. I thought to myself, *that's the second time I've been told this.* The time before was about thirteen years ago. When I was researching spiritualism, I read time and time again that the foetus survives no matter how old it is in the womb. Once conceived, it will either survive in this life or in the next.

Paul began to tell me of the survival of the termination. It was now in the spirit world, and it was a daughter. My eyes filled with tears, my immediate thoughts were that it must be true. This was the second time I had been given this information. *Oh my god, what have I done? I've killed a child!*

It was as if Paul had read my thoughts. "No, you haven't, Eileen. Your daughter wants you to know this: she understood your circumstances at the time."

The tears flowed down my cheeks. Then it was as if Paul was trying to lighten the atmosphere. "She says she would never have worn shoes like you are wearing right now. She loves high heels." At the time I was wearing a low-heel sandal, though not through choice; I had no alternative with my condition. But I also would have preferred to wear a glamorous pair of high heels.

"Your daughter went on to grow up in the spirit world, and she is now a young lady." He went on to describe my daughter in detail. He said she was the image of me and added that she is always with me. I must not have any regrets, because she knows that one day we will be together. We will share the times that we have missed on earth. When my time is over, she will be waiting for me on the other side.

He also asked me if I had a large space in the centre of my living room with a special chair in the corner. I did; it was one of those massage chairs. He said she often sat in it when she came to visit me. He asked me, "Don't you ever feel her dancing near when she swishes past you? She likes to wear a lot of white."

I think about her often. I talk to her as if she is here. Sometimes I get this sadness in the pit of my stomach that I missed out on a beautiful little girl. I think about all that could have been. But I have to stop myself because; if I'm sad, then my girl is sad. When I'm happy, so is she.

I have this strong desire to call her Ann. She would have been aged twenty-six at the time of this writing. She also says that she loves red peonies, and that I don't have any in my garden – which I don't, My intension is to plant some in my garden in the near future, as a tribute to my beloved daughter Ann. I hope my sons understand when they read this. I'm sure they will. They all have forgiving hearts.

My Little Red Car

After I had my leg amputated, I wanted to start driving again. I wanted my independence back. I put out a request to the angels to help me choose a car – something small, reliable, and not too expensive.

Harry and I went for a drive one day. We pulled up at a garage not far from where we lived. We both looked around the garage to see what was available. Harry spotted a small red car, a Daihatsu.

When I looked, I wasn't that interested because it was bright red. But on closer inspection, I noticed the car was in very good condition. It had low mileage, and it was an automatic with a small engine. I was thrilled. It had everything I needed it was perfect. Straightaway we took it for a test drive.

Harry lifted the bonnet of the car to get a closer inspection. I couldn't believe my eyes. "Look, Harry, look!" In the right- and left-hand corners of the bonnet; was written in white paint "E" and "R" – my initials! It was as if they had been painted on with a fine-feathered brush. It was the same white substance that they used to use in old corner shop windows to advertise their goods for sale. We looked at each other in disbelief.

Harry still thought there must be a logical explanation! I had a good feeling about the car and bought it the very next day. The angels had answered my prayers. We couldn't believe our luck, and to have my initials was more than a coincidence. There's no such thing as coincidence. Spirit guides and angels work at this to make it happen. It's supposed to happen.

We don't always realise what the angels and the spirit guides get up to. When we are in touch with these wonderful beings, they see and hear all our problems. They will arrange synchronicities and scenarios around the situations. They solve all our problems without us ever being aware sometimes. I keep thinking to myself, *there's such a lot we don't understand. I want to find out more.*

God created angels his messengers to make life a little less difficult for us all. It seems a pity not to take the offer.

I kept the car for about five years, it never let me down. I made many trips to visit Alan Bellinger, as well as hospital appointments. It gave me my independence back for a while.

As years passed I noticed one day that whenever I drove my car, my heart would beat faster. My blood pressure would start to rise. I started losing all confidence on the road, and eventually I gave up driving altogether. It had served its purpose for many years. I'd been driving for forty-four years and had only had one slight accident. Not bad hey.

Tony

When Harry and I were separated, Harry met a man called Tony in his local pub. They became good friends; Tony had also been through a divorce. Tony was a bus driver in Sheffield. When Harry and I decided to give our marriage another go, I became friends with Tony and his new girlfriend, Sandra. We all became good friends and shared many happy times in the local pub.

Time passed, we hadn't seen Tony and Sandra for a while. We assumed that perhaps they were both on holiday. It was only when Harry spoke to the land lord; Bill that Harry heard the bad news. Tony had been diagnosed with cancer. Bill thought we already knew. When Harry told me the news, we were both in shock. Finally we went to visit Sandra and Tony.

As soon as I saw Tony, I freaked out but tried not to show it. I remember looking at Sandra; she looked drained from the whole ordeal. I tried to act cheerful, but she saw straight through me. It was such a shock. What does one do in situations like this? Tony had only just turned forty.

At the time I didn't have any knowledge of the spirit world; I was simply at the tip of the iceberg with my research, there was such a lot to learn. Tony had shed so much weight that he was just skin and bone. It was bone cancer.

Tony was always complaining of backache; he'd put it down to driving a bus all day long in Sheffield. When we left and said our goodbyes, Harry and I got into the car, I remember turning around.

Eileen Veronica Richmond

Tony was waving to both of us from the living room window. We both thought at the same time that we wouldn't ever see Tony again.

Despite Tony's illness, Sandra and Tony planned to get married. Unfortunately we were going on holiday at the same time. When we arrived home from holiday, I made a point of ringing Sandra to see how Tony was. "Hello, Sandra," I said, trying to sound cheerful. "How are things? How did the wedding go?" There was a deadly silence, and I said, "Oh no!"

"Eileen, Tony died after our wedding. Not only that, on the morning of his funeral, our wedding photos arrived."

I remember sliding down the wall with the phone still in my hand, and we both cried. "Oh Sandra, I am so sorry."

About a year later, I was still searching for answers, going from one medium to another, and doing my research into spiritualism. I went to see a medium called Bill Campbell. Halfway through the session, Bill asked me if I knew of a Tony who was in spirit and had passed over with a bone disease. I thought to myself, *this man's good,* but I tried not to show any reaction. I nodded my head, careful not to give myself away. "He wants you to tell his wife that he is just fine, that he is out of pain. She has to stop grieving and to get on with her life."

Bill also told me lots of other things – personal things. How could he possibly know all this? It fed my spiritual hunger to find out more.

There's more to this world than we will ever realise. There's so much that we are unaware of, and it's up to us to find out.

When I arrived home, I thought I must ring Sandra to tell her the news. I was so excited for her. But what would she think? Would she believe me? We had never discussed spiritualism, so she'd probably think I was crazy. I began to have second thoughts and left it for a few days. No matter how I tried to push it to the back of my mind, the voice I was hearing in my head wouldn't let it go. One day I plucked up the courage to phone Sandra and tell her.

After telling her all that Bill had said, her response seemed subdued, but I'm so glad I plucked up the courage to tell her. No matter how silly I felt, it was important that I gave this information to Sandra. I will never know whether she believed me. All I know is that I had to tell her. Tony's voice was in my head all the time, nagging me to tell her. He wouldn't give up.

It has been about twenty-five years ago since I've heard from Sandra. How the years have flown by. We never heard from Sandra again, and often wonder what became of her. I'm so pleased I told her. If I hadn't, I would have regretted it for the rest of my life, especially knowing what I know now.

It's so important that we pass these messages on from our loved ones. Can you imagine how helpful this can be to ones who are grieving, and how frustrating it is for the ones who have passed over to try to get a message across?

Sometimes I find it hard to explain to sceptics about the survival of the spirit, the soul. But I know I have to. I can't say that I've met that many people who think as I do, apart from the spiritual church, and of course Alan Bellinger.

Some people will argue and look at me as if I'm crazy. I find this so frustrating. I know that I should accept other people's opinions about this subject, but I can't. It can be a very lonely road sometimes. I want to wake everybody up and say, "Smell the coffee!" But then, sometimes it has its rewards, such as when I do get through to people and it changes their lives forever.

Forget-me-nots

One day I was hanging the washing outside on the line. I had been thinking about Mum a lot lately, and I asked her to leave me a sign. I missed her so much. As I was pegging the last piece of washing on the line, the peg dropped at the side of my right foot prosthetic. I bent down to pick it up, and I couldn't believe my eyes. Where my foot was, there was this very tiny bunch of blue flowers growing in the lawn. I realised they were forget-me-nots, the flower.

I looked around the garden to see if there were any more growing, still trying to look for a logical reason. There weren't any. How could they have got there at the side of my foot, just when I was thinking of her and asking her to leave me a sign? I now know they were put there just for me. It's wonderful what the angels and the spirit world can organize; it's definitely not of this world.

I cupped my hands gently round the tiny bunch and pulled them from the ground. This little bunch of forget-me-nots meant so much to me. I knew that my mother was watching over me, and that she could hear and see me. There was more to come.

The same happened when I had picked some strawberries in the garden. There were six strawberries in total. I washed them under the cold tap and left them on the draining board. As I was wiping the kitchen tops down, I turned towards the sink. To my astonishment, the strawberries had been placed, one at a time, in an empty ceramic egg pot. It made me jump and laugh at the same time.

I have learnt to accept things. Anything is possible from the world of spirit. They can make things manifest or disappear. I love it when things like this happen – it's like playing a little game to let me know that they are around me. It's amazing that something so simple can have such a dramatic effect on a person, simply because it's not the usual.

Mum, I will never forget you. Thank you.

Joan

Joan used to be my daughter-in-law. She was married to my eldest son, Wayne. I have known Joan for about twenty years. Unfortunately they went through a divorce. They have two wonderful boys, Jason and Christopher It's so sad when this happens, but it does, and there's not a lot you can do about it. You simply have to let them get on with their lives and make their own choices.

I have always felt closeness to Joan. Perhaps it's because I haven't any daughters of my own – well, not living on earth. I know that she is a lovely person and a spiritual being. She can be very shy and easily blushes; there's a kind of childlike innocence about her. She reminds me sometimes of a frightened butterfly scared of this big, wide world.

I feel sometimes that we have been together in another life, and we may have come down in a group soul. I feel this also with Joanne, my other daughter-in-law who is married to my son Darren. I believe we are here together learning and working in a group soul scenario.

Joanne, Darren's wife, lost her mother, Hilary, to cancer at age forty-five. I once took Joanne to the spiritual church to see whether we could get a connection with her mother. Whilst we were sat together, I offered a little prayer up to the spirits to let a connection happen with Joanne and her mother. It was to no avail; it simply didn't happen for some reason. I was in no doubt that Hilary was with her that day, but it wasn't meant to be. It's not something you can command to happen. Was Joanne being tested by her faith in God and the spirit realm? I think that one day Joanne will find her spiritual path, but only when the time is right, like it was for me.

When you're in denial, you block off the connection with God and the spirit realm. You must have an open mind; you have to open up your heart. There has to be that longing within you, a passion to want to find out more. If you ask for help from God, you will be shown at some point in your future life. You must open your heart, surrender, and trust in God. Always stay within the light of God. Don't become a target for evil forces by not believing. Trust and faith are your weapons.

Let's get back to Joan. Unfortunately, Joan's father died at age seventy-six of emphysema. He had been unwell for years with his breathing. He became almost housebound for the remaining years of his life. About two months before he died, Joan had a dream about her father. She was fortunate to experience an OBE. I was so moved when she told me about the dream, and I encouraged her to write it down and give it to the priest so that he could read it at the funeral. I am sure that this helped a lot of people on the day. It may help someone who has lost a loved one to come to a greater understanding about how important our dreams are.

> I had a dream about two months ago. It had no meaning at that time, but will now stay with me forever.
> Mum, Dad, and I went to a café. It was raining and miserable. We walked inside. It was the usual busy, gray-walled café you see now and then. We were looking for somewhere to sit, but my dad carried on walking in front of us. Mum and I watched him walk to the end of the room towards a door. Dad opened the door and walked straight through it. Wondering where he'd gone, we followed him.
>
> Mum and I walked towards the door and opened it. What we saw next was amazing! In front of us was a long, beautiful green garden that seemed to go on forever. The sun was shining brightly and was warm on our faces. Down one side of the garden was row after row of bushes. They had the most beautiful flowers we'd ever seen – big and in every colour imaginable. The scent from the flowers was intoxicating.

What we saw next brought tears to our eyes. There at the bottom of the garden was Dad. He was skipping, running, and jumping up and down. He then ran around each bush, picking the flowers and smelling their strong scents. He had the biggest smile on his face, and he looked so happy.

But my dad couldn't run, and neither could he smell the flowers. He didn't smile that often, either, because he was so ill.

Joan was being shown this scenario in her OBE by the angels to ease the pain of grief. It proved to Joan that George was free from all his pain and suffering so that she could go back and tell her family. What a lovely way to prove that we all survive death in the end. The spirit world was preparing Joan for her father's inevitable death.

They always say that the colours in heaven are more vivid, much deeper, and more profound than the colours on earth. Everyone who has had the privilege of witnessing this say the same thing.

At about five thirty one morning, I was just about to turn over in bed. All of a sudden a picture flashed in front of me, like I was watching a movie. I was sitting in a big, beautiful garden and surrounded by the most beautiful flowers. I sat around a table with several friends, and we were all playing a friendly game of cards. I couldn't help but notice the clothes that we were wearing – such deep vivid colours. Then the picture vanished, was this another distant memory? Was I remembering my real home and where I really came from?

I'm left wondering: what was that all about. Was it more validation and proof that yes, we do go to a better place? Was I given a glimpse of heaven, just like Joan in her dream?

Sometimes unexplained things happen to me that leave me wondering what it means. More often than not, it's when I'm on my own, and especially when I'm at rest, completely relaxed in the early hours of the morning.

Daffodil

One day Harry had just left for work at about six thirty in the morning. I was laid on my side and feeling quite chilly at the time. All of a sudden it was as if someone was climbing into my bed. I felt the blankets turn back, and the bed sank with the weight. It seemed someone had just snuggled up to my back and put an arm around me. At first I felt a bit frightened, so I asked my angels to protect me. I didn't feel the usual fear and dread that I had felt on other occasions. Still, it left me wondering who it might be.

It turned out to be the spirit of my mum. I know that the spirit of our loved ones who have passed come around us, especially when we are ill. They still want to help us.

I have sensed my mum around me many times, especially when I go into the hospital.

Once I went into hospital for another operation to try to save my leg. I remember there was this patient on my ward, an elderly lady with a very posh voice. She was the kind who like to be seen and heard, who thought she was a cut above the rest. Every day her daughter would arrive. She practically stayed with her mother all day, waiting on her every whim. The daughter was in her mid-forties, but she still called her Mummy in a childlike way.

I sat up in my bed one day. I remember looking at this woman whilst the daughter kept fussing round her. I could also sense my mother around me at the same time. It was as if my mum was stood at the top right-hand side of my bed, looking at me sideways, close to my ear. She was looking and listening to the mother and daughter, taking it all in.

Then all of a sudden my mother chimes up with the words, "Huh! I can't imagine her been fucked, can you?" I was hysterical with laughter! People turned to look at me, to see why I was laughing. Only Mum would make a statement like that. She wasn't shy at using the F-word. Oh Mum, how embarrassing! It cheered me up to no end. How's that for proof?

When we pass over, we retain our own personalities, our character. Nothing is lost. We don't spontaneously become holier than thou and know all the answers. Not only that, but the spirit can still see and hear, although we cannot see them.

How do I know? Because I have witnessed the truth for myself. There was the time I was out of my body and trying to talk to Alan Bellinger. I banged my fist against my chest, shouting, "I'm here I'm here!" He was looking in the opposite direction, totally unaware.

What a privilege that was. How could I keep this to myself? This happened in broad daylight. I remember thinking to myself at the time, *so this is how it is. Nobody will ever believe me.* It filled me with such joy and excitement, that we all survive death. We all move to another dimension, that's all.

We have done our time on earth, so to speak. Have you ever heard that old saying "When your number is up, it's up"? This is very true. It is your time to depart this world to the next dimension. You have played your part. We have come down to evolve and progress, to find our true selves so that we can go home.

It is our choice whether we decide to come back again, so that we can evolve more; it's purely for the soul's progression. Life on earth is a continuous cycle. It goes on and on, just like the world rotates continuously. It's like the leaves on the trees: they die and grow back again. Birds migrate to the same place year after year. Life is an endless cycle. Life is really an adventure.

Wouldn't it be a wonderful thing if more people were given evidence like this? Yet I know that the world is receiving more information and knowledge than ever before from the spirit realms, especially towards our younger generations.

The angels are arriving in droves to help with our planet. The world is going through great changes as I write. All we have to do is open up to it. You don't have to be special and have magical powers or be religious. It is your birthright, part of your sixth sense, which we humans barely use.

There are places to go if you want to learn more about this, such as spiritual churches and psychic development groups. There are lots of books on this subject, as well as information on the Internet.

Daffodil

But be careful out there, especially about the places that ask for lots of money to teach you. It's not necessary – it's so easy to teach yourself. Why do you think you were given a sixth sense in the first place, if not to help you in your life? Please use the tools that God gave you!

You are not aware of it, but deep in your soul, you have all the answers, all the knowledge of life itself. That's what you are here for: to discover it all over again. You've experienced this time and time again in all of your past lives. You will be doing it all again in your future lives. You are eternal and everlasting.

You may ask yourself, "What's the point of all this, if I already have all the answers and the knowledge?" The point is your memory is erased every time you reincarnate after birth. You will have no knowledge of lives lived before. You will be starting your new life all over again.

Will you make the right choices in this new life? Will you make the same mistakes as in your past lives? How much will your soul evolve in this new life? How much has your soul evolved throughout all your past lives? How evolved do you think your soul is? At what level is your spirit progressing?

What kind of person are you?

1. Are you a racist?
2. Are you homophobic?
3. Do you look down on people with disabilities who have special needs?
4. Do you look down on the poor and the homeless sleeping in the streets?
5. Do you laugh at other people's misfortune – disfigurement, deafness, blindness, and deformities?
6. Do you have respect for the old and the infirm?
7. Are you kind to all animals?
8. Do you respect all plant life?

If you answered yes to some of these questions, then you need to do some soul searching if you want your soul to evolve. That is why you are here again. These are some of the reasons why you returned in a new body, in a new life to learn.

Don't you want to be the best you can be in the spiritual sense? The whole point of life is for our soul to reach perfection. We are given every opportunity for each life we have lived, so that we can make it possible. If we have committed terrible crimes and misdemeanours in our past lives; we will be given another chance to do so, so that we can amend this. God forgives us all, no matter what atrocities we may have committed in past lives.

It is never too late to ask God to forgive you in the life that you live now. After all, you have eternity on your side. Look deep within yourself. First, start by forgiving yourself. Learn to love yourself, and then you can love others.

Meditation

In order to meditate, all you have to do is find a quite room where you will not be disturbed. Play some relaxing music, dim the lights, light a candle or two, and sit in a comfortable chair with your legs uncrossed. Or you can lay on the bed and take three deep breaths, breathing out slowly.

As you do this, try to imagine you are breathing out all the negativity and debris of the day out of your mind and body. Imagine it coming out of your feet. If you listen to your breath, as you breathe in and out, it stops you from thinking things that keep popping into your head. Get used to listening to your breathing first. Imagination is a powerful thing, and your body will believe what you tell it.

Be aware of your shoulders: are they relaxed? If not, let them drop then go down to your arms and hands, all the way down to your lower body. If you already know about the relaxation technique, then you are halfway there.

Now you are breathing gently. You are feeling more relaxed. If thoughts keep popping into your mind, listen to your breathing more. Trying to empty your mind isn't easy, especially these days with the stressful lives we all lead. The more you practice, the more easier it will become.

Remember that life's not always meant to be easy; it can be very harsh at times. We are all evolving together. All souls are down here to learn.

With your eyes closed, imagine at the top of your head, your crown, that there's an opening. This is your seventh chakra. First ask the spirit world to protect you, to only let the pure white, healing light enter your body.

Then ask for your spirit guides to come in, and also the angels. Relax and keep breathing gently. Ask the spirit guides and the angels to give you guidance and understanding. You may want to tell them of any problems in your life, and ask for their help.

Remember that you have to ask your angels for help. They can only help you if you ask them. I can't emphasise this enough. The only time an angel will intervene is when it is not your time to die, or when you're in danger. Then the angels will step in to save you. If a loved one has died, the angels may appear to you. You can also ask for help for others, such as members of your family who are ill.

If nothing happens the first time, or you don't feel that your prayers have been answered, keep trying. You may find that a few days later, some of your problems have been resolved.

You need to get into the habit. It's like anything else: the more you practice, the easier it becomes. You will know if you are connected to the angels if you see beautiful colours. All the colours have meaning. For example, emerald green represents Archangel Raphael, the angel for healing and peace. All the colours represent the chakras: yellow represents the soul.

You may experience tingling all over your body, or heat. Imagine your crown chakra as a lotus flower opening up to receive the white light. That light goes into your body and all the way down to your neck, shoulders, hands, trunk, hips, thighs, legs, and feet.

When you think your meditation and healing session has reached an end, imagine your crown chakra closing up, sealing in all the white light and healing. Then thank the angels, the spirit realm, and your personal guardian angel. Remember that you don't have to be religious. It has nothing to do with religion – it's your birthright.

Usually when I'm meditating, I allow myself thirty minutes to an hour. But more often than not, I always fall asleep, especially if I'm laid on my bed. Its best if you are upright in a comfortable position, with your feet placed firmly on the ground.

Sometimes I have experiences. I always know when I have received a healing. Sometimes I feel strong heat or gentle heat spread over my body, or a tingling feeling of pins and needles in my hands. I always receive a strong muscular tightness around both my eyes just before my meditation comes to an end. It feels like a contraction, like electricity. My eyes squeeze really tight for a few seconds and then relax.

This is the vibration between the two worlds. It has been happening for ten or more years. Sometimes I see the colours that respond to the seven chakras and the archangels.

The Seven Chakra Colours

The 7 chakra areas

1. Base – crotch-red.
2. Genital – orange.
3. Solar plexus above the belly button – yellow.
4. Heart over the chest – green.
5. Throat around the neck – blue.
6. Intuition between the eyebrows – indigo.
7. Spiritual on top of the head crown – violet-purple sometimes gold-white.

Sometimes I feel a gentle hand on me in various places, wherever I need healing.

But most of all I always feel my leg has whole. 'You know the one that I have had amputated'. Sometimes I want to scratch my big toe, I can feel my ankle or I can feel a hand on my leg.

It's different from when I experienced the first phantom pains.

Just after I had my leg removed, the surgeon called it phantom pain. The doctors told me I would still be able to feel my leg, that this was normal.

It just felt like my leg was still there but it was painful. It lasted for about a year on and off.

When anybody passed by me, I would immediately try to hold it back. So they wouldn't catch it. It was an awful sensation.

No this is different there's no pain.

I feel completely whole again; more proof and validation that the spirit body exist.

Daffodil

When I meditate my body is between the two worlds; just like when I'm asleep, my spirit body hovers inches above my physical body.

That's why people that have lost their limbs. Always say that when they dream, they can run, and walk, again, just like the blind person he/she, can see again in their dreams and in colour!

The year I met Alan Bellinger was 1997. I was almost fifty years old. As I have already stated at the beginning of the book it changed my life forever. If it wasn't for Alan I may not have seen and witnessed what I did. I feel a strong connection to Alan, like it was all part of a plan, all part of the bigger picture that it was all meant to be.

If I hadn't had become ill in the first place, I may not have made the choices that I did –I may not have found my spiritual path.

I feel too that my dear friend Wendy Early is part of the plan, that is why we are together.

Can you imagine what a better world we would live in; if more people were aware of the meaning of life?

I'm sure one day it will come to that. Everybody at some point in their lives must ask themselves this question. Why am I here? Who am I?

I remember years ago when I was fit and well. I would wear the latest in fashions and would look forward to the weekends dressing up; socialising with our friends.

After a while it became monotonous. I would start asking myself questions. 'Is this all there is to life', its like there was something missing.

When I first went abroad with Harry to Spain. I had looked forward to it so much, but it became an anticlimax after a couple of days.

Mum used to say' "Our Eileen's never satisfied" and she was right. I knew something was missing from my life, but at the time, I didn't realise what it was. It's taken a lifetime to find out! Do you feel like this?

It's the same with rich people, they make lots of money. But how do they feel at the end of the day? Most of them are discontent.

Eileen Veronica Richmond

In my younger days when I was growing up. The girl especially; thought she'd have to find a boyfriend has soon as possible or she might be left on the shelf.

The next thing, she would be planning her wedding. She thought she had to find a man to make her complete it was the typical stereotype at that time. I don't think much has changed today.

After all, all her friends or either getting married, or having babies.

Then one day she wakes up feeling trapped looking after the family. Not having the time to do the things she'd like to do, maybe thinking, "I ought to have pursued my carrier, or gone to university"?

Then the resentment sets in. Her marriage starts to fail, heading for the divorce courts.

This is happening all too often ... marriage break-ups. It's the children that suffer.

This all happens because we all have become conditioned; to think this must be the right thing to do.

Because this is what our parents did, and their parents before them.

You have to get to know yourself first. Question yourself. Is this what I really want for the rest of my life?

Look to God and the Angels for answers. God has a plan for all of us.

I guarantee the answers will come, maybe not always straightaway; but they will, especially when the time is right for you.

There is always a right time for everyone.

The people we meet along the way, it's no coincidence we are supposed to meet them. The relationships we form with others. Life is all about making the right choices; all learning from the experience, how the soul is able to evolve.

Sometimes it doesn't seem fare. You may not get that promotion you were promised. Or the pay rise that you expected. You could have a tragic accident that could change your life in a split second. You could suffer the loss of a loved one.

It usually happens when we go through a crisis in our life; that we start to look at things differently. That we start to change. We start asking ourselves questions. What's it all mean? What's life all about anyway?

Daffodil

    I do believe that more and more people, especially today's generation, are becoming more aware and are more interested in the meaning of life. That they are opening up to it, not just accepting that death is all there is.

    I've noticed that there seems to be a lot of more younger people attending the spiritual church these days, looking for answers.

    As Colin Fry. A well known medium always says and I quote, "The biggest lie that we were ever told; is that "death is the end".

    I also think that this contributes to a lot of suicides. The ones who can't find no meaning to their lives.

    It all becomes too much; but I promise you all, there's a valid reason why you are here,

    Look within your heart-your soul, not your mind.

Katie

A couple of weeks ago, my second son, Darren; his wife, Joanne; and my two granddaughters, Emily and Katie, came to Sunday lunch. Darren happened to be looking at a photograph of my mum and me together. He had Katie in his arms at the time.

As he was looking at the photograph, he said, "Do you know, Mum, Katie only said just last week that she missed Big Grandma." All the grandchildren always referred to my mum as Big Grandma, so as not to mix the two of us up. She was not that big, just a little taller.

"Oh, that's nice," I replied, not giving it much thought. I carried on with the lunch.

A week later, it would have been my mother's birthday, 2 February 2007. I always make a point of speaking to her photograph, and wishing her a happy birthday. One year I poured her a drop of whiskey, her favourite, and put a cigarette in an ashtray next to her photo.

How I miss the old times, when we would have a drink together. I wished I could ring her on the phone, just to have a good gossip.

I raised my glass. "Well, Mum, happy birthday love." Then spontaneously I shouted out to her, "Oh Mum, can't you just come through? Can't you just show yourself again?"

On mum's birthday, Darren, and Joanne came with Emily and Katie. Darren and Joanne were going away for the weekend, and the children would stay with me. Darren told me that Katie had mentioned my mother again, on the way to our home. She said that she loved and missed her, and that she had pointed to the sky and said that Big Grandma was a star in the sky.

Daffodil

Katie also mentioned the number nineteen. The number nineteen was the age my mother wanted to be on her birthday. Remember, we can be any age that we want to be in the spirit world, by changing our thoughts. We especially choose the ages that we were most happy in life. Was it her sense of humour? She had a good one. Or was my mother at level nineteen with her spirituality?

We go to different levels when we die, depending how far we have come with our souls' progression. It is just like school on earth, when we take exams for instance. In some of my dreams, it's as if I'm in a lift going up to a different level, visiting the spirit realm.

Later that night, I went to bed. I couldn't stop thinking about it. Katie was five years old at the time when Darren was telling me this story, but she was only eighteen months old when my mother had died. She hardly saw my mother or knew her at all. Was my mother coming through to Katie, to let me know she heard my words that morning? I like to think so.

Often Katie will say to me, "I love you, Grandma, and I love Big Grandma, too." It's as if Katie has been getting to know my mother even though Mum has passed over to the next dimension.

You have to catch the young children early, around the ages of two to six, because they are more opened to spirit than adults. Kids are more accepting and think it's normal. Sometimes parents don't always listen to their children, thinking they are making it up or that it's some sort of imaginary friend.

Harry once told me about a friend of his at work. His friend and wife used to babysit for their granddaughter on occasion. She was about two and a half years old. Sometimes the little girl would say that she had seen an old lady at the bottom of the bed.

This happened quite a few times. One day her grandparents were going through some old photographs. Suddenly the little girl pointed out to her grandparents, "That's the lady I saw at the bottom of my bed!" It was the husband's mother.

I have always spoken to my grandchildren about the angels, and I tell them to never be afraid. We each have a guardian angel watching over us, and we only have to ask for help when we are troubled and need it.

I believe that one day something will happen on this planet to change everybody's way of thinking, and the majority will change for the better. Something spiritual and profound is going to take place. It has to, before we destroy this planet. You only have to look at the world to see what's going on around you.

Young, teenage gangs carrying guns and knives, and killing each other. The bullies at school, where victims commit suicide. The increasing break-up of family life, especially one-parent families. Drugs are one of the worst things that have destroyed and continues to destroy our society as a whole.

There is child sexual abuse and trafficking young girls into prostitution; not to mention what else is going on around the world. Global warming, nuclear weapons, the war in Iraq, man's greed – the list is endless.

What kind of world are we leaving behind for our children, and our children's children? We seem to be going backwards, not forwards. It paints a very gloomy picture, so what can we do about it? It's all up to us. What is needed is a massive shift in the collective consciousness all over the world, at the same time. We all can help this planet with our thoughts, by changing our thought patterns to spiritual thoughts such as, "We are all one. There is no separation. We are all brothers and sisters. We are all equal. We come from the same God."

We have to stop turning a blind eye when we see something that shouldn't be happening, such as people not having the basic needs, and pollution happening all around the world. We are destroying Mother Earth and her soil for growing healthy plants and vegetables. The animal kingdom is becoming increasingly extinct. Regarding dolphins and whales, it is estimated that over three hundred thousand drown in fishing nets around the world every year.

Daffodil

Look at the polar bear. There are an estimated twenty to twenty-five thousand wild polar bears remaining in the world. And to top it all, the arctic ice has declined by over 10 per cent since 1979. The arctic seals, the polar bear's main food source, are also under threat from loss of sea ice.

During the last century, over 95 per cent of the world's wild tiger population has vanished. At least sixty-six Sumatran tigers – one seventh of the population – were killed in one year. In 2005 eighty-three fresh tiger skins were seen on sale in the Tibetan capital over a three-week period. The Bali, the Caspian, and the Javan tigers are already extinct.

Why does man continue his cruelty to animals, killing God's wonderful creation? This has to cease if we want to save our planet. We can't carry on like this! We can all make the difference, no matter how small.

When we all depart this world, we will be asked, "What did you contribute to the world to make it a better place? How did you treat your fellow man? Did you make a difference? Did you contribute to stopping mans cruelty to animals?"

We can all help by praying each night for the animal kingdom and the plant kingdom. Ask for the rain forest to be replenished. Ask to bring peace and harmony to our world, and to end all wars. Ask to bring nations together and to end all conflict before it's too late. God and the higher intelligence will hear you. We need to live in peace and harmony. We are all God's creations.

The Ones Who Have Passed Over

When we lose a loved one, we may prefer to choose a cremation or a burial. Whatever choice we make, it is not always necessary to feel that we have to visit the graveside, although this can be helpful for the bereaved that are left behind. Our loved ones are always around us, anyway; they are only a thought away. I was told once that my mother, who had passed, was less than a foot away from me. It was comforting to know.

The greatest compliment you can give to your loved ones who have passed over is to acknowledge that they are still with you. Talk to them normally; even that's not always necessary, because they can pick up on what you are thinking telepathically. They can feel your sadness, your pain.

Try to imagine if it was you on the other side, and you left loved ones behind. You could see and hear them, but they couldn't see you. Can you imagine how frustrating that must be?

When your loved ones see you happy and settled after their death, it makes life better for them in the next dimension. They can get on with their new lives. When you're sad and still grieving, it holds them back. It stops them progressing on with their new life.

It makes it harder for them to say goodbye. That doesn't mean to say that they don't want to see you; they will always come to see you, and they will always be around you. It's simply that we can't see them.

They already have the knowledge now that life is eternal, because they are in the next dimension. Life goes on, and they know that we will all see one another again one day. You only have to think of your loved ones, and you draw them straight to you. I often feel my mum and dad around me, especially when I'm ill.

Mary

The last time I saw my sister was in April 2006. We were sat in her kitchen. Don, her husband, was with us at the time. I had been to the hospital prior. I'd had made a mistake with my appointment. I didn't feel like going home straightaway, for some strange reason.

Mary lived near the hospital, so I decided to call in for a coffee. We were having a good conversation about life. As always with me, I have to discuss my spiritual side, especially the weird things that happen to me. It's as if I can't help myself; I feel like I have to tell her.

All of a sudden Mary brought my father into the conversation. "My father was a bully."

I looked at her, it hit a raw nerve. I nearly blurted out, "Yes, Mary, and you were a bully to me." But I didn't. It would have caused one almighty row between us.

As I was ready to leave, I suddenly told her that I was going to write a book about my experiences. I felt compelled to get it all out on paper; I couldn't keep talking about it all the time. It was the only thing on my mind; the only subject that interested me.

Immediately I felt my mother around me. She must have been listening to our conversation. I heard the words, "Be careful what you say." It felt like a warning. I surprised myself, because I wasn't going to tell anybody about the book, but I couldn't carry on like this. I had this real strong passion to do something once and for all.

At first Mary looked at me in surprise. Then she said that if I wanted any help, I only had to ask her. She added, "I've really enjoyed our conversation today." So had I.

She also said, "It could take you years to write it." Well, it probably would. It's not a novel; it's about searching for the truth as my journey develops. Her prediction came true; it has taken years- eight years altogether.

Days later, I sat at my computer. I didn't have an ounce of experience, but I had a feeling of trepidation and excitement at the same time. I thought, *I know, I'll begin with my autobiography about my childhood and what it was like to grow up in the fifties.*

When it came to introducing my sister into the book, I was stuck straightaway. It was like a reality check. I couldn't remember one good thing about my childhood with Mary! It came as a bit of a shock. How do I introduce my sister into the book? This book was about truth, so I couldn't pretend that everything was normal – far from it. I had to be true to myself. I needed answers.

A few days later, with much anxiety and trepidation, I wrote a letter to Mary about our childhood. It took me ages to think of what I could say. How could I put it to her? But I needed to know. I must tread carefully. I didn't want more conflict between us; our relationship was already very fragile.

Mary could be volatile. I needed to know why we never bonded as children. Something must have caused it. She must also have realised this. I put it as tactfully as I could, but to no avail. Mary perceived it in the wrong way as usual; she accused me of having a vendetta against her; which was utter rubbish.

It was the last thing I wanted. I was hoping the book might bring us together.

Was it the fact that Mary was six years older than me? Or perhaps Mum put too much of a burden on Mary at an early age, too much responsibility? But in my heart, what I really wanted to say was, "Mary, why were you such a bastard to me over the years?" Even to this day, we have had our moments. Mary was always looking for confrontation. If I'm being honest, all I ever felt from my sister was anger, hatred, resentment, and jealousy; sad but true.

Daffodil

It was a hard thing to come to terms with, but it was a fact. *Why?* I kept asking myself. I couldn't deny that was how it was between us. I had to know the truth. It was as if I had pushed it to the back of my mind all those years ago, to try and pretend it had never happened.

After searching my memory as a child, I remembered one happy episode. It was the summer school holidays, and Mum and Dad were at work. Mary brought all her school friends to our house. We were all in the front room, playing dress-up; and singing songs like "Tea for Two" by the Beverly Sisters, as well as all the songs from the musicals. Laughter filled the room, it was a lovely day, and everyone was happy.

I was about five or six; Mary was eleven or twelve. But even then, I remember looking at Mary and feeling older and wiser than my years. I thought,

She doesn't usually let me in, let me play. Why now? I was so happy at the time that I didn't care. I remember thinking; *I wish it could be like this all the time.*

When I was growing up. I was always taught to respect my elders, and Mary was one of them. I always thought she knew best. I looked up to her and wanted to be like her. I suppose she became my role model.

But things went from bad to worse. I tried to keep out of her way, just like with my father. When we were alone together, as soon as Mum and Dad went to the pub, she would get me in a corner and beat the living daylights out of me.

It wasn't just the physical abuse – it was more. Regarding the verbal abuse, the intimidation I believed everything she said to me: that I was stupid, useless, and thick. Kids grow up believing the things that are said to them must be true. Especially when said by your elder siblings.

I always remember how her face would change to a dark red full of anger as she did this. I often stared at her when she wasn't looking; wondering what makes her like this. What made her so angry? Was I such a bad person? All siblings fight and fall out, but this was different.

I'm not saying that I was all innocent and light, but I knew her behaviour was wrong towards me.

What brings it home to me; is that when I watch my granddaughters Emily and Katie play together, although they can argue and shout at one another, Emily (the eldest) is so protective of Katie. They soon make up, and it's lovely to watch. Also, Karen and Lisa, my two nieces, Mary's daughters seem to share a close relationship.

When Mary was to marry Don, two days before the wedding, we were arguing and finished up fighting. I thought she had broken my thumb, and so did she. That was the first time that I had seen any remorse in her; although she never said she was sorry, I could tell that she was. It was as if she couldn't help it. She was very much like my father in that way, so volatile.

Nevertheless, the day she married, it broke my heart. At the time I didn't know why. I suppose looking back; Mary might wonder why I cried so much on her wedding day. It even shocked my mother. Why I would be so upset?

It wasn't till I got older that I realised why I was crying. It was the loss of what could have been a happy childhood. We would never get a second chance. We would never get to live it again. It was gone forever – lost, failed.

As the years went by, Mary never wanted me in her life. She was always looking for confrontation and any excuse to fall out with me. When I tried to end my life; she called me stupid. She has never been there for me. She once came close to admitting it once.

I'm sorry, Mary. If you are reading this, I don't want to hurt you; but you know it's the truth. It's no good blaming anyone; it's simply the way it was and still is. You can't blame Mum and Dad for everything. They weren't the greatest of parents, but they were never cruel, either.

But I'm not here to discredit my sister, to talk about all the hurtful things that she has said and done over the years. It doesn't matter anymore. I just want to understand why. What made her like that? Was it my father? Yes, he could be a bully. Did he turn Mary into a bully? They say that bullies tend to breed bullies. It's not that I'm making excuses for Mary, but something made her the way she was, and I would like to know the reason. After all, she started out as one of God's innocent children, like we all are.

It saddens me to think that my mother didn't help in that way as we were growing up. For some reason, Mum had her own insecurities, and she tended to play us against one another, especially in our adult years.

I always felt that I got on well with my mum – more so than my father – but sometimes I saw her in a different light. I wanted to trust her because she was my mother.

Sometimes Mum said and did things that I didn't agree with, but I still loved her.

Mary once said to Mum in later years; that she'd had a turbulent life as a child. Our parents were perhaps lacking in parenthood, and we didn't have much money, so I didn't find it easy to understand what Mary meant by it.

It saddens me when I look back at our life then. Why did our relationship have to be this way? What upsets me now, is that I would look at her sometimes and I could see the anger that she carried in her aura: a certain mistrust of everything and everybody. Sadly, I couldn't help her – at the time, I was afraid to even approach Mary.

The most fascinating thing that haunts me is why did we agree to this relationship, to become sisters in this lifetime before our birth? Or is it karma? Do Mary and I have past karma, past issues that we have chosen to come back to resolve?

Past Life

I had hypnosis for a past life regression about three years ago. It seemed to take forever before I succumbed, but eventually I did. I suddenly found myself in a small town. It was all misty and cloudy at first. Then I saw myself from a distance: I was male. I wore brown tan leathers, like a typical cowboy. My hair was blond and curly, just showing underneath a leather cowboy hat. I could see that I was walking on wooden decking with wooden poles, where cowboys used to tie up their horses. It was a sunny day.

My name was Henry Blackheart; I had my own cattle business. The year was 1874. I lived in a small town called Elsemere, Virginia. I noticed that the town was very quiet. Suddenly the atmosphere changed It was as if all the people fled the town suddenly, like there was some kind of imminent danger.

I found myself in my house. There was a bare wooden floor, and a large stone sloping fireplace to my right. There was a table with chairs in the centre of the room. The room was long and narrow with a small window facing me at the end. I sat at the table. As I looked straight ahead, I saw a young woman at the end of the room, in front of the window. She was petite and pretty, and we stared at one another.

She had a baby in her arms about eighteen months old, wearing a bonnet. I couldn't see the baby's face. The woman had another child by her side that was about six or seven. He was wearing a leather cowboy hat with curly brown hair around his ears. I recognised him straightaway, I shouted to him, "Jack!" I felt very emotional.

Daffodil

The woman was my sister Mary! Jack was my husband Harry. The atmosphere between the two of us was strained. They were leaving town, and she was taking the children. She wanted me to come with them.

I was a stubborn man, and wouldn't leave the town with the rest of them. I was not leaving my business and my home. I was about fifty-two years old.

I found myself staring at the woman, I felt sad. I hadn't been a good husband to my wife. I felt that I didn't always treat her properly. I wasn't a very nice person in that life.

That was it. I came round, my cheeks felt wet.

The more I thought about it after, the more it made sense. As I've mentioned before, sometimes we can come down in group souls, being born into the same family. When we pass over and look back at our lives, we witness some of the bad things we did. We want another chance to put it right, and maybe we wish to be born into the same family again in different scenarios so that we can make amends. It's purely to amend our souls.

We cannot escape the past if we have caused pain and sorrow to others. At some point we have to come back. Its karma, but it is still our personal choice. What goes around comes around; there is no mistake. It is universal law: whatever the misdemeanour, the soul cannot move on, cannot evolve.

We will keep choosing to come back till we make the right choices. Is this the trouble with my relationship with my sister Mary in this life? I want to be close to her and feel that she was always pushing me away.

All those years have been wasted. Am I paying for my karmic debt in this life? Is this why my mother behaved the way she did, not wanting me and my sister to be close? It's all part of the bigger picture. Were my mother and father playing their parts, moulding us into the adults we have become today? I'd like to think that this is so, to bring some closure.

I love my sister. She will always be my sister. If I never see her again, she will always be in my heart.

At the beginning of our lives, we are given free will. It's all about choices, remembering, and learning to love and forgive one another.

After the hypnosis, I asked Jason, my eldest grandson, to look up some information for me on his computer. I wanted to know whether there was such a place in America, in Virginia, called Elsmere. Sure enough, there it was.

Past Lives

These past lives took place with Paul Parker. He specialises in readings for past life regression. He told me that I have led a Buddhist life, and that's why I have a strong, placid nature in this life now. That is very true.

I also led a wonderful French life in Edwardian times, where I lived in a French city called Versailles, in a grand house with 120 staff working for me. I have always been drawn to French language ever since I could remember. I think it's the most pleasant, sexiest sounding language on this planet. My regret is that I didn't learn to become fluent.

I have also been a Chinese madam, working in London. This is where I think I knew Peter from a past life.

I've led many warrior lives, and Paul said I did my bit, whatever that means. I was also involved with the Christopher Columbus discoveries.

But the most disturbing life I have led makes me shudder. It was around the sixteenth century, I lived in Northern Italy, in Verona. I was a Dowager, according to Paul. I'd never heard the word before. It means a woman with a title or property derived from her late husband. I was a dignified, almost elderly woman.

He went on to say that at this time, I had a lot of power and authority over people. I worked for the church. And I could decide whether men lived or died. It was my job.

In this past life I used to work with my hands at crafts. However, someone in this lifetime was more talented at these crafts than I was. I didn't like the fact, and one of the atrocities that I committed in that lifetime was to have that person's hands removed! I found this very disturbing after the reading.

I don't think that I could have accepted the information, if I wasn't already aware of what my life was about and the things that I already knew. I don't think Paul would have been given the information from the spirit world if I wasn't ready to accept it.

The spirit world will only pass information on to a person when the time is right, when the person is ready to accept it. Let's face it: who would want to live with information like this? It could be enough to make one crazy. I'm living out my karma, which I chose to do. As Mother Teresa said, "I know God will not give me anything I can't handle. I just wish he didn't trust me so much."

Somehow it all made sense. As I have already stated, I developed rheumatoid arthritis at the age of forty-one. Apart from losing my right leg (which Paul stated was due to medical negligence), my hands are the worst part of my illness. They have become grossly deformed, especially around the wrist. They look awful, and there's nothing I can do about it. I remember Paul patting both his wrist and saying to me, "You are picking up the tab for it in this life."

Before they became deformed, the pain was unbearable. It seems now that all the damage that has been done, the pain has become easier, but my dexterity is very weak. Nevertheless, it shows as a reminder of that past life.

This information was very hard for me to take in. I hate any form of violence or cruelty, especially towards another human being. If you knew me in this life, you would never believe it. I consider myself a spiritual person; I would lay my life down for my family. All my life I have helped others to the point where I almost feel responsible for them.

I asked myself many times whether Paul might have made a mistake. Could he have possibly got it wrong? But what was to develop later confirmed that it was the truth it did happen. There was no doubt. All I can say is that I must have come a long way with my soul development since that life in the sixteenth century.

Daffodil

We have all come back to lead different lives, and we will continue to do so. People who commit murder, rape, and terrible crimes and are never found out by the law may think they have got away with it. Little do they know? This also applies to those who served only minimum sentences for terrible crimes.

That's the whole point: we can never get away with the misdemeanours we have committed, no matter what. We will be shown all this when we pass over to the next dimension. Then it will be up to us to make amends. At some point, we will choose the appropriate karma.

Some souls have completed their journey on this planet for the last time. They will pass over to a higher realm. It's another dimension where they will continue the journey to further the soul's progression.

Sometimes we may wish to come back and help mankind. We never stop learning. At some point I had made the decision, when I had passed over, to come back to pay for my karmic debt, and to make amends for the terrible deed I'd committed in the sixteenth centaury.

Although hundreds of years have passed since then, there is no escape. I myself decided at what point I wanted to come back. We are our own judge and jury. God does not judge us.

At some point we come down to live the opposite experience, to see what it's like to live at both ends of the spectrum. We will experience what it's like to be good and bad, man and woman, rich and poor, fat and thin, black and white. The world was created in this way so that we can learn from all our experiences.

Our souls have to acquire the experience of the opposite; it's the only way we can learn, so that we can keep progressing with the soul. That's our reason for life. We ourselves choose all these experiences, and we should try to remember who we truly are so that we can find our way back home, to God.

No wonder I felt that terrible dread when I was born; I didn't want to be here. Paul said that the spirit world let me have the happy French life that I lived first, before I came into this life. Is this why I felt such fear and dread the moment I was born? Is that why I didn't want to be here? Because deep in my soul I knew?

Some of you may be asking yourselves how could a new born baby experience the emotion of fear and dread?

At the time I didn't feel like a new born baby. It was my soul that was experiencing this, dread and fear, I felt like an adult, sometimes I think about the sixteenth century life, although I have no recollection whatsoever. I think most about the victim. I ask for forgiveness, and I have to put it to rest. If not, it could make me more ill. I sometimes wonder if that person is in my life today. Maybe he or she is in my soul group?

Months after I had been to see Paul, I was thinking about the readings, sometimes I would play the tape back. Every time it reached the part of sixteenth century, I felt myself cringe, did I really do that. How bad, how evil!

My children might get hold of this tape one day. I was going to destroy that part of the tape, but I'm so glad I didn't. It is so important. No matter how awful the situation, I had to face the truth. We have all led good lives and bad lives; they are part of the whole experience, or else we wouldn't be here. There would be no point to life if we couldn't progress with our souls.

When you look around and see all the suffering that people are going through – the disabled, the blind, the sick – stop for a moment and think.

Those people could be living out their karma. They could choose to live a life of suffering so that they can make amends for the misdemeanours they committed in a past life. They didn't have to come back, or they could have chosen a life of difficulty so that they could help others. Have respect for those people. We have all been in their situation. We are all trying to evolve. You mustn't judge.

Souls don't have to come back, but if they didn't, there would never be any progression with their journeys. Don't have arrogance in

Daffodil

thinking, "Oh, he must have done something wrong in a past life. Serves him right." Any bad feeling you send out is bad karma. We should never judge others. We all mirror one another.

Whether that person is suffering mentally or physically; that's not what life is about. You can help that person by sending out positive thoughts. Surround that person with love from your heart and soul. You will be amazed how well it makes you feel.

Don't worry about the suffering that one may experience in this life now, whether it is a mental or physical illness. The reward will be far greater when one passes over to the next dimension. It was the Buddha who said that life is suffering. He was right.

Remember that you chose this life to experience. It didn't just happen – you chose it. Your soul will continue the journey evolving till it reaches total ultimate perfection, so that it does not have to return to this planet. It will go to a higher dimension, a higher level.

If your suffering becomes too much for you to bear sometimes, ask the angels of mercy to give you a respite from your suffering. Say a prayer of forgiveness to the ones you may have hurt in a past life. It could be centuries ago, but remember that time does not exist in the real world. Although you will not remember your past lives, your prayers will be heard.

If you have chosen a life of suffering and are seeking a cure, it won't happen. It would be wrong for the angels or spirit guides to intervene and give you a miracle cure.

They would be interfering with the life that you have chosen for yourself, your blueprint for this lifetime. To receive a miracle cure wouldn't help your soul to progress. It would hold you back, and you would have to live it all over again in another life.

That's the reason why some people are healed and others are not. When seeking healing, remember you are not been punished; the people who are suffering on this planet now are becoming evolved souls.

We have all been here time and time again. We have all committed misdemeanours.

It's simply that we are all living on this planet at different soul levels. That's why we are all unique.

Take the relationship between my husband and me, for instance; we are complete opposites, chalk and cheese. When we were young, people would have never put us together as a couple. But I know we have been put together for a reason. Sometimes there is a side to Harry's personality which I find difficult to accept. We have many debates on different subjects; we can never agree, so we agree to disagree.

Sometimes I ask myself in frustration, *why have I been put with this man?* I have been really frustrated in the past by his outlook on life, his stubbornness not to have an open mind, his ridged way of thinking. But knowing what I know now, it all makes sense.

The good thing that has come out of our relationship is that my illness as brought out the best in my husband. He has been very tolerant of my illness. He can be very caring, and very patient, and he always looks out for me.

One of the lessons I have learnt from Harry – and I'm still learning – is to have more patience'. The people who are in our lives now may irritate us. However, the ones we have conflict with the most could turn out to be our greatest teachers.

Remember that the life you live now is not just about you; it's also about the people in your life. You may not know it, but by being together, whether you are a couple or they are your work colleges, friends, or siblings, the relationship is no mistake.

You chose to be put together, to learn the lessons needed in this lifetime, in order to help your soul progress. You will be learning from one another without realising it. You may not like it, but it has been necessary to put you together for whatever reason that will be revealed to you at some point. God has a plan for all of us.

Birth

Have you ever wondered why males and the females both have nipples? Because the embryo always starts off as a female first, before the baby's soul decides whether it wishes to be male or female. We are all born with male and female tendencies, as in yin and yang, weak and strong. The male and female balance is usually equal in babies, fifty-fifty.

But sometimes this is not so. Sometimes there is too much male hormone imbalance in the baby girl, or too much female hormone imbalance in the baby boy. This can cause confusion for all involved, especially as the child starts to develop. As soon as children are old enough, they will realise their preference.

Can you imagine a child growing up as a boy, and wanting to be a girl? Put yourselves in that position for a minute: The ridicule, the torment he will receive from his friends. Wondering to himself why he's not like them. Having all the feelings of a female in a male body reaching his teenage years. Trying to hide the fact from his parents and everyone around him. But worst of all, living a lie.

I can't think of any greater challenge, but for some reason his soul chose to be like this before birth. The spirit takes over the physical body; the spirit body is who we truly are. The soul does not recognise sexual preference; it doesn't know the difference. The physical body is simply the vehicle we chose for this lifetime.

Although this may seem like a misfortune in the womb, it is not. Instead of judging your fellow man, send out positive feelings and love for that person.

Every time you do, not only are you healing the person for the conflict he or she may have to endure, but you are also healing yourself. Try it and see. Count your blessings.

We are all human beings no matter our colour, race, or sexual preference. We are all a part of each other. We all have the right to be here. We are all connected. Love is the most important thing. We may have all lived lives as a homosexuals or lesbians. Remember, we've come to experience it all, for whatever reason.

The biggest challenge for homosexuals is what sort of life they are going to choose. Will he hide his true feelings, living out a lie for the rest of his life? I can't think of a worse position! Or will he face up to the world by telling his parents, friends, and work colleagues, "Look, this is who I truly am"? Will he have the courage and strength to face the world?

The greatest challenge would be to live a lie. Think of all the strain and stress, which this would bring throughout your life. It could make you ill. Have the strength and courage to face up to who you truly are. In God's eyes there is no shame; this has been happening since the world began.

Homosexuality is more explained in the book *Messages from Margaret* by Gerry Gavin. Margaret is an angel who gives Garry, the author, information. This developed into a book, which I highly recommend. Imagine for just a moment that your soul or spirit is without sexual organs, but is capable of sexual energy and expression far beyond anything you could currently comprehend. This is the essence of what your sexual energy is really like. There are many who truly believe that the greatest erogenous zone is the brain, but rather it is the soul itself.

All of the most profound perceptions and experiences you have as a human originate in your spirit form. Now imagine for a moment that your soul, your higher self, decides to experience lifetimes in many different forms. Some may be as men, and some as women. But imagine further that in some cases, an individual soul chooses to experience more of these lifetimes in one form than the other. What then happens is that the collective memory of the experience of

Daffodil

the soul is such that it becomes more accustomed to the feelings and sensuality of one form over the other.

This will cause the soul to have an overwhelming sexual attraction from the vantage point of that form that the soul has experienced most frequently. In other words, if you have come into this scenario as a man, but you have primarily lived out other scenarios as a woman, then there is a probability that your energy could be imprinted with the predominant characteristics of a woman. You may find yourself attracted to your same sex.

As a spirit, there is no judgment in this situation because sexuality is regarded as an expression of spiritual energy. But as human beings who are living within the social customs of different cultures, this can become a very difficult situation. This will cause many humans to repress and fight these internal feelings because they are told that it is not socially acceptable.

There's confusion that often arises when sexual energy – which is, at its root, akin to creative energy – leaves the unlimited capacity of the spirit and enters into the human physical form. Once this occurs, then the energy becomes limited by the accepted mores of society in which that person dwells. Should that soul be attracted to another form that is, in this lifetime, of the same sex, then it is considered by many societies to be an abhorrent behaviour. But what is actually happening is the true expression of the spiritual energy. I'm therefore speaking here of what I would refer to as the truth of homosexuality.

Again, it is something that many tribal people, especially Native Americans, knew and followed. The person who had the spirit of both man and woman in one body was deemed to be a sacred person. They were protected instead of abused.

***

Gavin goes more into depth in the book, but I thought it was important to mention this topic. I must admit, it is a subject that I have pondered over many times myself. But after reading what Angel Margaret had to say, it gave me a greater understanding. In fact, it made sense. There's a lot we don't know about the human spirit, and I'm sure we will get to find out when we all leave this world.

The worst thing you can do is fight against it, if you are a homosexual. You may not like yourself because of it. But on the other hand, you may embrace yourself for who you are. Your physical body will never overcome your spirit, your soul body.

This does not mean that in all your future lives, you will have to live your life has a homosexual again and again. You choose your own life – who you want to be, your own scenario. You may have chosen this life for the experience. You may have caused pain and suffering to another because of his or her homosexuality. It's karma, remember.

The secret of life is to love one another.

Christopher

Soul Mate

When Christopher, my grandson, was about to be born, I was so excited. Three days before he was born, I remember being in the kitchen and feeling butterflies in my stomach. I was making the Sunday lunch when all of a sudden, there was a tap on my right shoulder.

I heard a voice say, "The baby will be born on the following Wednesday." And he was! I knew I had heard the words. I definitely felt the tap on my shoulder.

At the time of writing this, Christopher his almost fourteen years old with a very wise head on his shoulders. He is very spiritual and caring.

When he was two, I knew that he was different. At first I used to wonder why I felt this way about Christopher. After all, we already had our first grandson, Jason, who was three years older than Christopher.

I used to feel guilty at first. I later found out that it's nothing to do with favouritism. I now realise it's because I recognised Christopher's soul. We have been together before. There can be a very strong feeling between two people when the souls recognise one another, like in soul mates.

Do you feel a close bond to someone, even one of your family members? You may have several children, but one will stand out more. You will feel more connected to one of them over the rest, yet you love them all equally.

You may have come down to work out a karma together, or you may have been together in a previous life. That person may have been your brother, sister, mother, or father.

It's the same when we become grandparents. We can have several grandchildren and love them all the same, but there may be one to whom you are more drawn to. It's not necessary the same child for both grandparents, or both parents. It's the group souls I talked about early in the book, being born back into the same family group time and time again.

At first I thought Christopher may have been the reincarnation of my father. Now I sometimes wonder whether Christopher is the reincarnation of my grandfather, Edward Molloy, to whom I was very close. I always felt a strong connection to my grandfather even though I was only a small child. He always insisted on calling me by my second name, Veronica, instead of my first name, Eileen.

Christopher happened to call one day when I was having problems with my leg. I asked him to place his hands on my left leg, which he did. We were chatting away as we always do. I can talk to him like an adult.

After Chris went home, about an hour later I tried to walk a few steps, it was a little painful. However, the next day I didn't need my wheelchair. It was the same when I broke my hip: Chris was there for healing my hip, although I didn't realise my hip was broken at the time.

This connected feeling to one child is quite normal among families, so don't feel guilty if you have a preference. It works both ways. The grandchild may prefer one granddad to the other, or he may prefer the mother rather than father. It's all to do with soul recognition.

Eternal Life

Harry took me to the cinema, and we saw the film *Ghost* with Demi Moore and Patrick Swayze. As the film came to an end, Harry and I made our way towards the exit up a flight of stairs and onto the balcony, to try an avoid the crowds.

I remember turning around to watch the remainder of the film, where Demi and Patrick are saying goodbye to each other. Then Patrick starts to walk towards the light.

I was left wondering to myself, *Is it really like this when someone dies?* I was thinking of my father at that second. I wondered whether we did live on, and whether we did go to a better place. Suddenly it was like an electric charge, a hot overwhelming feeling. I felt in my soul it left me breathless. I knew then that my dad had answered me. The feeling was so powerful.

I fully believe in the afterlife I know that we are all eternal. At the time, I couldn't stop thinking about the scene where Patrick Swayze is murdered. At first Patrick doesn't realise that he his dead, as he looks down on his body.

In 2009 Patrick Swayze died after battling a long-term illness with pancreatic cancer, at the age of fifty-seven. When I heard the dreadful news, I couldn't help but think, *He would have gone through the same experience as he did in* Ghost.

I wondered what his thoughts were as he looked down upon his body for real and realised that he hadn't died, that he was very much alive. Death is not the end– it is only a new beginning.

God and the Angels, give us a helping hand in creating movies of this nature, to make us think. They also do it through music. Have you noticed the amount of written songs that contain angels and love? I believe that the film *Ghost* was created to reach as many people as possible, in order to make them think. It was the same with the film *The Sixth Sense*, and many others.

When Alan Bellinger met his wife, Joyce, for the first time, he felt an overwhelming feeling in the pit of his stomach that left him breathless. "It was like a bolt of lightning. I just knew she was special."

Bessie

After fifteen years of love and devotion, I lost my best friend, Bessie the dog. I had to make the agonising decision to put her to sleep. It was like a part of me died that day, too. For the last fifteen years, Bessie was with me every day, twenty-four seven. I'm finding it very hard to come to terms with it. Knowing what I know about death and what happens after we die, one would have thought it would have been easier for me.

I have found it totally devastating. All our pets and animals live on in the next dimension, just the way we do, which is a comforting thought – we will see them again! Nevertheless, it hurts to lose our beloved pets.

I know my mother was waiting for Bessie to pass over. Three days before Bessie died, I woke up one morning, and for some reason I felt extremely melancholy. I couldn't bring myself together, no matter what I did; I simply wanted to cry all the time.

I thought, *what's wrong with me?* At the same time, I could sense Mum around me, telling me that now would be a good time to let Bessie go. *I can't. I can't! I love her so much.* Tears streamed down my face. Only people who have pets, who love them dearly as I loved my Bessie, can appreciate and understand the heartache, the pure devastation that this can bring.

I knew I had to make the decision. I had been asking Mum weeks before to help me out with Bessie. "Mum, help me out. Come and fetch Bessie. Take her up into those fresh fields of heaven. Let her run wild, free from all her ailments." For weeks I kept trying to come to terms with it.

Bessie had been incontinent for almost two years. She had to wear nappies at night. She was also deaf and almost blind, but I still couldn't let her go.

The problem began to worsen. It wasn't as if she was suffering in pain – or was she? She was simply old.

Three days later, on 16/6/07, we had Bessie put to sleep. I held her in my arms and buried my face on the top of her head whilst they gave her the lethal injection. As I held her, I could feel the life draining out of her body. She was gone – my beautiful companion, my beautiful Bessie. It was the hardest decision I have ever made in my life. Deep inside, I know we will be together again, but the pain of losing her hurts so much. It's like a great big hole in my chest that constantly aches.

That day when I came out of the vet's office, something changed in me. As I walked towards the car, suddenly I felt this strong connection, a sudden bond with all animals all over the world. It was something I had never felt before. It was a strange feeling and is hard to explain. It was like a realisation of something greater, something bigger, that had taken place through Bessie's passing.

We don't choose our animals; they choose us. In many cases these animals come down as guides and helpers, especially when we are going through problems in our life such as illness, bereavement, or a crisis. All animals are psychic. They can't talk, but they can pick up on your mood and your energy, especially when you are ill.

Bessie came to me just after I started with my illness. She had been a great comfort to me over the years. She always seemed to know when I was at my lowest. I will never forget her. I give thanks to God for creating such a beautiful animal such as Bessie, and for letting her into my life, if only for a short while. I know I will find her again someday.

It's now been a month since Bessie's passing. I feel there has been a shift within me, in a spiritual way. It's like a knowing: I seemed to have a stronger bond with all animals since Bessie left this world. It's as if Bessie has taught me that all animals have a soul.

Daffodil

If you have never felt the love from an animal, then you don't know what you're missing. The love from an animal can bring such joy. The love our animals give us is like Gods love for us: it is unconditional and much stronger than human love. They don't care what we look like in the morning. They continue to offer us love and loyalty for the rest of our lives, no matter what. Their love is unconditional.

All I know is that when the time is right, I need to put all this love I had for Bessie into another little pup before I burst! Probably it will be another rescue dog. Or maybe the spirit world will send her soul back to me.

A couple of nights ago, I was relaxing in a chair, and I started to meditate. I was thinking about Bessie and couldn't get her out of my mind. I missed her so much, wondering where she was and hoping she was in doggy heaven.

All of a sudden the tune "Somewhere Over the Rainbow" popped into my head. It's always been a favourite of mine, and I began to sing it in my head. I saw a vision of Dorothy holding Toto. I felt the spirit world was telling me, that yes, Bessie was over the rainbow, gone to heaven. I felt happy.

A day after she had died, it was Father's Day, 17/06/07. Darren and Richard, two of my sons came to see me after a game of golf. They were both saddened by the news that Bessie was no longer with us. "Hi, Mum," both of them said, giving me a hug.

Then Darren said, "I've got some news for you. You're not going to believe this, Mum!"

Katie, Darren's daughter, had drawn a Father's Day card at school. She had taken the card into her parents' bedroom that very morning. She had drawn a picture of two dogs in the park. One dog on the ground, the other dog climbing up to the sky. Darren has a lovely chocolate Labrador called Zak. I believe Zak was the dog on the ground in the park, and Bessie was the one in the sky, climbing towards heaven.

She had also been asking questions again: "Why did Big Grandma have to die, it's not fair." Katie was only eighteen months when my mother passed over. How could she remember my mother? Why did she keep saying it was not fair that Grandma had to die? I feel strongly that my mother and Katie have been getting to know one another. My mother has been dead almost five years.

When I'd previously told Darren the bad news about Bessie, he thought it best not to mention it to the children at the time. They weren't aware of Bessie's passing. Katie had made her Father's Day card at school earlier that week, before Bessie had died.

Harry

Harry and I went for a week holiday to Bournemouth with our friends. We felt lucky: it was 4 August 2007; the weather was wonderful that week, after all the rain and floods that Britain had endured – the worst summer on record. Whilst on holiday, Harry was to have a spiritual experience. Yes, Harry the sceptic!

In the evening we would go to another hotel called the Sands Hotel for a game of bingo. I hate bingo by the way. One evening it was about nine thirty, Harry had gone to the gents. As he was walking back to the table where we were all sitting, I noticed he looked quite pale. "Are you all right, love?"

"Am I all right? Am I all right!" He looked quite startled.
"What's wrong, Harry?"
"You're not going to believe this …" he began. "As I was going towards the toilet, this old man was in front of me, heading in the same direction. He was dressed immaculately and had a walking stick; he seemed frail.

He had a stoop as he walked in front of me at a snail's pace into the toilet. I watched him as the door closed. When I entered the toilet, I immediately saw a much younger man wearing a flowered shirt. He didn't seem to be using the toilets. It was as if he didn't know where he was.

He looked one way then the other, and he headed straight for the door. When I'd finished, I looked around for the old man, but I couldn't see him. Strange, I thought, he couldn't have possibly gone past me. I assumed he must have used one of the two cubicles.

There was no back exit door. My curiosity got the better of me. I bent down to see if I could see him underneath the cubicle. The hairs stood up on the back of my neck. There was no one there. Eileen, I know what I saw!"

I could see that it had disturbed him. I thought, *that makes a change. He always looks at me strange when I tell him the things that happen to me, always thinking they must be a logical reason.*

A couple of days later, we discussed what had happened that night. "There's no way that old man could have gone out of the toilet without me seeing him. It's impossible, especially at the pace he was walking," Harry insisted. "Eileen, you are going to think I'm daft, but –"

I stopped him mid–sentence. "I know what you are going to say. The young man with the flowered shirt and the old man were one and the same person."

"Yes," he said, shaking his head slowly while trying to comprehend.

Remember earlier in the book, how I explained about how we can appear to our loved ones at any age, young or old? Remember that you can travel anywhere you want to go? This was a prime example. It's possible the old man used to frequent the hotel when he was living, and he visits the hotel now and again. If someone was vain and very conscious about their appearance in life, then he would want to appear to you like he once was.

In the spirit world, everyone is around age thirty, but they have the ability to change their age if appearing to a loved one back on earth. For instance, if a grandchild only remembers her grandfather as an old man, then that's how the grandfather will appear to the grandchild.

This is why my mother and father appeared much younger to me when I saw them in an OBE, looking healthy and happy. Christopher always spotted my father in spirit as wearing a cap, which was fashionable when Dad was around forty years old. I myself only remember my father ever wearing a trilby hat.

I must admit, I had been asking the angels and the spirit guides to give Harry some kind of spiritual experience – nothing that would

Daffodil

frighten him, but something that would make him think. This certainly did. Thank you, spirit world!

The experience also reminded Harry of an incident that happened in the seventies. Harry was only in his twenties at the time. He used to work the night shifts at the Laycock Engineering factory near Millhouses in Sheffield.

One evening whilst working on the machines, Harry looked up and thought he had seen a man bob down behind one of the machines. He walked towards where he'd seen it, but there was no one there. He turned to one of his workmates. "Do you know, I could have sworn I saw someone hiding behind one of the machines?"

His friend replied, "Harry, I've often thought I'd seen someone out of the corner of my eye, on many a night shift."

Later that night, it happened again. Harry saw a Roman soldier from the waist up. It was as if he was climbing down from horseback. Harry saw the metal breast plate and helmet with the feathers of a typical roman soldier. Then he watched as it disappeared.

One day Harry was talking to the manager of Laycock Engineering. He happened to mention the incident to the manager. The man became very interested in what Harry had to say because he was a bit of an historian. The manager later found out from the library that Laycock Engineering was built on an old Roman burial ground.

When Harry was in his twenties, he was involved in a life-and-death situation at work, where he was almost crushed to death while driving a boom truck. Without going in to complicated details of how it all happened, he was being crushed with his chest against the steering wheel of the truck. He managed to escape at the last minute by reaching for the hand break with great difficulty.

He carried the imprint from the steering wheel on his chest for weeks. He was very lucky to have escaped; obviously, it wasn't Harry's time to die. His guardian angel intervened at the last minute. This often happens when we face death: our angels will intervene if it's not our time. What struck me was that when all this was taking place, Harry said it was as if his whole life flashed before him. It is quite a common thing when people find themselves in life-and-death situations.

Harry's best friend, David Hessell, was our best man at our wedding. They had known each other since childhood, and they worked at the same factory after leaving school. It had been a while since Harry had seen David. One day Harry bumped into David in the street. After a few exchanged words, Harry said, "I saw Harold the other day." Harold being David's father.

David frowned, "I don't think so, Harry. My dad's been dead for sixth months."

Harry said the hairs on the back of his neck stood up when David told him that. He had definitely seen Harold in the Plumbers Hotel in Sheffield. Harold frequently had a drink there after work, sitting at the same table. He gave Harry a wave from across the room as he had always done in the past. This really spooked Harry.

Sometimes when you have a funny feeling, like when the hairs on the back of your neck stand up, or you suddenly feel cold, or you have a prickly feeling down your arms; – that is when your sixth sense is speaking to you that its right, it's real. You did see and feel something. It wasn't your imagination.

Harry has been nudged by his guardian angels several times, to give him insight into his spirituality. But these few incidents **never** inspired him to look into it further. "Why?" I asked myself. I would be so excited to discuss this with my family and friends. How can one ignore what's happening right in front of them when it is not of this world? But it had very little impact on him he still remains sceptic?

I hope that someday Harry will have a more profound, divine experience that will change his mind. I know I shouldn't, but I do worry about Harry's spiritual status. I know its wrong for me to push my beliefs onto Harry and to expect him to change. I should accept it and let him tread is own path, make his own journey in this life. It's simply because I love him and wish the best for him. There must be a reason for it, and that's why we have been put together. I want him to find his angels and God, before his life's journey is over.

Daffodil

As God would say, I'm always here, but is anybody listening? We should all listen more to our angels, for they are God's messengers. God sent the blessed angels to help mankind since the world began. If you have a spiritual experience, don't ignore it. It has happened for a reason. There's a reason for your life, and that is why you are here. It is up to you – it is your choice.

Mind over Matter

If you are living a life where you are ill most of the time, and you suffer pain on a daily basis, the key is not to give your pain and illness the attention. I myself have found that if I have a task to perform, I haven't got time for the pain; I have to get on with the job in mind. This draws my attention away from my illness, even if only for a little while.

What you create in your mind will turn to reality, so be careful of what you think and steer clear from negative thoughts. Try to keep your mind on other more important things. It's easier said than done. For every negative thought you have imagine yourself pressing the cancel button and replacing it with a positive thought.

People don't realise how powerful our thoughts are; if you did, you would never have a negative thought again. You alone have the power to do this. God gave us enough tools to tackle any problems, to make life easier. It's up to us to use them. You don't realise what you are capable of, how powerful you are. It's all been forgotten through lost generations.

In 1997 when I decided to take up a reflexology course, I wondered how I would ever get through it; especially with the RA. Sometimes I would study up to two hours at a time at my desk. My body stiffened so much that when I tried to rise from my chair, I could barely stand, let alone walk into the kitchen to make myself a cup of tea.

I would stagger towards the kitchen thinking, *it's no good. I've got to get on with my work. I haven't got time for this. Besides I've invested money in this course. I have to manage somehow.* That was how I got through it. I didn't give the pain and discomfort my attention. Instead of thinking

Daffodil

how bad the pain was, I would change my thought pattern. My studies were more important to me.

Your mind will believe what you tell it. Thoughts can be very powerful. After all, when we die and go to heaven, that will be the way, we control our new lives, by thoughts and telepathy.

Why not try it in this life? It's the same when you send absent healing to someone who is ill. No matter where they are in the world, they will receive your healing thoughts one way or another. The healing has to come from the heart. Anyone who is genuine and sincere can heal. Why don't you give it a go on someone you know who needs help? You don't even have to tell them you are sending them healing. Why not try your own experiment and wait for the outcome?

Scientific studies have found that the heart is surrounded by neurons, just like in our brain. That's why the heart can feel physical pain and grief, around the heart area – as well as love and joy. When I lost my Bessie, it felt like a great big hole in my chest, and it was really painful. I can totally understand how one can die of a broken heart.

***

Sometimes I wonder why I am here, especially when people I've known for years let me down big time. Then I'm reminded that I am on this earth to evolve. Sometimes it can get too much – after all, we're only human. Life's not always meant to be easy.

One thing this life as taught me is how different we all are. We are all unique. I think of myself as a spiritual person. I would help anyone who needed help, no questions asked, because this is who I am; it's part of my character, my soul.

Sometimes you come across people in life who can be quite the opposite. You thought they were your true friends on whom you can rely, the friends you thought would help you without having to even ask. I have come across several people in my life that I thought where my true friends.

I always see the best in people in everyone I meet. But one day when I saw the bigger picture, it occurred to me that it's not supposed to be like this. We're all here to learn. Life's not just about the self. It's about the people we live with: our friends, our relations, our children, our parents.

When we are born, we come from different spiritual levels depending on how much progress the soul has made. We all have to try to blend together to teach and to learn from one another.

I have to learn that not everyone thinks like I do in the spiritual sense. There are people who don't always respond the way we'd like them to. I must admit I don't like living on earth. I've never felt like I belonged here, anyway; earth is not my real home, especially the world how it is today: wars, cruelty to animals, greed and corruption, damage to the rainforest, increasing violence, and starvation across the globe. It's not a nice place to live anymore. I want to be with like-minded, genuine, spiritual people whom I can trust.

When people don't act in a Christian way, it's because they don't know any better. They're none the wiser. Hopefully they have come back to earth to learn to make the right choices and progress. We have to accept that there are people like this in life, and we have to make the best of it and learn from it. That's one thing we all have in common: we are all learning, trying to remember who we truly are.

We are living out different scenarios, and when we reincarnate, we'll meet people along the way. Some of us may experience little love and find life hard. If souls don't experience love, it may make them resent others who are loved; they become bitter and twisted through life, therefore closing down their hearts. It's up to the soul to find love by finding God first and asking for help. Ask, and you will receive.

Some people don't respond as one would expect, if they have never been shown love. They don't know how to give love; it seems foreign to them. Yet love is what makes the world go round. We come from love. Love is food for the soul.

Love is all there is. That's why it is so important that our children are brought up in a loving, warm environment. Our children copy us

Daffodil

because we are there role models. It doesn't bear thinking about if they are brought up in a violent and abusive environment. They become desensitised and will grow up thinking it is normal.

This earth is made up of all different kinds of individuals. Some are well evolved, and some are not. Some don't know the meaning of spirituality, care, compassion, or respect. But most important, they don't know true meaning of love. That is why we all chose to come to earth: to learn and to make a difference.

I find that when life becomes too confusing, it's best to meditate. If you don't know how to, find a quite place where you can spend ten or twenty minutes or so. Sit in a chair, relax your shoulders, and take a few deep breaths.

Be in the moment and ask your angels for protection. When you feel ready, ask the spirit world or your angel why you are having all these problems in your life. Remember that you have to ask your angels for help – they don't come to you, so you have to acknowledge that they are there for you. Ask, "What do I need to learn? Is there anything I should know?" You will be surprised what will happen.

On one of these occasions I was listening to a tape about how to speak with my Reiki guide. At first all I could see was a thick mist all around me. It seemed that I was in a park, I could see two pathways.

Then I found myself sitting on a park bench and looking straight ahead. A Tibetan monk was walking towards me and smiling at me like an old friend. I seemed to recognise him. He looked like a young Dalai Lama; I took him to be my guide. He was dressed in a dark red robe edged with gold. He looked about thirty-five; he had a book underneath his left arm, and wore glasses.

He sat beside me, and I turned to look at him with tears streaming down my face. I said to him, "But it's so hard, it's so hard," referring to the physical suffering I had to go through every day on earth.

He put his right arm around me, drawing my head towards his chest. I could smell his scent, and his clothes brushed the side of my cheek. He spoke softly to me. "You are learning, and I am with you every step of the way." How amazing! I felt blessed.

We are never alone. There will always be spirit guides and the angels to help us. It's your birthright; again if you ask, you will receive.

We have to move on no matter how difficult our lives become. The most precious thing that I have learnt over the years; is that **death is not the end**. Life can be much more enjoyable when you can face your future without the fear of death.

I do not fear death whatsoever. In fact some days I welcome it, when the pain gets too much. I want to go back to my real home. You may think it's a selfish thought. What about my family? I know that one day we will all be together again. I know why I was born, and I accept it. We all have to die so that we can be born again.

I loved life when I was young and healthy, and the children were small. I was happy although life was a struggle financially. I realise now how lucky we were in those days. I was healthy, and my husband and children were healthy. But most of all, we were happy.

I was healthy up to the age of forty-one. I did have a life up until then. Some people don't even get that. I often ask myself how children who have a bad start in life through illness, especially juvenile rheumatoid arthritis cope.

You may ask yourself why a child was born only to suffer in this life. What's the point? There has to be a reason why. It's not that the child or the parents are being punished in any way. The child who chose a life of suffering is an evolved soul who may be helping the parents with their souls' progression, or vice versa.

It could be the parents that are the evolved souls, or maybe all three are evolved. This is the life that all three of them planned before they were born. All three wanted to evolve by experiencing this life in order to reach more soul progression.

When we are born, we are all innocent. Our memories of lives before this new life have been erased. We start our new life fresh so that one day if all goes well on this planet with our mission in life, we will find our way back home, back to God. Where the next life is eternal, there is no end. Amen.

It makes my life easier despite the daily physical suffering, knowing that life is eternal and that there is no death. One day I will see all my family again. It helps me to carry on with my life, no matter how unbearable it can be at times. I know there is no end, only a new beginning. I know that I will be free from all my ailments, and my body will be restored. I will be in an environment where I will exist at my very best.

At my funeral, I want everyone to celebrate my life. I want everyone dancing and singing – a right old knees up. They should play all my favourite records: Tina turner, Aretha Franklin, Stevie Wonder, Michael Jackson, and loads of soul music. I certainly will be dancing my socks off in heaven, now that my leg will have been restored to me. It's been a long time since I've danced!

I often talk to my dead parents as if they are still here, because I know they can see and hear me. Although the conversation seems one-way, I know they know everything that happens in my life. I know that my mother still comes to family parties and gatherings. She always comes with me when I have to go into the hospital.

My parents and grandparents pick up on my thoughts; they feel my pain. Remember, one of the greatest compliments that you can give to loved ones who have passed over is to acknowledge that they are still alive, which of course they are! It's simply that they exist on a different vibration level, one that we will all ascend too eventually.

For the last twenty years, I have been looking for a cure for my RA. I never give up. I want to enjoy the rest of my life. I keep trying different remedies. I don't believe in drugs and medication for my problem, although I have had no choice but to try the medication. It may work for a while, but sometimes the side effects can be horrendous.

When I started with my illness at times; when the pain was really bad, I would lay on top of my bed. I would hear a lady's voice in my head telling me repeatedly, "Eileen, the body will heal itself." This happened a few times in the beginning. I tried everything, and I still do so to this day.

The only drug that seems to help me is prednisolone, a steroid. By the time I knew how damaging this drug was, it was too late. I was never told of the disastrous effect this would have on my body. All I knew was that the drug helped me to lead a normal life at the time.

I have tried to come off the drug very slowly. Apparently it can damage the adrenal glands that sit on top of your kidneys, which in turn produce cortisone, a natural pain killer. Prednisolone is a synthetic hormone.

This is a powerful drug that, if used correctly, can help with a lot of diseases such as an autoimmune diseases, asthma, and lung disease. The key is that if you have no alternative, use it only in short spells – not more than a week if possible. Then wean yourself off very slowly.

I was left to take the drug for three months. Because I felt all right at the time, I assumed all was well with me. I am still trying to wean myself off the drug. I get to about six weeks, and then I have to up the drug again because nothing else works. My heart beats faster, and it's all downhill again. I have lost count how many times I have tried to wean myself off this drug. At the moment I can hardly put one foot in front of the other. If I were to come off the steroid altogether, my body would go into shock, and it would kill me.

I still believe in natural remedies for any illness. Reflexology is a three-thousand-year-old remedy used in ancient Egypt and in China. It is excellent for asthma. You can manipulate the lungs via the feet. It is so simple! It's the same with migraines, which are easy to treat. It's persuading sufferers to take the treatment.

Whenever I came across a client with migraine problems, I always asked first whether they have an ingrown toenail on the big toe, which represents the head. It's surprising that when the big toe is treated, the headaches disappear. I treated my former daughter-in-law, Joan, after years of her suffering with migraine. After several sessions, it soon disappeared altogether. That was eleven years ago, - she's not had one since.

I remember going to see a medium when I had been taking the steroids for about three weeks. Halfway through the session, he said to me with much concern, "Oh, you're not taking steroids, are you?"

The following week I tried to come off the drug, but I felt so ill. How I wished I had persevered in those early days.

It's been twenty years now since I have taken this drug. I can only imagine the untold damage this has done to my body. Because of the drug, my bone density is very low, my skin has become very thin, God only knows what damage it's done to my internal organs.

I have had to learn to live one day at a time. It's no good worrying about what you can't control anymore; you will only wear yourself out. I know I have been given extra protection against the medication by the spirit world, because I've have a mission to complete. No one would normally last this long on steroids.

Molly

One morning my friend Wendy rang. I told her that I still hadn't found a little pup yet. She replied, "There's a little Jack Russell pup nine weeks old going for £150 in the newspaper. Do you want the number?"

"Yes!" I replied with excitement.

By the late afternoon I had Molly sitting on my knee. The chap I'd bought her from was kind enough to bring her to the house that day when I told him of my condition. When I opened the door to greet Molly, my heart sank. I didn't feel that pull I had experienced with my other dogs.

I must confess I felt a little disappointed. I invited him in, and we both sat down to discuss the puppy. Somehow the atmosphere changed, and it didn't feel right.

As I looked at Molly sitting on his knee, there was something about the man I didn't quite trust.

He noticed my disappointment. Ho'he said, "She's a Parson Jack Russell."

"She looks terrified," I replied.

"Well, it's because she's never been in a car before."

"Is she healthy? Only I will be taking her to the vet tomorrow."

At this point my mother popped in my head. "Ask him for money towards the vet bill." I ignored her, thinking it must be my imagination. As I looked at Molly, I felt sorry for her. I didn't hesitate I paid for her there and then in cash.

Daffodil

When Harry and I took Molly to the vet the following day, we found out she was full of infection. She had an ear infection and also an anal gland infection, Molly was put on antibiotics straightaway.

The lesson I learnt here was never to go against my gut feeling. That was why I didn't trust the man. For all I knew, she could have been stolen. How could I have been so naive? I'm always too trusting of others.

I rang Alan Bellinger to ask for absent healing for Molly; because the antibiotics didn't completely clear up all the infections. She is now as fit as a fiddle! She was supposed to be a Parson Jack Russell, but it now turns out that she maybe a fox terrier? Nevertheless, she is the cutest little dog and fills that emptiness I felt within me. I feel whole again and have so much love for her.

A few weeks later, I had been suffering with my left hand. It seemed to be getting worse – some sort of trapped nerve probably connected to the RA. I sat in my armchair trying to eat my breakfast. The pain in my hand became very intense. No matter where I put my hand, I couldn't get any relief.

I remember looking across at Molly; who was sat on the corner of the sofa on the other side of the room. Suddenly the pain became too much, I started to cry, all the while looking at Molly.

She cocked her head to one side, looked at me, jumped from the sofa to my husband's chair, and then onto my chair. Then she came around my back and immediately started to nuzzle and lick my hand, as opposed to wanting to chew and bite as she usually did.

For a second or two the intensity of pain subsided. I was amazed. It was as if she knew the pain I was going through. But then, of course they do – they are such sensitive creatures. Bessie used to be the same way; she always knew when I wasn't well.

I'm amazed at times when I look at God's wonderful creations. I find myself staring at these wonderful animals time and again – the tiger, the deer, and the dolphin – in all their glory. It's the same with flowers. Have you ever stared at a flower in full bloom? I mean really looked at it, in all its detail: the colour and the shape. I find it therapeutic to stare at these beauties, especially when I first started with my illness.

When Molly was four and a half months old, I knew that she was special. It sealed the bond between us. For a puppy to sense my pain at such a young age amazed me. It was not like she was an old, established dog. As the weeks went by, Molly became stronger and more boisterous.

My mother popped into my head. "You know you are going to have to watch yourself!" That meant there was going to be an accident before long. Again, I ignored her. I knew she was right, of course: I had never seen such energy in a little pup.

I kept having doubts about Molly and whether I could cope with her. Whenever family and friends came to visit, she would run around with wild excitement. She showed no signs of calming down she was extremely hyper.

I started reading books and watching dog programs on behaviour problems. Although I learnt a lot, I didn't know about certain dog breeds. It didn't make any difference. I was getting nowhere with Molly. Nevertheless, my love grew stronger for her each day; to me she was a loveable joy. I learnt from one of the training programs; that this type of dog breed needed to be exercised every day; till they were tired out, this was the only way they could calm down. They had to release their energy or else they became frustrated and could be destructive in the home.

I thought the back garden would be plenty big enough for her, with her being a tiny dog. How wrong I was. Although Harry took her out quite often, it wasn't enough for Molly. Then one day it became too clear.

She was looking through the window and pining at the same time, looking at me. She was telling me in her own way that she wanted to go out, to run free. Suddenly it was as if I could read her mind. I spoke to her. "You want to be free, Molly, don't you? You're trapped, you need to run free. You're like a little bird in a cage. I can't do this to you anymore."

Here I was, trapped in my own body. I could hardly walk around my home, let alone take her for a walk. I would love to be out there with the

Daffodil

rest of the world – to walk, to be able to run, to jump on a bus – but I was trapped. And here she was, full of life, such a high-spirited little dog.

I had to let her go. It broke my heart, but I kept telling myself it was best for Molly. To keep her would be selfish of me. It's not all doom and gloom. Wendy, my dear friend, offered to take Molly off my hands if it got too much for me. I was an accident waiting to happen, with Molly running around at a hundred miles an hour.

Wendy has always rescued dogs from the rescue centre. She seemed to choose dogs that have issues; she was drawn to them.

Perhaps there was a lesson for me to learn here. Sometimes you have to let go, even though you love them so much. It's the best for them. I let Molly go because I loved her so much; I couldn't give her the life she deserved. She will always be in my heart. At least I will get to see Molly now and again, once she settles down.

When I look back now, I can see the bigger picture. Of course Molly was meant to be with Wendy. I was Molly's rescuer. My experience with Molly was to save her life by taking her to the vet. Wendy wasn't in a financial position to do this. I knew Wendy would give Molly a good life, providing her with all the love and training she needed. All was not lost.

"Until one has loved an animal, a part of one's soul remains un-awakened."

Anatole France

When we die, we go to different levels depending how evolved our souls have become. It's like taking exams at university. If we pass them, we go to a higher realm. It all depends on how we died. If we died through accident or illness, we will each go to a resting place where we'll be restored mentally, and physically, but most of all spiritually.

We will still have the same characteristics, the same personalities, and the same bodies that we had on earth. It's simply that we exist at a different vibration. That's why when we die and leave our bodies, our spirit bodies feels so light.

We have to become compatible with the new world at which we have arrived. That's how I recognised my father standing on the pavement at the traffic lights just after he had died. It all seems a long time ago now, but it's still so very vivid in my mind. Although he didn't appear as solid matter, the outline and transparency was exactly the same replica as his body was when he was alive.

Some spirits will stay behind a little longer after death, curious because they want to see their funeral and to make sure everything goes well. This is when they will know who their true friends were. Everything is exposed, such as lies, misdeeds, trust, regrets, and true friends.

When we have all been restored after our deaths, and we have become accustomed to our new existence, we will move on to different realms till the time is right to move on. It depends how far we have come with our souls' progression, with how evolved we are.

If we have done well on earth, and if we have made a difference, especially helping mankind, we will go to the appropriate realm. In heaven time does not exist. There are no clocks or watches; there is no day or night. The atmosphere is constant, serene, and beautiful.

You will not believe what you are seeing and feeling. It is so overwhelming, loving, and powerful. Yes, this is your real home I'm talking about, where you belong. Everything exists through thought and telepathy, where everybody helps one another. Life carries on but in a different way than what it was like on earth.

We don't need sleep, for instance, because we don't need to restore our bodies. But we can still lay on a bed if we want to rest, just by pure thought. Those of you who never got to travel the world and see different countries will have the chance now, simply by transferring your thoughts. You can travel to any place you desire. If you think of Miami, Florida, for instance, you will be there in a flash' - with no jet lag!

We may come back to earth to learn more. We may come back to live out a karma so that we can move on with our souls' progress. But it will always be our decision. All karma has to be healed.

Daffodil

If you committed misdeeds in past lives, then you will have to suffer the same consequences if your soul is to progress. You see, your soul has to become pure if you want to reach God, for God is pure and we are all born in God's image.

When our bodies and minds have been restored back to health, that's when we are given a choice of what we want to do. Most souls want to help others. Some souls stay in heaven, perhaps practicing to be doctors, nurses, surgeons, councillors, or teachers. All work is towards their next experiences for their next reincarnations on earth.

Some souls in heaven will rescue other souls who have just died on earth. Some souls get stuck on earth, not wanting to leave loved ones or possessions behind. They may remain in shock because they do not realise they're dead, especially children who may have died instantly in an accident.

Sometimes at the point of death, just before impact, the child's spirit is taken out of the physical body so that it feels no pain. This happens for some adults, too; it simply depends on what level the soul as progressed to. More often than not, our loved ones who have passed before us become the rescuers. If it's our time to die, no one can prevent it.

Before we come back to earth, we have all the help we need from the guides, the masters, and the higher evolved. They prepare us for our next encounters on earth in different scenarios, such as how best we can help the planet. Some come back to help the planet, such as Greenpeace, which works in a group scenario.

We will be asked to choose the right parents, which will benefit us most for the life we want to live. We get to choose the time of our birth and the timing of our death, if we want to. Therefore don't go blaming your parents for the name they think they gave you, when in fact you named yourself!

Souls keep coming back to earth because they realise that after death, there is no end to life, that life is eternal. It gets better and better! Most souls want to be born again. It's a great honour to be given life, especially when the soul is all-knowing.

It will always be your choice when you want to return. You will receive all the help and advice from the masters before you return to earth. Many souls want to rest, especially after a hard life. I myself I'm going to have about fifty years rest! There's never a wrong time to be born. There are many experiences for the soul to learn. There will always be opportunities to evolve even further, if we want to.

Some souls don't want to return and are happy where they are. We choose the soul who will be our mother, the one best suited for this new lifetime. Once chosen, the soul can either enter the foetus at the time of conception, or it can hover around outside the mother's body. It may not enter the womb till the time of birth. The baby will pick up on the mood of the mother; it knows whether she is anxious or happy about the birth. It can also be a frightening experience for the baby, especially at the time of birth. Before the baby is born. It is aware of its environment. It can pick up on the mother to be, even before birth. It can sense all the people that are around at the time of birth, such as the doctors, nurses, and midwives, and even the mood of the father.

This can be a happy environment or a devastating experience, especially if the baby wasn't wanted in the first place. The newborn senses everything as an adult. My first experience was one of dread and fear. I simply didn't want to be here. Although I was a newborn, I felt like an adult. This is my higher self, my soul, that has all the knowledge just before the birth and just after birth.

I suppose it's just as well that our memories are soon erased. Can you imagine the repercussions if we weren't welcomed into this big wide world; if we weren't loved or wanted? It is possible under deep hypnosis to be regressed back in time to just before your birth.

If you want to know more about this subject, I highly recommend Helen Wambach's book *Life before Life*. Helen studied psychology. Questions were asked of two thousand subjects under hypnosis about life before birth.

Dr Wambach's two-year study persuaded her that "90% of the people who come to me definitely flash on images from a past life. I am convinced that the time has come to study rigorously the plausibility of

Daffodil

reincarnation". Here is an example from some of her clients whilst under deep hypnosis just before the birth.

Case B-105
"When you asked about the birth canal, I remember my head been out and the rest of my body still in my mother. I was looking up at the ceiling. After birth I was aware of green hospital gowns and bright lights. I was aware of other people's feelings; I had the understanding of an adult, not a child".

Case B-1
"The birth-canal experience for me was like going through a tunnel, then blue clarity, then yellow, then pure light. After the birth I had a good feeling. I liked the water I was washed in – the warmth of being wrapped up. I was aware of the feelings of others in the room, and that my family was delighted that I was a beautiful baby girl."

Case A-588
"I was unsure of what was coming in the birth canal experience, but after birth I felt alienated and alone. I didn't want to be touched. I wanted to feel the warm water again.
I was aware of other people's feelings in the delivery room;
I was distant from them and didn't want to be close to them. I was in a world of strangers. Lost without Louis. (Louis is a twin who left the womb early because he had other things to do. I know his spirit is helping me".

That's why sometimes stillborn babies are born; it's no fault of the mother. It's simply the fact that the baby has changed its mind. It doesn't want to be here and has gone back home. Can you blame them? Who would want to leave such a beautiful place as heaven? Although devastating for the mother, she will meet up with her stillborn baby one day, they will be an instant understanding. Nothing is ever lost.

So you see, no one forces you to reincarnate – you can change your mind at anytime. It's the same with sudden infant death. Sometimes a healthy baby can suddenly die for no apparent reason. The medical profession cannot explain why.

When you are born into this world, you bring nothing but love. When life ends, love is all you can take back with you.

In an ideal world when a child is born, it would be beneficial to the child to be born in the right environment. That the baby has contact with the mother as soon as possible. The baby will recognise his mother's voice straightaway. It's important the mother holds the baby skin to skin, touching the baby. The baby should hear the parents' voices. That would be ideal for all concerned. But it's not always possible to have the perfect birth, the perfect setting.

Don't worry if you are a mother and are about to give birth. Everything is unfolding as it should. No matter how your baby is born, how difficult the birth, you and your new baby planned this a long time ago in a different dimension. The baby chose you in the first place to be its mother.

Far too many caesarean babies are being born. Sometimes this may be necessary if there are complications that can become a risk to the mother or child. A child should be born naturally, if possible. But C-sections should not be done when natural birth becomes an inconvenience – such as parents booking holidays, or they don't want to go through the birth pain.

Childbirth is one of the most wonderful aspects of life. I'm glad I was fortunate to experience it. At least, I did with three of my sons. My first son, Wayne, was born when I was only sixteen. He was planned. I wanted a baby. Harry and I wanted to be together. Neither of us were happy living at home with our parents.

I'm sure that this is the reason that there are so many young mothers getting pregnant purposely, because they are not happy at home with their parents. Also, they might have never received love from their parents. Having a baby gives them a purpose in life, a baby to love; love is so important.

My baby Wayne and I nearly died when I gave birth. It was a tremendous ordeal. When I regained consciousness after the birth, I inquired after my son; he wasn't at the side of me in a cot, like all the

Daffodil

other mothers. He had been put into an incubator in case he picked up an infection. I was frightened for my son after all that had happened prior to the birth, with a dreadful midwife.

Wayne weighed nine pounds, four ounces. I was only five feet two inches. He had a very bad forceps delivery. His forehead and the back of his neck were swollen and badly cut from the forceps. He was also cut above his eyes – hence the incubator.

I didn't get to hold my son or see him right away. Neither did Wayne get to hear my voice, or smell my scent, or feel my touch. Only his father was able to hold him. For Wayne, it was a lonely experience. Not having that special connection with the mother at birth can be traumatic for both mother and child. I'm certain that this has an effect on all newborns. I'm sure it can cause problems later in life.

What a terrible start my firstborn had into this world. But why? It was the second day when they brought Wayne to my room, but it felt like forever. He was battered and bruised. He looked like he had been in his own little battle to enter the world.

I myself lost half my blood. It wasn't discovered till three days later, I had to have an emergency blood transfusion. I also had an infection where I had been stitched. They transferred me to another hospital because I required an operation for the wound to be cleaned and re-stitched.

I was terrified for myself and for my baby. We went through a terrible time. I was a young, naive, terrified, immature mother trying to do the best I could for both of us.

I always remember when I was in labour, on my way to Nether-Edge Hospital in Sheffield. It was a hot, sultry day in July 1964. Harry was in the ambulance with me, and he looked terrified; he was only eighteen. When they found out it was going to be a difficult birth, they transferred me to Jessop's Hospital in Sheffield, where I was examined by a midwife.

When everything was starting to prove more difficult, the midwife lost her temper with me she shouted, "What religion are you?"

I was in terrible pain at the time, I thought; *what's that got to do with anything?* I replied, "I'm Catholic." She carried on shouting. "Huh, I thought so! Its women like you who have babies like this!"

Then I must have passed out. I don't remember anything after that. I woke up on a Sunday morning, 19 July 1964. Harry told me that we had a baby boy. I remember feeling terribly weak and fragile at the time. I didn't realise it was because of the loss of blood. Harry told me later, when he was waiting for our baby to arrive, that when the midwife came out of the delivery room, she was covered in my blood. She had made a derogatory remark towards him.

The nurses kept asking me if I'd always had a pale complexion and pale lips. I must have looked like death, I certainly felt like it. It never occurred to them during the delivery that it might be blood loss! What really disturbs me was that a week later, a sixteen-year-old girl died in that very same ward as a result of a difficult birth.

Obviously this dreadful midwife made the wrong choices, by treating me in this way. This will have a karmic effect on her soul. She will have to face the consequences one way or another. She will be given a review of this scenario when she passes over.

I have a feeling it wasn't the first time that this midwife was so cruel to a young mother. Everything is recorded with the angels, good and bad. This is all stored in the Akashic records, the book of life.

As I have said before, what happened at the time of Wayne's birth was meant to happen. The point is how we all deal with it at the time. It's always down to choice. It was all pre-planned, so there's no good blaming anyone. Harry, Wayne, and I agreed to this before we came here. It happened for a reason.

I believe Wayne and I are working out our karma. We have had our ups and downs, our arguments and disagreements. He's the only one out of my four sons with whom I have had confrontations. But that doesn't make me love him any less. It's simply the way it is.

Daffodil

When Harry and I separated, Wayne could never forgive me. Was this one of Wayne's lessons, to learn to forgive in this life? Especially when his marriage broke down; when he and Joan separated, could his children forgive him? We all have to learn to forgive and move on. It's not good for the soul to hold on to unforgivness.

Wayne and I have probably shared a past life together. Hopefully we will work out our karma. If we don't, we will have to come back to do it again in another life, in a different scenario. It's like the scenario with my sister, Mary.

Who knows – Wayne could have been my father, brother, sister, mother, friend, or enemy in another life, and we still have issues to resolve. All I know is that I love my son unconditionally, and that's all that matters. And I know he loves me too. If this was one of the lessons me and Wayne's had to learn in this life now; to learn to love one another then we have both succeeded.

I feel I have had lives with all of my sons before. There's a special connection with all of them. I feel that Richard was once my father in a past life.

It's the same with my sister; we agreed to be sisters before we were born. We are working out our karma. Over the years I've tried to have a proper relationship with Mary. It's as if she didn't want to know me right from the very start; even as children we never bonded. We are like total strangers. It was not for the want of trying on my part. All I ever wanted was for Mary to love me to look after me, to protect her little sister.

I have no happy memories really from my childhood, I find this very sad. What can you do when you have done all you can? You have to face up to it; no matter how much it hurts, you have to learn to let go. You can never change what happened in the past, but you can change your future. The only answer is to love that person no matter what.

Even if you don't agree, agree to disagree and then move on. Don't let it fester for years because of some dispute. Other people are a reflection of you. If you hurt others, you only hurt yourself. Sending continuous love to people will act like a soothing balm that will heal the wound one day. Love is the answer to any disharmony. It cures all.

If you are going through a similar situation where there can be no resolve; and you have tried your best to make things right but have made no progress, at least you know in your heart that you tried, and that's all that matters. This, too, will be recorded.

We can't make another person love us. We are at lots of different levels when we come to earth, as I've said before. That's why some souls are more advanced than others. They take it for granted that life goes on because they've been able to remember some of their past lives, and because they do, they usually choose a spiritual path.

***

When I was young in the sixties, I could never understand why young people I saw on TV news, who were not much older than me, went to third-world countries to help out with disadvantaged human beings. These people were living in squalor and did not have the basics to lead a normal healthy life.

No clean water, food, shelter, schools, or contraception. At that time I thought like most people: "How can they keep producing babies all the time, when the country is in such a dilemma?" The volunteers going out to help were mostly young. I thought they must be mad! Who would want to go to third-world countries and risk their lives? I was at home, snug in my own little environment, I thought, *Ha! Rather them than me!*

When I was young, life had so much to offer. Now I realise that I was being a selfish teenager. How differently I think now. People who help in this way are fulfilling a mission. They know that God had a plan for them, giving their souls an opportunity to further their progression. What will their choice be? Will they want to help, or will they turn a blind eye? Thank God there are people like this in the world. What would we do without these special souls?

It always amazes me when I see young carers wheeling around people with special needs. I think to myself, *they should be out enjoying themselves like the rest of their generation. Instead they have chosen a life devoting themselves to caring for others.*

Daffodil

Some days I remind myself how little I knew of life in those days, and how much I needed to learn about life. For instance, could I have helped the needy in Africa or any other third-world country if I had had the opportunity in my younger days? To be honest, I don't think I could. I suppose I was too wrapped up in my own needs at the time. Perhaps my soul was not ready, or maybe I'm not as advanced as these caring souls.

I may be in a future life, as part of my soul's progress. Or maybe I have already lived a past life as a carer. Who knows? That's the whole point: we are given free will to make the right choices. Many souls are here to make a difference, and that's why they made a choice to come back to earth—to reincarnate once again and be given more opportunity to make a difference.

There are earth angels on our planet disguised in human form. They walk amongst us, chosen by God to help the planet and its people with their problems. They are highly evolved souls that exist on this planet. That are not always aware of their high spiritual status, though. The angel soul may not be aware that she is an earth angel, because all memory is erased from the past life after she is born. Yes, even angels can experience what it's like to be a human.

Then there are the angels who turn up out of nowhere to help at the last minute. There have been lots of stories where people have found themselves in difficult circumstances, such as their car was broken down in the middle of nowhere. Yet out of the blue, someone appears to help them. When they turn around to give thanks, the helper has disappeared. Has this ever happened to you? This is a very common situation.

Angels have intervened at the last minute in life-and-death situations. The angels will appear to you, dressed in appropriate clothing to fit the scenario, to convince you at the time.

Questions Asked

Things can go wrong in our lives. We can lose a loved one to a terrible disease, or a child goes missing or is murdered. This has to be the worst thing that could happen: a pure, innocent child being killed for whatever reason. How do parents ever come to terms with such a heavy burden? They don't. They have to live out the rest of their lives with the knowledge that their child was taken away under such horrific circumstances. But why? Where was God? Why did he let a little innocent child die in such a terrible way?

Why were all those children killed in World War Two, in the concentration camps? Why did the Holocaust have to happen in the first place?

The answer is to make sure that this would never happen again. War is senseless and futile. Why were all those children shot and murdered in an infant school in Dunblane, Scotland, by the maniac Thomas Hamilton in 1996? Who would want to live in a terrible world such as this? It doesn't make any sense.

Why was Ryhs Jones, the eleven-year-old-boy, shot and killed for no reason? The police say he happened to be in the wrong place at the wrong time, but was he? This was meant to happen. Just like the McCann family, the Rhys family made a pact before they were born. Children killing children is not acceptable, and it can't be allowed to carry on. Something has to happen. People have to come forward and speak the truth. We cannot be held back by fear, or else we will let evil prevail.

Daffodil

Again it is all down to the choices that humans make. We can all prevent these atrocities happening in the first place by the choices we make!!

We have to stand together and fight this cancer. What kind of world are we leaving behind for our children? When I hear stories like this, my heart goes out to the parents. I have nothing but love and respect for them: they chose a life, a scenario such as this, to help mankind.

What can be worse than losing a child? But of course the parents don't realise this. They don't know the bigger picture, and they don't realise how advanced their souls are. I guess in a way, it's a good thing that our memories are erased after our birth, and that we can't see into the future. Take a look at my scenario, for instance. I couldn't have faced up to the coming future if I had known beforehand what my future entailed. I would have been hysterical knowing I was going to be crippled and in chronic pain for more than twenty-five years.

They would be many suicides committed if souls on earth could look into their future. Some wouldn't be able to face life. Take a moment to think about it. Take a look at your own scenario, or maybe someone you know. Ask yourself whether you want to have known the real reasons for your existence and what may happen to you in the future, especially if your life was a happy life beforehand.

I shouldn't just be looking at the negative side of life. There were many happy times, many happy memories in my life. The ones that stand out for me are the births of my four sons and my seven grandchildren. The most important aspect in life is to have experienced love, to love and be loved. There is no greater experience.

When we pass over, we all learn the reason why terrible things happened in our lives, and why we had to be a part of it. I know it's hard to believe that all the atrocities that are committed on this planet are not real, but at the time we are conditioned to thinking it's the true reality. Bear with me.

We are all acting. The idea behind it all is to show humanity to itself. Man is capable of the most heinous crimes. However, man is given the chance to undo all the atrocities that he has caused to his fellow men. Man will always have the opportunity to amend his misdemeanours in his future reincarnations. That's one of the reasons why we reincarnate. All man has to do is turn to God and ask for forgiveness.

When you look at all the terrible, unbelievable things that happen all around the world on a daily basis, the list is too long to write. Then ask yourself, "Well, if there is a God, why would he allow all these terrible atrocities to happen in the first place?"

Good question. There would have to be a reason why the world existed in the first place. When man was created, all was perfect. It was a brand-new world, a brand-new beginning. Then God gave man free will, and that was the main reason for your life. Got put us all into different scenarios, giving us all the choices to make.

We could create a wonderful world, but many mistakes were made as the world progressed. God forgave us and gave us another chance to try again by introducing reincarnation. We would always have the chance to return to earth to improve our souls' progress by making the right choices.

We are all a spark from God. We are all God's children. We were all created in God's image, and therefore we are God. We will all return to God as children. God wanted to know all of life, and the only way to achieve this was by God living in all of us. By experiencing all the good and all the bad.

It would be no good to learn only all the good that life can bring, because man would never learn anything. There'd be no point to life. There would be no choices to make. That's why everything in life has an opposite.

God created all that could be good in this world, and so he had to create all that could be bad. That's why God left it to all his children; to choose. He had to give us all something to do, to work out for ourselves by hopefully making the right choices in life. That's why we were given free will, without God interfearing.

Hopefully our souls will learn a little bit more, and keep on learning with each reincarnation. Even if we make terrible mistakes in our new lives, God will forgive us and allow us to try again and again, in our next reincarnations.

Do you still find it hard to believe the reason why you have been given this life? Can you think of a better reason for why God created you?

Disasters

When worldwide disasters happen, like tsunamis, they were meant to happen. You may find this suggestion outrageous, but remember it is not real! It's an act, a scenario being played out on the world stage. We are all actors! This was planned before all these souls were born. It was their way of contributing to the world and mankind, to make the world sit up and listen to global warming. We have to take care of our planet before it's too late.

Take a plane crash, for instance, where hundreds of people are killed at one time. When we planned our lives before we came to earth, some souls also planned their deaths. For some advanced souls, it was no big deal because they had been given the knowledge of many reincarnations they'd experienced. They did not fear death.

We choose when we want to reincarnate into this world. Also, we can choose how we wish to die. Some souls want to help mankind before they die. It may also depend on what soul level the soul has achieved. All these people have agreed to die in this way;

There's no such thing as an accident, these things happen for a reason. It's not just about the plane crash. It's about the soul's reaction toward his fellow man. -Will he choose to just help himself or his colleagues? We all have a choice. So whatever caused the plane to crash in the first place will never happen again. T

This is the souls' contribution to humanity. It could have been an electrical fault with the plane. It could be numerous things. Quite a few planes have had near misses in the skies, just so that planes are set off on schedule, increasing the risk of a mid-air collision. It may be due to human error or overtiredness. It's also down to money.

When there's been a plane crash, there's always an intensive investigation as to why it happened. They find the fault with the plane, and it's put right; this prevents more accidents happening with the same fault. Therefore saving maybe hundreds of lives in the future. The people that chose to die in this way did not die in vain. It was their time to die. They came to a decision to help mankind.

This is just an example of a scenario for the soul, so that it can decide on what choice it wants to make before its next reincarnation, forever advancing.

How many times do you hear of a child dying from a terrible disease – or any person, for that matter? Through their deaths, doctors are able to find a cure afterwards, preventing others with the same disease from dying and yet again saving more lives in the future. All this works towards helping mankind.

This is the reason why the soul chose this future scenario in the first place. It seeks to help others and it wants to progress to a higher level. In actual fact, we are all programmed before birth, but of course we will not realise this. That information will have been erased just after birth.

There's such a lot that we don't know about the world and life itself. Anything is possible. The best way to find out is through meditation. Seek your spiritual path. The higher self can be reached through meditation. The knowledge that you receive will depend on your spirituality, on your soul's level.

It was believed that the soul had only seven chakras. The higher self chakra is the eighth chakra, and it sits above the seventh chakra, about ten inches above the crown. It also was believed that the soul consisted of about fourteen chakras in Atlantis times. The Atlantean people were very advanced in a spiritual way; they had more access to the spirit world.

In meditation, it is important that you visualise the white healing light, even if you can't see it. All you have to do is concentrate. Imagine the white light in your mind coming through your crown chakra and all the way through your body. At the same time, visualize all the negativity going out through your hands and feet.

This same white light will restore your aura. It is important that you imagine this white light, cleansing any bad negativity that may have entered your aura. If any negativity stays in the aura long enough, it may lead to illness later on, such as depression or apathy. It may lead you to drugs and alcohol abuse. If one of the chakras becomes blocked, this will also have an effect on your health.

When cleansing your aura, imagine that you are under a shower, but instead of water raining down on you; it's nothing but pure white healing light, cleansing the whole of your aura. Bombard yourself with this wonderful healing light – its free!

A good time to do this is before you get out of bed in the morning, especially if you feel tired and sluggish. Remember that your spirit body is as important as your physical body, if not more so. Maintain it by regular meditation, spending time on clearing your chakras and your auras with the white light.

My advice would be to read as many books as possible on this subject, if you want to help yourself and others. Who knows, you could even turn this into a career for yourself by helping others. Remember that God gave us the tools to help ourselves.

If everybody was aware of how to heal themselves and given the knowledge, I'm certain this would save a lot of doctor and hospital appointments; not to mention the National Health Service.

We should all be responsible for our health and well-being. God did not intend for us to be pumped with drugs that have horrendous side effects which can lead to other problems! I'm sure the NHS has its place in human society, and we couldn't do without it, but surely prevention also has its place.

Sometimes after I have applied a healing meditation on myself, I will see a mass of white light through my mind's eye. It's so powerful,

Daffodil

like an explosion. It's then that I know I have received healing from the spirit world. It's the same white healing light shown at Stephan Tooroff's healing sanctuary, which was captured on photographs now displayed on the walls of the waiting room. Sometimes gold is also seen in the white light. If you should see it, it's all a good sign that healing is with you.

If you don't see this bright white light when the healing is coming to a close, that doesn't mean you have not received a healing. If you want to see more, then you have to practice more. I didn't see it for a couple of years. Once I did, I couldn't stop. Now I see all the colours: emerald green, indigo, purple, turquoise, yellow, red. All have meaning. Always ask you guardian angel to show you how, if you're not sure. That's why God gave us all a guardian angel, to help us with the trauma that life can bring. We are never alone.

Karma and Rebirth

What Is Karma and Rebirth?

The wheel of life, or Samsara, is an ancient symbol that has the same meaning in Buddhism and Hinduism. It symbolises the cycle of birth, life, and death. When one revolution of the wheel is completed, life begins again with rebirth.

Karma is a Sanskrit word that means "action". The word is used to refer to volitional acts as well as the fruits or consequences that arise from these acts. The idea of karma had existed in ancient Indian philosophy before the time of Siddhartha Gautama,

It became an important element of Buddhist philosophy. The Hindu and Buddhist concepts of karma are quite similar, although Hinduism makes a further distinction between different types of karma, such as present karma, latent karma, and future karma. In the understanding of both thought systems, the law of karma describes the connection between actions and the resulting forces as follows: wholesome actions lead to wholesome states, whereas unwholesome actions lead to unwholesome states, both individually and collectively.

What we are is determined largely by what we thought, said, and did in the past. What we are thinking, saying, and doing now will form our future. The karma of past, present, and future events are connected by the law of cause and effect. For instance, if one generates bad karma by hurting or killing sentient beings, one will have to endure the negative consequences of these deeds in this or other lifetimes. Similarly, if one generates good karma by observing the precepts, positive consequences will inevitably follow.

According to Buddhist Philosophy

The Buddhist understands karma as a natural law. There is no higher instance, no judgement, no divine intervention, and no gods that steer man's destiny. There is only the law of karma itself, which works on a universal scale. Deeds yield consequences, whether in the next second, hour, day, month, year, decade, or even in the next lifetime.

Rebirth

Buddhists believe that the retribution of karma can span more than one lifetime. Rebirth has always been an important tenet in Buddhism; it is often referred to as walking the wheel of life, Samsara, it is the process of being born over and over again in different times and different situations, possibly for many thousands of years.

My Simple Explanation

The Buddha means the enlightened one. The Buddha believes that emotional pain is the main cause of physical pain and disease, such as resentment, hatred, self-pity, guilt, anger, depression, and jealousy.

If a person commits an awful crime, such as the murder of a child, when the person dies and passes over, he will be given a review of the wrong choice his soul made. Not only will he feel the pain of the child, but also all the anguish from all the people involved with the child. He will feel the pain of both parents as well as siblings, grandparents, aunts, and uncles. He will be given an opportunity to come back in a future life to make amends for the crime committed. When this soul is ready to return to earth will depend on him.

He will have all the help and advice of the masters and the teachers beforehand, in the spirit world. There's no way it can be forgotten and put to rest; this is called universal law, with cause and effect. Even if that person is truly sorry, the soul has to be cleansed before it can move on with its spiritual journey.

He could come back in another life with the child that was murdered, or the whole family in a group soul scenario. He may devote his next life to the child he murdered. The child, in turn, may have chosen a lifelong disability to help the person to amend his soul, especially if the child is an evolved soul.

He may have several lives before his soul is strong enough to make amends. If he decides not to, then the soul can't move on; it can't make any soul progression. No matter what, karma has to be resolved. What goes around comes around, and nothing is forgotten. It is universal law.

It is not always karma when bad things happen, as in the Madeleine McCann case; or the Ryes Jones case. As I have said, some souls wish to help mankind to further their souls' progress. This is a different scenario altogether.

The Madeleine McCann Family.
Madeline McCann was abducted in Portugal in Praia de Luz May 3rd 2007 from her apartment whilst on holiday with her parents Jerry and Kate.
Madeleine was a very special child, a special soul. So were the parents. My heart goes out to this family and what they have put themselves through to help mankind. I have nothing but love and respect for the parents, Kate and Gerry McCann. They have been persecuted through this scenario, but then, so was Jesus Christ.

One day it will all become clear, when they pass over to the next dimension. Their lives were all planed before birth, working together in the same soul group. This little girl went through all of this to help other children, as did the parents. There higher souls agreed all of this before reincarnating. This is what they chose to do as a way to help mankind. It is also a test of strength for the soul the spirit. The soul will be tested throughout its life. It may have to face great adversity.

I want to make people realise that despite whatever great evil they chose for this life, none of it is real. It's all an illusion, just a scenario. Wouldn't this make your life a lot easier, knowing that it will all end one day? You will be restored back to health again, and all of your loved ones; at the same time realising it was all a learning process for your soul to progress.

Otherwise, there would be no reason for life to exist in the first place. Can you think of a better reason why we are all here? We are all being tested, and this is how we find out who we are, our strengths and weaknesses. We build our character. God would not create these terrible events that happen around the world to see his children suffer. We all put ourselves in different kinds of scenarios so that we can make a difference to this world. It's simply that some souls go for challenging scenarios above and beyond the call of duty.

This is down to their soul level. I know when bad things happen, it's bound to feel real. We are supposed to think it's real. That's why we were programmed in this way. I know it all sounds very farfetched, but try to understand the reasons for our existence on this earth. Think about what I have said. Turn it over in your mind, and go over my explanation for our existence on earth. Leave no stone unturned.

Examine your own reason for why your life exists. You will not find a better reason. I did what was asked of me, to search for the truth, and this is what I was told. All this information is from a higher intelligence far greater than this world, helped by God, the angels, and the spirit guides to pass this on to humanity.

This is my reason in the first place, for coming to earth to help mankind. This is my mission. I'm just an ordinary, down-to-earth woman. I lack in some academic skills, I guess, but perhaps this was why I was chosen to do this work in the first place. I feel honoured, privileged, and very humbled.

Kate and Gerry McCann visited the European Parliament to urge Euro politicians to put their names to a declaration demanding a US style system to track abducted children. In America, information about abduction cases is broadcast on radio and TV within hours of a child going missing.

Efforts to introduce a similar system in Europe two years ago failed because of insufficient support in Brussels. Kate pleaded with the politicians to support their declaration before another family had to go through what they were going through. Surely this comes down to common sense. You see, this is the bigger picture. It's not just about

Madeleine – it's about helping all children so that the event doesn't repeat itself. It's all about the decisions we make.

I remember watching the news one day, there was a gathering with the Pope and the parents of Madeleine. Whilst the Pope was giving his blessing, a butterfly flew on the shoulder of Kate, the mother; it flew away and then came back again to land in the very same spot. Buddhists believe that butterflies are spirits of the deceased. I truly believe that it was the soul of Madeleine and that they will meet again. If not in this life, then it will certainly be in the next.

You see, we give our souls different scenarios to see what may develop, by the choices that we choose in this world. Some soul scenarios come with great adversity – far greater than others, making it a difficult life. By making the right choices, our soul starts to progress through different lives; we reach a higher level, and our soul becomes more pure. God is happy to see his children progress. Nothing makes him happier. We can progress to a higher realm. That's what your whole life is about: finding your way back home – your real home.

When I had the reading with Paul Parker, he told me that my mother said she knew the true meaning of her life when she passed over. "It was like putting on an old pair of carpet slippers. I knew I'd been here before. I was home. I danced with Eddy." Eddy was my dad's brother, my uncle.

I was surprised that Paul said my mother and father weren't together on the other side, but when I look back on their lives, they were never compatible. They used to argue almost on a daily basis. I felt that my father was more of a spiritual person than my mother.

Paul said it was unusual for this to happen – couple's not together on the other side. You see, you might not live in a happy marriage or partnership, but somehow you've ended up with each other. You may have come to regret your life you share with your partner; you may look back on your life and think what might have been.

Life can be hard at times, and it's not always happily ever after; that only happens in heaven. We don't always end up with the person we want to share the rest of our life with. We may have many regrets, especially

Daffodil

if we are married with children. We can all be total opposites with our partners, but remember that there's a reason you are with this person: for you both to learn lessons. You are only on a short visit from your real home, heaven, to learn these lessons.

I was told by Paul Parker that Harry and I made a good team. Where's the romance in that? Yet in my soul I've always known we are supposed to be together, even if Harry wasn't my type or I, his. There are reasons behind it. Yet I feel I have shared many lives with Harry. I sometimes wonder if we have become partners in our learning experiences, in different scenarios on earth, to help one another's souls' progression. All will be revealed when we pass over to the next dimension.

***

My mother said that she was treated with the greatest respect at the funeral directors after she died. We had taken my mum's change of clothes for the funeral to the chapel of rest—the funeral directors John Heath's in Sheffield.

My mother watched as they changed her into her burial clothes. I must admit, it left me with a comforting feeling that my mother was treated with great respect. It also validated that she was still alive and could see everything that was going on after her death.

Also, for some reason my husband was never that fond of my mother, yet he always treated her with respect and pretended to laugh at her jokes, pretended to enjoy her company. Once Harry was in the same room as me, and I heard my dead mother say, "Ha ha, I know your true feelings towards me now, Harry!" When I told Harry about this, I could tell he was taken aback. I knew it was true, that he tolerated mum for my sake.

Who knows – they may share a karma.
Spirits see everything, feel everything, and hear everything. There's no kidding or pretending when we pass over. Egos do not exist in the world of heaven; everyone is equal. It doesn't matter whether you were world famous or a great icon, rich or poor.

If everything was perfect in this life then there would be no reason for us to be here in the first place. We would not make any progress, and we would have no choices to make. We couldn't help mankind or the planet because everything would be perfect. What would be the point to life?

There would be nothing for us to do. We would be like machines, zombies, all the same. But we are not. We are all unique, each and every one of us. That's why God made a plan for all of us. We all have a purpose, a mission: to help this troubled planet and one another. We are all one, and we come from God.

Peggy

As the weeks passed by, I began to miss my dog Molly more and more, although Wendy, my dear friend, said that Molly was doing really well. She was running in the fields every day and enjoying her newfound freedom. Nevertheless, my life felt empty without her.

I kept asking myself why this had to happen. Hadn't the angels heard my plea to find another little dog soon after I had lost Bessie – one that would be right for me? I know why I had to give up Molly, although it broke my heart. I had to learn about freeing the spirit; I suppose it taught me a lesson.

I carried on for weeks, trying to find another little dog to come into my life. I visited dog rescue centers, the Internet, and looked through the pets for sale in the local paper. I even wrote an affirmation on paper and kept it in my handbag: "Dearest angels please find me a little puppy, one that's right for me, to come into my life. Preferably Bessie's soul. I expect a miracle." I would read it almost every day. Still nothing seemed to manifest.

Then one day I read in my local paper, "Cross border collie pups for sale. A litter of nine puppies." I inquired straightaway, the lady told me there were seven dogs and two bitches. She lived on a farm called the Old Musgrove. I rang Harry at work with excitement. "Oh Harry, you have to come home. It's just what we are looking for. They may be gone by the end of the day."

"All right, I'm on my way,"

I rung the lady back and asked her if she would save me the two bitches to look at. It took us ages to find the farm; it was such a dark miserable rainy day. When we finally found the farm, it was terrible to approach due to the sludge and continuous rain.

"You'd better stay in the car while I check to see if it's the right place," He seemed to be gone ages. Then I saw him and the lady approaching our car, each with a little puppy in their arms.

I was thinking *angels; please help me to choose the right one. Please give me a sign.* As I opened the door, I took one look at the puppy Harry was holding. I felt a pull straightaway. Then I looked at the other pup. Although it was lovely, something stopped me. The pup seemed motionless in the woman's arms; it never moved. I thought it strange as she laid it across my lap; it still didn't move. I looked again at the pup Harry was holding. I fell in love with that little face, that bundle of joy. I held her in my arms, we connected at once. When I chose Peggy, the woman replied, "Oh, the spirited one?"

On the way home I cuddled her on my lap. Although she stank to high heaven, it didn't matter – I had my little pup. All the while I thought about what to name her. "I know, Harry. I'll call her Angel!"

He gave me a look. "If you think I'm going to take her for walks, shouting Angel when she goes running off, you're mistaken!" I could see he meant it. I couldn't help but laugh, trying to visualize Harry running off for the dog and shouting Angel. It would ruin is street credibility.

By the time we arrived home, I had decided to call her Peggy. She's brought such love into our home. I've never known Harry to be so affectionate towards a dog. She definitely brings out his gentle side. The love I feel for this dog is so strong. Could it be Bessie's soul?

Molly was a precursor for a spiritual happening. I believe Molly was meant for Wendy, because Wendy knew how to handle dogs with issues. Plus, Wendy wouldn't have been able to afford to buy Molly and pay the vet fees.

Molly was a little puppy who would need special training, which Harry and I couldn't give her. He has enough to do with caring for me. I knew that Wendy was looking for another dog to be a companion to

Daffodil

Smarty, her other recue dog. The angels engineered it so that this would take place.

My angel then led me to Peggy because she was the right one for me, and Molly was the right one for Wendy. As an added bonus, my angel introduced himself to me; through Peggy his name is David.

Angel in Blue Jeans

About a week after we brought Peggy home.

I was in bed about 2 am one morning. Suddenly as clear as day, I saw a picture in my mind's eye of a very tall, handsome man with dark hair and the most beautiful eyes. He wore a black sweater; I could just make out a few inches of his blue jeans below his sweater.

He had his arms folded leaning against a desk, he looked at me sideways. At first I was a bit startled. He had such a beautiful face. I looked straight into his eyes. I was surprised that I could see him so clearly because I wear contact lenses.

I kept blinking as he spoke to me. "Are you happy?" All the while he smiled at me. "Yes, I am," I replied. **"Absolutely!"** I knew he was referring to Peggy. "But who are you?" He was still smiling as he said, "I'm your guardian angel, David."

I guess they don't always come with wings! It's a funny thing; but I've always liked the name David. My prayers were answered. You only have to ask for help from your angel or your spirit guide. We all have them, they are there waiting to help us. We are not alone.

Animals play a big part in our lives. I can't imagine been without a dog or some kind of pet. Also, some dogs come down as spiritual guides for their owners, to help them through their lives. One example is Barbara Thompson with Bram, which I mention in the book.

You only have to look at dogs that are trained to work with the blind or animal rescue dogs. They play their part in human society. All they ask in return is for shelter, food, and love. Dogs and cats help us to relax, even by simply stroking them after a stressful day, which can bring down one's blood pressure. Hospitals, hospices, care centers, and old people's homes now recognise the advantage of using trained dogs in therapeutic healing. The animals improve patients' lives mentally and physically.

Elderly people should not live alone, especially when they have lost their partners after many years of being together. It's such a wrench. Dogs can be such good companions and healers at this time.

Regarding the dreadful stories you read in the paper about dogs attacking children, this one I can't seem to answer. Is it bad interbreeding? This worries me. I love all animals, especially dogs. All animals are God's creatures, so what's going wrong? Some breeds are brought up to be vicious, especially the ones that are bred for dog fights. Owners use them as a status symbol and to intimidate people. It's sad, I wish I knew. Perhaps my angels will let me understand why this is happening.

Sometimes I ask myself, "Do evil dogs exist, just like evil people exist?" After all, dogs have souls just like us.

When I was eight or nine, we had a little mongrel pup called Mickey. We had all grown fond of this little dog. Dad came home from the night shift he was in bed. Mum was about to pop out to the shops before going to work, and I'd gone to school. As Mum was going to the shops, Mickey escaped somehow. He was knocked down and killed by a lorry driver. I didn't know till I arrived home from school later that day.

I had made a trifle in a cookery lesson. I was feeling quite pleased with myself; we were to have it for tea. When I tried to open the door, I knew something was wrong. Mickey would always be at the door, as soon as I opened it, he would make such a fuss over me. I looked forward to this every day when I arrived home from school.

As I walked into the living room, I remember it was very quiet. Then I saw the note on the table. I froze I knew something was wrong; as I started to read it. It came as a terrible shock that our little Mickey had been killed. He was such a little, lively fellow, always up to mischief. Everyone loved him.

I couldn't stop crying, I was absolutely devastated. So was my dad; he was in the kitchen, trying his best not to show any emotion. I remember walking straight outside towards the bin and emptying the whole trifle into it. How could we have sat down and enjoyed a trifle for tea that day? My little Mickey was gone, my heart was broken.

Years later when I had moved to the secondary modern school, St Peters in High Green Sheffield, I was still trying to keep a low profile. I was in an English lesson one day; this male teacher came to the front of the classroom and told everyone he wanted us to write an essay, a story. The difference was that it had to be a true story. I could hear the sounds of all the disgruntled children in class.

Suddenly I felt excited. *Yes, yes!* I thought to myself. *I can do this. I have a true story to tell: the one about my little pup Mickey.* I had never felt so confident in the classroom. I thought, *I can be good at this.* It was the fact that the story was going to be true that inspired me most– like the one I'm writing now. It was such a contrast with how I felt about school, always frightened of the teachers and scared to raise my hand in case I got the answers wrong. I had knowing that yes, this was how I should feel in the classroom: inspired. All children should. With excitement and anticipation, I began my story.

A week later I was in English class with the same teacher. It's a pity, but I don't remember his name, only his face. He wasn't like the rest of the teachers; he didn't rant and rave and he didn't frighten me. He had a gentle disposition.

No sooner had I sat down in class that the teacher began announcing the winner of the essay. He began to read my story to the whole classroom. As he was reading, I picked up on the emotion in his voice.

I felt so embarrassed, my cheeks flushed bright red, but inside I felt so happy. One could have heard a pin drop that day. I certainly didn't win the competition for my grammar and spelling; it was the fact that my story was true; it came from the heart. That describes my personality. It has to come from the heart, so always speak your truth.

Daffodil

All my life I have never been interested in fiction books. The stories that I have read have all had to be true. They have taught me about people's struggles and adversity.

For me, it has to be true, and it has to have inspiration, substance, value, and experience that can be passed on to help others. That's simply my opinion. What's the point of it if it's just fiction? I've just read Anne Frank; she was so advanced for her years. I was so inspired by her.

Books help people in many ways. For some it's an escape from life, from reality. My granddaughter Emily described the book she was reading as her friend. I thought at the time how very mature she was for her age.

Julia Winfield

Psychic Medium

On my visit to the spiritual church one Sunday evening. A medium called Julia Winfield gave me an unexpected reading. Prior to the reading, for several weeks I had been suffering with my health. It was a really bad flare-up of the RA. As usual I was trying to get through the day, trying to get on with my life as best I could. This was one of the worst flare-ups in a long time.

Every bone in my body was hurting, I could hardly walk. My hips and thighs couldn't take the weight of my body as I tried to walk, although I only weighed eight and a half stone. My spine began to crunch and crack. My shoulders and arms ached, and even my skull hurt this time, which had never happened before. It was as if I wasn't responding to my medication. Had I become immune?

But as usual I put on my makeup and do my hair, and nobody was the wiser. To the world I would appear normal, and nobody would recognise that I was ill. To quote my own doctor, "Looking at you, you would never know you were coping with an autoimmune disease." But inside my body was screaming.

Julia suddenly pointed to me. In a loud, clear voice she said."Is it all right if I come to you, dear? You are very ill! I've got a lady here who is very concerned about you. She looks very much like you, only small in stature." This had to be my grandmother Elizabeth Molloy, on my father's side. Whenever I have gone to see mediums in the past, they always bring my grandmother through, although my grandmother died before

I was born. "Also, I have a gentleman not much taller than this lady. Tears are streaming down his face as he looks at you." This was my father. "They're telling me that you have been through so much." She went on to describe the pain I was going through in detail, touching the areas on her own body. She was so accurate, and she could physically feel my pain. "How the hell are you standing up? They want to wrap you up in cotton wool. You have to have healing – you need help!" All the while she said my grandmother was pointing to the healing room they had in church for anyone who needed healing.

When it came to the end of the reading, the medium said, "They are bringing you the biggest bunch of Daffodils, saying 'Give her daffodils at Christmas. It will be a time of celebration.'" Then the medium looked at me and said, "Daffodils mean something special to you, don't they?"

What followed next astounded me. I thanked her for the reading and settled back in my chair. As she carried on with readings for other members in the church; she stopped mid-sentence, looked at the audience, and asked if anyone objected if she brought her guide through. She told us that this didn't normally happen, but her spirit guide was insistent.

As I watched her on the rostrum, she had her eyes closed, and her face looked a bit distorted. Then she started to talk in a deep male voice! I felt quite spooked. At the same time the top of my head started to tingle. I heard my father's voice in my head, "Listen to this, Eileen."

She began to speak to a man in the audience in English, but she had a foreign, antiquated accent. She had the mannerism and demeanour of a male as she moved her hands and body. As she spoke to this gentleman in the audience, he broke down and cried. It seemed that he had many problems. The guide told him that he was getting all the help he needed from the spirit world. The guide spoke with such words of wisdom.

As I watched her speaking from the rostrum, I never took my eyes off her. She never faulted. Every word her guide spoke finished in rhyme – words of comfort and wisdom direct from the spirit world. It was a privilege to witness this. I had never seen anything like it!

Then when it came to the end of the trance, she went into a quite meditation whilst one of her colleagues held her hands. Then she came out of the trance slowly. As I watched her, I noticed her midriff suddenly drop. Then she was back to her normal self. Julia's spirit guide had actually entered her body so that he could bring these wise messages from the spirit world to everyone in church. I later asked Julia who her guide was, she said his name was Kasp and he was an Egyptian.

I also witnessed another one of Julia's readings. This was very sad and brought a lot of people to tears, myself included. As Julia started to give a woman in the audience a reading, Julia was suddenly interrupted by the presence of a little boy in spirit. He kept running to and fro past the women Julia was speaking to.

She asked the same woman if she could take the spirit of a little boy who had died in a fire. The woman answered no. Then another lady in the audience put her hand up. "Yes, I can. It isn't me, though – it's my sister in-law."

All of a sudden Julia put her hands up to her face, and she was very emotional "Oh my goodness! This little boy has no face."

"Yes, that's right," the woman said.
"But he's saying he has now got his face back. He's saying that he had a lovely face, and that nobody deserved to die in the way he did."

"Yes, that's true," the woman answered. "He was a lovely child." Julia went on to describe that the little boy also lost his arms in a fire. "Yes, that's also true. He saved my nephew's life. He was found with his little body on top of my nephew."

All the while the little spirit boy said that he was happy now, and that he had got his arms back. He was blowing kisses to this woman. Julia informed the woman, "My love, it's very, very important to this little boy that you get this message across to his mother."

I don't think there was a dry eye in the church that night. It was one of the saddest readings I have ever heard. Even the children who have died in tragic circumstances try to communicate with their loved ones no matter what. This little boy was determined to get a message to his mother.

Can you imagine how comforting that would be for the parents who have lost a child, especially in appalling circumstances? To know that the little boy survived death, and that he is happy in his new world. Children carry on growing up in the spirit world no matter at what age they passed over.

If more people visited the spiritual church, I'm sure that they would be comforted by stories like this. They'd know that our loved ones who have passed over still survive, and that there's nothing they could have done to prevent the deaths; no matter the circumstances. It was their times to die, to leave this world. This child gave his life for another. This is one of the ultimate gifts to bestow on one's fellow man.

Julia could see spirits from the age of five. She has also been working on the rostrum for thirty years, helping others bringing words of comfort. Sometimes I watch her closely while she gives out the readings, I can tell she's not a well woman herself. Julia must have helped a lot of people over a period of thirty years; she is continuing to do so. In my opinion, these are the true unsung heroes who ask for nothing in return. She works very hard, and she also helps to run the Spiritual Church at Wombwell, in Barnsley, South Yorkshire.

I believe Julia Winfield should be recognised for what she has achieved. For all the help this woman must have given to hundreds of people over the past thirty years. She is a truly remarkable woman. I would put her up there with the rest of the great mediums.

Julia could have been a wealthy woman by now. I don't think she realises what an astonishing woman she is. I feel privileged that I have come to know her.

The very first time I met Julia in church, I took to her straightaway. It was the feeling one gets when one meets someone for the first time and feels comfortable, at ease. I instantly liked her. It was as if I'd known her all my life.

Since getting to know Julia, I now believe we recognised each other's souls at the time, because she also felt the same experience towards me. We have both had proof of the afterlife and know that there is no death. We both feel strongly that we have to put this across to mankind – it's our mission.

I once asked Julia why she didn't make a career out of her psychic abilities. She could have been a very wealthy woman by now, maybe on stage and in TV. She told me she didn't believe in taking money from people for the gift she had been given. "To see that I can help someone who has lost a loved one, and to bring comfort and maybe a smile to their face – that is all the reward I need."

That's what makes Julia so different. She comes across so naturally when she is performing, there's no ego; it's as if she is driven by a powerful force. Julia continues to help others in spite of her own health problems. Julia came out of an abusive marriage. She now lives with her two teenage children in Barnsley.

***

I visited the spiritual church one Sunday afternoon; and I had a surprise visitor. Peter, the man with whom I'd had an affair all those years ago, when I became pregnant. He came through as spirit. The medium looked at me and said, "I have your mother and father here, and they are bringing Peter with them." I must admit I was shocked. Still, I always wondered why he ever came into my life.

Several weeks later. I was in bed; it was in the early hours of the morning. I heard Peter come through my bedroom door. "Hello, Eileen," he said in a clear loud voice as plain as day. Peter had a very distinctive voice. All those years ago, it was the first thing I noticed about him, even before I saw his face.

I was laid on my left side in bed. Has I started to turn toward him, he stopped me telling me not to I reached out my hand. As I did this, he bent his head forward so that I could touch the top of his head. As I patted his head. I recognised straightaway. It was definitely him.

Daffodil

I don't know what he died from; all I know is that he was part of my life, for whatever reason. It wasn't a chance meeting – it was meant to be. However, I've never understood why I was so infatuated with Peter at that time in my life.

I was also frightened of him. He could be very violent and aggressive, especially when he had been drinking. I later found out that he was some sort of gangster – or was it all a front? He had me fooled. Yet there was a gentle side to him. He could be very generous towards people; and he had a great sense of humour. I felt safe with him. I didn't have to worry about anything anymore; he would look after me. That was it: I had felt secure. But deep down in my soul, I feel that we knew each other in another life. Was it karma? All I know is that he had a big impact on my life. I have no doubt that he has met our daughter, Ann, in the spirit world.

When I look back at the time I first knew him, I was once talking to him outside the C&A store one Saturday afternoon. As I was looking at his face, I saw a small crucifix dangling in front of his left eye. I squinted, thinking I must be seeing things, but it was still there! Eventually it faded away whilst I talked to him. Sometimes when I look back, it makes me wonder whether the spirit world was testing me. When we broke up, it broke my heart, and I was devastated.

My children were far more important to me than this man. I chose my children first, and I'm glad I did. I had put them first, and I always will. I'm so proud of them.

My feelings were that the spirit world didn't want me to be with this man. It was like I was been given a warning. At the time my father was still alive, so I wasn't into my spiritual journey yet. Of course I know now that it was my guardian angel protecting me. It was only after my father's death that my life changed.

Red Meat

This is a subject that's always concerned me. Should I eat meat? The late Lynda McCartney, who was once married to Paul McCartney of the Beatles, ran a campaign against eating meat. Her views were very strong. She wrote books and even made her own vegetarian meals for the giant supermarkets. The thing that has always haunted me was when she said, "One should never eat anything that has a face!" At the time it stuck in my mind, and it still does to this day.

I have tried in the past to become a vegetarian, but to no avail. I ask myself whether it is right to slaughter God's animals and eat them, especially red meat. I was surprised to learn that the Dalai Lama, head of the Buddhist culture, eats red meat because of a medical condition he has that requires iron.

I think where man has faulted is in the way animals have been slaughtered. In some cases these animals are aware what's about to happen to them, and they become stressed and panic-stricken. The stress the animal feels at the point of death will have an effect on the meat itself by being tough and not tasting as it should. All that stress has gone into the meat!

I believe that all animals should be reared on healthy farms, given healthy food, and cared for in a happy and natural environment. Certainly they shouldn't eat the foods that they are given today that include antibiotics and unnatural substances that can be passed on to the consumer. Chickens should be reared roaming around on the farms, not stuck in cages, never to see daylight. I myself eat very little meat. I eat mostly chicken or fish now.

Then I ask myself, wouldn't the world be overrun with animals if meat wasn't included in our diets? There's one thing I do believe in: every animal should be humanely killed, with the offering of a prayer to God for providing us with this choice, and for this precious animal for providing it.

When the world first began, man and animals walked together in harmony. Animals did not fear man, and man did not fear animals. Then one day all the animals ran to the hills in fear of man. That is how it is today. Is it because man killed his first prey for food? Did this all happen at the beginning of the ice age? After all, man had to hunt food for his family to stay alive. They even skinned the animals for the fur, to keep warm in the winter months.

Yet animals will kill one another to sustain life and to feed their young. In the animal kingdom this seems normal and natural. How else would they survive? Is it the fact that man has been killing animals for food for hundreds of thousands of years, and so we have all become conditioned through generations before us, and it has become normal?

Or is it the fact that in today's culture, that we have a choice. We don't have to kill an animal to survive anymore. It's not like it was in the ice age, when that was our only means of surviving. Is this what God intended? To only kill an animal for food when it is necessary, when there's no other means of survival?

To me, this subject is a very gray area. I don't have all the answers, though I wish I did. All I can say is listen to your heart, your soul, for the right answers. Ask yourself, "Is this right? Am I making the right choice?" Go with your gut instinct.

Religion

Religion is the root of all evil, whether it be Protestant, Roman Catholic, or Islam. After all, religion has been the cause for most wars for hundreds of years, and it still continues today with so-called ethnic cleansing. What makes one religion better than another, one race better than another? There's no such thing – we are all the same. No matter what nationality we are, we all come from the same source.

We should be concentrating on looking after one another and making sure there's plenty of food and water for everyone in the world. We should educate third-world countries so that they can fend for themselves. We shouldn't spend all our resources on bombs and nuclear weapons, sending our solders to war.

Every day there are solders being killed on both sides, along with innocent men, women, and children? It's on our TVs every day, and we simply accept it. We carry on with our lives as if it's the norm.

I ask that not just our country but for the United Nations come together to try to resolve some kind of world peace once and for all. Where is the love? This world can never progress till all wars end. We live in a world where man kills his own species. How primitive is that? We are still selling weapons of defense to other countries.

I know that things won't ever be the same since 9/11. What is going to happen to our world if things continue like they are? What kind of world are we leaving behind for our children and our children's children? Every single one of us is responsible for what happens to this planet. Until all war conflict ceases, there will be no future.

Daffodil

Innocent people are blown up by suicide bombers in the name of Allah! In Afghanistan, American and English soldiers are killed every day, and some of them are still in their teens. Some of these young soldiers have probably watched plenty of war films and played video games about war.

They want to be just like their heroes. They become brainwashed that this is the best job in the world. It's the same on the opposite side. The Taliban teach little children how to use weapons at an early age, bringing them up to hate the Western world. These children have never known peace in their short lives.

It seems like legalized suicide, with all the young soldiers being killed every day. It must be a terrible culture shock for these young soldiers when it becomes a reality, when they see death and destruction happen right in front of their eyes. How sad that man has to kill another man.

In December 2009 the news announced that another soldier was killed, making it one hundred soldiers killed that year. When is this all going to end? Look what happened to the soldiers in the Vietnam War in the sixties. Many teenagers were called up for this war, and they had no option. Many of them came home traumatised; they were unable to cope with normal life. Many committed suicide or turned to drugs and alcohol.

Many ended up in psychiatric institutions. Marriages broke down. They all had one thing in common: these soldiers were never the same again. War had destroyed their spirit, destroyed them mentally and physically, even if they did escape death. So why are we still having wars? It all starts with religion.

It must end. We must find a way to live together; to bring peace once and for all for all the worn-torn countries around the world. We must come together and find a solution to live in peace and harmony for our children's sakes. We can make this happen.

When Paul Parker was giving me a reading, he brought through my mother. He said she had the Bible in her hands, and she threw it across the room, saying that there were a lot of lies written in the Bible.

Incidentally, so did Princess Diana when she passed over. There were lots of lies written in the Bible to suit the Catholic Church, and many were born out of fear over periods of hundreds of years. One of the rules is that if a child is not baptised, he will never go to heaven. How ridiculous is that?

In the Muslim religion, they say if you become a martyr, there will be seventy-two virgins waiting for you in paradise. Surely a man must have been responsible for that one! We are all responsible for ourselves, not to any religion that dictates how we should live our lives. Life is about philosophy – that's what spiritualism and Buddhism is about. How we treat others sets ours standards for life whilst we are on this planet.

I like to call God the Heavenly Father, the one who watches over the world and who loves us all unconditionally, no matter what. We are his children. We can do no wrong in God's eyes; he will always forgive. When we deny ourselves, we also deny God, for we are all a part of God, born in his image. The word God is not a person, as I was led to believe as a child growing up. He was a God that I feared, a God that said I would be punished for not going to church. He was a God who sat in judgement.

God is in all of us. God is in nature – the sea, the plants, the mountains. God is all around us, in all nature. He is omnipresent, and we are surrounded by God. God is the universe. God is our conscience. The word God means "all that there is". We are all one; we are all connected. We come from the same source.

Timing

When the time is right and you decide to open up to the spirit world, it will never let you down. I myself like to address the spirit world as the higher intelligence. The spirits will only come to you in your life when the timing is right. Usually this happens in a time of crisis. Sometimes it happens around midlife, but it can be before.

I started on my own spiritual path with the death of my father; I was thirty-five, but I'd always had this feeling that there was more to life, something much greater. I'd had this feeling since I was a small child. Then at the age of fifty, it started to take off all at once.

You will only be given a message from spirits when they think you are ready to accept it. In no way will they try to frighten you. God does not give you more than you can handle. The more open you are to the spirit world for your highest good and with the best intentions, the more information will follow.

I don't advise the Ouija board for several reasons. First, if you are new at this, you are opening up to the spirit world, and so you leave yourself open to the lower elements as well. Some spirits can also be mischievous, playing around like naughty school kids. This is why you need someone who is professional in these matters. You should always ask for your guardian angels and your spirit guides to protect you. It's the same when you meditate: you leave yourself wide open.

If you want to develop more, there are psychic development groups in your local spiritual churches. There are lots of books written on this subject. Never attempt to use a Ouija board on your own or as a bit of fun with your friends. Always seek professional help.

Eileen Veronica Richmond

I love it when things happen out of the blue, giving me more proof that spirits are around me. One sunny afternoon I was pottering around my garden. I was trying to re-pot a plant in the greenhouse, which was difficult for me because I was using my crutch to get around. To reach the greenhouse, there are three steps. When I had finished, I couldn't find my crutch. I leaned against the wall to get back down the three steps that brought me onto the patio. After a little while I needed to go into the greenhouse again. I stood in the middle of the patio thinking, *where I could have put my crutch? Oh, I'll manage without it.* Then all of a sudden the crutch was thrown down at my feet, within reaching distance, so that I could pick it up!

I must have left it against the door on the outside of the greenhouse. Obviously someone was looking out for me. I'm sure it was Ken, my neighbour who taught me about gardening. His face flashed in front of me, thank's ken.

Schizophrenia

Schizophrenia is a serious condition, what I'm about to write is purely my opinion. There is a fine line between schizophrenia and clairaudience. Sometimes the two can become confusing.

Clairaudience is a term used for psychic and mediumistic hearing abilities, it means clear hearing. Clairaudience is when the person hears spirit voices or spirit guides trying to communicate. This can be alarming at first, especially if the person has no knowledge of this subject.

The wisest thing to do is to visit a spiritual church first, where you will receive all the necessary information before visiting your general practitioner.

Schizophrenia can also start with voices in the head. It is accompanied by much more serious symptoms. According to The British medical dictionary, most cases start between the ages of fifteen and twenty-five. There are four types.

1. Simple Schizophrenia – deterioration of emotional reaction with apathy and withdrawal
2. Hebephrenia – "silly" behaviour; inappropriate smiling and laughter; coining of words and hallucinations
3. Catatonia – stupor, negativism, suggestibility, and impulsive conduct
4. Paranoia – preservation of thought and emotion to a late stage, but with delusions of persecution or grandeur

The medical profession doesn't have a cure for schizophrenia. The only treatment for this named condition is a concoction of drugs and tranquillisers.

It could be a loved one who has passed over, or maybe the person's spirit guide is trying to communicate. It could be the spirit of someone who is stuck and needs help. Remember' that we all have helpers if we need them in the spirit world; they are hear to help us. Sometimes this can go wrong. It could be an evil spirit that is trying to communicate with you. Remember that there are good and evil spirits that can surround us all.

If this is happening to you and you feel reluctant to tell anyone, sit in a room by yourself. There is nothing to be frightened of. Ask your guardian angel to guide you and protect you. Remember that you have to ask. Tell the spirit that is in your head to please go away and that you don't like what is happening to you.

Be firm and assertive. If the spirit is a good soul, it will abide by your wishes and tend not to bother you again. But remember this might be part of your soul's journey. It's simply that you are not ready for the experience. There will always be a right time. It may have been a test from the spirit world to test your reaction. I myself have had several tests over the years.

On the other hand, if the spirit is evil, you will know by your own instincts. You will feel apprehension and dread or fear, just like I did earlier in the book. Remember that you are always in control. If the spirit is evil, ask for help.

You can tell the sprit to go towards the light. Ask your guardian angel to protect you. You can ask for a spirit rescuer to come in and take the spirit away, or ask for Archangel Michael to assist you. You can keep repeating the Lord's Prayer in your head till the spirit has gone, like I did; you don't have to be religious. The spirit will soon get fed up and move on.

If you allow yourself to become intimidated and ruled by this evil spirit that has lost its way, it will only get worse. Remember that you are strong. The answers are deep inside of you, in your higher self. It's simply that you don't realise it because your memory was taken away after birth.

If you allow the evil spirit to take over your life, it will even take over you physically and mentally by entering the soul of the victim, if you allow it to. The people around you don't recognise the person that they once knew. You become withdrawn and depressed. You stop eating properly and neglect your hygiene.

You become possessed by the evil spirit, which takes over your life. It tells you to commit terrible crimes, filling your head with all sorts of evil thoughts. All the while those around you think that it is you, that there is something wrong with you, that you have changed for the worse. This is especially the case when someone has been killed.

You need help. Yes, of course you need help! But not with drugs and tranquillisers so that you don't know what day it is. For example, say you are arrested. Then you are assessed by the doctors and consultants, and you're labeled schizophrenic.

You are released from prison or a mental institute. Within hours of your release, you have gone straight up to another victim in an unprovoked attack and killed him with a knife. All of this is because you didn't receive the proper treatment. Instead, you were pumped with drugs that probably made you worse. Whilst on the drugs, your symptoms become worse, and the entity is still in your head. Sometimes the entity will leave you for a while, and you will become your normal self. Then the entity comes back. Your personality changes within minutes, and that's why all those around you think you're crazy.

This story once happened for real. Either way, you can't win. If you were to go to the doctor and tell him that you are hearing voices in your head, he's going to think you're mad. The same would be true if you were to tell the doctor that a spirit is trying to communicate with you, whether it's a good spirit or an evil entity.

You yourself can put a stop to this by seeking out professional help such as mediums, the spiritual church, spirit rescuers, or a demonologist.

They will put you in touch with the appropriate people who deal with this kind of thing. I recommend going to see a professional expert first before going to see the doctor.

The thing is not to succumb to the entity. Seek help straightaway. You are not going crazy; this is happening all the time on this planet, with evil spirits seeking out the vulnerable. There are a lot of evil things happening on our planet, and we need to get to the root cause.

The evil spirits love it when they find negative people, manic depressives, alcoholics, and drug users. They hang on to the negative energy and feed off the fear. That's why drug users and alcoholics experience demons and have hallucinations.

Always seek help from your guardian angel to protect you every time you have a bad experience. Seek advice from the spiritual church. You have unbelievable power and all the tools that God gave you, if only you realised it!

My son Michael is forty now. About eighteen years ago, he used to sleep over at his girlfriend's on the weekends. She is now his ex-wife. One particular night as they got into bed, Michael felt this strong surge of energy enter his body. It felt evil and tried to take over him.

He felt at one moment he was fighting for his life. It was a battle between him and whatever this evil thing was. Michael stood his ground till the evil entity left his body. He felt exhausted and drained after the ordeal. This is what's called a psychic attack. He didn't tell me about it at the time. It was only when I was discussing my book with him one day that it all came out.

"Mum, it was terrifying," he told me. After he told me what had happened, I was able to explain to Michael in detail about such matters. Michael has not had any more experiences like this since. He reacted in the right way by staying strong. Always ask for help. Remember we are never alone.

Daffodil

On a lighter note, don't have nightmares. The previous information is meant to help people who don't know what to do, especially the young and vulnerable. Always remember that you are in control. There is always help from God and your guardian angel. You only have to ask.

Precious Lives

May 2008

"No, Mr. Barry Mizens, it doesn't t have to be this way." That is a quote from the *Sunday Mirror,* May 18, 2008. It is about the murdered schoolboy Jimmy Mizen. What a courageous family, especially the parents, Margaret and Barry Mizen.

Margaret's words were true: "There's not enough love in this world." Anger breeds anger. There needs to be more love in this world. How brave of this woman to speak this way after losing her son to yet another senseless killing. When will all this unnecessary violence end? It won't until we come together and do something about it. Life doesn't have to be this way – it *shouldn't* be this way.

I believe it starts in the home with the way that we raise our children. If more families raise their children in the way that Margaret and Barry Mizen did, the world will be a better place. Obviously their children have been brought up in a loving, warm environment. It's a credit to both parents. One only had to watch it on the news, when the whole family were together and being interviewed at the time of Jimmy's murder. One could see the loving bond they shared between them all.

What a strong attitude to have towards this terrible crime. They don't feel hate or anger for the family or the son who committed the crime. Margaret was asked why she didn't feel anger. She was protecting her whole family from being destroyed. She is aware that anger and hate are the worst emotions that one can carry, because eventually they will affect the physical body. Margaret chose not to hate or be angered by this terrible event.

Daffodil

At least the whole family has happy memories of Jimmy. Although his life was cut short, it was Jimmy's time. Jimmy didn't die in vain; he came down to serve mankind by hoping that one day things will change for the better.

Remember that none of what happened to Jimmy is real. It's a scenario that Jimmy and the man who killed him chose for their lifetimes. It's always down to choice – that's important. Whatever scenario we are playing, will we make the right choices?

It also includes Jimmy's mother, Margaret. Margaret chose to rise above the devastation of losing her son in this tragic way. She addressed the world in this manner and said that there's not enough love in this world, that anger and hate would only destroy her family. All this senseless killing has to end. We have to learn to stop hating one another. We have to learn to live together in peace and harmony. A tragedy had to happen first, to show humanity that life is sacred.

I remind you that we live in a world of illusion. We are all actors acting out different scenarios. I can imagine the majority of readers out there will be shouting and screaming, "Ha! Try telling that to the parents who are still grieving for their loved ones! And to the people who have died in horrific circumstances, like 9/11 or the Japanese earthquake."

All this information is coming to me direct from the spirit world. I have no reason to disbelieve the higher intelligence. I have nothing to gain by making it up. All I'm aware of is that this is the truth about why God gave us life. This is why we will all meet up with our loved ones in heaven. What happed on earth was never true, never real; it was simply an opportunity for our souls to progress, by living in the illusion for a short while. **The choices that we make in this life are what's real.**

It's all down to the parents and how they raise their children. We have to create a warm, loving environment as our children grow. We have to instill in them how precious life is, including every living thing that is part of our world – the birds, the animals, and the plant life. It has to be taught in our schools from an early age. I'm sure that this is already happening in most schools, but it has to be a bigger part of the curriculum. This is how bad things have become. It can't go on the way it is.

We are creating a Mad Max society where everyday violence becomes accepted.

Have you noticed on TV how the big emphasis is on crime, violence, murder, drugs, pornography, rape, and torture? Not to mention bad language. Our children have access to these programs. In some families young children are allowed to watch adult programs and are given full access to the Internet.

What kind of thought pattern is going to develop inside these children's minds as they develop? They think, *well, this is how the world is. There's nothing wrong with it, so it must be okay.* They soon become desensitised.

Pat Regan was violently murdered. I have a tremendous amount of respect for this woman. What a wonderful, brave woman she was, to have stood up to these gangs of crime after losing her son Danny.

He was only twenty years old shot down dead in 2002. Pat started a campaign for mothers against violence. She helped other mothers who lost their children to violent crimes. She told a meeting of top politicians and policemen that violent video games were creating a culture of bloodshed. Pat also told them, "They are desensitising our kids."

That's exactly where it comes from. From an early age, children are allowed to watch violence and are going to grow up thinking that it's normal! This campaign must carry on in Pat's name so that she didn't die in vain. But of course, she didn't. It was Pat's time, she had done all she could. She made her mark on this planet to help mankind. Now, it's up to us.

What terrible times we live in. What is the world coming to when children as young as eight are carrying knives to protect themselves? I often wonder what children think when they hear on the news that a schoolboy has been killed by another schoolboy, or that a child has been found murdered. What a terrifying time for a child growing up.

I know that if I was a child, I would be terrified to go out of the house, let alone go to school. There must be lots of children like this who are scared to go out of the house. So what do they do? They stay in the house all day, sitting in front of computers or TV, or comfort eating and getting fat. They should be free to play with their friends in parks, but they've become trapped. What can a parent do?

Violence is on our TV almost every day. Is it simply becoming an everyday occurrence? We don't have to live like this, in a world where our children are so frightened for their lives that they are carrying weapons.

I often wonder how a person's life would change if he was given the proof that there is another world, a far better world than this. What if he felt such powerful love in the presence of a divine being? Well, this happened to me. It has certainly changed my life, and I'm sure there are many who have been fortunate to have had similar experiences.

How can anyone keep it to themselves for fear of been ridiculed by their friends and family? If you are fortunate to have had a divine experience like this, no matter how insignificant you may think it is, you must tell your story. Write it down in a journal because there could be more to come. It may be the start of your life's journey, your soul's purpose as to why you are here. It has happened for a reason, and it is not just for your benefit.

If the spirit world gives you glimpses and proof of another dimension, of experiences not of this world, then it is your duty to pass this information on to your fellow man. Spread the word that God and the angels do exist.

If a divine experience happens to such people as gang leaders, murderers, drug dealers, and rapists, who feel no remorse and are consumed with the material things that life has to offer, I'm sure they have second thoughts once they see the bigger picture. The misdemeanours they commit in their earthly life; will have great consequences in the next life. I don't mean God is sitting in judgment. God only observes; it will be you who judges yourself. It is only when you start to regret the misdeeds that you have committed that you start to feel remorse, that you can amend your ways. It is never too late.

Your scenario may have been such that the misdeeds that you committed were a way of showing you that you have a choice, a second chance to change your life, to evolve your soul. You will never be turned away no matter what deed you have committed. It is your birthright.

We are all here to help serve mankind, to help make a better world. God is within us. The heavenly father is there to teach us. We only have to ask to be shown the way, as I was in my hour of despair all those years ago. I believe that I owe it to mankind to tell my story. This wasn't just for my benefit – the more people that this happens to, the better. It will make a vast difference to our world. Humanity has to change if we want our planet to survive.

My experience has given me great spiritual confidence so that I do not fear death. I know that I'm here for a reason, and I know what my soul's journey has been about. When my time comes, I will be united with all my family – the ones who have gone before, and the ones that will follow me, as well as the pets I've lost.

If Life Is a Game,

Then These Are the Rules

1. *You will be given a body.*
2. *You will be given lessons to learn.*
3. *There are no mistakes, only lessons.*
4. *Lessons are repeated until they are learned.*
5. *Learning does not end.*
6. *There is no better than here.*
7. *Others are only mirrors of yourself.*
8. *What you make of your life is up to you.*
9. *All the answers lie within side of you.*
10. *You will forget all this at birth.*

– Author unknown

Holiday

In June 2008, Harry and I decided to hire a motor home for a week's holiday so that we could tour the west side of Wales. We took Peggy with us and were looking forward to it. About three days into the holiday, the back of my right knee started to irritate me. Sometimes when you wear a prosthesis, it can rub and cause abscesses and cists. This had happened a few times in the past, and I had managed to keep topside of it.

This time it became serious and developed into a large, infected abscess. "Harry, we are going to have to find an A&E in Wales,"

He took one look at it. "You must be joking. We are going home."
I was admitted into hospital for an emergency operation that same day. The danger was that I had metal implants, which could cause havoc if I had an infection. Whilst in the ward, there was an old lady in the bed next to me called Elizabeth Foulden.
She was in for a new hip replacement. I couldn't believe it, because she was eighty-eight years old. We seemed to get on like a house on fire; Elizabeth told me her life story.

She was married at twenty-two, and her husband left her with two small children. Then she found love again at the age of seventy! She had lived with her new man, Harold, for fourteen years. Harold's family didn't approve of Elizabeth.

Elizabeth had two sons from her first marriage; she said that both of them were no good. It was a difficult life, raising two little boys. Times were hard then. I could tell that she hadn't experienced much love in her life. It made me think of my own family and how close we all were. To live without love has to be the worst thing.

Elizabeth was also very frightened of the hip operation she was about to have. She was in excruciating pain: if she moved in the slightest, she would yell out in pain, but she wouldn't let it interfere with our interesting conversation. As we got talking, I tried to comfort her and told her she would be just fine. "Elizabeth, you know if ever you're frightened, you only have to ask for your guardian angels. They will come to you if you ask. You are never alone."

"Oh, do you think so? It must be nice to have a faith."

"No, Elizabeth, it's nothing to do with a religion or anything like that. It's your birthright. Help is there for you – you simply have to ask." After giving Elizabeth a chat about my spiritual life, the doctor arrived to give me some intravenous antibiotics.

Within a minute of chatting to Elizabeth, I was fighting for my life!

The nurse took one look at me and said, "Oh god, she's reacting to the drugs." I remember lying on my back, gasping for breath, and thinking, *this is it. I'm going to die. Please, God, not here – not here!*

By this time they had drawn the curtains around me. All of a sudden Elizabeth shouted three times "Your angels are here!" Elizabeth actually saw two angels come to my rescue. I thought of my family. The attack seemed to last for about five or six minutes, and then everything started to normalise. "What happened to me?" I asked.

"You have had an anaphylactic reaction to the penicillin."

I found this puzzling. Since I was a child, I had been given penicillin for tonsillitis. In all my previous operations, I had been given it in the past. Why should this happen now?

I've not been given any real answers as to why this should have happened. My own theory is that I was given 500 mg of flucloxacillin and 500 mg of another type of penicillin, together at once. I think the concoction of drugs became volatile because they mixed them together.

I could even taste the chemicals in my mouth. I was later to develop two leaking valves in my heart. I'm certain that this was caused by the anaphylactic shock. My heart was stretched to the limit, I thought my chest was about to explode.

By this time I could hear Elizabeth's bed being moved to another ward. I heard her say to one of the nurses, "Is she all right? Can I see her?"

I managed to muster the strength to shout to her, "You'll be all right, Elizabeth. I'll find you." I think she was relieved to hear my voice. It must have been a terrible shock for her to see me all right one minute and then wondering whether I was going to make in the next.

I kept my promise I found Elizabeth in another ward after her operation. We held hands, she became very emotional. Sometimes I wonder if what had happened to me was all planned for Elizabeth's sake, to prove to her that the afterlife does exist.

The events that happen to us in life are not always about us. Sometimes when people are approaching the end of their lives, the spirit world likes to comfort them by giving them glimpses of the afterlife: angels, and loved ones whom they knew.

Prior to all of this happening, I was asked by a medium at the spiritual church if the name Elizabeth meant anything to me. It didn't at the time. Whilst visiting the spiritual church once again, Julia Winfield was the medium on the rostrum, and she soon came to me with my mother and father from spirit. She told me that my mum and dad were aware of what I had just gone through, and they assured me it would be all right now. She also told me that I had been very poorly because the infection had caused a big flare up of the RA. Mentally I had felt so low, it put me back in my wheelchair for three weeks.

All of a sudden Julia asked the audience if anyone could take a young man who had passed over from bone cancer. His name was Mike Harvey. He played football and had taken a knock to his leg. That was when the cancer had started.

He passed over very quickly, but no one spoke up for him. Julia said that this young man was looking for his mother. Then Julia asked if everyone had turned up who had bought tickets on the night. The lady who was collecting the tickets said that one person hadn't turned up. Was this the young man's mother?

The spirit boy said to Julia, "If you go to Barnsley Cemetery, you will see my grave with my name on it." Had his mother missed a great opportunity by not turning up that night?

Never Give Up

One thing I have found; with the help of the spirit world and my research over the years. Is that when we come to earth in a new body, we are given a new start. We will be tested along the way, and we will discover our strengths and weaknesses. We will experience joy as well as adversity; some more than others.

No matter how hard life becomes, we all have to get through it. Remember that we are only here for a short while, even though it seems forever. No matter what hardship you are experiencing, you must have faith. When life becomes too hard for you to bear. Surrender to the universe, to your guides and your guardian angel; trust that all will be well when life ends.

When life became too much for me to endure with my illness, I tried to commit suicide. My religious background had taught me that this was wrong: if a person committed suicide, they would end up in limbo when they passed over. This is not so.

When a person wishes to end their life because of chronic illness, and a slow death is all that lies ahead, the spirit world understands. I mentioned this earlier in the section on euthanasia. But if a person commits suicide in a healthy body, this is a different matter?

The person has to face up to whatever adversity life has thrown at them. This is where they will find their strengths and weaknesses to face up to life's difficulties. They are being tested.

This is there soul's contract for this life. If you commit suicide in a healthy body, you will have to keep coming back to earth till you get over the difficulties in life that you have been given. Your soul will then start to evolve. This is what you want for yourself. You have to learn this all over again by remembering who you are.

I believe this is what happens to a lot of young people, especially teenagers who commit suicide. They see no way out, especially with bullying and violence that is happening in society today. That's why we must put a stop to all these street gangs and knife attacks once and for all. It doesn't have to be this way. It can be a frightening world, but we have to find the love for one another – the love we once shared when the world first began. We are all connected; we are all brothers and sisters.

Martin Luther King Jr

On the morning of 5/11/08, the United States of America woke up to its new president, Barack Obama.

Obama is the first black American president in history. He came from a mixed race family; his mother was white, and his father was black. I pray that this is a good omen, a reminder that we are all the same no matter what race we come from; we are all a part of one another.

This is what the great American activist Martin Luther King Jr. fought for in the 1950s and 1960s. King was born 15 January 1929 in Atlanta. He was a Baptist minister and social activist who led the civil rights movement in the United States. From the mid-1950s his leadership was fundamental to the movement's success in ending the legal segregation of African Americans in United States.

King rose to national prominence as head of the Southern Christian Leadership Conference for equal rights for black and white Americans – and not just for America but for people all over the world – to join together and put an end to discrimination.

It's hard to believe that only fifty or sixty years ago, a black man in America couldn't share a seat on a bus with a white person, there were no mixed-race schools, and black people were considered second-class with no real rights. How primitive.

I remember listening to one of Martin Luther King's famous speeches. I was a teenager at the time. The inspirational words he used in his speech, I felt strong emotions at that time.

Martin Luther King Jr. was responsible for banning discrimination in 1965 he was awarded the Nobel Peace Prize on 10 December 1964.

I was only sixteen at the time, but I've always remembered it. I thought discrimination was a terrible thing; I felt ashamed towards the people who were discriminated against, to the point where I felt like I needed to apologise for this atrocity that was happening. I felt outrage for this terrible injustice. Even then all those years ago, I promised myself I would never become raciest. Deep within my soul, I knew everyone was equal.

This great man was to be assassinated on April 4, 1968, by James Earl Ray. The world was devastated. King was our only hope at the time to resolving discrimination and bringing peace to this world. The day King was assassinated; he delivered his last speech at Mason Temple, in Memphis, Tennessee.

> Well, I don't know what will happen now.
> We've got some difficult days ahead.
> But it doesn't matter with me now,
> Because I've been to the mountain top.
> And I don't mind. Like anybody,
> I would like to live a long life.
> Longevity has its place,
> But I'm not concerned about that now,
> I just want to do God's will.
> And he's allowed me to go up to the mountain,
> And I've looked over and I've seen the Promised Land.
> I may not get there with you, but I want you to know tonight,
> That we as a people will get to the Promised Land.

King had a sign of his inevitable death. God gave him a glimpse of heaven so that he could pass it on to all his followers, giving them hope of the Promised Land.

I believe that although Barack Obama was only three years old at the time, he was and is' part of a great plan. Obama will be responsible for a big change in our world. He will bring peace and harmony at long last to this troubled world to end all racial discrimination forever.

I hope that Barack Obama is the one to bring change to this planet for the better; this will be the start of a better world where there will be plenty for every one where mans greed ceases to be; and all wars will end. I believe B. Obama. To be a peacemaker.

***

All corruption as to end: you only have to look at the financial economy today. It seems as if the men in charge at the top; are only looking out for themselves ; and their families; while the working man is still struggling to keep a job, if he is still fortunate to have one? It's so hard for the working man these days to have a job and keep it. There's no financial stability anymore for working families. It has all been caused by the powers that be.

***

There's no need for all the religions in the world, all this worshiping. It's between you and God, however you perceive your God to be. Simply know that the great divine exists. After all, didn't Jesus of Nazareth prove it to us by his resurrection, after he died on the cross?

It is the soul that is important – how we live our lives, how we treat one another, and the amount of good that we can do on this planet before we finally pass over to the next dimension. We will come to realise the true meaning for a life lived on earth.

That's the whole point: nothing ever ends, and nothing is ever lost. We all have complete control whatever happens in our lives; we have been given the power. All we have to do is search for the truth by listening to our hearts, our souls, our gut feelings, and our sixth sense.

We were never taught that we have a sixth sense. We should have been taught by our parents and at school about the sixth sense. Instead we grew up thinking it's something weird and not normal.

Some of us have experienced hundreds of lives. The purpose is to choose experience, remember, and evolve. Until then, each and every one of us will be reborn into the next life, in a different body but with the same soul and characteristics that we have always had. Life will begin all over again.

Make sure you live your life well. Treat others as you would have them treat you, with love and kindness. Helping towards making a better world no matter how insignificant your contribution. Nothing goes unnoticed, not even your thoughts. Your soul will know about everything you do in your life, as well as the great divine. Even when you have forgotten, your soul will remember. Your soul has all the answers, all the knowledge about your past lives and your future lives.

The Akashic Records

The Akashic records or the book of life is where every thought, word, and deed a soul has on this planet is stored. Each soul has its own book of lives lived. It's like the DNA of the universe since the time of all creation, a giant library in the spirit realm. Like a supercomputer, it contains the mind of God and is constantly updated. The Akashic records can be accessed through astral projection, or when someone is placed under deep hypnosis.

We will all go to this place at some point, when we pass over to the spirit world. A wise spirit guide, a master, will assist us with all our past records. He will be there to answer all of our questions. The Akashic records are a record of all the accumulation of good and bad that we have committed in our lives. It details how we have treated others, and whether we treated them with love, compassion, understanding, and respect. Also what have we contributed to the world, to humanity?

There are many books written on the subject. It's a wake-up call for all of us. We are in charge of our thoughts, deeds, and actions. It's never too late to change. We can all contribute to a better life by changing our thoughts and actions. Remember that nothing goes unnoticed, not the tiniest thought. You are a wonderful human being and don't realise how powerful and capable you are.

Each of us has made mistakes in our past – we wouldn't be humans otherwise. That's why we are on this earth right now, evolving once again. We alone have the power to change our lives for the better.

It's possible to access the Akashic records for yourself. It is best accessed through meditation. Be completely relaxed and aware of your

Daffodil

breathing. A good time is before you go to sleep at night. Ask your angels and spirit guides for protection. Also ask the angels and the spirit world to help you have access to the Akashic records.

Follow whatever appears in your mind's eye, and go with the flow. Don't dismiss what you see; it's not your imagination for the experience your about to have will stay with you forever.

The first time I tried this, I found myself in the grounds of a monastery. I remember looking down at the grass; the monastery was like an old ruin on a hillside. I felt happy I sat on a bench with the sun on my face. I was a male dressed in a monk's robe. As I turned to my left, I saw another male in identical dress. When I looked closer at the man, I recognised him as my brother in that life – and also my husband in this life, Harry. The feeling I had was of the extreme loyalty that my brother felt for me. That was the end of the experience.

In another out-of-body experience I had, I felt like I was floating above the ceiling in this magnificent white temple; it reminded me of Greece. I felt like a child with blond curly hair, I was about six or seven years old. I felt happy, laughing without a care in the world as I floated around this great temple.

When I was about to exit the building through large doors whilst still floating. Out of the corner of my eye I saw this lady wearing a cream Grecian gown with long dark hair down the middle of her back.

She looked at me and said, "It is important that you remember my name." Her name was Wanda Deek'a. The feeling I had at the time was that she was a little annoyed with me, as if I wasn't paying proper attention.

I also remember hearing the word Pythagoras. When I awoke, I had to write the dream down because it was so vivid. That was in 1998. I'm still trying to fathom out what it all meant. I've never forgot the name Wanda Deek'a; I'm sure all will be revealed one day.

Incidentally, Pythagoras, the great mathematician and philosopher, believed in the reincarnation of the soul. He said that the soul is immortal and that "We have had many lives and will continue to do so; till the soul becomes pure. So pure that the soul doesn't have to reincarnate". I feel in my life that this is where I'm heading, that my soul has become more pure because I have learnt the most important aspects of life as follows.

- To love.
- The importance of family life.
- To give help where needed.
- To love our brothers and sisters.
- To believe in God and the angels, and to spread the word.
- To give to the poor.
- To know that there is only one true God and that we all come from the same source.
- To know that all men are equal.
- To be kind to all of God's creations.
- To respect all nature and our planet.
- To do the best we can to make a difference while living on earth.
- To learn to forgive one another.
- To know that we are all connected and mirror each other.
- To know that we each have a guardian angel when we need help; all we have to do is ask.
- To remind ourselves that God always forgives our sins.
- To be the best we can be.
- To always have trust and faith in the things we believe in, and to never give up.

Past Life

Sixteenth Century

One should never dwell on the past, but I couldn't stop myself. I often think about the past life I lived in the sixteenth centaury, where I lived a life as a dowager. It had something to do with religion. Is that why I'm so against all religions in this life now? Because of the lives that have been lost through wars caused by different religions? It still continues to this day. When will man learn that there is **only one God, one religion, and one race?**

Why did I have this power over people? What awful decisions had I made on people's lives?

I guess I will never know, not until I pass over to the next dimension, where all will be revealed about why I chose to live the life I'm living now. I suppose in away; I can understand now why I chose this life: it's so that my soul will be cleansed, and I will be able to evolve.

It's only natural that you may think that you are being punished for your past deeds, but you're not. We may have chose a life of suffering for the benefit of others in our lives now to help another's progress with their soul, which I have mentioned previously. The soul has agreed to live a disabled life or suffer some terrible misfortune for the benefit of others. It could be the parents or siblings; it could be man and wife; it could be anyone.

When I think of this life, I always send a prayer and ask forgiveness for the people I may have wronged. It's all I can do. Whenever I think of that past life, I feel suddenly protected. I call it a knowing; I could send myself crazy with guilt and remorse. This also would hold me back with the job I have come to do in this life.

Whenever I allow negative thoughts to enter my mind, my contact with the spirit world becomes weak. The spirit world doesn't allow negativity. No matter what you are going through. You must not allow in the negativity! Press the cancel button every time.

***

You never meet anyone by chance – it's meant to be. Look around you at the people who are in your life. Look at the situations you're in, and the issues you may have with others. Even people you don't like or don't get along with can turn out to be your teachers. Ask yourself why. Is it something you recognise within yourself, and that's why you don't like them?

There is no ego in the real world; we become as one. As time went by, I was in my kitchen one day, thinking once more again about my sixteenth-century life. I wondered whether this person could be in my life now. Suddenly I saw in my mind's eye Marlene's face, my friend and neighbour! "Gosh, surely not! It can't be." The more I thought about it, the more it made sense to me.

Marlene and I have been thrown together in our later lives to try to resolve whatever issues we had in that past life. Maybe we had even more past lives together. I must admit sometimes I would look at Marlene, and there would be a familiarity about her – more like a mother figure.

We shared so much in common when it came to discussing things of a spiritual nature. After all, Marlene had introduced me to Paul Parker, the past-life regression psychic medium. Also, she took me to the spiritual church. We exchanged loads of books on this subject, helping one another. We were destined to meet up in this life.

I had become very fond of Marlene. It was so refreshing to come across someone like-minded who thought as I did when it came to psychic matters. We had learnt so much from one another.

The more I thought about it, the more emotional I became. I was convinced about the fact that Marlene was the victim in that past life.

The very same day I went round to her house. Marlene already knew the information that Paul had given me. We had sat down together one day to listen to the tape. How do I explain to Marlene what I had just discovered? How could I ever look at her in the same way again – or her me, for that matter? However, she had to know the truth.

"Marlene, I have something to tell you," I started, my voice already faltering. "You remember that awful past life I led in the sixteenth century?" Tears filled my eyes. "Marlene, it was you!" I walked towards her and held her in my arms crying. "Oh Marlene, I'm so sorry, I'm so sorry."

Marlene was as shocked as me. "Are you sure, Eileen? Are you sure?" "Oh yes, I'm sure." After a little while we both sat down. "Can you forgive me?"

She put her arms around me and said, "You know me, Eileen. Of course I forgive you." Both of us were still trying to take it all in; staring at each other in disbelieve.

However we carried on with our relationship as if nothing had happened. I suppose it was mainly due to the knowledge we had both acquired over the years of research, and that we could both accept it.

Sadly Marlene and I were to fall out several months later on an entirely different matter altogether. At the time of this writing, it hasn't been resolved.

During this time, Marlene went to see another medium; who also could read past lives. She asked him why she was having trouble with her next-door neighbour, meaning me. Imagine how I felt when she told me over the phone that the medium confirmed the gory details of this past life in the sixteenth century.

Perhaps we will have to keep coming back, sharing another life. That's one of life's problems. At some point Marlene and I decided to come back into this life, and at some point we would meet up again to try to resolve our issues. If we don't, we will keep coming back into future lives till all issues have been resolved.

It's so important that we make peace with the people whom we have issues with if our souls are to evolve. I tried to resolve the issues between us despite everything. I loved Marlene and told her so, but this made no difference.

Sadly, I can do no more. Marlene has made it plain she doesn't want to be my friend. At least I tried.

Perhaps it's not meant to be. We will come across people in our lives, and we will stay for a while with these people till we have resolved the issues — or maybe not. In that case, we have to move on. Maybe I simply have to let go. Yet I feel inside that I've have made my peace with Marlene, even if she hasn't with me. I can do no more.

Several months later the issue was resolved we both made peace, we became even closer, helping each other with books and spiritual experiences. We had both come to a greater understanding of our spirituality. Our friendship still continues.

At last Marlene has found her freedom. She divorced her husband, bought herself a lovely home, and has now become a bereavement councilor. I know Marlene and I have helped each other in this life, although our scenarios were different. Marlene's scenario was more emotional, and my scenario was physical.

I'm so pleased that I told Marlene that I loved her at the time when we fell out. Love resolves everything,

More Past Lives

One night I laid in bed thinking about my husband and how lucky I was to have a loving, caring person in my life, especially with my illness. Surely it must get him down at times, looking after me. If it does, he never shows it. I've come to rely on him so much. This is when I feel I'm becoming a burden, but I mustn't let it get me down.

Then in my mind's eye, just like a movie, I was given a scene from a past life. I was looking down on this man in a field of grass. The man looked like a sea captain – a bit like the advert in Captain's Birdseye fish fingers, complete with cap and beard. I saw a profile of his face close up.

Then suddenly I was aware of my body. I was dressed in a long skirt with a tight bodice and a nipped-in waistline that felt more like underwear. My hair was swept up on top in a chignon and was chestnut brown. I felt taller, and my hands were clasped together at my waist.

As I looked down anxiously at the man, I felt a great sadness. He was walking back and forth as if lost. He looked panic-stricken, as if he didn't know what to do. Spontaneously I shouted out, "His name, Harry!" Although he was in a different body, I knew it was Harry's soul. He didn't hear me. I felt I had passed over to the spirit world.

Why was I shown this scene? Was the spirit world giving me comfort, showing me that my husband couldn't live without me no matter what, and I couldn't live without him? We had shared a life before, or even many lives. It comforted me. Although the scene was sad, it was also beautiful.

This also made me think of my mother. Earlier in the book, I described how my mother was adopted. She had wonderful adoptive parents. When I was very young, I used to ask my mum about her real parents. I would inquire as to whom they were, but Mum became reluctant to talk about them. She only said that her real father was a sea captain! She would say her real mother was beautiful and had lovely skin just like a peach.

They would often visit Mum. Of course, Mum was never aware of who these people were. It wasn't till Mum was told at the age of fifteen that she was adopted that she was given this information.

Remember that I explained that we can be born into group souls continuously, born into the same family over and over again. Were Harry and I the real parents of my mother in that past life? There's no such thing as coincidence! Is that why I felt that my mother had abandoned me as a child, and I always had a fear of been abandoned?

I probably would have wanted to be born back into the same family so that I would have a chance to make up to the daughter that I had given up for adoption. It seems we keep coming back in the same family groups, to have the chance to improve ourselves, so that our souls will keep progressing.

One day while meditating, I asked the spirit world to show me another past-life regression. Again, it was like watching a movie.

From a great distance I was watching this Indian girl; she seemed like a North American Indian I was about fourteen or sixteen. She sat on a grassy bank staring into a stream. Her hair was dark with two long plats. I remember getting close to her profile and looking at the tapestry band that was holding her plats just near her ear. As I was staring at her profile, her energy felt subdued as if all alone.

Has I turned around I saw a beautiful horse, a stallion. I felt myself looking at its right flank. It was tan and shiny with sweat. I felt as if I recognised the horse, I kept staring at it. It was so beautiful. Then I was looking at this girl's face full-on. I was right in front of her as she rode the horse fast.

Daffodil

I don't know whether the horse was spooked, but she was holding on for dear life. She fell and broke her neck; death was instant.

I have always felt an affinity with the North American Indian. Also, I have felt an affinity towards horses. They're such highly strung creatures, and yet I find them graceful and gentle, yet so powerful. I love the sound of horses neighing. Where I live, sometimes I can hear the noises the horses make. I find it so soothing, like a distant memory.

Whenever we are out driving and I see a horse on the road, it grieves me! It's one of my pet hates. Horses aren't meant to be on the roads especially with today's traffic. They are such sensitive creatures that are so highly strung.

Answered Prayer

I finally plucked up the courage to have my left knee replaced in October 2008. I'm pleased to say that up to now, it has been successful. Two weeks later, I developed a blood blister underneath my foot – the same leg on which I had the knee replacement.

The danger was that an infection could travel to the knee replacement, causing havoc. The blister developed into a tiny ulcer, which became infected. Each time I was given antibiotics, but the ulcer would later reappear. It was suspected at one time that I may have developed osteomyelitis. My consultant said if it had, I would be up Shit Street – those were his very words. I already knew this and tried not to panic.

I was given weeks of antibiotics. Every time I finished a course, the infection would return. I finished up with four more ulcers. I'm not diabetic, so the consultant couldn't understand it. I was desperate to get help. The chiropodist was helping me with the problem, but I needed more help. I sent out a message to my guardian angel and the spirit world to help me with my foot and to leave me a sign that they knew all about it. I wanted to know that I was been helped.

Just after I had my knee replaced, I bought one of those memory form mattress toppers. I highly recommend it if you suffer with back pains or a restless night's sleep. They are magic. Several weeks later, I was changing the bed and decided to wash the covering of the mattress topper. I had left the bedroom door wide open. Not only had Peggy been playing on the bed, but she had taken about four chunks out of the sponge.

Daffodil

"Oh no, Peggy, you naughty dog!" As I looked at the damage, I couldn't believe what I was seeing. There as plain as day on the mattress, Peggy had chewed the perfect shape of a foot. The planter was about two inches long and an inch and a half wide. It was a miniature foot!

Not only that, but it was an impression of *my* foot! I have a small digit that is not connected to the foot and just hangs loose, thanks to another operation from the Doctor who had failed me. The big toe is bent and misshapen through the RA. I kept staring at the mattress; the shape was perfect.

My angel or the spirit world left me a message that they were watching over me and that I was getting help. They made sure by leaving an impression of my foot. How wonderful is that! That has to be one of the best connections ever!

This time I have a witness – yes, you've guessed it: Harry the sceptic! When Harry came home from work, I said, "Go on, have a look what Peggy's done to the mattress." I followed him into the bedroom. As he looked down at the mattress, I pointed out to the foot. "What does that look like?"

He screwed up his face and said, "It's a foot, the bottom of a foot."

"Look further. What else do you see?"

"But there are only three small digits …" Then the penny dropped when I pointed out the misshapen big toe. There was no denying; it was there as plain as day for everyone to see. He kept shaking his head in disbelief.

"Now do you believe me?"

I'm still not out of the woods, but at least I know that I'm getting help from my angel and that the spirit world heard my cry for help. You only have to ask.

The infection continued for almost five years, but eventually it healed.

Finding Dianne

As I was finding it more difficult with the house work, I asked my angel to find me someone to do my ironing. Sure enough, I found Dianne advertised in the local paper. She started coming to my home. After I had my knee operation, she told me that she also did cleaning. It was just what I had been asking the angels for: a lady that could do both jobs!

All I needed now was a hairdresser, and guess what? Dianne was also a professional hairdresser! Too much of a coincidence, don't you think? One day while she was cleaning for me, I asked her if she believed in angels, I told her that she had her very own angel since the day she was born.

She gave me a look and raised her eyebrows. I gave her an angel reading with my angel cards. It was very meaningful to her at the time. We spoke more about the angels, I told her more of my experiences.

Dianne is divorced after eighteen years of marriage. She told me that she could do with more work coming in, having to raise two children on her own. "Well, why don't you put it to the test? Ask your angel for help. You've nothing to lose."

That same day when she arrived home, she texted me to say her phone had never stopped ringing with more work coming in! She went on to have more encounters with the angels and told some of her clients to do the same.

Dianna came to my home for a couple of years. I thought she was a true friend, but things were to develop with our relationship to tell me otherwise. I had a beautiful little gold and diamond ring that was shaped into a butterfly. I love butterflies; it sat neatly on my finger. Dianne would remark on the ring; she loved it, too.

During Christmas 2010 I was suffering badly with my health. I didn't think I was going to make it, and so I promised Dianne if anything happened to me; she could have the ring. But I survived, and I decided to give her the ring anyway that Christmas.

After that I would phone to make arrangements for my ironing to be done, but she gave excuse after excuse for why she couldn't make it that day. To cut a long story short, I never saw or heard from her again.

Why oh why do I always see the best in people? I seem to put everything into a new friendship. Why am I so naive to believe that every time I make a new acquaintance, it could lead to a new friendship? I know I'm too trusting of others. I find it hard to change.

When I meet new people, I'm always opened and honest. I don't try to put on any airs, trying to impress. I'm just me, what you see is what you get. Is this because I know that no matter who we are or where we come from, we are all the same? It's been the same all my life, when I look back.

Then again, I have two true friends whom I would trust with my life: Barbara Thompson and Wendy Early. I'm eternally grateful for them. Still, it saddens me when this happens.

Jade Goody

What a shame for someone so young to die. Jade was only twenty-seven years old she had two little boys. It must be heart-wrenching to know that she won't be there to watch them grow up. But of course she will – just not in the physical sense. Jade won't know this till she has passed over to the next dimension.

When Jade dies, she will go to a place of rest till she becomes restored. Then everything will be explained to her. She will be so happy that she is still alive and out of pain with no more suffering. She will be able to see her two little boys, although not in the physical sense. She will feel more alive than ever with no more pain and an understanding of what her life was about.

Jade shot to fame in Channel Four's *Big Brother* series. She went on to become a celebrity on other reality shows. It was whilst filming that it was discovered Jade had cervical cancer. Nevertheless, Jade decided to continue with the filming, determined to fight the cancer. Even when there was no hope left of a recovery, Jade allowed the media to follow her story. It's true that Jade has made a considerable amount of money as a legacy to leave behind for her two boys. Like millions of other people, I followed her story. I couldn't help but see the fear in this young woman's face as she tried to come to terms with her imminent death.

I would love to be able to talk to Jade, if only to take away her fear of dying. I'd tell her that there's nothing to fear whatsoever. She would probably think I was some kind of a religious fanatic trying to push the Bible. All I can do is send her prayers for a miracle. If not, then I wish for an easy, peaceful transition into the next dimension. I feel it is Jade's time.

Daffodil

Jade has probably saved many women's lives by her television documentary. Because of the way she became famous, lots of young women have identified with Jade as a single mother of two young boys. She is a down-to-earth, ordinary girl who became famous.

She was a young woman with two young children and everything to live for, with a promising future. However, she was struck down with cervical cancer. Because of Jade, there was an urgent surge of young women having cervical smear tests, saving many lives. Although Jade wasn't aware of her soul's contract, this was Jade's journey, her mission She came down to serve mankind.

Jade died on Sunday, 22 March 2009. I am glad for her that her pain is over at last. She achieved what she came to do.

It doesn't matter whether you are a celebrity, film star, great icon, pioneer, or the president. Positions held on earth make no difference whatsoever. There is no room for ego in the spirit world. We don't brag about who we once were. We don't try to impress others in this new realm, for no one would be interested. We would only make fools of ourselves, and no one is given preference.

Spiritual worth is all that matters. I wish Jade every happiness as she looks down on her family and realises that her life is not over – it's only just begun.

It was discovered later that almost half a million more women went for screening tests after the death of Jade. Farewell, Jade Goody. Enjoy your new life, knowing that someday you will meet up with all your loved ones and your two little boys.

Near-Death Experience

The typical near-death experience is as follows.

- A sense of awareness of being dead.
- A sense of peace, well-being, painlessness, and positive emotions.
- A sense of removal from the world.
- A perception of one's body from an outside position.
- Sometimes observing doctors and nurses performing medical resuscitation efforts.
- A tunnel experience; a sense of moving up through a passageway or staircase.
- A communication with light.
- An intense feeling of unconditional love.

There has been much evidence of people dying in different circumstances only, to survive death after maybe twenty minutes or more, and in some cases even longer, especially in the operating theatre. Scientists are now taking it more seriously. I have read lots of books on this subject. The ones that strike me most are children's experiences, where they talk about the wonderful bright lights, the angels, and of not wanting to come back to earth. I like the wonderful drawings that the children do in such detail.

But what strikes me is the fact that each of these children talks about the tremendous feeling of being loved and how it has changed their lives for the better. Every moment they were out of their bodies, they remember every minute detail, never to be forgotten; it stays with them for the rest of their lives.

Daffodil

One of the books I read on NDEs was *Light Beyond,* by Dr Raymond Moody. Since 1976 Dr Moody has compiled more than a thousand new case histories of people who experienced clinical death and survived. In *Light Beyond* Dr Moody records this research. Here are two examples of his research.

> Sam, who almost died the previous year from a cardiac arrest, due to an adrenal gland disease.
> I was chatting with him about his illness. When he shyly volunteered;
> "About a year ago I died" He told me that after he died, he floated out of his body and looking down, as the Doctor pushed on his chest to restart his heart. Sam, in his altered state, tried to get the doctor to quit hitting him. But the doctor wouldn't pay any attention.
>
> At that point Sam had the experience of moving upward very rapidly and seeing the earth fall away below him. He then passed through a dark tunnel and was met on the other side by a group of Angels.
> I asked him if these Angels had wings and he said no. "They were glowing" he said, luminescent all of them seemed to love him very much.
> Everything in this place was filled with light, he said. Yet through it all, he saw beautiful, pastoral scenes.
> This heavenly place was surrounded by a fence. He was told by the Angels that if he went beyond the fence he wouldn't be able to return to life.
> He was told then by a being of light (Sam called him God) that he had to go back and re-enter the tunnel.
> I didn't want to go back but he made me," said Sam.
>
> The Case of Martha Todd:
>
> I found myself floating up towards the ceiling, I could see everyone around the bed very plainly even my own body. I thought how odd it was that they were all upset about my body.
> I was fine and I wanted them to know it.

It was as though they were a veil or a screen between me and the others in the room

I became aware of an opening. If I can call it that, it appeared to be elongated.

I came out of this tunnel into a room of soft, brilliant love and light. The love was everywhere.

It surrounded me and seemed to soak through into my very being.

At some point I was shown, or saw the events of my life.

They were in a kind of vast panorama. All of this is really indescribable. People I knew who had died were there with me in the light. A friend who had died in college, my grandmother, a great aunt, among others. They were happy, beaming.

I didn't want to go back, but I was told that I had to by a man surrounded by a bright light.

I was being told that I had not completed what I had come to do in this life.

I came back into my body with a sudden lurch.

An old friend of mine told me years ago that whilst in labour with her son, the pain was so unbearable that she left her body for a brief moment. She remembers looking down on herself from above onto the bed. What struck her most was that she was wearing a baby doll night dress, which was the fashion at the time. She thought how ridiculous she looked in it while heavily pregnant. The next thing she knew, she was back in her body, screaming in pain. When she told me the story, I didn't give it much thought. How differently I think now.

I researched lots of evidence of different accounts on people whose families have died and have visited them. Their spirit bodies travelled around the hospital, even into the waiting room, where some of the family were told of the death of their loved ones. Then those people made full recoveries minutes later. After talking with their loved ones later about their ordeal, the patients were able to talk in detail about the conversation they were having whilst in the waiting room. Not just that, but the patients could also describe the waiting room in detail, such as the colour of the curtains or the nurse who was trying to comfort them.

This is quite common in hospitals, especially in the operating theatre where patients have died and then been resuscitated, usually after a cardiac arrest. The patients were able to describe all that was taking place whilst out of their bodies: conversations between the surgeons, how many people were in the theatre, name tags, and more.

For my experience, when I left my body at Alan Bellinger's in broad daylight, I didn't have to die. I was transported to another realm for a brief moment – who knows how long – but I gathered enough evidence to bring back for it to change my life forever. I experienced the same overwhelming feeling of love and peace. I will never forget what I witnessed; it will stay with me always.

I knew I had a job to do on earth, and I promised that I would achieve this without being told what it entailed. That was for me to find out. It is part of my journey's struggle. I know my guides and the angels are helping me.

It seems that more and more people are becoming interested in what happens to us when we die. When I first saw my father in his coffin, a part of me wanted to laugh. My immediate thought was, *that's not my dad, especially the makeup they use to try and make his corpse look healthy!* Neither did I find it scary. Yet something deep inside told me this was not the end. I simply couldn't and wouldn't accept it.

That was the beginning of my spiritual journey. I have a lot to thank my father for. You see, my father's death changed my life. I had to find out the meaning of life. There had to be something else to life. We were not just flesh and blood; we don't simply die and turn to dust. What an awful thought! I don't think I could carry on with my life if this was true! What would be the point of a living in the first place?

When my mother died, my husband and I were on holiday in Spain. My mother was in a nursing home at the time, slowly dying. How I wish I could have nursed my mother, if it hadn't been for my illness. I was too weak. I don't think my mother ever realised how debilitating RA is. I did the best that I could. I know she knows this now that she has passed over.

On our way back from the airport, I remember saying to my husband that I would know if my mother had died. It was about 3.00 AM in the morning. We were both shattered after a long delay. By five in the morning we arrived home, we both fell into bed, exhausted.

However, something made me want to ring the nursing home, even though it was very early. I couldn't settle down.

"I'm so sorry. Didn't anyone tell you?" the nurse said on the phone. "Your mother died on Friday night in hospital."

I wasn't shocked, but in a way there was a relief. Mum wasn't going to get any better. I knew it was her time and had predicted that she was dying four months prior. Because we were close, I thought in a telepathic way that I would have known that she had passed over. Perhaps Mum didn't want to spoil the holiday.

Later that day, I insisted on seeing Mum at the morgue. I had to see that familiar face one more time. It didn't matter that she had been dead for two days. I walked into the morgue with my sister and her husband, Don.

My mother was wrapped in a blanket with just her face showing. Her face looked small and gray. Tears streamed down my face as I held both her shoulders, pressing both sides of her cheeks with mine; trying to find that scent I could smell as a child whenever my mother cuddled me. Her cheeks were so cold. It wasn't a frightening experience; after all, she was my mother.

Three years later, I was told by Paul Parker that my mother had said she was glad that I was there. I could sense her spirit in the morgue; I knew she was with me that day, watching everything that was going on. I miss her so much; I still talk to her as if she's here.

If only more people were aware that our loved ones never leave us. It's a natural process that we have all been through time and time again.

What Happens at the Point of Death?

What happens at the point of your death? I don't like to use the words death or dying anymore, because nothing really dies. You pass over and continue your journey. Death means change: you simply open another door.

All living things are a cycle, meaning they are without end. You go on living. This is why so many people who have "died" do not believe it, because they do not have the experience of being dead. On the contrary, they feel they are very much alive, so there's confusion.

You may see your body lying there all crumpled up and not moving, yet you're suddenly moving all over the place. You often have the experience of flying all over the room and then being everywhere all at once. When the spirit desires a particular point of view, it suddenly finds itself experiencing that. If the soul wonders, "Gosh, why is my body not moving?" It will find itself right there, hovering over the body and watching the stillness.

You may have read where certain people have had near-death experiences, have left their bodies, and have seen themselves lying on the bed. It's quite common. If someone enters the room, and the soul thinks, *who is that?* And then immediately the soul is in front of or next to that person. In a very short time the soul learns that it can go anywhere with the speed of its thoughts. A feeling of incredible freedom and lightness overtakes the soul, and it usually takes a little while for the entity to get used to all the bouncing around with every thought.

If the person had children, and should think of those children, immediately the soul is in the presence of those children, wherever they are. The soul learns that not only can it be wherever it wants with the speed of its thoughts, but it can be in two places at once – or three or four or five. It can exist, observe, and conduct activities in these places simultaneously, without difficulty or confusion. Then it can rejoin itself, returning to one place again simply by refocusing.

The soul remembers in the next life what it would have been well to remember in this life: all effect is created by thought, and manifestation is a result of intention. Focus all your thoughts on good things, not negativity, because all your thoughts will instantly become your creation, your experience. Then you will have a greater understanding what your life was about. Where you see only darkness, replace it with light. You still have power over your thoughts.

Nothing has changed – only that you have dropped the body, which is no use to you anymore. Your positive thoughts will leave you with peace, joy, and tranquility. By thinking positively and seeing only love, gratefulness, and perfection in all things, you will prepare for your next life. You will have the knowledge that life is eternal, a world without end. Amen.

The spirit world says, "The best day of your life is the last day of your life."

"What happens after death is so unspeakably glorious that our imagination and our feelings do not suffice to form even an approximate conception of it/ the dissolution of our time-bound form in eternity brings no loss of meaning." – Carl G. Jung, Letters, Volume 1

The best time of your life is at the point of your death. You already know this, but you don't remember. The people left behind would not feel the grief that death causes if they could remember what happens at the point of death. If they did, they would rejoice; they would be happy and give celebration. Like I said your memory after birth was taken away for a good reason,

Daffodil

Remember that you have nothing to learn – you already have all the knowledge. The point of your life is to create the person that you really are and want to be by the choices that you make in life. Eventually you find your way home. This is what is called evolution, to make earth a better place. We are evolving all the time, every time we are given a new life.

That's why we are given free will, and God will never interfere with that. God can only observe and hope that we make the right choices: that's why when all the terrible atrocities happen all around the world, God will never interfere. He will leave it up to us to make the right decisions, the right choices, so that our souls will evolve even more. When making these decisions and choices, ask yourself, "Is this who I am? Is this who I really want to be?" You can decide by making your choice; listen to your heart and soul.

Take for example the conflict in the Middle East with the dictator and despot Colonel Gaddafie. How can we allow such a man to rule over his people by taking their freedom away and threatening their lives with death and torture if they don't adhere to his rules and regulations?

What kind of thoughts do his soldiers have? Is it the fact that they are too frightened to stand up to him? Is it the money? This is when you should ask yourself, "Is this who I really am? Is this who I want to be, to serve under a man like this who is willing to kill his own innocent people?"

It would be like the Hitler scenario all over again. We have to think for ourselves, not leave it up to some despots. There will always be despots. By changing our thoughts for the good of man, we cause the collective consciousness to triumph over evil so that we all evolve together.

We have to put right what we see as wrong, or we will never evolve. The world cannot turn its back on situations like this – we have to make a stand. We are all one, God's children. There is no separation.

For hundreds of years, we have clearly been making the wrong choices the wrong decisions. Look at the world's terrible situations: wars, starvation, nuclear weapons, racism, greed, drugs, the destruction of the rainforest, pollution – the list is endless.

We come back to earth to help humanity, to improve our soul so that we can progress. Think of it as a diamond made up of hundreds of tiny facets. Each facet represents a new life. We are given the opportunity to come back to earth to make a difference, and if we are successful, we add another shiny facet to the soul, all polished, shiny, and clean.

Some souls are dull and in need of a good polish. Only you can decide. Only you can make the choice.

Miracles

Never give up, because miracles can happen. I was inspired by a true story I heard on a TV program the other day. A young married couple and their two small children, aged two and four, had their lives devastated when the husband was involved in an explosion at work.

The accident left him with his corneas burnt in both eyes, leaving him blind and totally dependent on his wife. After months, as you can imagine, this left the husband in a deep depression.

Not only had he had his livelihood taken away from him, but he couldn't see his two little girls growing up or his wife's face ever again. The future looked bleak.

Then one day it became too unbearable. He stood on a riverbank contemplating suicide. All he could see in his mind's eye were the faces of his family. He decided to accept his fate that life would never be the same, and he returned home to his family. Weeks later he enrolled in a university and studied to become an assistant physiotherapist.

Ten years passed. One day whilst at work, he happened to be taking a break and stood near the window. There was a bar across the windowsill, and suddenly he held on to the bar as he experienced a terrible pain in his head. He thought he was going to have a heart attack. Then he experienced a bright white light in both of his eyes. I have also experienced this light. Still worrying what was happening to him, he gradually opened his eyes.

The first thing he saw through the window below him were a block of separate buildings. Then as he kept blinking, he started to see colours.

Eileen Veronica Richmond

He couldn't believe it – his sight was returning to normal! He hadn't seen his two daughters and his wife's faces in ten years! He was too frightened to go to sleep that night, in case he should awake and find that he was still blind.

When he went to see his eye specialist, there was no explanation as to why this had happened, it had never been known before. His corneas were healed and he had clear sight.

It had to be a miracle!

I love stories like this. They inspire me and validate everything I believe in. If you know of people who are blind, I'm sure this story would help to encourage them that there is always hope and that God will perform a miracle if it's for your highest good. Nothing is set in stone remember; anything is possible from the spirit world.

The Right Time

It seems that as my life goes on, I am put in the right place at the right time. It's not always for my benefit, but I have been put there for the benefit of others. For instance, I had to go into hospital for another operation on my foot, yet again it was unsuccessful, so I had to go in for it to be repeated. I was in the hospital for four nights. It may not seem a long time, but when you're in hospital with people twenty-four seven, you can really get to know a person.

In this case I met a lady called Linda Briggs, and we got chatting. This lady had come in for an operation on her arm. It was plain to see that Linda suffered with many other medical problems as well.

One night there was a mix-up with her medication when the nurse on duty was giving out the medication to the patients. Linda got really agitated and started to panic. I said to her, "Linda, don't get upset, love. It will get sorted out. Just take a deep breath, and everything will be fine."

Later she told me that when I spoke to her, she felt an immediate pressure on the top of her head. "You're going to think I'm silly," Linda said, "but I kept getting a name like Anna at the same time. It's happened before, especially when I get myself all upset."

Here we go again, I thought to myself. "No, I don't think you're silly. That's easy: it's your guardian angel, or a spirit guide who is trying to help you. That's probably her name."

As I started to explain to her about the angels and the spirit world, I could see her face relax, as if to say, "I've not been imagining things, then! I'm not going crazy." She started to tell me the things that had happened to her over the years, and I was able to give her answers. I also told her about myself and my experiences.

In the morning we were both been discharged from hospital. Linda began to thank me for the knowledge I had given her about the spirit world and the angels. "You have given me back my confidence. All these years I thought I was going mad and that it was just my imagination. I'd been frightened to tell anyone."

Linda had been a carer for eight years before her illness. She finished up having a nervous breakdown because of colleagues with whom she worked. She thought nobody liked her, lost all confidence, and gave up her job.

While I was in hospital, there was also a young lady called Sophia who had been brought in by helicopter. She had fallen of her horse at a show display. She had to lay flat on her back because she had spinal injuries, which was quite worrisome because she had no feeling down one side.

After a couple of days, Sophia broke down. She had only been married for seven weeks. She was thirty years old with her whole life in front of her. That night I had a word with my angel to get in touch with Sophia's guardian angel, to help heal Sophia's injuries for a speedy recovery.

The next day I asked Sophia how she was feeling. "Have you got any feeling back yet, where it was numb?" "Yes," she replied. "I can feel something happening."

I knew I had to ask Sophia outright about the angels. I thought to myself, *how do I approach her without her thinking I'm some Jehovah's Witness or a religious fanatic?* Finally I said, "Sophia do you believe in angels?"

"Yes, I do!" she replied. "I also know that my granddad is around me!" What a refreshing change. I didn't have to go through all the explanations; she was already full of spiritual knowledge.

Daffodil

When I left hospital that morning, I came face to face with Sophia for the first time. I looked in her eyes and knew she was going to get better. I told her so. It was as if she knew already; there was a kind of knowing between us.

Angel Poem

A drunken man in an old mobile. ...

They said had run the lights that caused the six car pileup on 109 that night,

When broken bodies lay about and blood was everywhere' the sirens screamed out eulogies,'

For death was in the air.

A mother, trapped inside her car,' was heard above the noise; her plaintiff plea near split the air

'Ho, God please spare my boys!' She fought to loosen her pinned hands; she struggled to get free',

But mangled metal held her fast in grim captivity.

Her frightened eyes then focused on where the back seat had once been', but all she saw was broken glass

And two children's seats crushed in.

Her twins were nowhere to be seen; 'she did not hear them cry', and then she prayed they'd been thrown

Free,' Oh god, don't let them die!'

Then firemen came and cut her loose.' But when they searched the back,' they found therein no little boys.'

Daffodil

But the seats were intact.

They thought the woman had gone mad and was travelling alone 'but when they turned to question her.

'They discovered she was gone.

Policemen saw her running wild and screaming above the noise 'in beseeching supplication Please help me

Find my boys! They're four years old and wear blue shirts; their jeans are blue to match," One cop spoke up,

They're in my car. 'And they don't have a scratch.

They said their Daddy put them there and gave them each a cone.' then told them both to wait for mom to

Come and take them home.

I've 'searched the area high and low, 'but I can't find their Dad 'he must have fled the scene,' I guess, and that is very bad,'

'The mother hugged the twins and said while wiping a tear.' he could not flee the scene you see for he has been dead a year."

The cop just looked confused and asked.' 'Now how can that be true?' 'The boys said "Mommy Daddy came' He told us not to worry 'And that you would be all right and then he put us in this car with the pretty, flashing light

'We wanted him to stay with us,' 'because we miss him so,' 'but Mommy, he just hugged us tight', and said he had to go.

He said someday we'd understand 'And told us not to fuss',' And he said to tell you Mommy' 'He's watching over us

'The mother knew without a doubt that what they spoke was true,' 'far she recalled their dad's last words,' 'I will watch over you.'

Eileen Veronica Richmond

The fireman's notes could not explain the twisted mangled car.' And how the three of them escaped without a single scare.

But on the cops report was scribed.' 'In print so very fine',

An Angel walked the beat tonight on highway 109.

– Author unknown

Live in the Moment

As my life goes on, I try not to think of my illness even though it's a degenerative disease. I'm learning to live more in the moment. It's no good worrying about what you can't control, and neither can you change the past.

On a good day I'm really grateful, and I feel much happier within myself. It's no good dwelling on the future and what might happen. We all have to deal with it the best way we can. I'm simply grateful for the good things I have been given in my life, as well as the special connection I have with the spirit world and the angels.

My illness is not who I am; I am not my illness, and neither am I my body. The real me is within my soul, my higher self, which has all the answers. My body is simply a vehicle for this lifetime.

Sometimes the body becomes too heavy to carry the soul; that's why we need sleep. It's not because you become tired that you think you need to sleep – it's the soul telling you that it has to escape for a while to rejuvenate itself. That is why sleep was invented. The soul causes the body to fall asleep. It literally drops the body off when it is tired of the limits, tired of the heaviness and lack of freedom. The soul is due for a good rest before returning.

But when the soul embraces a body for the first time, it finds the experience extremely difficult. It is very tiring, particularly for a newly arriving soul, and that is why babies sleep a lot. Have you noticed how much cats and dogs sleep? Yes, they to belong to the spirit world.

When the soul gets over the initial shock of being attached to a body once more, it begins to increase its tolerance, and it stays with it more. At the same time, the part of you called your mind moves into forgetfulness, just as it was designed to. Even the soul's flights out of the body, taken less frequently but still usually on a daily basis, do not always bring the mind back to remembrance.

Indeed, during these times the soul may be free, but the mind may be confused. The whole being may ask, "Where am I? What am I creating here?" This searching may lead to fitful journeys, or even frightening ones. We call these trips nightmares. Have you ever felt yourself twitch and jerk while you are asleep, sometimes waking yourself up?

Sometimes the opposite will occur: the soul will arrive at a place of great remembering, and the mind will have an awakening. This will fill it with peace and joy, which you will experience in your body when you return to it.

Harry

Harry, my husband, has always worked hard, especially when the children were small. Wherever he has worked, he's always gain the respect from the management and his colleagues for the quality of the work he has produced in steel fabrication and welding. He's always been in the steel industry and is able to solve the firm's problems, to the relief of the management.

When I look back to when we where first married, I remember someone had given us an old washing machine, but it was broken. Harry dismantled it, with pieces strewn all over the kitchen floor. By the end of the day it was working just like a new one. He was only eighteen years old and was self-taught.

It was the same when the car broke down. Harry could always fix it – and other people's car's, for that matter. Nothing would faze him. He soon had a reputation for being handy.

Once while driving to work on the night shift, he was witness to a terrible car crash. As he tried to help the victims involved, he couldn't help but notice the horrific injuries inflicted on the young people in both cars. This was before seatbelts were compulsory. When he came home off the night shift that morning, he told me all about it. I could tell it had disturbed him. I looked at him, his head resting on his hands. His eyes were open, deep in thought as he stared at the ceiling.

Harry was the first person to invent the electronic seatbelt. This meant that you could not switch on the engine till you had put on the seatbelt first. We didn't have the money to have the plans drawn up properly or patent it at the time. About two or three years later, the Swedish car manufacturer Saab thought of it. What a shame that it had taken an accident for Harry to think that one up, because he was worried about me driving and making it safer for me and our children. It seems Harry has missed his way.

One day I sat down at the table and made a list of things I would like to happen in my life. This list was for my angels. I asked for a motor home so that we could have holidays in this country. It was getting far too stressful to go abroad anymore. I wanted something that we could afford. Also, I wanted a little pup, who is now Peggy. As I visualized this happening, I saw a little black-and-white pup on my knee in the front passenger seat of a motor home.

I specifically asked for Harry to be recognised for all that he had achieved over the years. I felt like it was payback time for Harry. After all, his nickname was Troubleshooter at work. I folded the list up and put it in the back of my purse.

Soon enough, Peggy came along, followed by the motor home just like I had asked for. We have had some nice holidays the last eighteen months, especially with little Peggy. But the most amazing thing that's happened is that Harry finally has recognition.

This year Harry was asked if he would like to take his redundancy, along with another seventeen men, because of the financial decline in 2009. Harry had only another year before retirement, so he decided to take it. Two weeks later, the firm sent for him to attend the office one day, with a view to return to work as a self-employed contractor and steel fabricator consultant – along with the appropriate salary. Wow! I knew the firm Harry worked for couldn't afford to lose him. This entailed working part-time two to four days a week, which was just enough for him. Thank you, angels!

Now I'm always writing little notes to my angels. Why don't you try it? You've nothing to lose. Ask for things within reason – not for things like winning the lottery. It doesn't work like that. Believe what you ask for, and it will come to you.

For instance, if you're worried about your child being bullied at school, start with, "Dear Archangel Michael." Write it down, date it,

Daffodil

fold it up, put it in your wallet or purse, and consider the matter already resolved. You must have faith.

Don't fret about it any longer, or you may block the communication. Remember that in the spirit world negativity does not exist. If you are asking for healing for yourself or for another, ask for Archangel Raphael; he is the appropriate angel for healing.

Archangel Michael is the one who deals with protection. I always use Archangel Michael when I am away on holiday or in the hospital, to protect my home from burglary. Don't forget to say thank you. Your angels will always be there ready to help you. You only have to ask your guardian angel to help you. Your angel is there to help guide you throughout your life. He or she has been with you throughout all of your past lives –and will continue to be with you through all of your future lives.

If you use the word I want when making a request out to the universe; that is exactly what you will receive. It will leave you wanting. Therefore you will not receive it, and you push it away from you. The universe hears every thought, word, and deed. It is so vital that you send your request out in the right order. Believe have faith that it is already there, ask, and you will receive, like it states in the Bible.

When you have real faith in God and the great universe, and you believe what God says, then before you even ask it, it has already been given. When you thank God in advance for that which you choose to experience in your illusion in this world, in effect you acknowledge that it is there. Your first thought should be one of gratitude before you even ask, not stating what you **want.** You can't kid God or yourself. Your mind knows the truth of your thoughts, and so does the universe. You cannot lie to yourself – you have to truly believe and have faith. God communicates to us through feelings and thoughts that contain joy, truth, and love. This is your birthright.

How to Become a Healer

Do you have a strong desire to help others? Are you willing to work with the angels and the spirit world? When healing a client, you should always ask for protection. You may pick up the client's energies and absorb them into your aura, making you feel unwell. You also leave yourself open to negative energies. You can ask Archangel Michael for protection. It's also good to use visualization.

You can make your own protection with your imagination. Remember that your mind will believe what you tell it. I myself visualize that I have stepped into a pink bubble where nothing can enter; I'm totally protected. Or you can imagine that you are protected from head to foot in a purple cloak. It's up to you; you can choose any method you wish. A favourite one is to imagine your angel wrapping his wings around you, protecting you.

I once was healing a client, and I had forgotten to ask for protection. I felt shattered after the experience. Don't go thinking that it's unnecessary to ask for protection; it's important that you do.

When about to heal a client, never promise that you can heal them, no matter what. Tell your client that you can only do your best. Most of the time a healing will take place, but on rare occasions the client may not receive a healing. It's not that the client is being punished in any way by the powers that be. It's already been written in the client's contract before he or she was born. This is part of the lesson that soul chose to learn in this lifetime.

Some souls have chosen challenging lives. If that be the case, then there's nothing you can do. Although the client will receive spiritual upliftment, if not a cure. That's why some people are healed and some are not. If your client should challenge you, then this is your answer.

Sit your client on a chair or stool, whichever is most comfortable for both of you. Or you may wish to choose a treatment bed; this is better when working with the chakras I spoke about earlier in the book. Treatment beds are used in Reiki.

To begin, stand at the back of the chair. It's best to offer a prayer up to the angels and the spirit world, or you can do this before your client arrives. A simple prayer will do. Ask for healing and guidance for yourself and for your client, for their highest good.

Ask your client to take three deep breaths through the nose and exhale slowly out through the mouth. Tell her to relax. Then start by placing your hands on the top of your client's head, the crown; this is the seventh chakra, where the healing enters.

Try to imagine a white bright light or maybe gold coming down through your client's head, face, neck, shoulders, arms, chest, trunk, hips, thighs, legs, and feet. Hold this light within your client's body. After a few moments you may feel heat in both your hands; or a tingling sensation like pins and needles, or maybe cold – or maybe nothing at all. This is normal. Alan Bellinger used to see a blue light emanating from his finger tips whilst healing his clients.

Place your hands over the forehead, just between the eyebrows and over the eyes. This is what they call the third eye, the sixth sense, the sixth chakra. Hold for a few minutes. Then move down to the throat area, placing your hands gently around the throat; this is the fifth chakra and it is for communication with the spirit world and the angels.

After a few moments, move down to the heart area. Place your hands on the chest around the heart; this is the forth chakra. Then move down to the midriff; this is the third chakra, the soul, a very important place. I always stay on this area a little longer.

Then travel down to the lower abdomen, the second chakra, and lastly go just above the pubic bone, the first chakra. If you feel uncomfortable on this last area, you can let your hands hover by raising them a couple of inches. The healing will work just the same.

The method above is used for general healing of the chakras and aura. Reiki is a much deeper healing method carried out by a Reiki master or someone who has been initiated in the first and second degree in Reiki. If you want to use a simpler method to heal a client, you can start off with the seventh chakra and place your hands on painful areas of the body. Alternatively, hold your client's shoulders and use visualizations. Do whatever comes natural; you will be guided by the spirit world and the angels.

As long as your intentions are for the highest good for your client, then you can't go wrong. Remember whilst giving healing that you will also receive healing in return. Healing time can take from twenty to thirty minutes; it simply depends. You yourself will know.

Never think that you are unworthy of healing another person. Remember that we are all one; we are a part of God. Thinking that we are not worthy is like saying that God is not worthy.

***

When I started with my illness, the first two to three years of pain were the worst. However, there was a driving force within me that said I had to help others. How could I let others suffer the same agony that I was going through? I had to find a way to try and get better. The force was so strong within me. I felt it in my heart and soul, in my very being, with a passion. It's what I wanted to do. Then I met Alan Bellinger, and my real purpose for life started to unfold.

If you are not sure about your ability to heal another person, then you can try experimenting on a pet, child, or the elderly. Simply try it – what have you got to lose? Like I've mentioned before, you don't have to spend a fortune on learning how to heal. It's in all of us. You will do what should come naturally.

My granddaughter Katie possesses the healing gift, although she is only eight. I came across this by chance one day, when I asked her to massage some after-sun cream on my back and shoulders. As she began to touch my back and shoulders with little circular movements with her fingertips, her fingers were like little hot, penetrating rods.

I was quite taken aback. Then I asked Katie to place the palm of her hand on my back and go in circular movements. I knew it straightaway! It reminded me of Steven Toorof, the psychic surgeon whom I went to see for some healing several years ago. It was the same intense heat.

The only way I can describe it is that it's like liquid heat, really hot but at the same time very pleasant. I turned around and looked at Katie in surprise. "Katie, you can heal!" She looked at me and shrugged her shoulders as if to say, "So what?" Then she ran off to play.

Alan Bellinger never charged clients for healing, and I agree with him. However, if clients insisted, Alan would accept contributions. He would let the money accumulate over a twelve-month period and then pass it on to charities. Alan was very particular in keeping a record of all accounts. This came from his experience of working in Barclays Bank.

He prided himself on balancing the books, and his figures always added up. That was how Alan preferred it. In the Second World War, Alan was posted to Palestine with the First Cavalry Division in 1939. He ended up paying the soldiers' wages, and of course the books always balanced, to the relief of the sergeant major.

I suppose it's up to the individual. For instance, if you have to travel around the country to meet your clients, then you have to charge for your time and fuel. It's only fair, and the spirit world understands this.

If you find that you do posses the healing gift, always treat it with respect, and never turn anybody away. Don't let yourself rise above it, with an ego. If you have been blessed with this precious gift, the spirit world can easily take it away.

The Pendulum / Dowser

When I want to get in touch with the spirit realm or the angels, or I need some questions answered, I use the pendulum, or dowser. You can buy one or even make your own pendulum. I myself have a pure, clear, faceted crystal which has a point at the bottom and a small chain threaded through the top.

It's best if you choose your own pendulum – no one can choose it for you. The reason for this is so that no one else handles it. You will know with your gut feeling the right pendulum for you. It may be the colour that you choose that attracts you straightaway.

Once you have chosen your pendulum, it's best to cleanse it first. You can clean your pendulum by rinsing it under the cold tap; visualise your pendulum being cleansed of any negativity. Then find a little bag or a silk scarf to keep it in. I keep mine in a little velvet pouch.

Always try to keep your pendulum next to you or in your handbag, or even your pocket. The idea is not to let anyone have access to your pendulum. The reason for this is that the energy, vibes, or negativity from others can affect it. The first time you use it, ask the spirit world, the angels, or your guardian angel to guide you and protect you from negativity that may surround you and your aura.

A simple way to activate your pendulum is to hold the chain between your thumb and index finger. Let it hang down about five inches. You can use the clockwise sign for yes, and anti-clockwise for no.

Sometimes when asking a question, the pendulum may stay centered; this can mean it's wiser if you don't know. Refusing to move; or moving

Daffodil

backwards and forwards can mean its best if the question is not answered. However, you can try another way of asking the same question.

Try to stay calm and relaxed when asking questions for yourself. Try to stay impartial when asking questions for family and friends. Always remember to protect yourself first when opening up to the spirit realm. I always test my pendulum before asking the main question. If it's a nice sunny day, I will ask the pendulum "Is it raining today?" I'm always given the right answer. You can ask whatever you want when testing your pendulum.

The other day as I was testing my dowser, I asked Harry to give me an answer to a question that only he would know the answer to. "All right," he said. "Did I have a dream last night?"

As I started to ask the question, the dowser began to move anti-clockwise. Not only that, but it was a very strong, vigorous move. Sometimes when this happens, it means a very definite no or yes to your question. "No, you didn't have a dream last night," I replied.

To my surprise Harry said, "Yes, I did."

This puzzled me, so I started asking it other questions, and it came back with the right answers. "All right then, tell me about your dream. You say that you never dream."

Harry told me about his dream. A couple of weeks ago, Eric Kettelwell, an old friend of his who used to play snooker at the same club, suddenly died at the age of eighty-three. In the dream Harry was playing snooker with several of his friends, like he always did on Fridays and Sundays. Eric walked into the snooker room. All Harry's friends looked shocked with their mouths opened. Eric turned to Harry. "Would you like a game, Harry?"

"Sure, Eric, why not," Harry replied.

When the game was over, Harry moved over to shake Eric's hand. As he did, his hand went straight through Eric's hand.

I then realised the truth. "No, Harry, you didn't have a dream! You had an out-of-body experience!"

This is the difference between a dream and an OBE. In an OBE this did really happen – in the spirit world. Harry travelled to the spirit world while his body slept, and that was why he could remember the OBE in detail and would never forget it.

It was Eric's way of saying that he was all right to all of his friends. He told them that he is still alive and still up for a game of snooker. Therefore the question I asked the pendulum was correct. Harry didn't have a dream – he had an OBE!

More about the Angels

At my first day at school, the teacher told all the children in the classroom that we all had a guardian angel, which I mentioned earlier. We had our very own angels protecting each and every one of us. I remember feeling happy about it at the time. As I grew up, I never felt alone; I always felt as if I was been watched. When I look back, it also could have been my grandparents as well as my spirit guides.

My first experience was when my Uncle Eddy was in hospital. Harry had taken me, my mother, and Aunt Biddy to see him. Mum and I were helping Uncle Eddy out of a chair and onto his bed. I remember that same feeling, as if someone was watching me, and I felt compelled to turn around.

I could see two giant angels up in the far corner of the hospital ceiling They were both face to face as if talking to one another, passing the time of day and watching me the whole time. At the time I thought it was my imagination, but I never forgot it.

In the years to come I discovered that we are never alone, even when we are dying and about to pass over to the spirit world. It's the same when we come to earth in a new body: our guardian angel is with us. The greatest time of our lives is at the point of our death. It is a wonderful experience for the dying, but not for the loved ones left behind.

For the first time, the dying will experience the true reality of life. They will know they are about to embark on a wonderful journey, and they don't want any interference. They want their loved ones to head home or maybe go for a cup of tea. The worst thing that can happen is if the loved ones left behind ask the dying not to leave them, or they get terribly upset. This is more upsetting for the dying – they simply want to be off.

The best way to help a dying loved one is to tell them how much they are loved, and to ask the angels to help them on their way. This will help the transition for the spirit and the soul into heaven. Loved ones on the other side come to collect us, such as grandparents, husbands, wives, and children who have gone before. They are happy to see us, and it's a cause for a great celebration. Even our lost animals are waiting for us.

These wonderful, divine angel beings are here with us straight from birth to help us through our lives, and they will be with us till the day we die. They don't always appear with wings. My guardian angel appeared to me in jeans and a sweater. It was only when I inquired as to who he was that he told me he was my guardian angel.

When I was taking my Reiki course, there were several other students in the classroom. As I turned my head sideways to look at the line of people, every one of us had a giant Archangel standing behind us. These huge angels were as tall as the ceiling and looked down on us. My first thoughts were, *Whoah, this can't be real!* I kept it to myself, but it was real, all right!

I have seen angels dressed in robes; these are the masters, the ones who come to teach and guide us. Angel stories always interest me, I have read many books about angels, and they validate my belief.

To be in touch with your angels, you have to acknowledge that they exist and that they are here for you, as I have explained before. Your angels have to wait for you to approach them. Sometimes your angels will try to reach you through dreams or OBEs, just to nudge you. You may hear your name being called. This happened to me many times while growing up. I would turn around, but there would be no one there.

Once you have acknowledged your angels. You can ask for their names, and you can ask any questions you want. Offer a little prayer; make it personal by making your own prayer. This is best done at night before you go to sleep. Make sure you protect yourself first, because you are open to both elements.

Look for signs the next day. For example, a tune may keep popping into your head over and over again. If it does, listen to the words of the song – there may be a message in it for you. Your angels' names may come to you.

The other night I awoke at about three in the morning. This happens quite often when the spirit world or the angels want to get a message to me. A tune popped into my head: Susan Boyle's "I'm Who I Was Meant to Be". It was not one that I was familiar with, but I seemed to recognise the tune. I played it in the morning. As I listened to the words, it had great meaning for me at the time. I felt very emotional.

When you ask for help from your angels, you find that synchronicities happen all the time to help you along. Whatever your problem is, it will eventually resolve itself. The spirit world and the angels work tirelessly together to make things happen; nothing happens by chance. They put you in the right place at the right time. They may put a thought into your head, but you will think it was your thought. They are very clever at bringing things together; it never ceases to amaze me.

Christmas Day

Christmas Day 2009 was a day I will never forget. I sat on the sofa, looking straight through the window and tucking into some tea and toast. It was about 8.00 on that cold, crisp morning. The sun was just about to rise. *How nice,* I thought. *I will be able to watch the sun rise on Christmas Day morning.*

As I waited for the sun to rise, all of a sudden the sky started to go all pink, and at the same time it started to pulsate. I was able to stare at this bright pink, pulsating light without it hurting my eyes. At the bottom of the circle of pink light, there was a straight line pointing directly at my heart. I blinked my eyes several times, and there were pink clouds surrounding the sun. I rose slowly from the sofa and walked over to the window, still staring at the scene. All I could think of was how amazing it was!

When I closed my eyes, I saw the colour emerald green. This happened several times as I kept opening and closing my eyes. As I sat back down on the sofa, I looked towards my left, towards the fireplace. I saw a soft fluffy ball of yellow light hovering over a three-foot decoration I had placed in the hearth for Christmas. I stared in disbelief at what I was witnessing. It then gently disappeared. As I looked back towards the window, the sun suddenly rose, and I had to turn my eyes away.

What did it all mean? I know what I saw was for real. The colour emerald is the healing colour from the Archangel Raphael, which also represents the heart chakra. Pink represents love from the Archangel Chamuel and means love from the angels.

Yellow represents the colour of the soul chakra, and it also means happiness.

I believe the angels were sending peace, love, and healing out to the world on Christmas morning. But what did the yellow fluffy ball of light mean? Was it a present, a gift from the angels? Did the fluffy yellow ball represent my soul? Whatever the message, it left me peaceful and happy. We should all strive to be happy in this world.

I was told at the age of sixty that all the people I knew in the sixteenth century lifetime were coming into my life now. But why? Are there issues that have to be resolved before I die? Now I'm very wary when I meet someone. This will happen to all of us. We may have issues with different people, and it's best if we can resolve them while we are still on this earth. If not, as you already know by now, we will have to keep coming back with the same souls time and time again, in different bodies.

Lots of souls have chosen lives that will be challenging. The purpose is to purify the soul. That's the whole point of reincarnation: so that the soul becomes so pure that it does not have to return in another body, another lifetime. Still, that's up to the soul. There's no reason for its return unless it wants to be of help to mankind. There are many different levels of the soul's purity.

Life can be wonderful, but it can also be very harsh. I am fortunate to have experienced both. Our higher selves have all the knowledge. I feel very grateful and honoured to have this connection with God, the angels, and the spirit world.

I am glad to have learned all that I have. For example, how many people can turn round and say that they do not fear death? You can achieve this by listening to your soul. You only have to ask – the guides above will be listening.

At times when it all becomes too much, I ask myself, "Why did I choose such a hard life? Why did I choose to have this illness?" Although I had all the advice and guidance from the masters before I came to this earth, God does not punish past misdeeds.

We are all responsible for the lives that we will encounter; we write our own stories right from the beginning, and we choose every scenario that happens to us. We even choose what we will look like, which country we live in, and which languages we speak.

Is it that I want to experience the pain I may have caused others in other lifetimes? Why would I choose a sibling who never wanted me in her life? Why would I choose a spouse totally opposite to my character? All will be revealed.

We all come down to experience a life completely opposite to the ones we have lived before. For instance, if we were very happy in one life, we will also have to experience what it's like to live the opposite. By experiencing every opposite, our souls become more experienced in a spiritual sense. That's why everyone's soul is at a different level.

You will be given all the best advice by the masters, the teachers, before you come down to earth. I know deep down in my soul that I have had different lives. I've been a male and female. Sometimes I have flashbacks of these lives. For instance,

I saw myself coming out of a barber shop where there were several concrete steps. As I looked to my left, I saw one of those red and white barber poles they used to have near the door entrance in the old days, in America. Although I was a female I remembered looking at the clothes I was wearing: a gray two-piece suit. The skirt was a pencil skirt at calf length, with a fitted jacket and a white collar blouse worn over the lapels. The connection is that in this life now, I've always had a flair for cutting and styling hair, and not just my own but other people's. No one has taught me; it simply came natural to me.

It was the same Beethoven. He was so professional at very young age. It's because his soul remembered a past life, it came easy to him. The soul remembers everything. It's the same with children who are brilliant at different subjects far beyond their years: the soul has remembered. It has to do with their soul levels at the time. Although we are not supposed to remember any of our past lives, some of our past lives may seep through the veil that divides us.

I often remember my mother saying when I was growing up, "You know, they say that your life is all mapped out in front of you before your born." I've never forgotten that. It's true!

My Peggy

I awoke, raised my head from the pillow, and staggered into the kitchen to put the kettle on. *Here we go again. Another day I have to try and get through.* I entered the living room with my breakfast and sat down on the sofa. I took the medication for my condition. After a while I relaxed with my head on the pillow, I closed my eyes.

My whole body felt like I had been involved in a terrible car crash. There was not one part of my body that didn't hurt. I opened my eyes, and there was Peggy staring straight at me. I looked into her eyes, and I knew she realised that I was in pain.

She never leaves my side all day, and she knew today was a bad one. I don't know what I would do without her. I know my condition is getting worse. The pain is constant now, and there is very little respite these days. I increase the pain killers, and it helps for a little while. It's hard to get through another day. I try to keep a cheery outlook, but everything I do takes great effort: whether it's making a cup of tea or getting dressed, the simplest things are becoming harder and harder.

I try to occupy myself with my computer work. Anything that will take my mind off my physical condition. I am constantly meditating. Anything that will take me away from this constant torture.

I manage to get through another day. Soon it is night, and I can escape the pain. I fall asleep, and sometimes I escape to the spirit world, where I am normal; there is no pain there. My dreams can be pleasant. Then I awake. It is morning, and it starts all over again.

Daffodil

My family keeps me going, as well as the book I'm writing. It's so important to me that I finish this book. It's my whole reason for being here. It would be lovely to rise one morning and be free from pain, if only for a day.

I have to keep finding the strength within me to carry on with my life, no matter how hard it becomes. Although I'm ill, I have an awful lot to be thankful for: a loving husband who takes care of me, as well as the love and joy my sons, and grandchildren bring. I never lose hope that I might be better one day, that there may be a miracle at last.

I do know one thing: I am receiving all the love and help from the blessed angels and the spirit realm for my highest good. I know they hear me.

To change my blueprint for this life would be to interfere with my soul's progression, and that would only hold be back. I have chosen this life. I must live it.

I know one day that I will be free from pain. The purpose for the life I have lived will be successful. There are lots of people all over the world suffering on a daily basis. Some are worse than others; they perhaps wonder what's the point of living, if only to suffer for the rest of life

Each and every one of us has a reason for being here, whether or not we are suffering. We will evolve throughout our lives. If being ill is one of them, then this was accepted before our birth. We chose this life so that we may make the right choices, so that our souls may evolve. Throughout the book I know what I say may seem repetitive at times, but don't ever think you are being punished.

We have to find a way to live our life no matter how difficult it becomes. There's nothing wrong with having a good cry when it becomes too much. Others might think we are feeling sorry for ourselves, but if it does you good, go ahead and bawl all you want!

You will find that you feel much better for releasing all the stress that has built up over time. It's the same with men who have been conditioned to believe that it is weak for a man to cry. What nonsense! Crying releases all the pent-up emotion we feel inside. It's a natural form of release. Man is no different to a woman in that sense.

It's the same when men think it's weak to confide in a male friend, or for a woman to talk about her problems. Instead, they bottle it up, or turn to drinking to help with their problems. Or even worse, they suffer a nervous breakdown. Men shouldn't suffer in this way. There's always help. What could be better than pouring your heart out to your guardian angel? I swear to you that help will come if you have faith and trust in your guardian angel.

The best medicine in the world is laughter. It's a great healer and releases endorphins into the brain. You can get through your everyday life even when you're in pain. Especially a good old belly laugh – when tears come streaming down – makes you relax instantly and provides a feeling of well-being.

My Harry can still make me laugh, even after all these years; that's one of the reasons we get on so well.

There was a film made in 1998 with Robin Williams called *Patch Adams*. This was a true story about a medical student in America in the seventies who treated his patients illegally, using humour. Many of his patients were children. It turned out to be a very uplifting spiritual film. In the end, Patch proves this to the medical board. All his patients were quick to recover from illnesses and operations. It's a wonderful story, and I highly recommend it.

I once heard a story of a man who was sent home from hospital with cancer. He was told he hadn't long to live. He went out, bought lots of comedy films, and watched them over and over again till he laughed his way into remission from the cancer.

Then there was the twelve-year-old boy who had leukaemia. His favourite pastime was playing video games, especially the ones where he scored points by knocking out his opponent. One day his consultant was watching the boy from a distance playing the game, and he noticed how happy the boy became every time he scored a point.

He also saw an opportunity to include this in the boy's treatment. "Every time you score a point, I want you to imagine that you have killed off one of your bad blood cells." The boy went on scoring points; so much so that he went on to make a full recovery!

Know that you are being monitored by the angels and the spirit guides every day. You are never alone, even when you think you are. Your illness may be so that you find your spiritual path, the journey that you are supposed to be on, just like me.

How would it change your life if you were receiving communication from another world, from a divine source? What if you find out gradually that you are communicating with another world, seeing angels, and hearing messages and advice from your spirit guides?

Wouldn't that make more sense of your life, if you were receiving information from a higher intelligence – a divine intelligence? Wouldn't you be able to cope much better with your illness and all of your problems? All we have to do is ask for help! You don't have to be religious.

This was my prayer many years ago, when I was in agonizing pain when I was totally desperate. I laid in my bed one night, and it had all become too much for me to bear. "Please, please help me! If there is a God out there, please show me the way! Tell me what to do!"

After that night, my life slowly began to change. Synchronicities started happening. I was led to one thing after another in a spiritual way, as if someone was guiding me. I followed my intuition and listened to the guidance. This is where it has lead me today. This is why my life has made sense, the reason why I'm ill.

Surely this will help you, knowing that your pain is recognised by a divine intelligence. All they want to do is help you. Sometimes my illness seems forever. I wonder what's going to happen to me, but really, we are only here for a short spell.

One day it will be all over, and we can go home. We will be free from the trauma of life, happy and healthy once again. Pain and suffering does not last forever. Life is eternal in God's heaven. God's love for his children will never cease to be.

Bram

Bram was a beautiful, long-haired Alsatian dog who belonged to my best friend, Barbara Thompson. He was so handsome; his fur was the colour of shimmering shades of gold. He always looked as if he was smiling at you with a big grin on his face. The eyes said it all. He would stare at you with such mutual understanding; he had such a wise soul. Every time Barbara took Bram out for a walk; strangers would stop to say hello. He became quite a celebrity in his hometown. Everyone loved Bram.

Barbara rescued Bram when he was just a puppy. It was love at first sight for Barbara it was the happiest day of her life. From the very beginning they became inseparable. Barbara would only leave him for short periods at a time if she had to nip out to the shops. She rushed round to get back to her beloved Bram. They went everywhere together; the bond they shared was like no other. They became as one.

Bram was a special dog in the spiritual sense, although Barbara didn't realise it at the time. He was also her guide and teacher Bram came down to be with Barbara for a special reason: to teach and guide her.

Bram's passing opened up a whole new world, the spirit world, by the communication she received. The angels gave her step by step guide; all she had to do was listen and look for the signs. Barbara has always had an affinity with animals, especially with dogs and cats. She's achieved lots of charity work over the years, standing on street corners in the cold collecting for her charity on behalf of Dogs Trust, as well as rescuing her three-legged cat, Casper, when no one wanted him.

Then one day tragedy struck. Bram slowly started deteriorating, and soon passed away. Bram lived to be twelve years old – quite a good age for an Alsatian. However, it was to have a devastating effect on my dear friend

As soon as I heard the news, I knew Barbara would be in a terrible state. How could I help her to get through this terrible tragedy? Where did I start? After all, I knew how much Bram meant to her. He was her life, her reason for living.

Barbara reached the depths of despair; she didn't want to live anymore. "I want to be with my Bram. It's like a part of me has died, too." Everyone tried to rally round, but it didn't make any difference. Barbara would take to her bed and cry herself to sleep.

I spoke to my angels to ask for their help. What was to follow has truly been amazing. I wrote to Barbara regularly with a tarot reading from the angels, about twice a week. These readings from the angels eventually guided Barbara. It opened the door to her spiritual path.

She would have dreams about Bram. One day when Barbara was getting out of the shower, she heard a voice in her head distinctly say, "I can be in any puppy you want me to be." She knew it was Bram. By this time it had been several weeks since Bram's passing. I was trying to persuade Barbara into acquiring another rescue dog or puppy. I knew that with the help from the angels, this would be the only answer. Barbara has so much love to give to animals. It was like when I lost my beloved Bessie, and I had to find another little soul to love, another rescue puppy. I needed the love from an animal in my life; it made me feel complete. I can't imagine life without the love of a pet, whatever it is.

As time went by, Barbara tried to move on with her life, but some days it would become too much for her, and she would break down once again. Even though I would pass the messages on from the angels, which were always meaningful at the time, she would have her doubts.

What was materializing over the months of messages that Barbara received from the angels and in her dreams was proof of Bram's survival. He lived on, and the Angels and the spirit world were showing her step by step. All Barbara had to do was trust and have faith. That's all it takes. When we ask for help, we will receive it.

Eventually Barbara found a nine-month-old cross border collie. She named him Bronte. When Barbara introduced Bronte to her cat, Casper, they seemed to recognise one another with sniffs and licks. It was a tense time for Barbara. It was important that Bronte and Casper were compatible. Not only that, but Bronte seemed to know his way around the house. Even on their walks, he seemed to be familiar with everything.

At last Barbara slowly came to terms with the loss of Bram, especially knowing that Bronte is the reincarnation of Bram. What gives it away are the eyes. It wasn't noticeable at first, but slowly Bram has entered Bronte's soul. She remembers his words: "I can be in any puppy you want me to be."

Barbara was so stricken with grief at Bram's passing that she failed to realise all the wonderful things that were happening around her from the angels and the spirit world. Why Bram was taken away at this point in her life? By Bram's passing it opened up Barbara's spiritual path. After all the evidence and communication from above, it strengthened her belief that life carries on after death, even with our animals. She realised that angels did exist.

Bram wasn't just a dog – he was Barbara's guide and teacher. That was why they shared such a strong bond between them. The love they had between them will never die. Real love can never be destroyed.

Barbara wanted to share her story in order to help others who have been devastated after losing a beloved pet. All animals live on, just like humans. Look to the angels, ask for their help, and look out for the signs. They will never let you down.

Plants

Some consider animals a lower form of life. In fact, animals act with more integrity and greater consistency than humans. Plants, which some consider an even lower form of life, respond to people who love them far more than those who couldn't care less.

Some people might scoff at this, but why not try it? I have I have three lovely plants in my home that respond to affection. Prince Charles was ridiculed for his belief in that plants responded to touch and voice communication.

Tests were carried out by which plants were divided. One section was given all the attention, and the opposite section was just given water. Although the second group of plants were still alive, they did not grow and flourish like the plants that were given all the love and attention. In a way, it's very much like raising our children. If they are given love, attention, and the nourishment needed as they grow. It will bring out the best in them.

We have to look after the rainforests. Many of the trees and plants have healing properties that are used for medication worldwide. Cannabis has so many beneficial properties, especially in reducing chronic pain. Yet man is responsible for tampering with this beneficial plant, mixing it with other plants, making deadly hybrids, and damaging the human body in the process.

Neale Donald Walsch, in his book *Conversations with God, Book Three,* speaks of the beneficial benefits of Cannabis.

Do you have any idea how many trees it takes just to supply your world with daily newspapers, to say nothing of paper cups, carry-out cartons and paper towels? Not one tree would have to be cut down if cannabis-hemp was used instead. Help saving the rain forest!!

Hemp can be grown inexpensively and harvested easily, and not only used for paper, but the strongest rope, and the longest lasting clothing: and even some of the most effective medicines the planet can provide.

It has so many wonderful uses, that there is a huge lobby working against it.

Too many would lose financial gain to allow the world to turn to this simple plant; which can be grown almost anywhere.

This is just one example of how greed replaces common sense in the conduct of human affairs.

When I was young in the sixties, drugs were rife, yet I could never understand why anyone would want to take drugs. I was the opposite – I wouldn't take an aspirin for an headache. I exercised three times a week and had a go at yoga, although I wasn't very good at it. However, I felt that the stretching it involved did me the power of good. I tried to eat healthy foods and took vitamins. I looked after my body.

At this present time I'm in the process of discussing cannabis with the consultant at the hospital to prescribe Cannabinoids for my pain relief.

Cannabis has been prescribed for patients with multiple sclerosis, which has been more successful than any other pain relief. I believe cannabis should be made legal for the right reasons. If cannabis works for my pain relief; then I should be able to reduce some of my other drug treatments, which some I've become immune to. Not only that, but the NHS would save millions of pounds a year. However, that would only happen in an ideal world, because like everything else (such as alcohol), it would be open to abuse.

We all have to become responsible human beings. That also goes for teenage children in schools who have easy access to cannabis. They should be taught the benefits when used in medication, as well as the dangers of this drug. People also add toxic chemicals to enhance the drug, which can be deadly in long-term use.

One day my pain was so intense that I bought some cannabis off the streets. I was fed up with the pain. I didn't want to smoke it, so I tried it in some chocolate brownies. That was my intention, to put it into my cooking. I had the most terrible experience! This is a warning to you all out there. If you have a healthy body, then look after it and treat it with respect.

In the end the medical profession turned me down for cannabis treatment. They said there had been no proof in the case of rheumatoid arthritis. I didn't believe them.

Knowing

The angels say that when we need help, we should look for the signs. In my office on the windowsill sits a small clock that is fairly secure. When I walked into the room a couple of days ago, the clock was on the floor next to my computer chair. I picked it up and checked that the window wasn't opened. I didn't give it much thought and was thankful that it wasn't broken.

A couple of days later, laid across my desk was a birthday card that had fallen off the shelf above my computer. This card was an old birthday card; I had kept on my shelf for about four years because it had special meaning for me at the time. My friend Wendy chose the card because it had a bunch of daffodils on the front of it. "I thought this would inspire you with your book, with you calling it *Daffodil*."

This made me think of the clock. Why would it be on the floor, and why did the card fall onto my desk? Was there a message for me here about timing and daffodils? Were the angels giving me a message, telling me to get on with it? There is no such thing as coincidence!

This is what happens when the angels and spirit world want our attention. They will put obstacles in our way to grab our attention. We of course look for a logical reasons, which is normal, but that is not always the case.

'Only love and peace can save our planet –
If we all live together in peace and harmony'

By Eileen Richmond

Miracles

Several weeks ago, Harry and I decided to decorate the living room. "How can you help in your state?" he asked.

"Well, if I sit on a chair and paint the bottom of the wall, you can paint the top. I'll just take my time, nice and steady. Besides, it will give me something to do." Reluctantly Harry agreed. We also managed to decorate the hall.

After a couple of weeks of decorating, one morning I put the kettle on. When I tried to lift the kettle off the stand, I yelled out in pain. The pain shot through my shoulder and upper arm, it was excruciating. I couldn't believe it. Whilst decorating I hadn't felt any pain or strain at all. In fact, I felt good within myself to have managed to do a job! I couldn't even brush my hair; it was so difficult to dress myself. I refused to believe it was anything to do with the decorating.

After a week there had been no improvement, so I went to see my doctor. After examining my shoulder, he said, "I'm afraid you have torn the muscles that control the movement of your upper arm when you try to raise it up or down, and when you try to move your arm outwards."

"Oh no! What does this mean?"
"I'm sending you to see a specialist. You'll probably have to have MRI scans. And an operation and then months of physiotherapy."

"Is there a chance that my shoulder will heal by itself?"

"I'm afraid not. Torn muscles don't heal by themselves."

I tried to hold back the tears. *Not again,* I thought. Another operation followed by months of physio. I came away devastated. I went to see the specialist, who told me the same story: torn muscles don't heal by themselves.

I prayed to my angels to help me once again. "Please, Archangel Raphael, please help me to heal."

It took several weeks, but there has been a 98 per cent improvement!

Rheumatoid arthritis doesn't just affect the bones; it also affects the muscles, ligaments, and surrounding tissues. The repetitive movement of painting must have caused the muscles to tear, but I never felt a thing. I won't be doing anymore decorating!

The angels had healed me once again! Then I asked myself, "Why is it that other parts of my weary body haven't been healed when I have asked for help?" Some things are meant to be, and others are not. To be completely healed would interfere with my blueprint for this life. I'm so grateful to have the angels in my life. How would I ever get through all the difficulties that have happened to me, if not for the angels?

You can always rely on your angels to help you through difficult times in your life. Whether it is illness, mental problems, problem teenage children, bullying at school, or any problem at all, the angels are there to help and guide you. It is your birthright. All you have to do is pray to the angels for what you want for your highest good, either for yourself or for others.

For instance, maybe you are a married couple or partners having difficulties with each other You're arguing between yourselves about who is in right or wrong, and it gets out of hand. Here's what you can do.

Find a quiet place to relax and clear your mind. Speak to your guardian angel about all of your troubles. Ask your guardian angel to have a word with your husband's or wife's guardian angel, to help resolve any issues you have between you. While you are doing this, see in your mind's eye that the issue has been taken care of and resolved already.

Daffodil

Wait and see what happens in the next few days or weeks. Keep a journal. It may be that you are meant to stay together, or maybe not. Whatever the outcome, know that your angels have your best interest at heart, and they will guide you accordingly. All you have to do is have faith and trust.

Joanne

When my son Wayne finally divorced from Joan, my first daughter-in-law, she and I maintained a good relationship. We have continued to do so to this very day.

Eventually I met Wayne's new partner, Joanne. We also seem to get along very well. As our relationship started to develop, I noticed that Joanne became interested in angels. When we were discussing angels one day, she told me that her sister Haley was a big believer in angels, so I didn't feel self-conscious about telling her about the experiences that I'd had.

Joanne had to have some medical investigations at the hospital along with a colonoscopy. She was apprehensive about it, I advised her, "On the day of your appointment, I will send in the angels to help you. All I want you to do is concentrate on your breathing. Keep listening to the sounds of your breath. The more you do this the better; it stops you from thinking."

I was talking to her on the phone several days after; curious to know if anything had happened. She told me that as she was trying to concentrate on her breathing, it wasn't always easy to do. Joanne told me that she felt pressure on the top of her head as if someone was pressing down, but it felt like it was inside of her head. This is what I expected. The angels were healing Joanne's spirit body as well as the physical body.

Then at one point she felt that she was laid at the side of her body, out of her body, all the while conscious of what was happening and aware of her surroundings. I didn't tell her what to expect – she told me! I was simply grateful that the angels and guides had helped Joanne.

This is typical of the angels: whenever I ask for assistance, I will feel the pressure and tingling on the top of my head. Why don't you try asking for help when you need it, especially if you're going to have an operation? Always concentrate on your breathing when you are in the operating room or in the dentist chair. The concentration on your breathing will also stop you thinking about what's happening to you at that moment.

Joanne also told me of a dream she'd had of her grandmother. She's had the same dream several times. "I dreamt I was at my gran's house. I'm in the hallway, and hung on the wall is a telephone underneath some coats. But my Gran didn't have a telephone."

Obviously her grandmother was trying to communicate with her; that was why she was shown the telephone. "Next time you have this dream," I told her, "try to pick up the phone."

Joanne sat in her bathroom one day when Archie, her spaniel, followed her. He was looking at Joanne's face and then Archie suddenly looked to the wall. He continued to stare at the wall, barking all the while. Joanne said it was really spooky. I felt that this was her grandmother trying to make contact with her. She also told her sister Haley, who confirmed she also thought it was their grandmother.

I have a strong feeling that her grandmother is trying to tell Joanne; that life goes on and that there's nothing to be frightened of. Her gran is happy in her new life and wants Joanne to know it. She probably wants Joanne to seek out a medium so that she can prove to her of her survival. We shall see.

Finding God

One day I was reading from an angel leaflet that recommended a trilogy of books by Neale Donald Walsch. It was the title of the book that caught my eye first: *Conversations with God*. I thought this sounded interesting, with a bit of cynicism thrown in. It was the fact that I had discovered it through my angels that made me think, *I'd best see what God has to say.*

I began to read the first book, I began to find it very challenging. I kept going back over the pages trying to take it all in, thinking, *Well, this has thrown a spanner into the works.* I felt so frustrated that I wanted to cry. Nevertheless, I knew I had to carry on whether I wanted to or not. Not only that, but I had to send for books two and three.

I knew I had to read all three books. I had to get to the bottom of this and leave no stone unturned. After reading all three books. I still didn't feel confident enough to take it all in. It left me depressed, outraged, happy, and frustrated – a multitude of mixed emotions.

Finally I read each book three times over. I defy any person who has read these books once' to say that he or she understood it straight from the start – unless the person remembers who he or she is. That's the whole point of the books, the whole point of your life: to remember who you are and where you come from?

What struck me most, as I finally started to understand and absorb all three books, was the fact that it goes back to the very beginning, when God created the world from nothing.

This information in the book has nothing to do with the Bible; it is straight from God himself. No matter how you perceive God, God communicated with Neale Donald Walsch through words, thoughts, feelings, images, and a knowing. I have done the same, and so have many other authors on this planet.

Too many myths and lies are written in God's name. I strongly recommend that you read this trilogy of books, *Conversations with God* by Neale Donald Walsch. I believe that this man has been chosen by God to tell the story to humanity.

The beauty about it is my own explanation for life and why we are all here. It came from my soul, from feelings. I had a deeper knowledge inside me, and there was all the work and research that I put in over the years. It has been preparation for what was to come. This is me, remembering myself. It comes from the soul, a knowing. We all share this knowledge; it's a matter of finding it.

I believe that God and the angels want me to pass this on in layman's language so that every man, woman, and child can understand.

There are more angels appearing on our planet as we approach 2012. This is not because the world is going to end, but because there will be great changes taking place all over this planet. We have to sit up and listen. Be willing to have an open mind, and open up your hearts. Give God a chance.

The Beginning

The next pages are extracts from the book *Messages from Margaret* by Gerry Gavin. After reading this book, I felt it important to include it. This is my personal paraphrasing, with the author's kind permission.

Margaret is an angel who spoke to Gerry with information as to what really happened in the beginning, when the world first began. Many of us were taught that in the beginning, there was only darkness, and that the creator gave birth to the universe. God thought of which he desired to create, and then there were the words "Let there be light." This is a myth that has been presupposed for hundreds of years.

In the beginning there existed only thought, and that thought existed in the form of pure and omnipresent light, which is called the origin of positive magnetic charge. This charge existed in bliss and in a state of pure consciousness, but it wanted to share its consciousness, which was the beginning of the power of conscious thought.

But to expand, the creator realised that he would have to set this energy in motion, and there would be a need for a polar opposite – a negative charge that would allow for the creation of matter and antimatter, finite particles of creation that would come to be called cells and atoms.

The creator contracted its energy into a small, dense form, creating the first fusion. The resulting explosion of energy, which some have come to call the big bang, gave way to matter and antimatter, positive and negative charges, and darkness and light.

All of the particles, however different, were interconnected to the creator and were a part of its essence. There were new beings that sprang from the creator's original thought, and they began the process of what has now come to be known as creation.

The first of these beings were the angels. Some were created of the positive matter, and some of negative; some were beings of light, and others could not connect to the light. These angels contained the consciousness of the creator and continued to create, in concert with the thought of the creator, an entire universe. They sought the perfect balance of all things light and all things dark, positive and negative in charge. The magnetic resonance of these things allows the universe to be held in place by the pull of these polar opposites.

The creatures of the day and night were created and so existed; until humankind found fire and realised that its light and warmth would allow them to inhabit the night in a waking state.

We are at the end of another age of darkness, and humankind is about to discover another form of light that will change the face of the future. All that exists is therefore interconnected to the creator, the originator of the thought that gave birth to the creation, following the creation of the angels.

The creator shared with the angels the plan for the rest of the universe, and the angels in turn continued the process and gave birth to the next level: the spirits that would come to inhabit all with what would follow. We are human beings, the whole spirit, the soul, the higher self.

We are connected to each other and to the creator by the strands of what we have come to call DNA. The angel that created you also aided in the creation of thousands upon thousands of other humans, plants, stones, and creatures that share a common creative thread with us.

Our connection with the angel is what establishes it as our protector or guardian angel. We are a part of that angel's consciousness, just as we are a part of the consciousness of the creator. All beings share those thoughts in a universal or collective consciousness. Just as there is no snowflake that is exactly like another, so are our souls. Part of what makes us so unique is our ability to continue to reinvent ourselves through our own creative thoughts.

Most cultures will agree that the best way for a story or a truth to be relayed is through one who is an eyewitness to that story or truth. Angels were and are the eyewitnesses of creation and all that followed.

Angels do not ascribe to judgment about how history or humankind has evolved. Rather, they are witness to the true sense of the word. The angels are a part of us, and we are a part of the angels. Together we can partner with the creator into an entirely new world of creation.

We were told the story of Adam and Eve, and that these were the first two human beings born on this planet. But Angel Margaret states the original human spirits were not the biblical Adam and Eve.

The story that revolves around them was created to give humankind a background into the understanding that there were many who came from the direct design of the creator but who were all interconnected. There were many souls that were created at the time of the big bang, and these original souls knew everything of the creator and basked in the light of its pure love. But they were also aware of the energies of darkness.

You cannot create density with light alone. There must be spaces of darkness as well. There must be matter, and there must be antimatter. There must be a positive and a negative charge for there to be the electricity that sparks something to experience life. It is what holds everything together.

Angel Margaret says, "Please do not interpret my use of the word darkness as meaning evil. I speak of darkness merely as absence of light, and light might also be interpreted as complete understanding."

As I mentioned earlier; read the book for greater understanding – it could change your life! I highly recommend this book by Gerry Gavin. You can also contact Gerry by emailing him at gerry@gerrygavin.com.

Second Version

I have left it up to you to come to your own conclusion as to what happened in the beginning. In the beginning, some say that Adam and Eve were the first two people on earth, the father and the mother of the whole human experience. The act of Adam and Eve was not original sin – in truth it was the first blessing. We should thank them from the bottom of our hearts for being the first to make a "wrong" choice, or else this world would not exist.

Adam and Eve produced the possibility of making any choices at all! Also, in our mythology we have made Eve the temptress, the bad one who ate of the fruit and invited Adam to join her. This mythological setup has allowed us to make women man's "downfall" ever since, resulting in all manner of warped realities and confusion, not to mention distorted sexual views.

In the very beginning nothing existed. God wanted to experience life itself, and the only way this could be achieved was to divide parts of himself into his spirit children, his offspring, to experience life on earth. In that way God could live through every one of us, and we in him.

The part that I found difficult to understand was that if God could only experience life through each and every one of us, and he wanted us to know everything, then we would have to experience everything. For example, everything has its opposite, like alpha and omega.

That's how it is with life. If you lead a life where you were continually happy, how would you know the difference? You would have to experience it by living an unhappy life at some point. It's the only way we can learn.

At one time in one of your lives, if you were born of white race, sooner or later you would then want to experience what it's like to be of black race.

We have to experience both opposites so that we can learn. That's why we were given free will: so that we could choose, hopefully making all the right choices in our lives. God wanted to know all of it, for us to know all of it. We are all of it. We are all one source. The point is how will we create ourselves in our lifetime? What choices will we make? Who do we want to be? Will we remember who we truly are?

We have all been both good and bad, fat and thin, weak and strong, short and tall. Do you get the picture? We've come down to experience it all. We were born out of pure love; we are all part of God, and there is no separation. We were made from pure love, and we are all born perfect in the spiritual sense. Each and every one of us is a spark from God. We are God, because God made it that way.

Do you see how both the stories interconnect with one another? Is this one of the many lies that was told in the Bible, when in fact Adam and Eve never existed??

***

The third and fourth planets are more intelligent, more advanced in technology. They are a highly spiritual, enlightened race. Some of these evolved species are living on our planet, trying to help with our technology, but most of all trying to help save planet earth.

They see that we are destroying the earth, the animal kingdom, the rainforest. Man is still killing his own species; wars still exist. This is because we haven't the intelligence worldwide to sit down and resolve the issues that need to be resolved in a peaceful way. This is how it was in the beginning: a peaceful planet.

Once women ruled the world, and the family environment was governed by the matriarch. Issues were resolved around the table with the elders; making it fair for everyone. People didn't think they were better than the next person. Everyone showed love and respect for one another, and everyone had equal rights; there was no racial discrimination. Fear did not exist in the way it does today.

We live in a very primitive world where man prefers to live in a material world. Man's goal is to reach for power and success no matter at what cost. He no longer wants to share the fruits of life with his fellow man. In the beginning, God provided enough for all, but man became greedy, wanting more and more. You have only to look at the state the world is in now to realise this.

Once we all lived in a society that was caring, where humans cared for each other. We were a far more intelligent race, and no one had to go hungry; there was enough for everyone. Murder, rape, and torture were unheard of. We were once this highly intelligent spiritual race in Atlantis.

There are thousands of other planets in our universe. Some of us are arrogant enough to think that we are the only intelligent planet in the universe. We think we are an advanced race along with our technology.

On a scale of ten, we score about a three. Some of the other planets are more advanced, and they can even control the weather. The perfect crop circles that are seen everywhere on this planet are other planets telling us that we are not alone, or maybe it's a wake-up call. Still the scientists refuse to believe, always assuming they know better.

Take a look at our world now. A third of the humans are without food and water and the basic needs. Our young children are killing each other. Wars are never ending, mostly in the name of religion.

There is the financial decline of the world's economy – while the big bosses at the top continue to award themselves with massive bonuses. Money is spent on nuclear weapons all around the world. China is one of the world's biggest polluters; it is also becoming one of the richest by sacrificing its natural environment. China is the most materialistic country in the world. And to top it all, we are now tampering with life itself by experimenting with cloning.

How primitive our planet has become, where man still kills his own species. How can that be progress? Why should there be a need for any nation to build nuclear weapons? Why should there be wars in the first place, when we all come from the same source, God? By killing others, we are killing ourselves.

Till this is realised, we can never evolve as a race. There have been some changes taking place across the globe – changes for the better – but we still have a heck of away to go! We are receiving help from a higher source trying to help our planet before it's too late. Its species are more intelligent and evolved than ours; they are far more spiritually advanced.

We all have to do our best to help the planet and the human race to become more spiritual. We must show love and respect for one another, no matter what race, colour, or gender. We have to learn to respect Mother Nature all over again. We have to stop sacrificing the natural environment.

I believe our next generation will be our salvation and will save our sick planet. In some parts of the world, more young people are becoming spiritual. It has increased already since the beginning of the eighties. Groups and organizations have been working hard to improve the planet's situation. Some of these souls born at this time may not know that they were chosen to do this before they were born. This was their mission in life, to help the planet. Are you one of them? A special soul, come down to help our planet?

Why not ask your angels or spirit guide? They may answer you through words, music, or dreams. Sometimes when our guardian angels want to contact us; a song that we know will pop into our heads. We may not even like the tune; it may keep repeating itself. However, listen to the words because there could be a message in it for you. Or you may want to use a pendulum, giving you a straight yes or no. Reiki can also open you up to the spirit world.

In my first initiation to Reiki, I found myself with a dolphin on a boat. It was a warm, sunny day, and I was happy tickling the dolphin's belly while it laid on its back looking up at me. It seemed to be smiling at me. Many people have said that at the first initiation of Reiki, they experience wonderful things happening. One lady told me she once saw a giant angel come towards her and wrap its wings around her, giving her great comfort.

The Planet

The soil is running out, and so are the nutrients. When a crop of potatoes is picked from the field, or any vegetables for that matter, that part of land has to regenerate naturally for the next season, in order to be ready for the next crop of vegetation. But the powers that be demand fast turnover for the sake of making more money.

It's all down to greed. Scientists have had to invent chemicals to put into the ground to make up for this. Eventually it will have an effect on the consumer, our physical bodies, and we will begin to suffer. Have you older readers noticed how vegetables don't taste the way they used to, compared to fifty years ago? This is especially true for the potato.

People were talking about 2012, saying that the world would end, Let me assure you now that the world will never end, but it is going to change dramatically. We are heading for great changes; the world will not be as we once knew it. It will progress to a far better world. It has to, if it's to survive.

This will take years, but it's up to us. Before the world reaches this stage, it will get worse before it gets better. There will be storms, floods, fires, droughts, and terrible disasters occurring all over the globe. There will be a great purging of this earth.

People will look at the world in a different way. They will see the devastation that man has caused, the pollution, the damage to the animal kingdom – man's cruelty. Man will come to realize the world isn't what it once was. This is where we are heading. It is only then that man will turn towards God Almighty, our father, and ask for his help.

The light workers already know what is taking place all over the world; they are here to help humanity in this great magnitude of change.

Daffodil

The angels will come here in droves to help humanity. Eventually humanity will realise that what is taking place in the world is for the best.

It will be a golden age, where man will begin all over again. We will build a better world where only peace and love exist, and where the importance of family life will reign even greater. Human life will become sacred once again.

All humanity will be responsible for making this happen. Man's greed and power will not exist. There will be no need for wars or starvation. There will be enough for everyone man will come to realise, that there is only one God and one religion that does not separate one being from another.

Every one of us belongs to one another. Men and women will become equal.

Love means the opposite of fear. Once men took pride, they were happy to protect their families and children, and to hunt for their survival. They were proud of their physical prowess and strengths. Eventually man was responsible for introducing fear into the world. Fear means "false evidence appearing real". That began our downfall: the failure for our world to survive.

Instead of the old days, where decisions were made to resolve all problems through love and respect for his fellow man, threats and fear took priority. The world has never been the same since. We've been on the decline ever since fear was introduced.

Nations are still fighting one another; wars still exist after all this time. Our young fight and kill one another. How can this world ever evolve? It's no good blaming the children – it's what they have learned from their elders. They lack the wise ones that once governed our peaceful nations, the matriarchs, the peacemakers.

Television has become the camp of our culture. How many people these days pick up a non-fiction book, a book about real life with, useful knowledge that can be passed on down to the family? People have spiritual experiences that can benefit others, especially if one has lost a loved one.

We can learn so much from one another, from other people's experiences of life. We have to live in the real world, **instead of going along with the rest of the world.**

How many of you ask yourselves, "Why am I here?" If you don't, then you should. What's the reason for your life? Have things happened to you in the past – experiences that you thought were your imagination? Don't you feel inspired? Don't you want to know more? I tell you this: I found it very exciting, it gave purpose and meaning to my life.

I'm so happy I chose this path. That's why I want to share it with you. I want you to find your purpose and real meaning, the reason why you are here. Every single human being has a purpose on this planet. There's not one of you that can escape the eyes of God. Even for souls who have lost their way in life and have made the wrong choices, God knows them personally and loves them as equals.

Now, doesn't that give you some idea about how great and powerful God is? And this is coming from me, the one who wasn't sure about God before I started this book. As I sit at my computer writing all this information down for you. I know the spirit guides are by my side, helping me. I feel so happy and very humble.

I always seem to know the answer when I have any doubts about this project. Sometimes I wondered why it has taken me so long to write this book. Why all the gaps in between? There were weeks and months when I had nothing to do, it just seemed like wasted time. Then suddenly I'm on with my book, and the information comes rolling in. I can't stop! It can't be writers block, because it's not a novel. It's real.

It's like I have had to wait. I, too, have had to learn and experience whatever the subject was about before I could write about it. Neale Donald Walsch also experienced the waiting and the gaps in between, waiting for more information to come through.

How many of you do the same thing day in day out? Where does it get you? Are you satisfied with your life? Can you honestly say that you are happy? Do you feel like something's missing? This can't be all there is.

Most people think, "If only I had more money, or I could win the lottery. It will solve all my problems. If I could only find the right partner, or the right job. Turn to God. Ask your angels and the spirit world to help you find your purpose for this life. I promise you that with pure determination, that answers will come. You must have faith and trust always. God bless.

Take a look around the world right now. Are you happy and content with the world in which you live? Does it affect you when the media shows you harrowing pictures of starving people with no basic needs, while your sit having your evening meal? What about another suicide bomber blowing himself up, killing innocent women and children? Another soldier has been killed, or some innocent victim is murdered. Our children killing one another. Then there's the drug and booze culture, the gang culture,

Take heed, my friend. This could be the reason why you are here, to make that difference. Listen to your guides, your angels, and God.

Do you feel safe living in a society such as this? Is this what you want for your children? You were born on this earth to find out who you are, and to help make a difference. This is not who we are!

This is not how it should to be. I can't emphasise enough what a wonderful, powerful human being you are, if only you knew it. Your soul holds all the knowledge with all the lives you had before this life, nothing is ever lost.

You only have to look at a newborn baby to see its pure perfection before it enters the illusion of this new life. It is innocent, a brand-new beginning, only this time it is not all-knowing. That is why it's here: to find out whom he / she is by starting all over again.

We have been taught by our parents, teachers, historians, and politicians, and particularly the religious scriptures, regarding the rights and wrongs and their ideas of the world. **And that's just it – these are someone else's thoughts**, *not yours.* Some of us have accepted what we have been taught by our elders as gospel. We have to go deep into our consciousness and examine everything that confronts us, when it comes to making decisions about right and wrong values.

It may seem frowned upon not to believe what our parents and teachers taught us. We don't want to render them wrong. They probably thought they had been taught the truth, and they felt it disrespectful to think otherwise; so they went along with it, teaching the falsehoods to future generations.

Ideas form the shape of your thoughts and create the substance of who you are. If your values serve you, hold on to them, argue for them, and fight to defend them; be true to yourself. If there is such a thing as sin, this would be it: **to allow yourself to become who you are because of the experience of others.**

Is this the reason I could never go along with my father about the Catholic religion, or any religion? His thoughts were becoming my thoughts, and inside it didn't make me happy. It wasn't the way I thought, and it didn't make sense to me.

But even then, I knew there must be something else other than religion. This was an example of me being adamant, rebelling, and being true to myself. I was creating myself; building my character. I'm glad I did this because I found out who I was. I also found my holy father in the end, my best friend, my confidante: God.

We have to make a start by making the world a better place. Time is running out, and the world cannot carry on the way it is with starvation, wars, drugs, greed, and pollution.

Cross Breeding

The liger – now man is interfering with nature and God's creations. They are interbreeding the lion with the tiger and calling it the liger. It can grow so big that it cannot stand. It is prone to its hips breaking because it is too top heavy. Also, it is prone to deafness, blindness, and numerous other ailments, along with a short life expectancy. Is there any wonder!

This breaks my heart. How cruel! What good can come from this? We let these poor animals suffer. This would never happen in the wild, only in captivity. This is also happening with the zebra being cross bred with the horse, and the whale being cross bred with dolphin. It all sounds bazaar to me. Why does man continue this cruelty?

If this is not natural, then it shouldn't be happening. Science shouldn't be interfering with God's wonderful creations. Let's make a stance together. This is not what we want for our world; this is not who we are. Instead of turning a blind eye, let's do something about it as a collective conscience.

It's only a matter of time before man tries to clone the first human being. It has to stop! This is not a world that God intended. People will say, "Well, why doesn't God do something about it, then?" God can only look down on this planet and observe his children. God cannot intervene. The idea was for us all to create a heaven upon the earth. What a joke – it's hardly that, or anywhere near.

A New Beginning

Let's discuss our children, for they are our future. Instead of starting with the three Rs in school, let's teach our children the importance of human life, and how important we all are to God. We all come from one the God, and there is no discrimination in heaven. We are all the same, and we should treat everyone with love, respect, and kindness. There is no difference between the colours of the skin – we are all the same, all brothers and sisters. We are on this planet for the advancement of the soul, to become enlightened.

We have to teach children honesty, responsibility, and integrity from a very early age. We have to build the right foundation for our children as early as possible, so that they grow into responsible human beings with love, compassion, and respect, and so that they teach their children.

We should teach them to respect the environment, the plant life, the animal kingdom, and all living things.

It's no good that Molly is at the top of her class with her reading, if during playtime she bullies the new Asian girl in the playground because her parents are racist. She doesn't know difference. It doesn't matter that Johnny came top in maths when he disrespects an old couple in the street.

It's got to start with the parents and the school's curriculum. What's the point in teaching a child to become academic if she has no values, no morals, no respect, and no integrity? What kind of an adult is she going to become when she matures?

Future generations are going to pass it on to the next generation, so that it continues and becomes a vicious circle. Don't you wish you could change all this? I know I do.

Don't you think a children's meditation session with trained professionals would be a wonderful idea to bring into the school's curriculum, starting with the infant and primary school? Try to imagine all these little children sitting on the floor in front of their teacher, just like when she's reading them a story.

They are told how to breathe and relax properly. In between; they learn thoughtful messages on how to love and to respect friends, parents, and teachers. They can also learn to appreciate all living things which God created.

Can you imagine what a calming effect this would have on a nervous child who comes from a broken home and feels insecure? Even if the session lasted for only fifteen minutes, I'm sure there would be significant improvement all round.

I'm sure this would reduce the bullying culture in schools. The main thing is to teach these children as young as possible so that it becomes second nature. They will grow up into more confident, responsible human beings.

It would be wonderful if the parents of these children were to be more involved, but this is not always the case. Some of the parents don't know how to raise their children, especially if they were never taught the fundamentals themselves.

A school near where I live did a trial for children on meditation classes many years ago. I thought at the time it was a good idea from the ages of ten upwards. Some of these children experienced another world, which must have been heaven.

They spoke of angels and the feeling of being loved. All the children that took part in the meditation session had one thing in common: a look of calmness and serenity. Some of the children improved with their school work. They all seemed happy and stable.

Now let's take a look at the other end of the spectrum. These same children were sent home from school. Their parents allow them to watch violence and play awful video games. They are exposed to bad language and pornography. Some of these children drink alcohol.

It's normal for the parents to abuse one another in front of their children, not caring what effect this may have on them in the future. No wonder our culture has taken a downfall. I know in which world I would prefer to raise our children. To have a stable relationship with their parents, teachers, and friends.

When my four sons were small and all under school age, there had to be some level of discipline. I was getting on a bus on my own, with my four children. It was quite a struggle, as you can imagine, with the twins being in a pushchair at the time. The two little ones were not much older. However, it was one of the proudest days of my life.

Before we had set off on our journey, I had told them to be good. As we settled in our seats at the back of the bus near the platform, the four of them were in a line on the double seat; I sat on the opposite side, nervously watching them in case they misbehaved. I had nothing to fear – they were so well behaved and did not make a sound. They simply had cheeky grins. As people started to get off at various stops, I received nothing but compliments. "What well-behaved children!" "How nicely dressed they are." "They're a credit to ya, luv! As I write this memory, I can see it so clearly, and it brings tears to my eyes.

The moral of this story is that I must have been doing something right in the way I raised my children, for people to be so kind with their remarks. I'm not saying I was the perfect parent – far from it. But no one had shown me how to be a good one, especially my own parents.

Was it the fact that I vowed I would never bring a child up in the way I was raised? My own experiences as a child taught me a better way of raising my children. If I look back, my only regret would be that I wished I had shown my children more love and given them more hugs. This is so important when children are growing up. I know as a child I craved for my mother's love.

Daffodil

No one is perfect. We all make mistakes – we wouldn't be here otherwise. I believe that we learn from our parents as to how we will raise our children, whether it is good or bad. Remember we chose our parents for the lessons we had to learn in this lifetime.

That's why we should never blame our parents, and we should never judge either. If you really think about it, it makes sense. You are not born into this world as a victim. You are here to learn.

We Can All Take Part

If every one of us on this planet was to change our thoughts from negative to positive; by doing one good thing on the same day; sending it out to the universal law of attraction for our fellow man, there would be a massive shift in the world's collective consciousness; all of that happening at the same time on this earth would work towards good.

That is why when disasters happen in the world and people offer prayers to help the victims, it can be so powerful. The more people who pray, the more powerful we become together

Once earth was a wonderful place to live. It still can be – we all have to come together to make a better future. God has been given a bad name through the false teachings of our elders. Many things were written in the Bible about Jesus of Nazareth that simply isn't true.

The writers of the New Testament never met or saw Jesus in their lifetimes. They lived many years after Jesus left the earth. The ones who wrote the Bible were great believers and historians, and they took the stories that had been passed down to them until finally the Bible was created.

Not everything was included in the final documentation. There were certain individuals within these churches or enclaves who dictated what part of the Jesus story was going to be told. This process of selecting and editing continued till the Bible was published.

God is our friend, our teacher, and the creator of all things. God is all that is good. Why was I brought up to fear God? Why did I feel like a bad person for not attending church, disappointing my father in the process? Deep in my heart, I knew that it shouldn't be this way. I didn't have to fear God at all – I simply had to listen to my heart. Was I remembering who I truly was?

I was supposed to go confession the night before we buried my father; it was a Requiem Mass. I remember being in church with my sister and my mother. I had the strongest feeling that all this pomp and ceremony wasn't for me. I told my mother and sister that I didn't want to go to confession and Holy Communion. I truly loved my father, but I would have felt like a hypocrite if I had followed the rules of the Catholic Church then. It didn't mean anything to me at the time.

My mind was full of mixed emotions. Was I a bad person for not going to confession and Holy Communion? After all, it would have been my father's wish. My sister said afterwards that she respected my feelings.

I tried to look for God a year after the death of my father by attending midnight mass on Christmas Eve, looking for answers. I still couldn't accept the death of my father. I wanted to find out whether there was a God; I wanted to know the meaning of life.

I needed answers. I found no comfort, just an emptiness and a deep frustration inside me. There had to be something greater – I just knew there was. There must be answers somewhere. I had to find out, and I made this my mission.

The irony is that God doesn't want your worship. He does not need your obedience, and it is not necessary for you to serve him. These are the behaviours of the church, who demanded it, as well as the monarchs who were egomaniacal and insecure, introducing fear into the church. This is never what God intended. I am here to vindicate my friend, my teacher, my creator, my real father.

God does not punish; he observes us all through our lives past, present, and future. When bad things happen in the world, people keep saying, "Well, if there is a God, why didn't he do something about it?" Because to do so would interfere with our souls' progress. The only time that God will intervene is if it's not our time to die. There's a great plan for every single one of us, as I mentioned earlier.

God says we have nothing to learn in this life because the soul already knows all. We only have to remember who we are and make our choices about who we really want to be. That's why we have no memory of our past lives: so that we begin all over again without the knowledge.

What does God look like? He has no shape or form. He could adopt a form or shape that we would understand, but that would be impossible. People would assume that what they saw is the one and only form of God, rather than one of many. God is omnipresent and is everywhere. God can appear in any shape or form – whatever is right for you at the time. If you had an idea what God might look like, then that's how God will appear to you.

I once met a girl at the spiritual church. There were whispers going around that she had actually seen Jesus Christ when she was in her bathroom one day. His image was portrayed across the bathroom tiles. I was intrigued to know more. I asked her, "But how did you know it was God?"

She looked at me in all sincerity as she put her hand to her heart and said, "I just knew it was him."

I had no reason not to believe her. You are all capable of greater things – you have to be, for God made you in the image and likeness of himself. That's why we are a part of God. There is nothing that separates us from God; that's why God does not punish or sit in judgment. God would be punishing and judging himself. God is made of pure love and is all–knowing. We are all a part of this grand scheme – every single one of us. The thing is you do not know who you are. You think you are a great deal less...

Where do you think this belief stems from? You thought your parents were right – after all, they were your role models and the ones who loved you. It was your parents who told you that love is conditional. You have forgotten what it's like to be loved without condition. Your parents didn't know any better – they were told that by their parents, and so on.

The first thing that comes to mind is that if we are all perfect, what about the despots and serial murderers? What about the terrible crimes that have been committed over the centuries? Why didn't God intervene and put a stop to all these terrible atrocities?

Because otherwise the world would not exist, and there would be no challenges, nothing to put right. Man wouldn't have the chance to evolve, to right all the wrongs he committed. Remember that everything has to have an opposite.

***

All wars must end, or else mankind will never make any progress towards bringing peace and harmony to our planet. Neither will man's soul progress. In the Second World War, hundreds of millions of people were killed and murdered, not to mention being maimed with atrocious injuries and psychological problems.

The Vietnam War also springs to mind: lots of American soldiers turned to drink and drugs because they couldn't adjust to a civilian life once the war ended. Lots of soldiers ended up in mental institutions, and the war destroyed many men's souls.

I believe that the Second World War happened to show humanity to itself. Mankind cannot go on living in fear. Something of a great magnitude had to happen, if the world was to change for the better and we were to live without fear.

Fear has always been man's greatest downfall since the world began. We have to learn to resolve all our problems without war. The world belongs to all of us, to all races, nationalities, and generations. It's not just the men at the top who have the power to change the world!

I was born in 1947, so I don't remember much about the war and its aftermath. I'm thankful for that. But often something would remind me, has to what it must have been like in those days. Especially for the children. My parents were always watching documentaries, about the Second World War, as I mentioned earlier. It was one of the greatest catastrophes that ever happened to our planet and to mankind. I believe it happened so that a new world could begin.

Marlene

Is it possible that I volunteered myself to commit the atrocity in the sixteenth centaury with Marlene? Also, Marlene agreed to be the victim. But why? For what reason?

I was willing to help Marlene; with the lesson of forgiveness. When I committed the atrocity in the sixteenth century, Marlene was unforgiving – and who could blame her? This would have been the last thought in her mind before she passed away: unforgiveness.

She took this thought with her when she died. When she was given a review of the life just past, it is only then that she would realise that she must learn to forgive in her next reincarnation. We all must forgive others no matter how atrocious the matter.

In that past life, I would have agreed to take on the emotion of a jealous person and all the consequences it entails. We could both learn from it, so that both our souls will evolve. That's why Marlene and I chose to reincarnate together once again: helping each other so that our souls will progress.

When we fell out in our present life, it took Marlene a while before she could forgive me. Is that why I have never felt the emotion of jealousy in this life? Because of that past life? Marlene learnt how to forgive me at last.

You are probably saying to yourself, "It's all a bit too drastic to learn a lesson." But remember that we live in a world of illusion. None of it was, or is, real. Only the choices that we both made at the time are for real, giving us the chance to cleanse and heal our souls.

Eventually this led me towards searching for the truth: God does exist. The reason is to teach the readers of this book and to help humanity. Never forget how precious human life is.

To Make It Clear

1. We all come down to learn lessons.
2. We may come down as a group soul.
3. Or with a partner.
4. Or on our own.
5. We then choose a scenario together.
6. Usually it's one that will benefit mankind.
7. The offering may be small, or very challenging. In the case of a murder, or a killing, or war, or good against evil, or of great magnitude.
8. One will play the victim, and the other plays the perpetrator.
9. This will depend on each soul's spiritual level.
10. Some souls will succeed. Some will fail.
11. You will be given the choice to repeat lessons that went unlearned.
12. With lessons that are successful, your soul will evolve.
13. You will die; this is when you will realise that there is no death, only change, a continuation of life.

We are all actors playing on the world's stage, playing the game of life. We make choices and mistakes. Some try to do the best they can; some succeed, but some fail. No matter what the outcome, God will continue to love all souls unconditionally. We are all given the chance to amend, to turn towards the light to ask for forgiveness. That's why we have to learn to forgive ourselves and others.

At the point of death, you will realise that your life was just an illusion, although it seemed very real at the time. The first thing that will enter you head is, "So that's what life was about!" All the pain, all the heartache, all the adversity you had to go through will become clear. You will leave the trauma of life behind to be where you are at your very best, the real you. In your real world, you belong in total bliss. It is a place called heaven.

Whether or not you believe it is your choice. You're probably thinking, "How do you know all this?" Simply because God told me. This is my mission in this lifetime.

Can you think of a better reason for your life, your existence, on this planet? If so, please let me know.

Remember that God created man so that God could experience life on earth through man. It was and still is the only way. That's why God can only observe his children. That's why at some point in our lives, depending on the life we have led, we will remember who we once were by the choices we have made in this life. That's why life will never end. That's why death does not mean the end, only change.

All our lives we think we are our bodies; some of the time we think we are our minds. The most difficult thing for people to do is to hear their own souls. God speaks to us all through feelings, because feeling is the language of the soul. The question is- is anyone listening? He also uses pictures and images and colours. Sometimes I see a deep indigo or a vivid purple which is the highest spiritual colour. What colour do you see? The colours all have meaning.

The Original Ten Commitments

I felt it important to include the original Ten Commandments. The real title was "the Ten Commitments".

The word of God was not a commandment, but a covenant.

You shall know that you have taken the path to God, and you shall know that you have found God, for there will be signs, these indications, these changes in you.

1. You shall love God with all your heart, all your mind, all your soul. And there shall be no other God set before me. No longer shall you worship human love, or success, money, or power, nor any symbol thereof. You will set aside these things as a child sets aside toys. Not because they are unworthy, but because you have outgrown them. And you shall know you have taken the path to God because …

2. You shall not use the name of God in vain. Nor will you call upon me for frivolous things. You will understand the powers of words, and thoughts, and you would not think of invoking the name of God in an ungodly manner. You shall not use my name in vain because you cannot, for my name – the Great I am – is never used (that is without results), nor can it ever be. And when you have found God, you shall know. And I shall give you theses other signs as well:

3. You shall remember to keep a day for me, and you shall call it holy. This so that you do not stay long in your world of **illusion**, but cause yourself; to remember who and what you are. And then

Daffodil

shall you soon call every day the Sabbath, and every moment holy.

4. You shall honour your mother and your father —and you will know you are the son of God when you honour the mother / father God in all that you say or do or think, And even as you so honour your father and mother on earth (, for they have given you life) so, too, will you honour everyone.

5. You know you have found God when you observe that, you will not murder (that is, willfully kill, without cause). For while you will understand that you cannot end another's life in any event (all life is eternal), you will not choose to terminate any particular incarnation, nor change any life energy from one form to another without the most sacred justification.

6. Your new reverence for life will cause you to honour all life forms —including plants trees and animals — and to impact them only when it is for the highest good. And these other signs will I send you also, that you may know you are on the path:

7. You will not defile the purity of love with dishonesty or deceit, for this is adulterous. I promise you, when you have found God; you shall not commit this adultery

8. You will not take a thing that is not your own, nor cheat, nor connive, nor harm another to have anything for this would be to steal. I promise you when you have found God, you shall not steal. Nor shall you …

9. Say a thing that is not true, and thus bear false witness. Nor shall you …

10. Covert your neighbours spouse, for why would you want your neighbours spouse when you know all others are your spouse?

11. Or covert your neighbours goods, when you know that all goods can be yours and all your goods belong to the world? You will know you have found the path to God when you see these signs.

12. For I promise that no one who truly seeks God shall any longer do these things. It would be impossible to continue such behaviours.

These are your freedoms, not your restrictions. These are my commitments, *not* my commandments, for God does not order about what God has created. God merely tells his children, "This is how you will know you are coming home."

> For whom shall I command?
> And who shall I punish should my commitments not be kept?

"There is only me."

God Space

To be in touch with God, however you perceive him, remember that there is a great, divine, higher intelligence out there – more than you can ever imagine. It is best to meditate even if it is only fifteen minutes a day or once a week. Even if you simply sit there and nothing happens; the higher intelligence will know you are trying to get in touch. Keep practicing till something does happen; once it does, you will want to do it all the more.

Tell God exactly how you feel. You don't have to speak right out to him; I talk to him in my head. Remember that God does not need your worship. He is your friend, your father, your confidante. He is the one who created you, the one who loves you unconditionally.

By meditating you take yourself away from this world; this earth we live in, this illusion, even if only in your mind. It will do you the power of good, and you will feel much calmer and restored. You will find that you can cope with problems better, especially if you live a busy, hectic life. Plus, eventually you will start to remember who you are.

You will be guided to your spiritual path, the path you need to come home. You have to find your God space. Try to make the effort for your own sake. What's ten to fifteen minutes a day, or even once a week, out of a whole lifetime? God has provided us with the tools, and it would be a shame not to use them. This is what man has forgotten.

Here is one of the best ways to get yourself into a relaxed state of mind. I find this pure heaven. If you are completely alone in your home, and you know that you won't be disturbed, sit in a comfortable chair. Take three deep breaths, sit back, and relax.

Then listen to the quietness, the stillness while breathing gently. Keep doing this for as long as possible. Every time I do this, I find such peace within myself. I find it hypnotic. It's as if my soul becomes detached from my body without going to sleep.

For a little while I leave this world behind, all the hustle and bustle, all the troubles and sufferings the world endures. Its sheer peace and tranquility – nutrition for the soul.

This also turns your aura golden, the highest spiritual colour, a feeling of well-being –hence the old adage "Silence is golden". If only I had had this knowledge years ago, I may not have suffered with my health so much.

Do this frequently to get the best out of your life, especially if you have health issues. This eventually will lead to healing. It will also lead you to your spiritual path, towards God and the angels. You owe it to yourself, to take the tools from God. God does not want you to suffer.

> I think immortality is the passing of a soul
> Through many lives or experiences,
> And such as are truly lived, used and learned,
> Help on to the next, each growing richer, happier and higher,
> Carrying with it only the real memories of what has gone before …
> – Louisa May Alcott, letters

Changes

The world will never end, but have you noticed the changes that are already taking place? In January 2011 dead fish washed up on the shore in America. Black birds fell dead from the sky in North America. Note the floods that have taken place in Brazil, Australia, and Haiti, as well as the decline of the animal kingdom.

The ice caps are melting. The world's economy is in decline. Not to mention the uprisings in the Middle East. And then there was the great earthquake that happened in Japan in March 2011, what's this telling us? The change has already started.

Japan now has radiation leaks that have already spread to some of the local people, endangering their health. There has to be a better and safer way to produce electricity. These nuclear electricity plants are all over the world producing electricity. T

There are also nuclear bombs, weapons of mass destruction, and nerve gas that can cause devastation. If there were to be an earthquake in these areas, how can our world be 100 per cent safe?

Still Japan continues to build on its fault lines. The United Nations has to come together to resolve the potential destruction of our planet. We have to stop making weapons of mass destruction. All wars have to end. We are all one nation, one people, coming from one source, one God. Until everyone on this planet realises this, there will be no future, no resolve.

Why not make our world a safer place by disarming our weapons worldwide, demonstrating for world peace, and putting all our resources into making a safer way to produce electricity? Why should there be a need for deadly weapons of mass destruction in the first place? Who wants to live on a ticking time bomb?

They are dangerous nuclear weapons sitting on this planet as I write. Does that make you feel comfortable? Now we have the economic recession. Although it is slowly recovering. We all have to contribute in one way or another, no matter how small our contribution may seem. We have to stop being greedy and materialistic. If nations all over the world took a decrease in wages by only 10 per cent, the economic recession would end tomorrow. For this to occur, it would have to happen worldwide, with the United Nations coming together. It's as simple as that: all working together in harmony as one, as it should be.

All my life I have never felt like I belonged here. It always felt strange to me, like living in a foreign country. "This is not where I want to be. I don't belong here." Is it because deep in my soul, I know there's a better place where we all belong?

When I was young, life could be magical. When you're a child, you can escape and live in your own little world. Living in my fantasy world freed me from the illusion of this world, although I thought the world was real at the time.

When you grow to be an adult, that's when the problems start; that's when our lessons begin. I am now sixty-four years old, and I would say that the last ten years of my life have been the most trying times, both physically and mentally. I have not found this life easy at all – in fact it has tested me to the limit on many occasions.

What has happened to our world? How could mankind get it so wrong? Given the amount of evil that exists on this planet, I sometimes wonder whether this planet is the real hell. I find this world so very depressing; at the moment. The fact that wars still exist, When 9/11 happened, we all knew that life would never be the same again. Why are some people so obsessed with evil and violence?

Even the dramas on TV, such as the popular soaps *East Enders* and *Coronation Street*, have turned to violence for their story lines. Is all this necessary? What used to be fun for the whole family to view is not safe anymore. What does this teach our children? That violence is okay, that it's normal?

After writing the above, weeks later I was to hear in the media that a fourteen-year-old boy, Daniel Bartlam, murdered his own mother, by re-enacting a scene from *Coronation Street,* where a mother is murdered by her son.

Daniel Bartlam was obsessed with horror movies, violence, and *Coronation Street.* While growing up, he was probably exposed to such scenes of horror that he thought it was the norm. He had been totally desensitised.

I know that I have been shown the reasons why we all exist on this planet. It saddens me that we are going backwards. We keep making the wrong choices. It will take hundreds of thousands of years to recuperate; to what this world was capable of at the beginning. It could have been a heaven upon the earth, so what happened? What can we do to help to put it right?

***

God made it so that here would be different races. There were no mistakes. God's wish was that someday we will all come together and live in peace and harmony.

I know as you read that it all sounds repetitive, what I'm saying about God and us all being one source. But I have to do the best I can with the knowledge that I am being given by the spirit world. I can't emphasize enough the importance of this knowledge. All I know is that I have to pass it on to humanity before I leave this world. I've never written a book before, so I ask for your patience.

Surely life is too sacred. Are we so primitive that we can't sit down and resolve all the problems of the world together? A third of the world is starving, when there's enough for everyone. Everyone has a right to food and shelter, a right to work and earn a decent living.

Our world is dying, and it cannot carry on the way it is. Do you like what you see and hear? Man has to stop his greed. There's enough to go around. How can these bankers who earn massive bonuses live with themselves? Don't they have a conscience? How do they sleep at night? What do they think when they see people in great need of the basics?

We can't keep turning a blind eye. It is happening, and it has to stop. We have to start somewhere. We could all start by respecting one another, because we are all sisters and brothers. No matter what colour our skins are, what race, what religion we come from, we all belong to the one God.

God cannot interfere and put it right. That is why we were given free will. It is up to us to put it right by the choices we make on this planet. We have to learn to love one another. Love is all that matters, for love is all there is. The love that I experienced in heaven was not like human love. I could feel it in every fiber of my being, my entire body. It soaked into my skin and bones I could breathe it in, I will never forget it.

If everyone on this planet did some good every day, it would make for a better world. That would be a start. This aggression against one another must stop. The children in gangs **have to learn to become children all over again.**

As adults we have to become more responsible, especially towards our children, for they will inherit this world. Take a look what's happened to the family unit, and the breakdown of family life. Every aspect of human life that once was good is crumbling.

After World War Two, people started to experience their freedom once again. Realising that no good can come from war. People came together and helped one another. They cared more for each other, especially the family unit. Having nearly lost their children to the war, they were given a second chance to build their lives once again. It was a time when one could rely on next-door neighbours if one needed help. People appreciated life and one another.

Does it have to take another war to make us all realise this? It can be like this once again: we can all become happy, living together in peace and harmony. This is not just with humankind, but with the animal kingdom, the rainforest, and plant life – all of God's creations. We have to stop the pollution that is destroying our planet.

Family

So what went wrong, and what did war teach us? Absolutely nothing – only pain, misery, and suffering. The world turned greedy to where money mattered most, and materialism became the ultimate goal. This has lead us to the world we live in today, with the financial decline. If there are no jobs, then how can you earn any money to buy a house or raise a family?

Where is the food going to come from to feed the family, if you have no money? We can't keep relying on state benefits, which come from the taxpayers who are fortunate to still have jobs. It is only a matter of time before they lose their jobs. It has become a vicious circle on the decline. What does a desperate mother and father do if they can't feed their family because they have no income? They're going to borrow or steel.

Say, a father borrows money from a loan shark at high interest rates that are well above what he can afford. He has no other option. He can't let his family down, and they need a roof over their heads. They need food, shelter, and clothing.

Then when the funds have run out, the loan shark offers more financial help. The client has no option but to borrow more money because he is desperate. There is no way out of his predicament. He can't afford to pay back the high interest rates, and he is threatened with violence.

The worst scenario is that you hear on the news that a father or a mother couldn't cope anymore, and they've killed themselves – or worst still, they've killed their children, too. This is happening all too often.

But what is being said about the loan sharks who are offering what's supposed to be financial help to these poor unfortunate people?

How can the government allow this to happen in the first place? They allow these loan sharks to charge such vast amounts of interest. There should be legislation brought in by the government. It's no different from the fat cats who are running our banks now, still taking vast bonuses every year.

What the bankers and loan sharks don't realise is that when they pass over, they will be given a review of these activities that took place in their lifetime, with all the choices they made. They will know what it was like for these unfortunate people. They will be the judge of their own misdemeanours, and hopefully they will want to make amends. When they reincarnate, they may choose a life scenario in which they can help mankind in a financial way. Or this could turn out to be karma, in which their souls will have to experience and bear the consequences what it was like to be destitute and in financial crisis. What goes around comes around – nothing is forgotten. It is universal law, cause and effect.

Surely legislation has to come into it. We can't allow this to continue. The world has got into a terrible financial state, mainly through man's greed, even when there's enough to go round for everyone. Man does not see it this way; the only thing he sees is profit and more profit. That's why the world has to change if it's to survive.

Vanity

There's far more attention paid to the physical human body instead of what human life was intended for: the progression of the spirit and soul. The soul does not die; it lives forever. It's the soul that needs maintaining. At some point the body starts to deteriorate, this is normal. But your soul never deteriorates – it is everlasting. That's why older people feel much younger in their minds, when the body starts to age.

I'm sixty-four this year, but in my mind I feel about thirty-three. Don't you think that this is a wonderful feeling, to know that when you die, all these physical problems will be healed? You will become the perfect human being that God intended you to be. All the people out there who are suffering in this world with terrible diseases, illnesses, deformities, mental problems, and blindness will be restored back to health one day!

Meanwhile, we should all be taking good care of our souls and making sure we make the right choices. Instead, we are more obsessed with the way we look. There are more and more people having plastic surgery and Botox, risking their lives for it and taking it to extremes, all to look good.

Why would you want to inject a poison such as botulism into your skin? Eventually regular injections are bound to get into your bloodstream and build up in your body at some point, possibly causing side effects detrimental to your health, especially to the immune system.

People are becoming more desperate to hang on to their looks. Nobody wants to grow old, but it is a fact of life. This is a natural process, and it happens to everyone. **It's keeping the soul healthy that matters most.)**

The young generations today are fed on a diet of how you are supposed to look, what's acceptable and what's not acceptable, by the media: magazines, fashion shows, and TV. It affects their future careers. Some young teenage girls are now asking their parents for plastic surgery for birthdays and Christmas presents. Some of them are not even fully developed yet! Now in the news there are stories that suggest these implants are leaking. This is bound to cause detrimental side effects to the human body. It's simply a matter of time.

One young girl was asked, "What do you want to be when you grow up?" She replied, "I want to be a famous model and marry a footballer, because they have lots of money." We are sending out all the wrong messages to the young generation.

What a pity that girls think that by having the perfect look and the perfect body, that this is all they have to do to make it in this world. They are blinded by a supercilious media society. **It's the importance of the soul that matters**, not how well you look for your age.

It's the little person that God will look down upon. God can only see a shining soul that's done more good upon this earth for his fellow man in his short existence upon this earth. Yes, the rich man may give to the poor "because he can", but it's the poor man who's willing to give his last penny to help another soul who makes a difference. It's all about the good intention.

We have so much to learn about the human soul and the need to nourish the soul with our spirituality. When we pass over, it will be the soul of that person that will be examined, not the way he or she looks. It seems today you have to look a certain way to be accepted in today's society.

It's the same with age. If you're past fifty, you're classed as old, and you can't get a job. But what about all the experience and wisdom you can bring? You may be fortunate to be a fit and healthy person who feels young at heart with bounds of energy, but someone will always say, "Sorry, you're too old." They will always prefer someone prettier and younger. Common sense has gone out the window!

William Roache

They wrote: William Roach who plays Ken Barlow in Coronation Street had lost the plot in a TV interview with Kevin Moore.

The seventy-nine-year-old told a stunned chat show host; that all humans will soon communicate through telepathy. He also predicted a series of earthquakes, hurricanes, floods, and tsunamis. He claimed that these disasters would be necessary to disperse negative energy.

He also said of his late wife, Sara, that he was pleased to bits that she had gone home. He told the host that the earth was a living being with consciousness, and it has an understanding. And just like us; we can become enlightened, and raise our vibration levels into a higher spiritual level, the earth can also do the same. This is what's happening.

Unfortunately, there are some cleansings that will have to take place, where negative energy has to be discharged. These will be in the form of earthquakes, hurricanes, floods, and tsunamis. The prediction that the world will end in December 2012 did not take place, but it's the change and the end of a lot of things as we once knew them.

He predicted that we'll move into the golden age, which will be a wonderful age where we will all love one another. We'll communicate telepathically, we'll all be aware of our spiritual selves, and it will be a beautiful place to be. He said a lot of people who are sensitive will be aware of it, whereas a lot of people will simply be aware of all the awful things that are going on.

Daffodil

But we need to look at all the bad things as a glorious process of birth. We're going to be moving into this wonderful period where people will be more loving and caring.

This is a world that I wouldn't mind being born into again. This is how it should be, not as the world as it is today. What a nice surprise it was for me when I read Ken Roache's predictions. It was exactly the same thoughts and feelings that I had been carrying around with me for years. It's not that we should be afraid – it's a new beginning for all of us; especially our children's children. Doesn't it make you feel better knowing that our children will grow up in a better world, where human life is sacred once again, as it was in the beginning? What a wonderful world we could create.

I want to be a part of this new beginning by helping mankind. I want share my thoughts and feelings, if only to take away the fear. That there is absolutely nothing to fear, only fear itself, and if every one of us can think positively, the transition will be made easier. God will never let us down, for he is our father, and we are all his children. He will take care of us.

William revealed his struggle to find happiness early on in his Coronation Street career. It was solved by a homeopathic doctor who was able to communicate with him while he slept. William said the spirit guide doctor appeared on several occasions and spoke to him. He said that now days spiritual things are more accepted, and it's going to keep getting bigger. But when I started these things were very unusual, and one had to be careful who one spoke to, because people would become hostile. Spiritualism helped him deal with the death of his eighteen-month-old daughter, Edwina, in 1983. "I've had messages from Edwina saying her role in the spiritual realms is helping young babies who have gone over and are crying for their mummies, she is able to help children in the spirit realms. I don't worry about Sara as I know I will join her eventually."

How refreshing I found him when I read this in the paper, and how brave of William Roache to explain this on national TV. Of course the journalist who wrote it was trying to make him look like a fool. The journalist has a lot to learn.

I was experiencing all these thoughts and feelings years ago, but it's nice to know that somewhere in the world, someone else was, too. Yes, William was right about us speaking telepathically. This happens in heaven, and also when we communicate with our loved ones who have passed over, as well as communication with higher spirits. In the early days, I had to be careful who I spoke to about the spiritual things that were happening to me, but now I don't care! I'm willing to talk to anyone who's willing to listen. I never tire of it. I find it so exciting to have been witness to things that were not of this world.

Whenever I think of what may happen to this world, there's a sadness inside me. It's like when you have to say goodbye to someone you love. However, deep inside me there's the knowledge that it can only be for the best; it has to happen. Remember that we can never die. Just like the world, it will continue as it always has done.

We will share a life without end. Amen.

A Visitor

I was in bed one night when I suddenly felt a presence coming from the right side of the room. I didn't want to look but I knew I had to. I thought to myself, *Oh dear, what's this all about?* As I turned my head slowly towards my right, I saw this man from the waist up, and everything was in black-and-white.

He had a full head of dark hair streaked with gray, and a bit of a beard. He looked about forty-five to fifty. He sat on a chair and was wearing a gray suit jacket; He had both his hands on his knees. All the while he was staring at me out of the corner of his eye, and he looked so nervous and anxious.

At the time I didn't feel scared. I could see and sense that he was frightened and was in need of help. As I looked at him, I could see that he had an injury to the right side of his head that came across his right eye; this area was all bloody.

I closed my eyes and thought, *what's all this about?* The energy I felt from this man was that he had been bludgeoned to death with just one blow to his head. I prayed for the angels to come show him to the light, and for any deceased family members he may have had; to come fetch him and take him home. After a while, I felt a sense of peace wash over me.

The next day when I began to think about what had happened the night before, I couldn't help but think how frightened the man looked; the plea in his eyes for help. I was happy to help this poor spirit. God only knows how long his spirit had been waiting for someone to help him cross over.

You see, this is happening all over the world with spirits that haven't moved on. Some spirits think they are still alive, or they don't want to leave behind their possessions, or they may have unresolved issues.

Once you have died, there's nothing else you can do on this earth – your number has been called. Go towards the light, and you will be accompanied by angels or your spirit guides, or deceased loved ones who have already passed over. There's nothing to fear. They can only help you to pass over to the next world. But if you don't want to go, there's little that can be done. It's entirely up to you. It is your choice.

It's the same when we are born into this world. We make our own choices, and we decide when we want to come back here. Wouldn't you rather move over to the other side, with all of the loved ones who have passed before you? You don't want to be hanging around in limbo, waiting for a bus that never arrives, or for something that's not going to happen. Your time's up, so go home. There's a welcome party waiting!

Revelation

On the same day as I had the revelation with Marlene, my neighbor. I had a premonition. I remember after the conversation with Marlene; that I was walking back to my bungalow. I was just about to walk across the lawn up to my home; when all of a sudden it was as if time stood still. I felt I was in two places at once. I stared up at my front door, although I was several meters away.

Then I had the premonition. It was as if a fine veil was in between me and the next dimension. I knew that I was going to write a book that would help mankind. But in my mind I thought; I can't do that, I haven't got the skills needed. Wendy would have to write it. I didn't feel capable at that time. I was also given information that when the book was completed, I wouldn't be around. My work on this planet would be over, and I will have left this world.

A slight sadness came over me, but I seemed to readily accept it. I knew it was the reason for me being here on this planet. It was my mission.

In early 2012, further information came through. I would be in my sixty-fifth year when I passed over. In my mind's eye, I was shown the months May, June, and July, written across the palm of my left hand. It was as if I was in two places at once yet again, time stood still.

Did that mean I have three months to live, or did they mean my book would take three months to finish? It was 15 June 2012, and my book was almost complete. I tried to make sense of it, letting it play over and over in my mind.

I'm not at all afraid, for my life had purpose. I know I will be going home. I will see all my relatives and friends, and especially all my dogs that have passed over. I know I will be surrounded by that very special love that only God and the angels can give.

I will be sixty- this year in October 2012, so it could happen anytime after that, or before my sixty-sixth birthday. I'll have to wait and see. If this is more validation and proof to the reader, then I'm all for it.

***

One day Paul Parker was giving me a reading over the phone. I was bent over the computer desk with the phone in my hand. As I turned around, Paul was sitting in my computer chair and looking up at me. He said, "It's all to do with the mind." It was as if we were carrying on with our conversation in the same room, as well as on the telephone! Obviously it was Paul's spirit body in my office chair.

Paul mentioned at some point that he felt like sometimes; he was in two places at once. I took note, without mentioning this to anyone. Then later I remembered Stephen Toorof, the psychic surgeon, saying to me that he had been in two places at once, giving a seminar to all his followers in India whilst still in England, in his tiny clinic.

Depending on your spirituality level, your spirit body can split off and go to other places, like it can when we have passed over. Your physical body is still attached to your spirit body by the silver cord, which only breaks at the point of death. Similarly, when we are asleep we can go anywhere as long as the silver cord is attached, and we are still earthbound.

All I know is that anything is possible when it comes from a higher intelligence like the spirit world. I'm sure I'll understand all this sooner or later.

***

Life has become too much to bear. The human body can only tolerate so much. When the internal organs start to deteriorate through

Daffodil

illness, and I'm having to take medication just to stay alive, it seems pointless – but I know I have a job to do.

That's why you should look after your body and try to prevent illness. I can't wait to be free from this heavy load that my body has become. This is not a life. It has become an existence on a daily basis. I know there are a lot of people in similar circumstances who think as I do.

I know it sounds has if I'm clinically depressed, but I can assure you that I'm not. I'm aware that there are hundreds of people all over the world who are suffering like myself, or in much worse conditions. But there's one big difference, and I feel very humble and privileged for it: I was given an insight into human life itself. I have all the spiritual knowledge that was bestowed upon me, which has given me the confidence to do something about it.

The book is the only thing that keeps me going. It's my saviour, apart from my wonderful family. I feel truly blessed. My life has been a struggle but also an exciting journey.

I have learnt the secret of life itself: all that really matters is love. God bless you all, my brothers and sisters.

Useful Knowledge

These are the things I have learnt through my life; and that I wish I had known when I was young. I'm certain I would have had less health issues. I would like to pass this knowledge on to all of you.

1. First, acknowledge your guardian angel. Let him know that you know he is there for you. Speak to him like a friend. Find your God space and spend at least five to ten minutes a day speaking with God, your father, just Relaxing and talking to him like you would your best friend – which of course he is.

2. Always stay true to yourself, follow your gut instinct, and listen to your sixth sense and your heart. Pursue your dreams. Know that you are loved by God and the angels. Always have faith in God and the angels.

3. Avoid anxiety at all times by deep breathing three times and then letting it out slowly; relax your shoulders at the same time. Surrender all your worries and anxiety problems to God and the angels, especially when it becomes too overwhelming. Whenever negative thoughts enter your mind, use the cancel button and replace it with a positive thought. No matter how hard it may seem; your mind will believe what you tell it. Your thoughts are so powerful. Remember that all illness starts with the mind first.

4. You only need to use gentle exercise throughout your life, by stretching all your limbs like a ballerina or by taking up yoga. This is what the Buddha recommended thousands of years ago. You can learn by watching your cat as it moves and stretches; this is all that's required to keep yourself supple. Swimming is

excellent for the body because it is a gentle, all-round activity for the body. You don't have to abuse your body at the gym by using heavy weights and wearing yourself out. Be gentle with yourself in mind and body.

5. Try to balance a healthy lifestyle with the foods you eat. You don't have to drink litres of water a day to stay healthy; this can lead to strain on the kidneys. Make sure you drink six glasses of water a day. Sip the water throughout the day rather than in one gulp. Drink only herbal teas. Earl Gray is a nice refreshing tea, but there are lots to choose from. I only drink one cup of coffee a day. One cup is good for the bowel. When dieting, don't deny yourself your favourite foods. Calorie counting works for everyone as long as you count the calories. Everything should be considered in moderation, not just in food but in all things. Chew your food more before swallowing; this gives your digestion less work to do. It also gives you a sense of being full. If you eat slower and chew more, then more often than not you cannot finish all of the meal.

6. This will help your weight to reduce. The foods that you crave are the foods you should avoid; they don't suit your metabolism. And of course, try to eat your fruits and vegetables, even if it's only one piece of fruit and one vegetable a day. Learn about alkaline and acidic foods. You should balance your food intake: It should be 80 per cent alkaline and 20 per cent acidic. Eat healthy and let your thoughts be positive. Try to fast for one day to give your internal organs a rest, flushing out all the toxins, but remember to drink reasonable amounts of water.

7. Always treat one another with love and respect. Acquire a pet, cat, dog, or whatever you prefer. The love you receive from your pet animal is unconditional love, just like the love you receive from God. God spelt backwards is dog. The connection is unconditional love, which is a reminder to all of us what real unconditional love feels like.

8. For people who suffer with bad headaches such as migraines, don't forget to check the big toes. This represents the head, and

if you have an ingrown toenail, this can be the cause. If it's not an ingrown toenail, massage the whole of the toe, especially the tip of the big toe; this will send a fresh supply of blood to wherever it has become blocked in your head and is causing the pressure.

9. You will find this information in any reflexology book. This also works on any other areas of the body, especially on the internal organs. With reflexology, by working on the whole foot, you can manipulate all the internal organs in the body, sending a fresh blood supply to an area where it has become stagnant. It's the same with acupuncture. This could save the sufferer from taking years of medication, when all that was needed was a natural remedy. You can save on years of untold damage that the medication may have caused, such as the side effects.

10. If at any time you become ill with a disease, especially if it is a degenerative one, my advice is to read everything you can about it. **Educate yourself** – don't be in denial. Don't be afraid of it. Hit it head-on. Stay positive at all times, because you can help yourself. I think it's important that we equip ourselves with some knowledge of how the human body works. We are responsible for ourselves, our own bodies.

11. We can't always rely on doctors. For instance, we can tell a lot about urine by the colour. It should be a straw colour, the clearer the better – although alcohol can make the urine appear colourless. If the urine is dark or cloudy, it could be a sign of infection, or you may not be drinking enough water and liquids, causing dehydration and also headaches. This is common, especially in older people. If the urine smells and stings, this is a sign of infection. That's when you should to see your doctor. Don't leave it and think it will get better on its own. You can help yourself by drinking lots of water to flush out the kidneys. Most adults will overcome infection if they have a good immune system.

12. If you suffer from a disease and take medication, chances are your immune system will be weaker. It's the same with faeces: check for blood, or if the stools are black and accompanied by a

Daffodil

putrid smell. Note sudden changes in bowel movement, such as diarrhea followed by constipation. Always have it checked out by your doctor, because it could be infection, and the visit could save your life.

13. Bowel cancer is one of the easiest cancers to cure, if caught in the early stages. All you have to do is check on yourself now and then, especially when you are not feeling well. Don't be alarmed if you see blood in the bowl; this could simply be hemorrhoids, also known as piles, which are easily treated. Also, certain foods can cause constipation, which can also lead to hemorrhoids.

14. A warning: I once put bleach down the toilet. Later when I went to use the toilet, when I looked down the toilet bowel the water had turned dark brown. Bleach and urine are volatile. It gave me a fright, though. You can find everything you wish to know on the Internet or at the library. I know the spirit world is protecting me from the side effects from the medication. No one would ever last this long on the medication I have taken over the years. I know it's because I have had a job to do. I simply hope that the end of my life is quick and that I don't suffer too much.

15. If you need to see a consultant, at least you will have a good understanding about your condition. Don't become too obliging to follow the doctor's suggestions or advice. Before making any decisions about surgery and operations, ask questions such as anesthetics, blood monitoring, side effects, and possible infections. Remember that doctors don't know everything, and sometimes they make mistakes. They're only human, after all.

16. We all need sunshine. We also need vitamin D for our bones, which we get naturally from the sun. Steer clear from sun-tanning machines because they are not the same as the real thing. The fairer your skin is, the less time you should spend in the sun. You are more prone to wrinkles and skin damage.

17. Scientists now believe that the sun prevents skin cancer! For years we have been told that too much sun causes skin cancer. What are we to believe? I must admit I'm a big believer in everything in

moderation, as the Buddha suggests. Over the years it has always puzzled me how well the sun can make you feel, refreshed and vitalized. It depends on the colour of your skin. I would suggest little at a time but often, depending on the type of skin you have. Just don't overdo it.

18. There's been an increase in rickets in children since strong sun creams came onto the market. Also, women who are going through menopause need sunshine and vitamin D to help prevent osteoporosis. For menopausal women, try to sit in the sun for ten to fifteen minutes a day, even with your clothes on. The body needs sunlight just like nature. Our bodies are accustom to bright light, for light is where we come from.

19. We are not used to the dark winter months. That's why so many people suffer with depression in winter. It even has a name: sun affective disorder, also known as SAD. The medical profession has brought out a remedy for artificial light to be used for so many minutes a day. Although results were found, my gut feeling says otherwise. For more information go to the website.

The Adrenal Glands

The adrenal glands are attached to the kidneys. They work together with the pituitary gland and the hypothalamus, which is situated in the brain. The adrenals produce natural hormones such as estrogen, progesterone, steroids, cortisol, and cortisone, as well as chemicals such as adrenalin, norepinephrine, and dopamine. I can't emphasise enough how important these glands are. This important gland governs the whole body.

When the glands produce more or less hormones than required by the body, disease conditions may occur, as in my case. The steroids that I have had to take daily since I was diagnosed with RA; have had an effect on my adrenal glands, and they've also thinned my bones. At the time of taking prednisolone for my RA, it gave me a false sense of security that all was well.

At the beginning it helped take away the pain. Little did I know what the drugs were doing to my adrenal glands, not to mention my bones? That's why I felt the need to pass on this information to help others. Always look for the natural way to heal yourself before taking years of medication. You'll be surprised at what you can do to heal yourself. For me it's too late the damage is already done. Still, I try.

Reflexology is used in hospitals and hospices. It's very spiritual and therapeutic for the patient. It is also used in hyperactive children. Babies love it; it has such a calming effect.

We all have the power to help ourselves, instead of going to the doctors or the A&E as soon as we feel unwell. Sit in a chair, calm yourself down, breathe deeply, and then ask for guidance from your guardian angel and the spirit world. Listen to your body and your soul; always trust your gut feeling.

This is what I did once in A&E. It was a kidney stone that I had passed while waiting to be seen by a doctor. My soul was telling me it was all right to go home. I knew my mother had helped me; it wouldn't be the first time. We have all been given this power to help heal ourselves, so why not use it? This wasn't the first time I had asked for help by just listening to my soul.

My sister Mary sent me these inspiring words from God. she sent me this after I had been in touch with Don, my brother-in-law, by letter, after one of my sons had told me that Don had been suffering with a back problem with severe pain.

I gave Don all the instructions about how to get in touch with his angel. I also said that I would be sending him healing, especially on the day of his operation.

I hope and trust that Don is recovering well.

The Interview with God

I dreamed I had an interview with God. "So you would like to interview me?" said God.

"If you have the time," I said.
God smiled. "My time is eternity. What questions do you have in mind for me?"
"What surprises you most about human kind?"

God answered, "That they get bored with child hood. They rush to grow up and then long to be children again. They lose their health to make money, and then they lose their money to restore their health. By thinking anxiously about the future, they forget the present, such that they neither live in the present or the future. They live as though they will never die, and they die as though they have never lived."

God's hand took mine, and we were silent for a while. Then I asked, "As a parent, what are some of life's lessons you want your children to learn?"

He replied, "To learn that they cannot make anyone love them; all they can do is let themselves be loved. It is not good to compare themselves to others. Forgive by practicing forgiveness. It only takes a few seconds to open profound wounds in those they love, and it takes many years to heal them. A rich person is not the one who has most but is the one that needs least. That there are people who love them dearly but simply have not learned how to express or show their feelings. Two people can look at the same thing and see it differently. It's not enough that they forgive one another, but they also must forgive themselves."

"Thank you for your time," I said humbly. "Is there anything else you would like your children to know?"

God smiled and said, "Just know that I am here always." As I read the interview with God, it reminded me of my sister's conflicting views.

I wondered whether Mary recognised some of these traits within herself.

*"Only one thing can make a soul complete,
And that is love."* Eileen Richmond

***

When I nearing the completion of my book, I thought I'd better start looking for a publisher. The thought scared me; I hadn't a clue on how to go about it, so I went scouring on the Internet.

Then it dawned on me – what a fool I was! Why hadn't I asked my angels to help me? I don't know why I hadn't thought of it before. Why not ask the angels to help me publish my book?

One day just before going on my computer to write, I sat at my desk and did a quiet meditation. I asked my angels to help me finish the book and to find me a publisher. After a little while in my meditation, I could see a page of writing in my mind's eye. Although very faint, it was clear to me what it signified. Next I was shown the front of a book – a book which was completed. Then I heard a faint voice state that I would be given more. Wow!

When I came to write the same day, as I sat at my computer, I wondered where to start. Then I heard a faint voice in my right ear say, "Go to the beginning of the book."

I found myself going over the pages adding more. I thought I'd covered everything, but there were still things I had forgotten. Memories came flooding in. All the information is coming from the spirit realm, so I'm not finished yet.

Friends

Friends come into our lives for a reason: so we can learn from one another. We draw them to us, whether they stay for a long time or only for a short while. It was prearranged. You may remember some of these friends with fondness, or you may have bitter memories of your relationships. Nevertheless, it was destined. Once the lessons are learned, that friendship may break up, and you move on. Or, it may become a long-lasting friendship.

When I was about ten years old, I had a friend called Jean, who was twelve years old. Jean had a sister called Sandra. One day Jean tried to instigate a fight between me and Sandra, who was two years younger than me. There were a bunch of us kids playing at the top of a hill on some wasteland. Suddenly Jean said, "Go on, hit her!" She meant Sandra.

I thought to myself, *Oh no, not again. Why do we have to start fighting?* Besides, I didn't want too. It was the fact that Jean was four years older than Sandra, and so she couldn't be seen bullying her younger sibling.

I could tell the sisters didn't like one another, and Jean wanted me to do the dirty work. No sooner was I thinking about this that Sandra thrust her fist into my face without touching me. Then she shouted, "Come on then, Catholic!" with such hatred. Jean pulled her away from me.

I was bewildered I didn't know what to think. What a strange thing to say. What did she mean? I didn't even know about other religions at that time. Sandra was Protestant and had been brought up to hate and disrespect Catholics. It never seemed to bother Jean or me. The years passed, and my friendship ended with Jean, but I've never forgotten the incident all those years ago.

Then in my late twenties, I was working at the C&A stores in the town centre in Sheffield. I was serving on the desk, and as I looked up, I could see we had a new cashier assistant. She looked familiar to me, but at that moment I couldn't place her. After a while, when we had no customers, Sandra said, "Well, don't you remember me?" As I looked at her she, said, "I'm Jeans sister."

We kept looking at each other. I didn't know what to say, but I remembered the past incident at once, and it became very clear. "It must be twenty years ago since I saw you," I said.

I don't know whether Sandra remembered the fight incident. We started with the usual small talk first. She was married with one child, a boy called James. Yet she seemed to know all about me. She knew that I was married with four children, and she said she'd seen me on occasion when I gave my parents a lift home, waiting for them outside the pub with my children in the car.

At the time I didn't know whether this was a good thing; I doubted the situation in which we had met again, but after that day we were always together.

One day she offered me a lift home, and she insisted I come in for a cup of tea. I really didn't have the time. I had to get home to do some housework and cook for the family; life was hectic. Then the penny dropped about why she was so insistent. She really wanted me to see her new home to show off; and to let me know how well she had done for herself. I played along and threw her the odd compliment.

As I sat having my cup of tea, Sandra went to change into some shorts, because it was a hot summer's day. She sat on the floor facing me.
Suddenly I was drawn to the size of her thighs. They looked enormous compared to the rest of her body. She was about five foot two, flat-chested, and a size ten.

She was chatting away, but I couldn't stop staring down at her thighs. I don't know whether she caught me or not. It just looked so odd. It's funny how things stick in your mind, but there you go.

Daffodil

Years later we had become firm friends. Sandra decided to leave the C&A to work for a supermarket, an upgrade job working in the cash office. She left C&A because she didn't get the promotion she was expecting. When we were discussing whether she should leave her job, I suddenly said to her, "Sandra, this could be the making of you." It was like a premonition, and it was. She climbed to the top of the ladder. Sandra was a high achiever and was very good at figures. I was proud of her but also a little sad at the same time.

Work took over her life. Her work became the most important aspect of her life. It was as if she had to prove to the world that she was capable, that she was worthy, always reaching for the top. If you asked her about her job, she would be in her element. She didn't know when to stop talking about it. I could always tell, because when she got overexcited, there would be white spittle drooling from the corner of her mouth. I pretended to ignore it, but I was sure she was aware of it. It was like a drug to her. She had to have more ... but at what cost?

Then one day she told me she had applied to become a Magistrate. I nearly choked while spluttering my cup of tea. Had I heard right? After digesting what she had just told me, I said, "Oh come on, Sandra!" with a kind of cynical humour. "Somebody would only have to look at you in the wrong way in court, and knowing you, you'd slap another ten years on their sentence!" When I look back, it seemed so funny at the time, but I was serious. I knew her all too well!

"Oh no," she replied, "There are guidelines that you have to follow."

In all my years of knowing Sandra, I always tried to encourage her to go for it, to reach the top. I don't know why, but on this occasion I just couldn't. Something stopped me. It was like a knowing. Something deep in my soul was remembering why I reacted like this. Why didn't I feel happy for her?

Nevertheless, Sandra reached her goal of becoming a Magistrate. After that, I knew somehow our friendship would never be the same. You may think that I was perhaps jealous of Sandra's achievements over the years, but it wasn't that. Sandra would be the first to agree: if anything, I encouraged her to go for it. The feeling I had was more like, "Why do you want to go and do that?" But at the same time it eventually destroyed our friendship. That's why I felt sad when she first told me; I must have known.

It was always a fact that Sandra was the academic one in her family. Despite everything, she always came home with high grades from school. Sandra used to say that she could write a book about her life. I would think to myself, *yes, but you would have to tell the truth*. I sometimes wonder what she will think of her old friend now, who has written a book!

My sister Mary once said to Sandra while pointing a finger at me, "She's the beauty, I'm the brains." They both thought it was funny. I couldn't hide the hurt. I'm very sensitive, and Mary knew this. It was one of the many hurtful things Mary would do over the years.

It was the same when I passed my driving test. When I told Mary my good news, she looked at me straight-faced and across at Don, "Well, if she can do it, you can!" There was no mention of "Well done, sis", only a look of resentment.

Sandra did well to achieve what she had, and I'll always be proud of her for it. She went out into this world to prove that she was worthy. No matter who you are, where you come from, whatever your background or financial status, you can be successful.

After Sandra remarried, things between us were never the same. We lost the closeness that friends share, plus I was ill. I lost my mojo, I suppose. I wasn't the fun person I used to be. Although I tried to be, it wasn't the same. We parted in October 2000 after all those years together, just after me and Harry moved into our bungalow.

I sometimes wonder what's happened to Sandra. I once got in touch with her just after I lost my leg in 2002. She already knew that I had my leg amputated; someone must have told her. But there was no real response from her, no compassion over the phone. She wasn't the person that I once knew. I asked her about work, trying to be polite. Then she went on and on about her new job and the new company car she was waiting for. I remember holding the phone away from my ear and thinking, *I wish I hadn't bothered to phone her*. Sandra hadn't changed. I felt abandoned, but I still felt love for my old friend.

Past Life

In a past life, I saw Sandra on a hot summer's day. It was inside of the Great Arena in Rome. It was a time when gladiators fought for their lives and Christians where thrown to the lions. She was dressed in the typical attire for an upper-class lady of the day. She wore a gown and headdress as she stretched out on a chaise lounge, propped up by her elbow.

The day was hot and sunny. Servants were scattered everywhere, waiting on all the people and serving them grapes and wine. I could hear the roar of the crowd in the background.

As I gazed at her profile, she raised her right hand high; fist clenched, and pointed her thumb towards the ground. This was an expression used to let the Christian or gladiator live or die. Thumbs up, he lived; Thumbs down, he died. Was I one of her subjects in that life?

Is this our connection in this life now? Is it karma with the religious issue Catholic and Protestant? Is this why I didn't want her to become a magistrate a judge? Is it because I had the same power in the sixteenth century, whether a man lived or died. And now Sandra has that same power? Why did I feel abandoned by her?

Even though I don't yet understand the reason for our being together in this life, I know that one day I will. I have more fond memories than regrets of the friendship we shared in this lifetime together: the laughter, the parties, the tears, the fun we had, the chats we had on spirituality. Sandra believed there was something else to this life, and she often had experiences like me. She often saw spirits.

Sandra came from a large family; I think there were six of them in total. She lost her mother to cancer when Sandra was only eight years old. Her mother was only thirty-one when she died. Her father did his best to keep the family together. He did what he could under the circumstances, but he also was a drinker.

Sandra was the odd one out at home. She didn't want anything to do with any of them. If the truth be known, she was ashamed to be connected to them. She kept to herself. Even though the children all went to the same school, she kept a low profile so that other pupils and teachers didn't realise Sandra had relatives at the same school.

She went on to marry her first husband, Peter. She wanted everything that she didn't have at home: a nice house, nice furnishings, and a nice car. Her home was immaculately clean. Sandra had very high standards, and she also had the energy.

Then she started putting on an act, pretending to be something she wasn't. Peter nicknamed her Mrs. Bouquet, the lady who played Hyacinth in the TV sitcom in the eighties.

Sometimes I would tease her. Then she was faced with the fact that her one and only son, James, was gay. I'd known for years about James; while watching him grow up, it was so obvious to everyone who knew him, even my own family. But Sandra never mentioned it. She was in denial till the day James told her.

What did it matter? He was still her son, after all. She never spoke about it. I felt sorry for her, because James was her only child. She seemed to hate the fact she'd be denied grandchildren. It was something she was going to have to come to terms with. Sandra chose a lot of tough issues for this life.

Sometimes I overheard bits of conversation Sandra would have with other people.

"I have a very high-profile job, you know. At work I have to dress accordingly. My father was a coal merchant, you know. He had his own business." In actual fact, her father was illiterate; he had an old truck, which he used to deliver coal, potatoes, or the odd job. He did everything he could to make a living and to put food on the table.

It must have been very difficult for Robert Sandra's father. He did very well raising his children without a mother. At least they were together and not in foster care. He managed to keep his family together which is important.

Sometimes I would find it all too embarrassing. One night we came back to our house for a bite of supper after a night out. I had gone to the toilet as Sandra put on the kettle. She was still going on about how well she was doing with her job. All of a sudden I blurted out, "For God's sake, stop blowing your own trumpet!" while I was still in the toilet. Then I shut my eyes hard. Why had I just said that?

True, she was getting on my nerves, but I didn't mean to come out with it. When I went back into the kitchen, the mood was a little quiet, but we carried on as if nothing had happened. When Sandra left that night, I thought, *why did I come out with those words? It doesn't seem like me. I'll have to apologise the next day.*

The next day when Sandra came round to my home, I said, "Listen, Sandra, I'm sorry about last night, but –" As I was trying to explain, she said to me, "Eileen, it's all right." She looked at me strange and added, "Because it wasn't you – it wasn't your voice! It was a male's voice!"

"Thank God for that," I said, relieved. "I knew something was strange about last night." "Me, too." She said that it sounded like her father, Robert, who was deceased.

She once said to me that she thought she came straight from royalty in a past life, and that she had been thrown into this life now to experience the complete opposite, in order to learn lessons. She was to experience both ends of the spectrum. This happened well before I was into my research. Looking back now, I think she was right; it makes sense. She always had this air of grandeur about her; even her first husband called her a snob.

Yet I could see beyond the false pretence that Sandra presented. I knew her much more than she knew herself. Like me, she craved to be loved by her mother and father. Her mother died from cancer at the age of thirty-one, leaving six children behind. I felt sorry for her in many ways.

She once said to me, "Do you realise how lucky you are at your age, to still have your mother? To talk to and be able to phone each other, and go shopping and have a laugh together?" As she said this, tears filled her eyes. I'd forgotten that Sandra had never experienced this. Of course she was right: I took things for granted. I thought Mum would be around forever.

Sometimes you have to face up to the harsh reality that life has given you and deal with it the only way you know how. We should be truthful to ourselves and to others. It's no good trying to be something that you're not. You can't kid yourself, and you certainly can't kid God or the angels. Just be yourself, and you will feel a lot better. Be proud of who you are, whatever your background or financial status.

Remember that life is just a game where we all participate. Feeling negative about life's situations will only hold you back. Try to be the best you can be, and always stay positive no matter what life throws at you. Try to make a difference in this world no matter how small it is; it will be noticed by the powers that be.

Don't hold regrets, and don't keep looking back and saying to yourself, "If only I'd done this or that, things might have been different."

The best way to live your life is in the present, not worrying about the past or the future. Look for the bigger picture. Keep your spirit healthy and your aura sparkly and clean by thinking positive. Remember to use the cancel button whenever negativity enters your head; not only will it help you spiritually, but it will also keep you healthy. Ask God and the angels to guide you.

Say that you have been born into a life you do not like. You don't like your parents or your brothers and sisters. You don't like your peers. You just don't like life. So what are you going to do about it? It's no good thinking, "I'll take drugs. That will help numb it. Or I'll just kill myself." You'll simply have to come back in another life to do it all over again. Who knows, in the next life you live, you may have given yourself even tougher issues.

You gave yourself this scenario so that you could learn from it, and so that your soul will evolve. You chose the tough situations. You will have received all the guidance you needed. God would not have given you something that you were not ready for. You wanted this so that your soul can keep progressing throughout all of your lives, moving on and reaching for perfection.

Drugs and Alcohol

I don't have to remind you that drugs and alcohol are destroying our society, and the situation is getting worse. In February 2012 the media announced the death of Whitney Houston at age forty-eight. She was found dead in the bath.

She was one of the most gifted and talented young ladies of our time. I loved the song that she recorded back in the nineties, "I Will Always Love You". It was one of her greatest hits. She was such a talented young lady and earned six Grammy awards over three decades.

The year before, Amy Winehouse was found dead. It was related to alcohol addiction. Yet again another talented young lady. Then there was the death of the great Michael Jackson, another death related to a drug overdose. It seems to follow a pattern. They were all in their prime, were very talented, and were very famous.

There's always the same set of synchronicities prior to the event, regarding why these three people died in these particular circumstances. Before all three were born, they saw what drugs and alcohol were doing to our young people, and destroying society. They wanted to help. By becoming extremely famous and talented, they could reach as many young individuals has possible across the world. They had to get the attention of the young ones, and what better way than through music? The more talented they were, the more people they would reach.

They chose a scenario in which young people hopefully would take notice of, hoping that one day they would realise that drugs and alcohol can harmful and even kill. All three famous people chose this scenario to help others.

Daffodil

You choose the time when you wish to be born, as well as the manner and timing of your own death, if this is what you wish. I hope that the deaths of these three famous people haven't been in vain, because the drug culture has become so dominant in our society – it's taking over the world.

I hope it's been a wakeup call for thousands of young people all over world; for the good reason it was intended for.

In Peru where they make cocaine illegally, the toxic waste left from this deadly drug is tossed into the rivers and the ocean! Also, a large amount of rainforest has been destroyed. In the process; it makes me cringe. Can you imagine what this is going to do to the fish, and other sea creatures?

Not only does it destroy human life, but it is destroying nature on a vast scale.

The Saviours

Some souls that have reached such high levels; volunteer themselves to come down here simply to help people on this planet. They walk amongst us and can arrive in groups. They are like an army of soldiers, but without the violence. Some are known as earth angels.

Some groups that are down here are known as thunder-beings, and they help the planet itself by preventing world catastrophes; such as meteors colliding with earth and earthquakes. They help the animal kingdom, and they fight pollution and anything that can be a danger to this planet.

Sometimes disasters occur, but sometimes they have to, especially when there's a build-up of energy, like the tectonic plates coming close together. That's why volcanoes explode over time. The planet itself is a living, breathing entity with a conscience. It has to release its energy, its build-up. If not, the world would explode! It's not rocket science to try and understand; it's all to do with nature.

This information was brought to my attention by the book *The Lighted Path,* by Risha Henrique. As I was reading the book, it became familiar to me. I wasn't at all surprised by it. It was my soul remembering.

We also receive help from other planets. We've had a lot of help with our technology. This group of souls helps our scientists with ideas. Obviously the scientists are not aware of this; they think it's all down to their own inventions.

Haven't you noticed how far and how fast we have come with technology in the last thirty years? The crop circles are a nudge to let us know that we are being helped by a higher intelligence. They are not here to harm us, like most people assume. They are here trying to save us — from having to save ourselves! They see that man is destroying the planet.

Can't you see now why we are entering the big change, and why it's inevitable? Man's greed and the destruction of the planet has gone too far. There has to be a purge, a cleansing, of the world's evil destruction. It will be the only way we can save the earth and our future generations.

Like I said before, the new world will enter a golden age and become a wonderful, peaceful, spiritual planet. We will all experience this new and wonderful world with future reincarnations. Nothing is lost. We will be reunited with our families once again.

Jealousy

Jealousy is one of the worst emotions one can carry around. We have all had lives where we have suffered jealousy in one way or another. Some feel it more than others. Not only does it affect the ones who are jealous, but it also affects the person one is jealous of. By being jealous, you are sending out bad vibrations to that person's aura, to the point where the person can become ill. Also, you are damaging yourself because what you give out will come back to you; this is karma.

I myself must have carried this emotion around with me in the sixteenth century, to the point where I made another one suffer (Marlene). It was through my jealousy at the time that this terrible atrocity happened. I must have learnt this lesson in my reincarnations after that life. Now I do not carry this emotion because I've never felt it in this life. Yes, I can feel admiration and awe for others, which is healthy, but never jealousy.

However, my mother would try to instigate jealousy between me and my sister. Mum once said to me, "Our Mary gets really jealous of you, but you don't, do you?" I can't even remember what it was about. I was more concerned with why my mother would want to cause jealousy between us. My mother would test me over the years to see how I would react, but it would never work because deep down I knew what she was trying to do. Or was my soul remembering? Our souls remember everything, even the thoughts we have had.

Whenever you feel jealousy coming on, stop yourself straightaway. Be in control of your emotions because you don't want to feel this way. It's normal to have such feelings, but look at it more with a feeling of admiration. Be happy for them. It's when jealousy spirals and gets out of hand that it breeds hatred towards others, sending out bad vibrations surrounding that persons aura – and also your own aura. Remember the laws of karma.

When we carry negative thoughts around all the time, the spaces between the heart and just above the belly button become blocked. These areas are the chakras, and they should be clear, but what is seen instead of emerald and yellow, bright and shining and running free, is a muddy, grey, brown, or even black, causing illness eventually. You are inflicting harm on yourself.

A lot of mediums and psychics are able to diagnose what's wrong with a client by first examining the aura. Once the client has received the healing, not just physical but also spiritually, he will have a positive way of dealing with his emotions. These areas will start to disperse.

All continuous negative emotions carry a price and will have an effect on your health at some point. All illness starts in the mind. To feel homeostasis, the mind, body, and soul have to work in harmony. This makes you feel whole and gives you a sense of well-being.

Whilst I don't feel jealousy in this life now, I've come across many people in my life who are – and they're quite open about it, not even trying to disguise the fact. When this happens, I think to myself, *Oh no, not again*. It can ruin friendships and causes animosity, even with your best friends.

This is what happened between me and Marlene. She once said to me, "I want what you have." I already knew that Marlene suffered from jealousy. I tried to ignore it and hoped she would tire of it eventually, but it was in her nature. It wasn't just me – she could be jealous of anyone. It was her workplace, her colleagues, and people she met for the first time.

What a waste of spiritual energy. The more I thought about it, it began to make sense. Why was Marlene like this? After all, she was supposed to be a spiritual woman. It was because Marlene and I had shared a past life in the sixteenth centaury, where I was the jealous one. *Have the tables turned?* Remember that we come down to experience both ends of the spectrum. Was it Marlene's turn to be jealous? Was this another lesson for both of us in this life?

Was it the fact that when all this occurred in the sixteenth century, she couldn't forgive me? Did she carry hatred towards me and unforgiveness? Who could have blamed her, given the terrible crime that I committed. But she is now my dear friend in this lifetime. At the point of Marlene's death in that past life, she would have carried these feelings over into her next reincarnation.

A word of caution: at the point of death, take only love and loving thoughts with you. Forgive all. If you have any negative bad feelings at that time in your mind, you will take them with you. Think of only love and forgiveness when it's your time. Especially forgive yourself.

This all goes towards a smooth transition into the next world and beyond. You came into this world alone, but you brought love with you. You will exit this world in the same way. It's best if you take the love back with you.

I have always felt a closeness to Marlene. I've felt that we have had lives before, trying to solve similar issues over and over again but without success. Marlene's had a difficult life. I would say it's more mentally and emotionally, rather than physically. Maybe she found it hard to forgive in this lifetime, but I feel strongly that we have resolved our issues at last. I love my dear friend Marlene – may we always remain friends. I know she will understand my explanation for the above.

All her life, Marlene's was starved of love, which is a tragedy. I think that this is worse than living with a chronic illness. That's all Marlene needed, to be loved. We all need to be loved. Love cures everything. If only we all realised this, the world would be a better place. Give love wherever you see it lacking. Remember that when you send out love, it will return to you tenfold.

Remember, we are all at school on earth learning lessons. We may have been learning the same lessons before in past lives and failed. We can be reborn and try all over again in a new life a new scenario.

The beauty about it is that we will always be given the opportunity to try to conquer our misgivings, if not in this life then in future lives. We have been given forever to achieve this; there is no time limit. Remember that God loves a trier.

"Love is the elixir of life. It has no limits."

Eileen Richmond

Fear

Remember that fear is the one thing that holds us back. As I said earlier in the book, man introduced fear into this world, and it has been man's greatest misfortune ever since. In some situations it is necessary for the fight-or-flight experience, and that's all fear is good for. When you become fearful, because it is a negative reaction, you become blocked or trapped. You can't properly progress with your life or your soul.

Why is it that you have become so fearful? Is it a fear of losing your job? Have you been told you have cancer? Do you fear death itself? Do you have a fear of flying in an aero plane? It could be a mountain of things that we are frightened of. Fear plays a big part in our lives in one way or another.

So the question is how do you deal with it? The best way to deal with the fear in your life is to meditate on a daily basis. Hand it over to God; let God deal with your situation, your fear, all of your problems. Let him become your friend as well as your father. Speak to him of all your fears and anxieties. If you allow yourself to do this on a daily basis, depending on how fearful you are at the present moment, I promise you that answers will come to resolve all of your issues.

In some cases, you may feel all of your fears have been resolved. However, it might take a little longer for others. Remember that this is nothing to do with religion or your beliefs. It's simply one of the many tools that God gave you to help you in this world.

Even if you only meditate for five minutes a day, the only thing you have to fear is fear itself. Fear means the absence of God.

To help yourself, keep sending thoughts out to the universe by refusing to be fearful. Tell the universe that you are not going to let fear into your life, that you are going to stay happy and positive as God intended you to be. Do this on a daily basis. Now sit back and watch as your life starts to change for the better! This is what I meant when I spoke of the power you posses. You don't realise how powerful you are.

Forgiveness

When we forgive, we open up our hearts. When we can't forgive, our hearts close down.

We all need to forgive one another, no matter the cause. It could be anything. We may not forgive our parents, our siblings, our spouse, our partners, or our work colleges. When you can't forgive someone and hold a grudge against that person, the poison starts to set in.

Your heart starts to close down. The feelings start to build up, and it slowly festers. It starts to hold you back with your soul's progression. You become stagnant and can't move on freely with your life. Eventually this starts to have a physical effect on the heart. Whatever affects you in a spiritual way will affect you in a physical way.

That is why a lot of people suffer from heart attacks. The arteries become clogged, and then there is a massive build-up, causing the person to have a heart attack.

To stop this from happening, the person needs to practice love and forgiveness. If you feel that you can never forgive, that it's gone too far, that the situation seems hopeless, then this would be a good time to meditate. Find a quite place where you won't be disturbed. Even if you don't believe in what I say, give it a try. Give God and the angels a chance to help you. Ask them why you find it hard to forgive. This is the only natural way that the heart can be healed.

Sometimes the person has carried the bitterness inside his heart for years. He may have become stubborn and ridged in his thinking. The only person he is harming is himself.

Have you ever found yourself in a situation where a fight broke out in the school yard? Then after it was over, you both reconciled and remained friends? Can you remember feeling better about yourself for coming to that decision. It wasn't worth falling out over and losing a friend. This is because you knew better as a child; you were remembering who you were. It's when we grow up that all the animosity begins.

Often when children fight, the parents intervene and say it was the other child's fault, causing an argument. By the time it is all over, the children are back playing with one another the next day, but the parents will continue to ignore each other, causing animosity amongst themselves.

It's the kids who are the wise ones. It's just not worth it.

We all have to look at life more through our spiritual eyes. We are all going the same way, on the same journey. Wouldn't it be better if we had a little more patience and understanding with each other? We could create a better society, especially for the children's sake.

When children are small, they are very impressionable and look towards the parent for guidance. It's important that we carry the right set of values, the right mindset, so that we can pass it on to our children. That way when they grow up, they become responsible, wonderful, spiritual human beings.

Love

As you have already realised by now, love is mentioned throughout; along with the soul's progression. You may have thought that some of the chapters may have been repetitive. The whole book is centered on love because **that is all there is**. Love is the most important aspect of your life and the most important thing on this planet.

The world cannot exist without it. Love is the greatest, most important lesson we can learn. It is what makes the world go around. God is pure love. You are a spark from God, and that makes you pure love, for God is within you right now. You are a part of God.

I used to whisper to my grandchildren when they were little, "What is the most important thing in this world?"
They would always answer, "Love," as they looked up at me with a cheeky smile. I always felt it was important to instill this in them at an early age.

For thousands of years, people have mentioned love. What does it really mean? I suppose it's hard to explain. We are all made of love. It's mentioned all the time in. songs, music, books, films, poetry, and Christmas and birthday cards. We even made a special day to celebrate love: Valentine's Day.

Love means many things, and there are varying types of love. The love you have for your newborn baby won't be the same love you have for your husband or partner. The love you have for your parents varies. The love for a true friend isn't the same as for casual acquaintances.

The word love is somehow special. It means to care deeply for one another. When lovers love and become intimate, it can also cause confusion because it is tied up with lust and infatuation; it becomes hard to define.

Then there's Gods love, and this is very different. This is not human love. You can't define this love. When I was at Alan Bellinger's house the day I was taken out of my body to a different dimension, I cannot describe the feeling that I experienced. It was so overwhelming, so overpowering. Here I stood in what looked like a little chapel with a small choir, and angels sang on my behalf. I felt the love from God, the angels, and everyone in the room. Oh, how I want to go back to that place. The love I felt was in my skin, in my bones, in every fiber of my being, especially my heart. It was the most wonderful, powerful feeling ever. This wasn't like human love; it was a lot more than words can explain. I felt intoxicated with love.

If that is God's love for all of us, then we all have a lot to look forward to. It's no wonder that when some people have near-death experiences, they say they've experienced the love from God and the angels, and they don't want to come back here. They want to stay. Even little children mention this special love. They never forget what it was like; it stays with them for the rest of their lives.

So you see love is important to all of us. It's life itself. You must learn to love yourself first, before you can love others. Love is the answer to all of your problems.

Problems are always solved where love is involved. Then there's the wonderful, unconditional love our pets give to us. This comes close to the love God shares with us, because it is unconditional. This is true love.

Happiness

On 23 February 2012, Frank Carson, a Northern Irish comedian, died at the age of eighty-five. He became famous in the 1960s after appearing on *Opportunity Knocks*. His famous catchphrases were "It's the way I tell 'em" and "It's a cracker". His comic material was never dirty or obscene. Frank could make people laugh without any obscenities.

He was also famous for his charity work. Frank Carson was a good man. He was a religious man and a great believer in God. When he wasn't performing on stage, he would be passing out leaflets to various people, and the subject was always God.

When he was performing round the country, he would leave his leaflets in all the hotels and in all of the bedrooms in which he stayed. He was a real God fanatic. He was also a very funny man, and he always made me laugh. In the early days I always thought he was a bit of a crackpot and a bit of a Bible basher, taking it all a bit too seriously. But one couldn't help but like the man. He would have me in stitches with his silly comedy.

Frank came down to this planet, and his mission was to make us all laugh and feel happy. He did it very successfully, like so many other comedians. Before Frank was born; he must have looked down upon the earth and saw what a miserable lot we were.

Frank decided, "This is what I want to do. When I return to earth for my soul to progress, I will try to make people laugh and feel happy. That will be my goal, my contribution to the world, my mission." He set up the scenario for this to happen for his next reincarnation. All of life serves a purpose, and we have to have balance in a world of turmoil. Let's face it: with the state the world is in, we all need to let go and have fun.

Have you noticed how well laughter makes you feel, especially a good belly laugh? You instantly feel good, and you forget about your aches and pains and worries, even if it's just for a short while. Yes, laughter is a good medicine for all of us, because it heals us.

We should all strive to be happy. It's important that you are happy in your relationships and your occupation. If you're not, then get out of this situation.

God did not intend for you to be unhappy. God wants all his children to discover happiness. If you're not happy, it's no good staying in a marriage for years, just for the sake of it, or for the children. It's unnatural and holds you back.

It's up to you to get the best out of life. Nobody can do it for you. If your circle of friends doesn't make you feel happy, and you feel you're not stimulated anymore by being in their company; then it's time to move on and make new friends. If you find it hard to find happiness, know that in your heart and soul, one day you will experience true happiness – on the day you go home.

I loved it when the children were small. I could hear them playing and laughing at the same time, and it gave me a sense of fulfillment and satisfaction. That's the trouble with this world: most people take life too serious. We all need to laugh more and lighten up.

Racism

I despise the word racism, but our culture has become racist. There's not a day that goes by without hearing something on the news about another racial attack. Again, this is all to do with religion. Why does it have to be this way? Hasn't it been going on for too long already? This is one of our greatest downfalls.

Take a look at the state our country is in. Who do we blame for this state of affairs? Is it the government? Is it EU Congress?

That is why there has to be change. And change is on its way that's for sure. The racist culture at this particular time, March 2012, is beyond repair. It's been exacerbated by the influx of immigrants into this country, but government officials forgot to use one thing: **common sense.**

I'm not particularly motivated by politics, so I don't feel inspired to discuss the state of this country. Not only would it make me feel depressed, but I don't wish to paint a doom-and-gloom picture for the reader. I'm sure you all have your own opinions. However, anyone with any common sense can see the damage that immigration has brought with it. After all, we are a small country.

We can't keep allowing more immigrants on to the ship when it is already starting to sink. We have to start resolving the problems that are creating these dire situations in the first place. Every man, woman, and child has a right to freedom and to live in a democratic society. We have to find a way to solve this influx of immigrants, but at the same time we must find a way to help theses unfortunate people. After all, they are our brothers and sisters.

Daffodil

If I was in there position, I'd like to think that some government body across the world was trying to help solve this problem. Immigration was never thought out properly; no one looked at the future consequences this could have on Britain. I hope it's not too late for Britain to recover.

You only have to look at the employment situation and the economy. We are not in a very good place. Where do we start to put it right? It will take decades. I know it sounds all depressing, but we have to face up to it. We've made the wrong decisions, the wrong choices, and it's our mistake. It's going to take a lot of undoing. There will be a cleanup of this terrible scenario. There has to be a new start, a new beginning.

The Titanic

Everyone's heard about the story of the *Titanic*. It was supposed to be the strongest, biggest ship ever to be built. But on 14 April 1912, at 11.40 PM on her maiden voyage to New York, the ship struck an iceberg. Around 2.20 on 15 April, the *Titanic* disappeared beneath the northern Atlantic Ocean. The disaster resulted in the loss of more than 1,500 lives. Almost two-thirds of the people on board perished.

In those days, class distinction was very prevalent. The *Titanic* was divided up into three classes of passengers. The second- and third-class passengers were not allowed upon the first-class deck, or even to mix with the first-class passengers, which proved detrimental the moment the ship started to sink. The iron gates were locked, keeping the lower-class passengers below.

Also many mistakes were made. There were not enough lifeboats provided for all the passengers. Some of the lifeboats weren't even full to capacity; one boat only carried twenty-four passengers despite having the capacity for sixty-five. There were no lifeboat drills performed in case the worst should happen. The captain of the *Titanic,* Edward Smith, cancelled all drill exercises which should have taken place the day before the ship set sail. This was despite him having forty-three years experience at sea.

Snobbery prevailed. Money, status, and social standing were all that mattered in those days. There was a lot of prejudice. If you were poor, you were looked down upon as unworthy, not fit for you to be in the same company of the upper classes. In some cases, this is still happening today; snobbery still exists.

Money talks. What is most noticeable is that the class structure was not based on the ability to pay, as we would do today, but upon the social strata in which one was born. In other words, it was breeding. My father always said that class distinction was all to do with breeding and what type of background one came from.

I understood what he meant at the time. However, my father wasn't a snob. No matter where you come from, we are all souls trying to do our best, trying to be the best we can be. Unfortunately, sometimes we get it wrong. We make the wrong choices and the same mistakes. That's why we come back: to try to amend our mistakes.

This was another disaster that had to happen, to show humanity to itself so that it never happens again. There shouldn't have been class division in the first place, just because of one's financial and social standing. No matter what, everyone should be treated as equal. Because of this class distinction, many lives were lost.

The *Titanic* disaster changed a lot of people's outlook; when it came down to class distinction.

When all of this was happening, when the *Titanic* was about to sink, spontaneous decisions were made. People knew they were facing death. It didn't matter where they came from, what their social standing or financial status was. Everyone was fighting to stay alive, to save their loved ones. That was all that mattered.

There were stories of heroism, choices being made, and sacrifices to save others. In that moment, most of the people became as one, working together to help one another. This is how it should be in all aspects of life, for this is what God intended. Instead, it took a disaster to make us realise that we can never allow this to happen again.

The human soul does not recognis class distinction; we are all the same brothers and sisters; we are one.

The souls that were lost in the *Titanic* disaster were volunteers from the spirit realms. They volunteered to come down and show humanity that social standing was wrong. They showed that we are all one, that we are all God's children.

They all agreed to help humanity in this way. Of course, none of these souls would be aware of what was going to happen in their life. It's just as well that our memories are taken away at birth. None of these people died in vain. By their deaths, their spiritual souls progressed more towards God.

When the *Titanic* disaster took place,

God brought them back to their real home. All these souls went over to the spirit world together. Most families would have been spontaneously reunited on the other side. All looking down on this terrible tragedy; they would have all realised that they were still alive! Therefore it is not as tragic as it may seem. The supposed victims would have all known this by now, by being in the real world and not in the world of illusion.

In the Early Hours

The spirit world usually likes to connect with me between two and three in the morning. That's when I seem to receive more communication from the spirit guides or angels. I get a flashback, see faces, or hear music or words.

Apparently we should always listen to our dreams, because there could be a message for us. The other morning, the link I had with the spirit world seemed rather busy. I was thinking to myself, *I'm not going to remember all of this. I really ought to be writing down what I am seeing and hearing.*

But there was one thing in particular that stood out, I remembered it vividly. I could see a large birdcage; I was standing up in the cage looking outwards.

Wow! Does this mean that God is soon going to set me free from all this pain and suffering? Does it mean that my mission is complete and I can go home?

Then I found myself lying on the cage floor and looking towards the sky. It was as if someone was laid next to me. It felt identical to me. Was this my physical body? I remember looking upwards, and a smile came across my face. It was a knowing that only I knew.

Later that week Harry heard a noise coming from the computer room. "Have you forgotten to switch your computer off or something?"

"No, why?"

"Can't you hear that noise?" Then suddenly it went off.

"Ho I'll check it before we go to bed,"

I had left the computer in sleep mode, as I always do. As I switched the computer on, suddenly I heard Eric Clapton's music, and the words; "Would you know my name if I saw you in heaven". He wrote the song "Tears in Heaven" for his little boy, Connor, aged four, who tragically died in an accident due to falling out of a high-rise hotel window.

It stopped me in my tracks. I became emotional as I listened to the words. This wasn't in my music collection, and I had not downloaded any music. Where had it come from? I knew it was meant for me, another message from the spirit world. There is no such thing as coincidence.

The next day, in the early hours of the morning, I remember been awoken by a horrible smell. It filled my bedroom, but it was familiar to me. It was the smell of death. They say that once experienced, you never forget the smell.

Perhaps it was from a past life. Then in my mind's eye I saw Alan Bellinger. He was wearing a dark blue silk shirt and dark trousers. He looked about fifty, but as he was looking at me, he seemed confused and upset. He was holding a book in his hands. I got the impression it was an address book; it was as if he was trying to tell me to get in touch with him.

I kept thinking of Alan that day. Obviously he was trying to tell me something. Alan was over ninety by now. That morning I tried phoning him several times, but the operator kept saying it was the wrong number.

I got in touch with Alan's son Robert via email about two years ago, inquiring after Alan health. He said that Alan was all right, but he got a little confused at times. When I searched for Robert's email address, I couldn't find it. I was prompted to write a letter that very same day to Alan, in the care of Robert.

I'd tell Alan that I was near to the end of the book and was searching for a publisher. The book was as important to Alan as it was to me. I had promised to give Alan and Joyce recognition for all the healing work they'd devoted themselves to over the years.

A week later, I still hadn't heard from Robert, so I went back to my old emails to see if I could find it again. At last I found it with the help of the angels. Robert emailed me back to confirm that Alan had passed away with double pneumonia that came and went four times over a period of six weeks.

Alan died on 16 November 2011. Robert said that Alan was at peace, even though his death took six weeks to reach the end.

No wonder I could smell death that morning in my bedroom. Alan certainly wanted me to notice him. As for why Alan looked upset and confused, apparently Robert had notified all of Alan's friends from Alan's personal address book. Robert had tried to let me know several times by phone, but I had forgotten to give Alan my new telephone number!

Later in an email, Robert said that Alan was fine, was with his wife Joyce on the other side, and was almost over the trauma of life. He said I should not grieve for Alan, for he was where he was at his best.

I hope that Alan comes through to me with more information.

A few months later, I must have travelled to the spirit world in my sleep. It felt like I was in a park on a sunny day. "Oh look, there goes Alan!" I shouted. I started running up behind him to surprise him; I put my arms around his neck. "Hi, Alan, how ya doin? How's my book? Can I come home yet?"

We carried on walking, and then he shouted out, "Ha! Let it hang out to dry for a bit."

I was disappointed. He meant it was not ready yet. I wouldn't be going home anytime soon."

By the way, when we use the word soon, it doesn't always mean the same in the spirit world. There's no such thing as time in the real world; therefore soon could mean tomorrow or in years to come.

Tina Nash

The Tina Nash story has to be one of the most disturbing cases I have ever heard in my life. Just when you think you've seen and heard the worst atrocities that man is capable of committing towards his fellow man, something comes along that floors you. You can't believe what has just been disclosed on the news – its content so evil. You say to yourself, "This can't be real, it can't be true. No one could do that to another human being." You're stunned and don't want to believe it's true.

Tina Nash was thirty-one years old and was a pretty mother of two children. She became a victim of domestic violence. In a diabolical act of brutality which has horrified the nation, Shane Jenkins deliberately blinded the mum by gouging out her eyes. Not only that, but Tina suffered a broken nose and a broken jaw as he tried to suffocate her in an attack at her home. Tina was left with her injuries for twelve hours before help arrived.

Every time I think of this woman, it breaks my heart. I pray for her in my meditation I send her healing. Nothing has ever disturbed me as much as this story. We can all help Tina by sending our healing thoughts. The more people who send prayers and healing, the stronger Tina will become. Let's all pray to God for a miracle to happen, and for Tina's eyesight to be restored one day. Miracles do happen, and there's no harm in trying.

Every time I think of Tina, I think of what she must have been thinking at the time, when all this was taking place. I try to picture what it must have been like for her, but I can't – it is too horrendous, and I have to stop myself.

One's eyes are so precious. They are the windows to the soul. To have that suddenly taken away from you has to be one of the worst things known to man.

Tina bravely spoke about her terrible, twelve-hour ordeal. "It's like being buried alive. This isn't me. I miss the world. I feel like a ghost. I can hear everyone around me, but I can't even see my hand in front of my face. He has robbed me of one of the most precious things in life. The hardest thing is I'm never going to see my kids' faces ever again."

Try closing your eyes for about twenty minutes and going about your daily life. It's a frightening experience.

Tina revealed that she actually looks forward to going to sleep, because she can see in her dreams. Tina's two sons were aged three and thirteen when this took place in April 2011. They witnessed all of this. They thought that Jenkins was trying to kill their mother. Can you imagine the damaging effect this has had on the children?

Tina is going to need tender loving care to get through all of this. She is helped by her family and friends, and her two sons. Tina sent out a message to all victims of domestic crime. She pleaded, "Seek help and get out before it's too late. Your situation isn't going to get any better."

Two women a week are killed by domestic violence, by their partners or former partners. Refuge hopes Tina's case sends out a strong message to the government and local authorities that domestic violence services are necessary and must not be cut.

I will never forget this lady. Sometimes when I think of Tina, I wonder what she's doing. Is she reading a book? No. Is she watching her favourite soap on TV? No. Did she have any hobbies that she can no longer do? Did she drive? I think of all the things that a pretty young mother would do at her age.

What would be my message to Tina?

Whenever you feel down, listen to your favourite music. Reiki music will sooth your mind, body, and soul. Music is so important because it helps the healing. Take reflexology sessions. Dance whenever you care to – in your bedroom, living room, wherever you feel safe.

Listen to the birds and to nature when you're outdoors. Spend as much time as you can with your children. Give them plenty of hugs and tell them you love them. Try to keep that bubbly, outgoing nature that you always had and that made you the person you are today.

But most of all don't let this man destroy your life by feeling hate and bitterness towards him. One day this man will have to face the consequences for the atrocity he committed. No one is exempt from misdeeds committed towards another human being.

He will reincarnate one day, returning to this earth in a different body and a different scenario. Hopefully he will try and make amends for what he did in this life. He will not be aware of this past life. The life that he chooses may be a hard one; for instance, he could lose his sight or even be born without sight. He may have to look after his blind child, who also has other disabilities.

He may wish to reincarnate in another life with Tina when he has seen all the terrible things he did to her. He may wish to care for her and devote his life to her. He will experience all Tina's pain and suffering at the time this happened, as well as the pain Tina's family went through, seeing her almost destroyed in this way.

Tina is determined to be a mother to her two children; they are her motivation to carry on with her life.

It was later found out that Jenkins tried once before to gouge out a man's eyes in a pub brawl. The victim was six foot four and was able to defend himself. Obviously Jenkins is a very dangerous man; he is well-known to the police for violence. At the time Jenkins was serving a five-year ban from local pubs in the area for violent incidents, including punching a policeman.

It will make no difference what Jenkin's sentence will be. He will have to face up to the consequences sooner or later in another life. He will be given a choice as to what happens in his next life. He could come back straightaway, or it could take him years to decide. Or he may want to remain on the dark side with the lower realms. Evil does exist on this earth, and it's not always for a good cause. Nothing is set in stone.

This also applies to all souls who commit terrible crimes towards mankind. Nothing is forgotten; it is universal law of cause and effect. Every action and thought you make on this planet will be recorded in the Akashic records, the book of lives.

19 May 2012

Three days ago, I hadn't been feeling well, which wasn't unusual for me. I had all the symptoms of yet another UTI, making me feel nauseous and sweaty. It seemed to get worse as the day progressed.

I put myself to bed with some paracetamol and stayed in bed the next day because my symptoms worsened. I finely rang the doctor to tell her the familiar circumstances of my condition. It was coming up to the weekend, and so it was too late to take the usual urine sample. She prescribed the usual antibiotics to cover me over the weekend.

The next day I could neither eat nor drink. Every time I tried to drink, I brought it back up. Therefore I couldn't take my medication for my other condition. How was I going to keep down the antibiotics?

It was now Saturday, the third day of being unwell. I didn't know what day it was and felt delirious. In the back of my mind, I didn't want to go into hospital. I felt so bad and wanted to die. In all the years of being ill, I had never suffered anything so evil.

Harry was concerned, but I had made him promise me that if anything should happen to me, he mustn't call the ambulance. I simply wanted him to make me comfortable. When I look back now, I shouldn't have laid the responsibility on Harry. It was just that I had had enough of being ill.

My chronic arthritic condition wasn't going to get any better. I certainly didn't want to end up in the hospital with all the horror stories you hear in the media. If I was going to die, then I wanted it to be at home with my family and little Peggy. This is still my wish.

By late Saturday afternoon, I'd gone past caring.

There was a knock at the door. It was my eldest son, Wayne, and his partner, Joanne. I hadn't seen them for almost eight weeks. As heard them enter the living room, I could hear Harry and them whispering. Joanne's mother, Jean, had been ill at the same time, hospitalised with a liver condition. When Harry was telling them about my symptoms, Joanne mentioned, "Oh, that's just like my mum."

Harry asked her if she could persuade me to go to the hospital.

I had managed to sit up in bed, with a jug in my hand, in case I was sick for the umpteenth time. Joanne took one look at me, I could see she was shocked at the state I was in. "Oh Eileen, come on, love. You can't go on like this."

I gave in. It didn't take much persuading, and I let them take over and send for an ambulance. In the back of my mind, I knew I had a book to finish! I finally arrived at the hospital after a very bumpy, uncomfortable ride in the ambulance.

They had given me morphine for my arthritic condition, because I was unable to keep any medication down. All the time I was being ill, my right stump felt tender and hot. I didn't dare look at it when I was in my bed;

I had enough to contend with. When I did finely see it, I was shocked. It had ballooned to twice its normal size, and it looked red and angry. I thought at the time, *I'll never be able to fit my prosthesis ever again.*

It turned out that I had septicemia! Within another twenty-four hours, I would have gone into toxic shock, and that would have been the end. I was given massive doses of two types of antibiotics, every day for nine days, after they had first been given intravenously. I'm astounded that the human body could absorb this amount of antibiotics in such high quantities.

After nine days, my mouth and tongue had become cracked, swollen, and very sore. I asked the doctor if he ought to be reducing the antibiotics by now. He took another blood test to check for any infection left in my body. It was clear; I could come off them altogether- big mistake.

I was so pleased that there had been improvement! I felt much better. But at the time I needed the strong antibiotics because they had to blast this poison from my blood. The thing was that now I had cellulites in my stump caused by the infection! *Oh no, not something else!* Why were the spirit world and the angels making it so hard for me?

What unfolded prior whilst in hospital was unbelievable. I remember arriving at the hospital A&E in an ambulance. All the time I could smell this beautiful aroma of roses, a powdery fragrance like talcum powder. It was all around me. Then later I was moved to the trauma ward; this smell followed me all around the hospital. At first I thought it might be something they had coming out of the air-conditioning. I seemed to recognise this fragrance from years ago.

We once went to Doncaster Market to do some shopping. I was using my mobile scooter at the time. I remember passing a chemist. Suddenly I stopped, and as I turned my head, I could smell this same fragrance.

At the time I was looking for the logical reason. No one had passed me, so was it coming from the chemist? Had someone sprayed some perfume, and it was wafting out of the doors? What I do remember is how it made me stop dead in my tracks. At the time I thought of the angels. When angels are near you, you may smell a perfume. They bring it so that you know they are with you. This is common.

When I arrived on the ward, as they pushed my bed through, the nurse on duty said to me, "Oh, you smell lovely. Just like roses." I knew then that my angels were with me, keeping an eye on me and comforting me.

There were four beds to a ward, and I looked around at the other three lady patients. There was an elderly lady of eighty–five, Margery, who had come in with a lung condition; she couldn't respond very well when I tried to speak to her. There was Pat, a nice, warm, friendly woman with gall bladder problems.

Daffodil

Then there was **Doreen.** As soon as I turned to look at Doreen, I knew she was trouble. She sat in the corner on my left side. She looked like a character from the Australian TV series in the seventies "Prisoners in cell block H". For those who remember it, you'll get a good idea of the character.

My heart sank for a little while. Then I thought, *it takes all kinds. Never judge a book by its cover.* We eventually introduced ourselves to each other, except poor Margery, who just stared. That night I asked the spirit world and the angels for healing for myself and the other three ladies.

The next day I met a nurse called Kath. As I watched Kath on the ward, I was compelled to ask her if she believed in angels. I felt a little reluctant because I didn't know her. However, it was as if the angels were prompting me to ask.

When I did, to my relief she said, "Yes, I do," with a smile on her face. She began to tell me of some of her experiences. Somehow; it was as if I had to get across to her that it was important she acknowledge her angel was there for her. I told her that angels will only come to her when she asked; no one could do it for her. Kath didn't realise this and was grateful.

The next day I could sense something was bothering her. She was having trouble at home with her son, and she'd been having trouble with the sister on duty for about a year. There was some kind of conflict going on between them.

I said, "You know, Kath, all you have to do is ask your angel to help you resolve this issue. There's a method where you can ask your Angel to have a word with the sister's guardian angel, to try and resolve the matter between you both."

She looked surprised. "Really?"

"Yes, it's as simple as that. But don't expect all answers at once. The outcome may not be to your liking, but if the angels have anything to do with it, it will be in your best interest, you can be sure of that."

As the week went on, I noticed that Doreen seemed to have a routine to her day. She would watch her TV and then play games. She was always eating and making vulgar sounds. Then out of the blue, she would have regular panic attacks, and they had to attach her to an oxygen machine that made a loud noise. This would happen in the day and also during the middle of the night.

One day when the doctor came to do the morning rounds, Doreen switched from being active to the ailing patient, to the point where she couldn't even rise from her chair. I could hear the doctor inquiring if there had been any improvement. She would continue the story of all her ailing problems.

One day Kath interrupted Doreen and the doctor. "Doreen! I've just seen you out of your chair, walking round your bed and going into your drawers. Kath shook her head in frustration as she looked at the doctor. Doreen was putting on a show.

Doreen had two sons that she didn't get on with. Later that day Doreen had a fall. The nurses came rushing in and said, "Oh Doreen, are you all right, love? Put your head on this pillow and take deep breaths."

I couldn't help but think at the time, *was the fall deliberate?* Doreen came to no harm. But I'm not here to judge.

She had osteoporosis as well as other problems. One night when I was trying to advise her with the help from the spirit world, I asked her, "Doreen, what happens prior to the panic attack coming on?"

She said it was as if something in her brain suddenly switched off. She had been told that only she could help herself, that it was all down to her.

Again I could feel my angel say, "Ask her the question."

"Doreen, do you believe in angels?"

To my great surprise, Doreen answered yes. At the same time Pat also said that she believed in angels.

Daffodil

"Brilliant!" I said. "We're halfway there!"

I gave them a rundown of all I knew about the angels, the important things they should know. I also gave information about the reasons for our lives and why we are all here.

When I told Doreen that we choose our parents, siblings, and scenarios for our best development, she frowned. I could tell she didn't agree. She didn't agree with choosing the parents. She turned her nose up and said, "I wouldn't have chosen my parents, especially my dad. He was always drinking."

I could see Pat was really interested and wanted to know more. I tried to explain to Doreen that she could take control of the panic attacks with the help of her guardian angel.

When all this was taking place, I was surprised I had the energy, but I knew I was being helped by the spirit world. Not only that, but I found that everything I was explaining seemed so easy. I was articulate, which didn't always happen with me. It was as if the angels wanted me to get in touch with as many people as possible, in order to get the message across.

With every person I came across, when I asked whether they believed in angels, they would share some of their experiences with me. But what they all had in common was that none of them knew they had to acknowledge their guardian angels and could ask for their help at any time.

It was easy to see what Doreen had planned prior to coming into hospital. Doreen had been in the hospital for six weeks, and she didn't want to go home. Apparently she had sold her home and was living with her daughter. God only knows how hard it must have been for her daughter, if this was the way Doreen was carrying on at home.

That night I asked for healing for Doreen. I asked my angel to talk to Doreen's guardian angel and resolve this awful situation somehow. I must have spent a good half hour concentrating on Doreen. Then I fell asleep.

It was about four in the morning when I awoke. I remember it being dark and very peaceful. There had been no disturbances that night –no oxygen machine and the usual panic attack! Doreen's curtain was drawn across from me. All of a sudden, I could hear Doreen shuffling around. Then I heard the rustle of a packet of sweets, and I could hear her munching on them!

I waited for a while, till her mouth was full, and then I asked in a very calm voice, "Are you feeling a lot better now, Doreen?"

I think she was shocked that I must have heard what she was doing, but I must confess I found the situation so funny. It was hard not to laugh.

"Huh. I don't know about that," she said, disgruntled. She had changed from the poor ailing patient to munching sweets at four in the morning.

Later that morning, a male nurse came to do the rounds. "Good morning, Doreen. You've had a good night, haven't you? No panic attacks, no oxygen machine."

Again she replied, "Huh. I don't know about that."

That day she gave me the cold shoulder. I could tell she didn't like me because I'd sussed her out. She wasn't aware I'd been asking the angels for help.

At the time it would have been easy to retaliate to someone I was trying to help, when she was being nasty towards me. But I felt that this was a test for me. I made a choice to help this woman. Doreen made a choice not to accept my offer of help, and she made it plain that she didn't like me. She knew I had sussed her. I knew the game she was playing.

I sat up in my bed and carried on talking to Pat about the here and now, and the angels. Doreen was pretending to read a magazine. Pat was eager to know more; she was suffering with her illness, but I knew she was going to recover and told her so. She looked relieved.

Daffodil

A little later Pat shouted across the ward to Doreen, "Well I feel a lot better for that. It all makes sense! She's done me the world of good!" All the while she looked at Doreen, waiting for her reaction. There was none.

Later, one of the nurses came to move me from the ward to the orthopedic ward. Pat was saddened by this and said so. "Oh, just when I was getting to know you." As they pushed my bed towards the door, Pat thanked me for helping her. I'd written more information on a scrap of paper in a hurry about the angels, and I gave it to her as I said goodbye.

Meanwhile, Doreen had buried her head in a magazine so that she wouldn't have to acknowledge me. As I was almost through the doors, Doreen shouted, "Byeee!" in a sarcastic tone. I answered in the same way. That was the very first time I had ever come across anyone person I was trying to help. It was like a smack in the face.

I met two nice ladies in the next ward. Betty was an eighty-two-year-old woman who had come in with a broken shoulder, due to her husband driving the car away and not realising Betty was leaning on the door. Her eighty-five-year-old husband was so shocked that he passed out.

"There just happened to be an ambulance at the scene," she said. That was the angels' intervention – no such thing as coincidence. What a lovely couple they made; they were so affectionate towards one another. When Terry, her husband, arrived at visiting time. I saw him stagger around the entrance to our room with crutches. He looked shattered.

The weather was so hot and humid towards the end of May 2011, but fortunately my bed was by the window, where I could feel the breeze on my face. It was as if the angels had thought of everything to make my stay in hospital more pleasant.

I later found out that Terry received damage to his lower back when he was dragged from a plane in the Second World War. He lost three inches in height over the years, which developed into arthritis. He was really struggling, the poor man. Terry came every day to see his wife no matter what. They had been together for over fifty years. They had both worked together as school teachers at the same school in Barnsley till retirement.

I had many debates with Betty about the spirit world, and about the angels. Despite Betty's injuries and her age, she remained a very bright and articulate lady. Betty had always been Church of England, if I remember correctly, but it wouldn't have made any difference what Betty's religion was. It made no difference because there's only one God. Which she had to agree.

Betty accepted what I had to say because she had allowed herself to have an open mind all her life, which all of us should have. They say you have to have an open mind to be an intelligent person.

Whenever Terry came to visit Betty, upon leaving they would always shout to one another. "Love you!" she would say. "Love you, Daddio!" which was a term used in the fifties and started in America. It means you are cool in today's language. I found this so endearing, that they still loved each other after all the years and weren't afraid to show it in public. That's what real love is. It never ends.

Then there was Doris in the next bed, aged eighty-three. She had fell and injured her lower spine, she also had osteoporosis. Doris used to be a nurse. One day when I was compelled to bring the angels into the conversation yet again, Doris looked across at me and shouted, "Yes! I do believe. I have two angels, and when I was eleven years old, I saw two fairies right in front of me, running across the wall!"

Then she held her head down as if it was something shameful. She said, "I've never told anyone this before, for fear of being ridiculed." She looked relieved when I told her that I had also seen a fairy.

This happened in 1997, just after I had that out-of-body experience at Mr. Bellinger's home. Harry was on nights at the time. I had gone to bed, switched off the lights, and climbed into bed. I laid flat on my back. Then all of a sudden I saw all these sparkly lights and orbs surrounding the top of my bed. Right in front of me, inches from my nose, was this tiny fairy with little wings flapping, just like what you see in the fairy tale books and films.

I didn't know what to think at the time, but I definitely saw the one fairy and all the sparkly lights. I didn't tell anyone – they would all think

Daffodil

I'd lost the plot. Besides, I was more excited about the spirit world and the angels that I was discovering. However, it was a lovely experience that I've never forgotten. And for Doris to confirm that I wasn't the only one to have seen a fairy made it even better!

We are all at different levels with our spirituality when we reincarnate. That's why some of us will be given glimpses of the spirit world, experiences which are not of this world. That's why there are mediums, clairvoyants, visionaries, and others with such great talents. That can see spirits clearly and are able to help loved ones left behind, to make them realise that there is no end, that it's just a new beginning.

Doris was in a lot of pain with her back. They don't operate now on older patients with broken bones, especially with osteoporosis, for fear of creating more damage. The patient is simply strapped up and given pain killers while the bones fuse. Doris was a widow who lived on her own. She led a lonely life that was made harder when she was ill. Her only daughter lived down south.

She often told us stories from her past. She must have seen a lot of changes in the nursing industry over the past years, but one story disturbed us all.

One day she was preparing two children patients for theatre. They'd been starved twenty-four hours prior in preparation. A little boy had decided to give them both a sweet. Somehow Doris found out. She marched the little boy to the bathroom and stuck his head under the cold water tap! When she was telling us the entire story, she laughed and said, "Woo! I wouldn't have got away with it today – I would have got the sack."

I couldn't help but feel sorry for the little boy. I felt he did it with good intentions. No operations on the children took place that day. The boy must have been terrified! We all looked at each other, as the room went quiet.

Then later that day, two of the cleaners came into the ward. One of them shouted across the room to the other, so that we could all hear.

"Oh my God, I had a right day yesterday! I saw an appreciation) in my kitchen."

I had to laugh because she meant to say she saw an apparition. She was quite funny. However, I could see she was flustered and disturbed by it all.

"Why, what happened?" her friend shouted back.

"I saw my dead grandfather as clear as I am looking at you now! It's put me about, I can't be doing with this!"

I sat listening to what was being said. I thought, *I've got to intervene here. The woman's terrified.* "Excuse me, love, but why are you so frightened?"

"Well, it's not normal, is it?" she said.
"Of course it is."
"What do you mean?"
I went on to explain to her what happens when a loved one passes over.

Doris intervened and asked the woman, "Have you anybody in your family who is ill? "Oh yes, I have! My aunt – she's eighty-three she's very poorly at the moment."

"Well that could be the reason," Doris explained. "He's probably come to help her to pass over."
"Oh, don't say that. I couldn't live without her!"

This took some more explanation. Eventually she calmed down and felt much better about it. I told her about the angels, which she already believed in. Her friend looked at me and said, "Oh, I believe in it all. Do you know: if it's not every day, it's every other day that I find white feathers in my bathroom? Why is that?"
"Is it because you like having a bath? Is it your sanctuary?" I asked.
"Well, it's funny you should say that. I do all my thinking in there, all my crying in there. I guess it must be."
"Well, there's your answer."

"What do you mean?" she asked.

"Your guardian angel hears your cries, and he knows when you're sad. He keeps leaving you the feathers so that you will hopefully get in contact with him."

She was shocked. "Really! The feathers are like a calling card?"

"Tell me, have you ever acknowledged your guardian angel and let him know you know he is there for you?"

"Well, no. I didn't know you had to."

"That's why God gave us all a guardian angel in the first place. Life can be traumatic, and it is so harsh down here on this earth sometimes. All you have to do is say hello to him and talk to him like an old friend. After all, he is. He's been with you since your very first incarnation. He knows you better than you know yourself. He's the same one in your life now, and he will be the same one in all your future lives."

Meanwhile another two members of staff had entered the ward and were listening to the conversation. This must have gone on for about thirty minutes. I seemed to have crammed so much information into to those thirty minutes. The information came through so easily. Yet again I felt so confident and articulate. I knew I was being helped by the spirit world and the angels. I'd forgotten all about my illness.

The next day it was going round the hospital. I soon got a reputation as the angel lady in ward thirty-three: "Go and see the angel lady – she'll explain it all." After that, staff would filter onto the ward. I would repeat myself to them, or I would answer their questions. It was amazing that I could get across to all these people the information they needed to know. I knew it was helping them.

But I'd been so ill. Where was all this energy coming from? When I look back now, prior to going into hospital, I had made Harry promise me that if I should become ill again, he should not get the doctor or ambulance. I should never have made him responsible for that.

The spirit world had to engineer a way to get me into hospital, and it had to be serious enough to keep me in hospital for over two weeks. They knew how stubborn I was once I'd made my mind up not to go into hospital. They wanted me to reach as many people as I could about the spirit world and guardian angels, and why we are here on earth in the first place. That's why I was given all the information, and the energy required. I find it all amazing, weird, and wonderful!

The next day the same two cleaning ladies came to the ward. "Well?" I asked the one who had seen her dead grandfather. "Did you have a word with your guardian angel?"

"Yes I did. I asked all sorts of questions."

"Any luck?"

"No! But that same day she went on. I walked my dog through the park and asked my guardian angel questions. Out of the corner of my eye, I could see something white, long, and flowing." As she said this I was given the same picture. She said, "Every time I looked around me, it disappeared."

"Well that's not surprising, is it? Your angel knows how frightened you were when you saw your grandfather. Your angel doesn't want to scare you. Still, that's progress."

I asked the same question to the other cleaning lady, who kept finding white feathers. "Yes," she said. "I asked my angel as soon as I arrived home."

"Any luck?"

"No." Then she said, "But lo and behold the next day I found a white feather laid across the remote control in my bedroom!"

"Great," I said. "You were being answered!" They both looked at each other and smiled.

Later that night, a black male nurse walked on to our ward. We all said hello and asked him his name. "Moses," he replied. What a lovely name – it seemed so appropriate.

After a little while, I couldn't resist the urge. I stared at him while trying to size him up. "Moses, do you mind if I ask you something?"

He turned to look at me. "No, go ahead," he said with his arms folded.

"Do you believe in the angels?"

He went a little quiet; it wasn't easy to tell what he was thinking. Then he pointed his index finger at me while his arms were still folded in a relaxed mood. After a pause Moses replied, "Angels are heavenly beings, sent by God, and they are there for you to use."

As he spoke, I felt that he had a lot to say about this subject and could teach us all.

The next thing I knew, my mobile phone went off. It broke the mood. The conversation came to an end as another nurse came onto the ward. I could tell everyone was disappointed that this had happened.

I thought Moses may come back later, but we were all bedded down for the night. I couldn't help think that he was quite knowledgeable about spiritual matters. He could have given us more information, but it wasn't to be.

Eventually I made a full recovery, but the illness had taken its toll. I was sent home. I said goodbye to all and promised to keep in touch with the nurse Kath when I came for my clinic appointments.

23rd June 2012

Can you believe it? Out of the hospital for twenty days, and then I'm back in. On the Friday afternoon prior, I began to feel unwell again. I felt so weak and lethargic. I decided to have a sleep on the sofa for half an hour I woke up later feeling a little restored.

At about six in the morning, I couldn't stop shaking, though I tried to hold my body still. *Oh please,* I thought, *not again not another infection.*

This time we sent for the ambulance, but they sent a paramedic, which didn't do me any favours. Although she was very helpful, it only delayed my waiting time to be seen by the doctor and for drips to be administered and blood taken. By now the infection was increasing by the minute. The next thing I knew, I was given an ECG and put to the top of the list to be seen. The sweat was dripping off me and running down my face; my hair was soaked, I felt terrible.

Finally they had me stable once the antibiotics and drips were administered. That night I was moved on to ward thirty-three, room six, in isolation. The nurse on duty said, "We are moving you to the isolation ward in case the infection is contagious."

Then I started with diarrhea and more sickness. *Oh my God, what is happening to me?*

After a couple of days, I felt like a new woman, I thanked the doctors who had been attending me. They were very pleased with my recovery. The consultant said that he had been very worried about me and was considering putting me in the ICU when I first came into hospital.

Daffodil

Meanwhile, they were running all kinds of test; they didn't know what it was.

At four the next morning, I had been sleeping soundly. All of a sudden it was as if someone had pulled me by the scruff of the neck back into my body. Remember that when we are asleep, we can leave our physical bodies and travel. Or remain hovering above them. I had a shooting pain across my midriff. I sat up in bed and was sick again!

Whatever was happening to me; it was not of this world! I knew that this experience was evil. I felt that awful dread in the pit of my soul. It was evil versus good, testing me to the limit. My belief in my God and my angels would never falter. I became very ill once again.

To make a long story short, I had an infection somewhere in my body, and they didn't know where it was coming from. All they could do was to keep monitoring me while they found the cause, and to try and find the right kind of antibiotic. It was the most terrifying thing that I have ever experienced. **I was dealing with the devil.** The atmosphere in the room was thick with a dark, heavy feeling. I thought I was going to die, I asked the nursing staff to get in touch with my family.

However, no one would listen to me. It even caused an argument between me and Harry when he arrived early that same morning. He thought that I wanted to discharge myself that he had to come and fetch me. When all I wanted was to not be on my own if I should pass away.

The hospital sought the advice of a microbiologist. Eventually they found the antibiotic that killed the infection. Let's hope this one has killed the infection once and for all. Whatever the infection was, it wasn't contagious. I was asked if I'd like to join the other ladies on the ward, but my heart wasn't in it. I couldn't be my jolly self, and being alone did have its advantages: I was guaranteed a peaceful night's sleep.

But what was this infection in my body that the doctors couldn't find? When the doctor came round to see me the day before I came home; we were discussing what might have caused it - He shook his head; he still didn't know.

Something keeps niggling at me. On my right thumb just below the bottom of my nail, there's a tiny spot, like an injection mark. I first noticed it when I went into hospital. It's bright pink, but it has never faded and still looks fresh. Sometimes I look at it and wonder how it got there in the first place. Then I'm reminded of that awful, evil experience, where it felt like I was being dragged out of my body. A powerful evil force was attacking me!

No, I wasn't hallucinating with hospital drugs. Besides, I have the scar to prove it. But why does it bother me so, when I look at the spot? I think maybe I was meant to be ill; maybe some unforeseen evil force had injected my thumb with some deadly substance. How could I go from one extreme to another within twenty-four hours of feeling so well? It doesn't make sense.

Consider the fact that the doctors didn't know what the infection was, or whether it was contagious. It felt like I was fighting for my life. Over the last few years, some strange things have happened to me that are not of this world. Sometimes it's so hard to explain that I don't even try.

But one thing I have come to realise is: there's a lot we don't know about this world and the universe. No doubt I will find out sooner or later when my time comes. Then on occasions when I do watch SKY TV, I find out I'm not the only one who has scars and a strange story to tell that is not of this world?

Meanwhile in hospital, I met some of the same people again – nurses and cleaners. My work was not yet finished. I met Kath, the nurse whom I first spoke to about the angels. I asked her if there was any resolve with the sister on duty who had been unkind to her.

She looked at me and started laughing. "You're not going to believe this. After I had spoken to you, I gave it a try and asked my guardian angel to help me with this problem. The very next morning, the sister rang me to say she wouldn't be coming into work. She had tumbled down the last three stairs and hurt her ankle!"

Kath and I both laughed out loud. I said, "It wasn't anything serious, though, was it?" I felt a little guilty.

"Oh no," Kath said. "I was just like you when she told me over the phone, trying hard not to laugh." Kath's guardian angel wanted to impress her, and he certainly did.

Regarding Kath and the nursing sister, the atmosphere between them has calmed down. They even had their coffee break at work together, so that's progress. It will take time. It's like the angels wanted to give the sister a slap on the hand, like one would a naughty child. No great harm was done.

I met a few new nurses, and we talked about the angels. It was exactly the same scenario as before. I came out of the Hospital on 5 July after twelve days. It was a great ordeal for me. My body felt traumatised by the whole event; but mentally I felt calm and able to cope. You'd think by now I would have cracked up. It's because I know I'm being looked after by God and the angels.

After coming home from hospital, I went to see the consultant for my follow-up. About the wound on my knee; where they had to drain it. The surrounding skin has been slow to heal. Although the wound is only small, this means I haven't been able to wear my prosthesis for three months. The wound looked clean, and there was no sign of any inflammation, so they didn't think it necessary to check my blood or give me a swab test.

On my second follow–up, appointment I insisted on tests. The consultant thought I was being too fussy and didn't think it was warranted. He saw the look of concern on my face and said, "Oh, if it pleases you, then," looking at me rather annoyed.

Guess what? When I went back two weeks later, yes, there was an infection. Also, my blood enzymes levels had risen! My own GP had failed to notify me of the results from the hospital. Eventually I was put back on antibiotics. I shouldn't have had to ask for these test to be done in the first place. They should have been done automatically, especially with my medical history.

I'm losing all faith with the medical profession. It's certainly not what it used to be. Thank God I have my guardian angel looking out for me.

Whilst I'm on the subject of hospitals and them not being what they used to be, I'll add that I've seen a lot over the years, with so many changes. For instance, junior doctors and senior registrars don't wear white coats anymore.

They come to work in their everyday clothes so that patients can't distinguish one person from another. I always thought that the white coat looked clean and professional. One attractive lady registrar who was attending to a patient wore trousers. The thing that stood out; was that I could clearly see the thong she was wearing underneath the trousers. Hardly professional!

Once, I asked why the medical team had stopped wearing white coats. "To put the patients more at ease," they replied. In other words, it was to avoid white coat syndrome. Call me old-fashioned, but I think it causes more confusion.

Whilst I've met many nice nurses and doctors, I could easily pick out the ones who shouldn't be in the medical profession at all. A male orderly who brought tea in the afternoon placed the tea in front of an elderly patient so that she couldn't reach it. I was watching this, and I interrupted. "But she can't reach her tea."

The orderly made no attempt to move it closer to the patient. "Oh, the nurse will see to her," he replied, How *cruel*, I thought. I couldn't help the poor woman due to my knee replacement. The care and compassion isn't what it used to be, and it's not something that we should have to learn – it should be in our hearts and souls already.

But sometimes I would come across nursing staff who would put themselves out to help me all they could. Some would have a little chat and share a joke or two. It can make all the difference when you're in hospital.

Too much emphasis is applied to the paperwork the nurses have to do, instead of concentrating on more important jobs. It's the same with serving meals: the nurses shouldn't have to serve the patients meals. That's not the reason why they applied to come into the nursing profession in the first place.

Important Synopsis

To summaries. I want to make it clear to every reader the reason for your life; to make sure I've not missed anything important and that you can understand clearly in your mind.

Why not ask for the help of your guardian angel to help you understand, if you find it difficult to take in. You may experience a connection from your guardian angel as you do this. Don't look for it – you will feel it.

Firstly, we are all God's children, so that makes us part of God. Therefore we are God itself. We hold the same power as God, but we think that we are a lot less. We do not realise how powerful we are – we can be anything we want to be through the choices we make in this learning process. All the answers lie within our souls.

For instance, you may have chosen a life where you are suffering a debilitating disease in order to learn, so that your soul will progress. You make a choice: you either become the victim, or you turn it into something positive like I did. Ask yourself, "Why did I choose this life?"

You may think that God is punishing you –most people do. It may be that most of your incarnations have been fairly happy and easy ones, but with very little progress with your soul. Open yourself up to God and the spirit world and of course your guardian angel.

Ask them to guide you through this scenario you have chosen. You will find that you will be guided all the way through it. There will be times when you have doubts; you will be tested along the way. Things will only happen for you when the timing is right. What you must sustain is **faith.**

However, if you decide to become the victim, this is exactly what you will become. You will create your reality; what you think, you will become. Now, wouldn't that be a complete waste? After all, you chose this scenario to learn from it. Great things come from little acorns.

God wanted to experience it all through his children. This was the only way this could be achieved. God created the opposite to everything because he wanted to experience both. He left it to his children to make the choices – hopefully the right ones. That's why we were given free will.

When you live in the spirit realms before you incarnate. No soul is forced to do something he doesn't want to do. You will never be given a task so hard that you could not deal with it. You dwell in the spirit realms till you are ready; this could be years, or hundreds of years. There is no such thing as time or clocks. Because you're real life is eternal.

I find all this so exciting. Don't you? You will have the advantage of studying and learning all your favourite subjects, as well as the current state of the world. Then you find out one day that you would like to put all this knowledge to use by incarnating to help humanity and the planet. Not only that, but you have the opportunity for your soul to grow! What could be better? Isn't life wonderful? You will always have these opportunities – forever.

When you were born, you were pure, whole, and innocent because you came straight from God. But you were born without memory. The idea was for you to start your new incarnation without memory of lives lived before. However, your soul still knows the all, so nothing is ever lost.

You were put on this planet to reach enlightenment; for your soul to progress by the choices you make to reach the path of consciousness; so that you find your way back home to God.

By this you will remember who you are: God's pure, innocent child. You will be forgiven for all your mistakes, all your downfalls. You will be given a choice to try all over again by reincarnating into a future life to learn the lessons once again. It's entirely up to you.

This applies to all the despots who ever lived on this planet, and all the despicable human beings you can think of. God forgives all. Right now I can feel your outrage, especially if you have been a victim or have lost loved ones to such crimes. I also had to think very carefully before I could totally accept it.

Then I ask myself; who am I to question God? God speaks of the truth and nothing but the truth. He explains the reasons for this through me, so that I could write about it. This is my mission. Remember that this world is just an illusion. All the atrocities that take place on this **earth are not real.**

First, your real home is heaven. That is your real reality. That is where you truly belong. When you arrive in heaven after you have passed over from earth, you become the real you, the person you truly are. You will remember everything instantly because your soul remembers the all. Your memory is given back to you. You still have the same character and personality you've always had.

The question will be has your soul progressed in the life you have just left behind? You will be shown a review of that life; it will be like watching yourself on a big movie screen within a matter of seconds: all the good you achieved, all the mistakes you ever made, all your good and bad thoughts.

You are not your body! You are not the illness or disease that you suffered on earth! You are not that blind person anymore, or the physically handicapped person, or the mentally handicapped person. You are now whole, perfect, God's innocent child. You are now back to the real you, the one whom God created, whole and pure as you always were.

At the time we live on earth, it all seems real. We are all programmed in this way to think it's our real reality. The pain feels real. The sorrow and the heartache feel real. The loss of loved ones feels real. The baby you miscarried seemed real. The wars on earth seamed real. The Holocaust seemed real. The starving children in Africa seemed real. The 9/11 terrorist attacks seamed real. It was all **an illusion** to make us think that it was real and really did take place.

Do you honestly think God would have allowed all these terrible things to have happened for real? He didn't create the world so that all his children would suffer. Besides, God would be punishing himself, so what would be the point? We are all a part of God and this is not what God intended. God loves each and every one of us. He is pure love, and we are pure love.

To All the mothers whose sons were killed in wars can rest assured that it wasn't reality at the time. It was only an act we are playing out. The soldiers are in heaven, looking down on their parents and wives and children. They know full well that they will be together again one day. They will come realise the truth. They will have had all the knowledge given back to them as soon as they passed over.

These soldiers volunteered themselves in this way to try to help humanity, to put a stop to all wars and killing.

Probably conversing with one another before reincarnating; saying "Look! We can't go on living in a world like this, killing one another. It has to stop once and for all. It's up to us to make the right choices and put an end to all this fighting and suffering. We have to learn to live in peace and love, as God intended."

Doesn't this all make sense to the meaning of life? Ask yourself right now. Can you think of a better one? Wars will keep happening till someone comes up with a solution to end all wars once and for all. The world must come together to put down all weapons of mass destruction. We should sit down and resolve all conflicts, problems, and greed, turning our minds to saving this planet. God cannot intervene, and so it is up to us.

God watched in sorrow as he saw all his children make the wrong choices. Don't forget god had to make bad situations as well as good situations so choice would be possible in the first place; god left it to his children to resolve. It seems that in this experiment, if you want to call it that, man has been making too many wrong choices, too many mistakes. You have only to look at the world around us now and see the terrible state it is in.

***

Evil was created so that we could make choices to become a good person, or a bad person. Unfortunately, some of God's children like to dwell on the darker side; they prefer the evil side to life. We have not helped this situation. We have allowed our children to grow up and become exposed to violence and horror by men creating evil films and games for the media. It's so prominent that some adults and children want to go out and create the violence and evil for real.

You probably saying, "Wait a minute. Didn't you just say that life on earth is an illusion, that none of it is real, that we are all just acting?" Yes! So what do I mean, then?

The decisions we choose for our souls to progress is a fact. It is the only one real reality we possess. Like I said, some of God's children prefer the evil side to life, and that is why **evil exists on this planet**. However, God will always forgive his child if the child is willing to turn to the light and ask for forgiveness.

There will always be room in God's heart for all his fallen children, the ones who have lost their way. We have to learn so that we can make the right decisions; the right choices, so that all souls will ascend together with all their brothers and sisters.

For the record, first we choose a scenario in the new life we are about to venture. We may come to earth in a group soul scenario, learning together. We will choose our parents, siblings, husbands, and wives. It's not because we favour them, but because they are the ones who will serve us the best in the lessons we have chosen to learn in this new life.

Our planet is slowly dying. The world continues its downfall as I write this in 2012. People are living in fear all over the world. The starving children that we continue to see on our TV screens are volunteers; evolved soul's to remind us all. They have always been there to remind man of greed and how man can change if he chooses. Man is making the wrong choices. They are there to remind us all. "Are you going to help us when there is enough for everyone? Are you going to share with us all the abundance you were given by God? Or are you going to turn a blind eye and pretend we don't exist?"

The innocent women and children who were slaughtered in Syria; were due to the wrong choices made by man. **These are evolved souls.** What is happening when we allow children to become victims through the wrong choices that man has made? We are destroying our planet.

There's no turning back – this world has to be cleansed if it's to survive. It has gone too far. This world is a living, breathing planet with a conscience. All the evil in the world has built up; it has to be expelled if it's to survive any future.

You are probably asking yourself, "Why has God created us all in the first place and the scenarios that we choose for ourselves, anyway?" It's because the world would not exist, and **there would be nothing to do**. God would have had to create something that would keep the world turning forever. But his intention was to create a heaven upon the earth. It will take forever to reach that goal.

Besides, can you think of a better way to give us all something to do? It would be pointless if we came down to earth, and everything was perfect and we didn't need to learn anything. If we had no choices to make, we'd all be like zombies or machines, going nowhere and making no progress with our souls. There would be no reason for a life in the first place. That's why God created the opposite to everything. God thought of everything.

Will we make the right choices? Will we choose to love our fellow man? Or will we choose to kill him through continuous wars and murder? Will we treat our brothers and sisters with love and respect? Will we treat others as we wish to be treated ourselves?

The only way God will interfere if it is not your time to die. God created the guardian angel and gave us all one for every life that we incarnate into. They are with us from our very first life, up to the lives that we are living now, and all our future lives.

There are no secrets, and you cannot hide from your angel.

How many of you have shouted out, "Oh God, please help me!" Have you called on God in your hour of need, or to help someone else? Even though some of you didn't believe there was a God in the first place, we all do it automatically. This is because our soul is remembering who we truly are.

I've been searching for God all my life. It was only when I became ill in 1989 that I was desperate for help. I shouted out for God's help. "Please! Please! If there is a God out there, please help me! Tell me what to do. Show me what to do!" From that day on, my life had new meaning. I was led to my spiritual path that I was destined to walk. I found the real reason why I had chosen this life – a life of pain and suffering starting in 1989, which has tested me mentally as well as physically.

This is why we are all here. God wants us all to find our way back home. We have to do it all by ourselves with the help of our guardians angels, and we can. For those who chose a life of suffering, whether it be physically or mentally, don't become the victim of your illness, or else you will make this your reality. You will remain stuck with your soul. The mentally handicapped are guided more so by the soul. You will not move on with your life if you become the victim. You will waste it; you will simply wallow in your own self-pity and suffering. Choose the positive side for what it was intended for. This way, you will find your strengths and weaknesses. It may not be an easy journey, but with the strength and courage from the angels – in this case, Archangel Michael – you will have all the help you need. And of course, you'll have help from God.

Archangel Michael is a strong angel; he can be as big as a jumbo jet, if need be. He is our leader in battle, and he will protect us from danger. He will give us strength and courage in all matters.

When I was in the hospital, I asked for his protection every day. "Please, Archangel Michael, give me wisdom, guidance, and understanding. Protect me from any evil that may hang around my aura, my soul, and my body. Keep my aura bright, clean, and shiny."

It has taken me years to find my God, my real father, and the reason I had to come here in the first place. All of this was to tell humanity the truth and nothing but the truth: the reasons for your life. I'm totally convinced that what I have written in my book is the truth. God and the angels made it so easy for me, as more and more guidance and information poured into me.

When I look back on what happened, I feel so humble and blessed that I was chosen for this experience, although I didn't think I was a good enough person. Maybe this is why God chose me in the first place. I am good enough. This is a tendency with all humans, to think we are never good enough.

There are human beings scattered all around the world and doing exactly what I am doing. They are trying to teach the world that God does exists, and that we have a reason for our lives. Some work alone, and some come down in armies, soul groups, and the like. These are called the light workers.

Never in my wildest dreams did I think for one minute that I was going to be given such powerful, divine information from God and the angels, as well as the spirit world. Weeks and months would pass by without me writing a word. In between the gaps, I would carry on with more research, reading book after book about other people's experiences. I would come across authors with the same views, thoughts, and experiences that I was having. It validated everything I believed in and had already written. This gave me the impetus to forge ahead.

I asked God and the angels to give me more, to be shown more. I know I needed much more for my book, if they wanted to make an impact and provide more verification, more substance. Boy, did they deliver!

What we have to believe and remember is that there are no mistakes, no accidents, no chance meetings, and no coincidences. Everything that is happening to all of us is unfolding as it should. In relationships there are no what-ifs. In that way it should make life a whole lot easier. Go along with the flow. The life that you live is supposed to be the way it is, with all its ups and downs.

There's always a reason why things happen the way they do and the reason why we are all here, to make a difference. We are all on a mission. When a person dies in an accident, then it's his or her time to die. There's nothing you could have done to save the person. It's the same with people who adopt babies and children, or who foster children. There's no mistake that they may have chosen the wrong baby. I hope that this brings comfort, joy, and reassurance to all adoptive parents and children out there. All was meant to be by their choosing, for both parents and children. It was all that the people involved had planned together, before they were reincarnated into this life; each and every one of them agreed.

If you are the parent of an adoptive child, or you know of someone who is, then tell them of your finding. At least give them the benefit of the doubt. I know firsthand, because my mother was adopted, and it upset her more than she let on, especially at the latter end of her life. As soon as my mum passed over, she would know the reason why.

Evil

Evil will always raise its ugly head in life. There is no denying that this world has its fair share, when you think of all the horrendous atrocities that have happened all over the globe over the centuries' up to this year 2012. Our job is to conquer evil as best we can. Sometimes good can come out of an evil situation.

A mother's son may have been killed by a gang member, which unfortunately seems to be on the rise with the drug culture of today's youth. The mother may wish to turn this tragedy into something positive, so that her son has not died in vain. She can set up a campaign and expose these gang leaders and drug dealers, once and for all.

I believe that a lot of these youths come from broken homes and have no sense of belonging. They have never experienced a loving family environment. Then when they become members of a gang, they find there is no way out. They've lost their freedom, and they are bullied and threatened. In some extreme cases, they are asked to prove their allegiance by killing a rival gang member for whatever reason. It could be a case of kill or be killed.

What always strikes me most is when the parents of a victim are interviewed on the TV news of the terrible tragedy, and they answer, "We don't want this to happen to anyone else. We don't want anyone else to go through what we are going through. I've lost count how many times I've heard this remark. It always restores my faith in humanity.

Euthanasia

Today, on 17 August 2012, I heard the devastating news that Tony Nicklinson has been denied the right to end his life by lethal injection. Tony, aged fifty-eight, is the father of two sons. He had a stroke five years ago on a business trip to Athens, leaving him with locked-in syndrome.

This means Tony is paralyzed from the neck down. He can only communicate by blinking with a device on his computer. Tony was absolutely heartbroken when he heard the outcome of the verdict. He has become totally dependent on his wife and family to care for all his needs, taking away all his dignity. Try to imagine what it must be like for this man on a daily basis.

Tony is here for the benefit of others, to put a stop to man's suffering. When a person's health comes to such extreme circumstances such as this, then man should have the right to die. Tony described his life as a living nightmare. "I am saddened that the law wants to condemn me to a life of increasing indignity and misery."

Why can't this man die with peace and dignity, in the presence of his loving family? It must be horrendous for his wife and family to see him like this every day, knowing that there's nothing they can do to help him. It's slow torture.

How can we let millions of people suffer in this way; with similar extreme health problems who don't wish to live any longer? How can we say no when there is no hope of a recovery, no future, just the guarantee of a slow and painful death? What gives us the right?

I know people will say, "Well, it's open to abuse." But this has always been the case with man. At the end of the day, man is responsible for his own conscience; he has to make the right decisions. Surely it's down to common sense. We don't let our animals suffer in this way; we are given a choice to make when we take our beloved pets to the vet. Of course we don't want them to suffer! We use our common sense.

This was Tony's scenario, his mission prior to birth, for the right to end man's unnecessary suffering. Tony is going to appeal to the courts. I pray that he is successful and that he completes his mission in life by helping humanity in this way. They should be a government policy procedure brought into action; it should not be left to the courts to decide. What gives us the right that we can create a law that says man must suffer, even when there is no hope of a recovery? It seems so primitive.

22 August 2012

Today Tony Nicklinson died of natural causes; they said it was pneumonia. I for one was pleased to hear this wonderful news. Well done, Tony, your mission is almost complete, and you could do no more. God bless you.

Just let's hope that by Tony's tragic circumstances, the government sees the necessity to change the law. No one should have to suffer in the horrendous way that Tony did. His last message to the world was, "Goodbye, world. The time has come. I had some fun." Rest in peace.

***

August 27, 5.30 AM

A tune popped into my head, waking me up. I recognised the song: "You've Got a Friend" by James Taylor. It was one of his best hits in the seventies. I let it play over and over again in my mind. How wonderful to have a connection from my guardian angel. The lyrics were so appropriate at the time. If you listen to the words, you will understand why I became so emotional. The messages were clear in the song. Always listen for your guardian angel, especially when caught off guard.

7 September 2012

In the early hours of this morning, I saw a clear picture of my father from the waist up. He stood at the side of my bed, looking at me. He wore a short-sleeve shirt; he looked about forty-five years old, with graying at the temples. He was holding a jacket open for me, about to help me put it on. He gave a nod and said, "Come on, then." Has Dad come to fetch me home? I can't help feeling it won't be long now.

There is no such thing as time in the spirit world. When things like this happen, it makes me think it won't be long; I'll be going home soon. On the other hand, it could mean years, because there is no such thing as time in heaven. Nothing is set in stone. The spirit guides could change the original plans for a soul. Or maybe one's soul has a bit more work to do.

Casey Watson

Over the years I've read many books, all nonfiction. As I've mentioned earlier, it has to be real for me, a true story of people's struggles through life. It's the same with a good film: if it's based on a true story, then I'm interested. It can also be a learning experience, too. There's one thing that never fails to impress me, and that's the power of the human spirit.

There was one lady in particular, Casey Watson. She is the author of *Little Prisoners*, published in 2012. Casey and her husband, Mike, are foster parents. These two people are definitely earth angels!

The book is about Casey and Mike's experience and how they brought two little children, a girl aged six and a boy aged nine, into their home. These children were practically feral children. I've never heard or read anything as harrowing as this in my life.

Despite having two children of their own and a grandchild at the time, they found it in their hearts to show these children love, compassion, security, and stability that they needed so desperately. Where did Casey get the strength and courage to carry on when problems arose, and when the outlook looked so bleak?

Most humans would have given up. I believe this strength comes from God, through his angels, wherever there is a genuine need. It also reminds me of the strength I needed when I had to go into hospital and was desperately ill. I found the strength to help others.

Obviously Mike, Casey, and their two grown-up children all gave a hand. They became involved, giving Casey the support she would need in helping these two poor children a start in life. At times I wondered whether I could carry on reading the book. I found it so overwhelming, but it was so compelling. I had to see the outcome and hope for a happy ending.

Thanks to Casey and her family for showing these children the way life should be. This experience also restored my faith in the human race. There are good people out there who are willing to go above and beyond in order to bring love and peace to troubled souls.

More details are given in the "Books Recommended" section. I strongly recommend this book. It's a wake-up call for all of us to learn what's going on behind closed doors.

The London

2012 Olympics

As you know already, the year 2012 brought the Olympic and the Paralympic games to England. Despite the money it cost, I'm glad to say it's been an overwhelming success in more ways than one. It brought nations together, bringing peace and happiness to all those involved. It gave people a purpose in life.

Instead of all the usual daily bad news that we see on our TV screens, we were able to escape, even if only for a few weeks. Nevertheless, it seemed to make everyone happy. There was a wonderful atmosphere in the air, with the anticipation and excitement of nations competing all together.

I've never seen as many smiling faces on my TV. Contestants had tears of joy in their eyes when they were interviewed and congratulated on their success and gold medals. But for me, it wasn't about the wining. It was about the peace and harmony, and most of all the love it created throughout the games. It showed how, as nations all over the world, we are all capable of building a better world.

We can all strive to live in peace and harmony. It also inspired the younger generation: they could be Olympic contestants one day. I guess it's changed many young lives. Let's face it, the young generation need guidance and direction in their lives today, more than ever. They need something to aspire to.

God says we can be whatever we want to be. We have the power that God has, because we are all a spark from God. As his children, we can use this power. All that is required is to have belief in yourself, and faith and trust in God. You can do it, whatever your aspirations may be.

In the years to come, people will remember how the Olympics made them feel, the feel-good factor. Let's hope that it carries on creating a better world to live in, especially for future generations to come.

Full Circle

One Sunday morning Harry shouted out "Come on, love. Shall we have a run out in the car somewhere?"

"Why not. It's a lovely day. Where shall we go?"
"I know. Let's go back to where it all began. Let's visit our old house, our very first home where the kids grew up. We can have a Sunday lunch out somewhere. We could go through Graves Park and walk to the other end, like we used to when the kids were little. This time we can take Peggy – she'll love it!"

At the time I didn't feel too good, but I knew I had to make the effort. I had to push myself, especially now that the summer was coming to a close. "Come on, then. Why not." As I was getting ready for the journey, I had this feeling in my soul that this journey would have some spiritual significance.

When we were first married, we moved away from my mother's house because we simply couldn't live together. It's not always a good thing to live with your parents, but we had no option at the time.

We found a little back-to-back, terraced house with two up, two down rooms. It was in Woodseats, Sheffield, South Yorkshire. Although we would only be renting, I felt very excited at the fact that we'd have our very own home at last. We moved into the house in 1966. Darren, my second child, was due to be born the following April. It was a happy time, and we soon made the house look homely after we'd decorated it from top to bottom.

Daffodil

We lived in the house for eleven years; its one of my best memories, living in that little old house, with tin bath and all! As already mentioned, life was a struggle, especially when the twins came along, but we were all healthy and happy.

That saying always springs to mind: "Your health is all that matters." How true. It doesn't matter who you are, or how rich or famous. If you don't have good health, what good is being rich?

Harry and I set off. We parked the car outside the top of Graves Park; I was riding my electric scooter, Peggy and Harry toddling behind me. It was such a lovely sunny day with a gentle late summer breeze.

At first I couldn't believe how big the park was. Obviously there'd been many changes over the years. The trees looked so mature; after all, it had been thirty-five years since we were last in the area. It looked much better, with play grounds for the children and all the usual facilities provided for today's convenience.

We sat outside the cafe in the park and had a lovely cup of cappuccino. We started to walk on the path to reach the other end of the park, we hardly recognised it. However, near the very end, before we came to the gates, it hadn't changed at all. It still had its babbling brook with its twists and turns on either side of the path. It brought all the memories flooding back.

We used to push the pram with the twins in it. Wayne and Darren would follow behind, exploring, and throwing stones and sticks into the stream, laughing and giggling. There was always the promise of ice cream when we reached the end.

Eventually we came to the end, which brought us out to the busy shopping area known as Woodseats Bottom in the old days. "Look, there's the old pub, the Big Tree. Fancy a bit of lunch there, love? We can sit outside," "Why not," still thinking about the old days and how it all seemed like yesterday.

After lunch Harry said, "Tell you what: why don't we have a stroll through the shopping area and go back to the top of the park that way? Then we could have a stroll past our old house."

"Okay. There's nothing to rush back for," I agreed. All the while I was glad Harry had the idea to visit our old neighbourhood. It felt good to reminisce, and at least it got me out of the house.

Woodseats consists of a plethora of shops, pubs, butchers, supermarkets, and hairdressers on either side of a long road that stretches for about half a mile. Lots of the original shops still existed, although they were under different names.

It was nice to see the old Woodseats School that the children had attended all those years ago. It hadn't changed from the outside. Then we saw that the old shop where I used to buy products on the weekly for the home, as well as clothes for the children, still existed. It looked up to date from the outside, all modern and trendy.

As we were passing by and reminiscing all the while, we soon came to the end of our old road, which was on a slight hill. The first thing that struck me was how tiny the houses looked. They looked the same on either side of the road, modernised with new doors and windows.

How did we ever manage in such a tiny house all those years ago, with no bathrooms or inside toilets? In those days there were four houses to one back yard, each with an outside toilet.

Harry was handy and managed to squeeze a shower in the corner of the kitchen, next to the sink, which was a luxury in those days. The house gave him the opportunity to learn his DIY skills, which set us in good stead over the coming years. How proud I was of my Harry. He seemed so clever and was always self-taught. He could fix anything, make anything, and invent anything!

As we slowly walked up the hill, we came closer to our old house, 34 Broxholme Road. Suddenly I saw this man standing on the doorstep. This would have been the fourth house at the bottom of the yard, number 28. It must be Craig! He was gazing upwards, towards the hill.

Daffodil

I could just see his left profile, before I knew it, I said, "Do they call you Craig Russell?"

He looked at me with a slight frown. "Yes, but who are you?"
"It's Eileen. This is Harry."
"Bloody hellfire! I don't believe it!" He looked at Harry again and recognised him this time. "How long has it been?"

"It's been thirty-five years since we last saw you!"
"Well, well, who would have believed it, hey? June will be back in a bit." June was Craig's wife. "Oh – she's here now, coming up the hill. Shush, don't say anything. See if she recognises you."

I sat on my scooter facing up the hill so that I couldn't see her approaching, unless I turned my body around. But even that was too painful to do at that time.

As she approached me, I turned my head slightly to look up at her, I recognised her straight away. "Hello, June. Long time no see."

After a while she recognised Harry, but she wasn't sure about me. "Oh blimey! I wondered who it was as I was walking up the street. What are you doing back this way? How longs it been?"

"Thirty-five years, June."
"Wow!"

June and Craig were our neighbours for eleven years. One day when I was hanging out the washing; June happened to be in the yard at the same time, and we got chatting. Then all of a sudden she said to me, "Do you believe in God?"

My response was, "I don't know. Why?"
"Oh, I do. I don't think I would want to go on living, if I thought there was nothing left after we die."

I thought to myself, *she must be a religious fanatic or a Jehovah's Witness, or something like that.*

But after all the years, I've never forgotten those words; they stayed with me. June had a girl at the time, Collette, who was around the same age as my eldest son Wayne. Later, June was to give birth at home to her second child, a girl.

Unfortunately it was stillborn. I was sad when I heard the news. In those days, one didn't know what to say or do. All the neighbours in the yard carried on as if nothing had happened. When I look back now, it makes me cringe. How different it was in those days. We were all there for June, but we were afraid of upsetting her and making the situation worse.

A few months later, after June had lost the baby, I went to her house. I asked her if she was all right. She replied, "Yeah, I'm fine. Com on in I know my baby's with me. I feel her round me." She also made a reference to other spirits being around at certain times in the evening.

To be honest, June spooked me. I thought at the time, *this woman's got a screw loose.* I didn't want to know – it scared me. I laughed it off at the time. June would always insist that she saw spirits all the time, and she continues to do so up to this day.

After our reunion, she invited us in for a cup of tea, but there was no access for me. It was a shame, but we carried on talking anyway. I knew I had to bring the subject up at some point. I had to mention her stillborn child and the spirits June had seen. I felt like I was being nudged by the angels and spirit world.

I had to tell June how right she was all those years ago, and that it is all true. We all survive death. There is no end, and that her stillborn child lives on in the spirit world.

But I could tell in her eyes that June didn't need any convincing. "You know," she said, turning to look at Harry. "We are never alone. And sometimes they stroke the side of your head, like this." She demonstrated."

I've been experiencing this a lot lately. It's like it comes over the left part of my head and face, and it can reach down to my left shoulder. To me it means someone is there who's taking care of me. Whether its spirit, or my guardian angel, it doesn't really matter. All I know that it comforts me when I experience it.

Sometimes my old neighbour Marlene would stop in her tracks when we were having a conversation. She gave me a demonstration of what she

Daffodil

was feeling at the time by stroking the side of her head and downwards. This happened regularly. It seems to happen to me when I'm on the sofa in the evening, or whenever I'm relaxed. As I'm writing now, it is happening!

As I was saying, we laughed and carried on with June and Craig, reminiscing. Then June looked down at my hands and said, "How bad is it?"

"It's bad – very bad," I replied.

We were about to make tracks home, but then June said, "Oh, it's a pity you can't come in for a cuppa. Perhaps another time then, hey."

Harry replied, "I tell you what. We'll see you in another thirty-five years."

We all laughed, but it made me think, *you never know. In another life, perhaps.* It's the same with that old expression "You only live once". I always want to shout out, "No, you don't!"

We waved, said our goodbyes, and carried on walking up the hill. One thing struck me: Peggy never made a sound. In fact, the whole time we were talking, I forgot she was there, and so did Harry. Since we've had Peggy, she's become very protective of me when other people are around.

No one can approach me in the street. No one can come up and pet her, or have a chat without Peggy barking her head off. Once she starts, there's no stopping her. People will stop and say, "Well, it's a good thing that she does protect you." If Harry helps me on with my coat, she'll carry on barking no matter what. This can be so wearing at times.

Where have I gone wrong with raising her, to make her like this? It's the same when the post man comes. Then she'll show me her lovely, gentle side, and I melt. One would think she can't be the same dog.

The reason I've brought up Peggy is that the whole time spent with Craig and June, we never heard a peep from her. Even when Craig and June approached me and put their arms round me, Peggy didn't react. I found very strange. Harry also realised Peggy never made a sound during the conversation.

If Peggy had been her usual self, she would have been barking loudly. It would have been impossible to have a conversation with Craig and June, and we would have continued walking up the hill, apologising all the while. The spirit world must have intervened that day to keep Peggy calm and peaceful; while we were all chatting; the spirit world knew the importance of this scenario and had engineered it so that it could bring us together.

I knew I had to pass this knowledge on to June, to confirm the survival of her child and all that I had learned over the years. She was right about it all along. Although June needed no convincing, I'm sure it still gave her comfort and validation.

Perhaps June needed this information at the time; I'm not sure. I bet she felt much better that day after our conversation. I know I did. There is no such thing as coincidence, remember!

It seems now that I have come full circle with my life, by going back to where it all started. I'm glad I did; it brought me answers.

April Jones

There's another horrific story in the media: April Jones, the four-year-old girl abducted near her home

Why do things continue to happen like this? Our kids should be safe no matter what.

On 6 October, at 2.45 AM, I see the back of a white camper van. It has no windows; this usually means the bedroom is situated at the back of the caravan. Next I'm shown a man from the waist up wearing a white vest. He's between the ages of forty-five and fifty, with receding hair. He is shaving himself in front of the mirror in the caravan.

I hear the words from the spirit world: "Opportunist belongs to a paedophile ring." Then I'm shown a white plastic bag about two feet long drawn at the top with a black cord. I sense the bag to be full of DNA evidence. I see no signs of April. And that was it.

I lay on my side in the early hours of the morning, trying to make sense of it. I realised the spirit world was showing me what had happened to April. Or were they? Was it meant for April? I asked for more information, but none came.

Why was I shown this? It couldn't have been any clearer. Or was the spirit world trying to warn me that this was going on, but on a much larger scale? This was what I felt. They later arrested a man named Mark Bridger. Because this information came to me so clearly, I felt I had to document it.

On 11 October I read in the *Daily Mirror* about April Jones. The police investigation had cordoned off a caravan, and forensics were taking it to pieces??

***

Every day when it comes to the afternoon, I can become quite lethargic. All I want to do is curl up and go to sleep. The feeling overwhelms me sometimes. This has been happening to me lately over the last three weeks.

I close my eyes once again and feel myself drifting off to sleep. At the same time, it's as if all the life force is draining out of me. I become weaker and weaker, I think to myself, *Is this it; am I going to pass over anytime soon?* But I survive yet another day. Why? I think of the premonition: when I was told that I will pass in my 65th year

The more I have become attached to the spirit world and my angels, the less interested I am in the world as it stands today. I don't feel part of this world anymore; it's like I'm on the outside looking in. I ask myself how long can this go on for. It's like I'm in a room waiting for my turn to come. I'm not afraid. I don't see any future for myself in this world. I simply want to be free, especially from the pain and all this heaviness.

This may be because there is no cure for my illness. For the first time in my life, I have money to spend, yet I don't feel the need to do so. I don't plan a holiday or have the house decorated. It all seems pointless. Yet everything must end at some point.

***

Zak, Darren's chocolate Labrador, passed over to animal heaven today, 3 October 2012. He suffered with chronic arthritic conditions towards the end. He won't be suffering now – he'll be running with all the other animals, free from any pain. I hope he's with my Bessie!

Jimmy Savile

Jimmy Savile was a disc jockey, media personality, and TV presenter in the late sixties and seventies. He was a national treasure – or so we thought. He was best known for *I'll Fix It,* a popular TV program for children, and of course for raising money for charity.

Like everyone else, I was fooled into thinking what a great guy he was. I wondered over the years why he was never associated with women, relationships, or marriage. I wondered whether he might be gay.

The thing is some people in the BBC association; knew that the sexual abuse was going on, but they were too afraid to come forward and do anything about it! Now, after Jimmy's death, hundreds of people are coming forward to state that they were sexually abused over the years.

What a shame to read all this scandal, and about a man who did so much for charity. We find out behind this charade that he was a paedophile. It's a total shock, and we don't want to believe it. Things are never as they seem?

Many people will say that he got away with it, that he was lucky by dying before it was discovered. Jimmy Savile will be aware of all the scandal that came out after his death. He will be aware of everything that's been said about him in the media, and what people are saying and thinking about him.

No, Jimmy has not got away with it! If he is a good man deep down, then he will ask God to forgive him. He will want to come back to earth to live in another body, to be reincarnated so that he can make amends in some way. He will punish himself as he sees fit. It won't be God who gives out the punishment. I have a feeling that Jimmy is going through great shame. He's beside himself, overwhelmed by his shocking behaviour while he lived on this earth; He let himself down in this shocking way.

God will always forgive his children for their sins. It's up to Jimmy now to help is soul and make amends. There's only Jimmy that can do this

Later we heard about other celebrities who have been accused. Most shocking is Rolf Harris. What we mustn't do, no matter how shocking, it is we must not judge these people. How do we know for certain? Perhaps we committed a similar crime in a past life. We don't know, and that's why we should never judge our fellow man. This goes for any heinous crime committed.

On 15 October 2012, my sixty-fifth birthday, I received a birthday card from my sister, Mary. We still send cards to one another. It's been six years now since we've seen each other. Inside the card was a little note.

Dear Eileen,

I can't believe it's been ten years since Mam died. Time flies.
We are both getting old; and I would hate anything to happen to either one of us without us making peace.
So for what it's worth, I want to say I'm sorry for our falling out. Let us put it behind us.

Love, Mary
I sent a note in return.
Yes, Mary, let's put it behind us.
It's a shame our life had to be this way.
Love, Eileen

This was a great relief to me, that Mary finally said sorry to me after all these years. It was totally unexpected it unlike her. This means that we have made peace in this life and will have progressed with our souls. This is so important for both us before we leave this earth. We would have had to come back at some point to do it all again, perhaps under different circumstances.

This is why it's so important to clear up any issues you may have with family, siblings, and friends. You don't want to carry them on to the next life. But like I said earlier in the book, if I never saw Mary again in this life, she would always stay in my heart.

Sometimes I wonder what our lives could have been like together – you know, like proper sisters. It saddens me, but it wasn't meant to be. There were lessons to be learnt. Let's hope we've both learned them. When I pray for my family's healing and protection, I always send out healing for Mary. I still do to this day, and my prayers were answered.

***

Another tune popped into my head in the early hours of the morning: Kate Bush's "I'm Running up That Hill". It was a great hit in the eighties. I listened to it on YouTube. It was proof again that appropriate lyrics appear at the time that I needed. Oh, how I long to run again!

"I'm running up that hill with no problems…"

Angel Message

Once you communicate with your guardian angel, he will never let you down. You will always be led in the right direction; never will he leave you to walk alone on your journey. At all times he will carry you, help you, give you strength and courage on the spiritual path that was set for you. Your guardian angel is with you always, whether you like it or not. God sent angels to look out for his children.

The angels are saddened by the response of God's children. There are not enough souls reaching out for help. This is the reason why God created the angels in the first place, to be his messengers. God knew that each and every one of us will need help at some point in our lives on this earth. It is the job of the guardian angels to reach as many souls as possible.

At this point in time, I think more young people are reaching out for help especially the younger ones. The world is heading for great change. Now would be a good time to turn to your guardian angel and get to know him. You don't have to wait till a crisis happens in your life.

If we were to measure the universe against our planet, we are all but a grain of sand.

The more I read, the more I see that all the authors seem to have one thing in common. No matter how their book begins or what story they have to tell, it all seems to have the same ending as to why we are all here: the meaning of our life, heaven, and the spirit world. They talk about the great love they experienced whilst there. All say that it is not like human love – it is much more. You would have to experience it first to realise its overwhelming power.

They experienced the angels, the guides and teachers, the learning temples, the vivid colours. They saw how perfect that realm is compared to ours. They viewed the flowers, the trees, the grass, and how everything comes to life. Everyone's skin who lives there seems to glow and be translucent. They communicate without words and have a complete understanding via telepathy. There's no ugliness, only beauty, and everyone seems to be around the age of thirty!

All the authors that have written their life stories in this way did so for a purpose: to help mankind. This work will continue, helping others to have their own divine experience towards God and then tell their stories, changing their lives and many others for the better. They can pass on the information to their children so that nothing is forgotten. We don't want our planet to end up the way it is today.

All the information is out there for you to discover. It opens up a whole new meaning to your life: you will find out who you are, as well as your purpose for your life. We all have one.

There were times when I found my journey so exciting. Once I started, there was no turning back. The more I researched, the more I found out. I had to tell everyone – hence the book!

If you're not sure how to go about it, turn to your guardian angel and ask him to show you. It's a good thing to keep a journal as you begin your journey. There will be times when things happen to you, and you will put it down to your imagination. Later on you will realise that it wasn't.

Remember that you are never alone. The most important thing is to trust the process and always have faith. Faith is a big word in the spirit world. I can't imagine what my life would have been like if I hadn't found God and the angels.

Changes will continue to happen on this planet till we reach perfection. All human beings will become spiritual, where love will reign and family will be the most important aspect of our lives. The world is changing, and I'm afraid it's going to get worse before it gets better.

It's not that I want to frighten anyone, but we all have to face up to it. We will be changing the world for a better one; we will all take part in this great transition. We have such a lot to do. There is nothing to fear because God is on our side. We are all heading towards a wonderful realm that is hard to describe in words. It has magnificent beauty, tremendous tranquility, peace, love, and serenity.

At the beginning of this book, I spoke about the war in Afghanistan and our soldiers been killed every day. Six years later, I'm still writing about war, but in a different country: the conflict in the Middle East between Israel and Gaza.

It is now November 2012. Without going into details, I'm sure you have heard all about it in the media. I have a bad feeling about this conflict. All peace talks have failed to resolve the situation. Meanwhile, innocent men, women, and children on both sides are being slaughtered. It breaks my heart to see the suffering on my TV day after day. I ask myself how can help these people.

I was astounded to hear that the BBC has defended a decision not to air a TV funding appeal for Gaza, saying it wanted to avoid compromising public confidence in its impartiality! It also said a decision was taken with other broadcasters not to show the Disaster Emergency Committee crisis appeal on any network in the UK.

The DEC said that there was clear evidence that the British public wanted to help. Of course the British want to help! We are talking about innocent children being killed on both sides every day. It needs as much publicity as soon as possible to send help and medical supplies.

Soon it will be Christmas. How can anyone be thinking about Christmas when we see the suffering on TV and in the media? For heaven's sake, let's get real! If I was in this terrible position, I would like to think that somewhere plans were being enforced to help my country, and that I wasn't going to be abandoned. These are our brothers and sisters. They need all the help we can give them.

Over the years I've accumulated many different kinds of medical supplies; bandages, special dressings, medication, sterile equipment, cleansing skin sprays, and saline washes. I was amazed at what I'd collected. Antibiotics, morphine in liquid and tablet form still in date, saline, and lots of special dressings for wounds.

I made a box of medical supplies to send to Gaza, hopefully for free. No such luck! The royal mail has had no instructions to deliver free mail to these war-torn countries. Why not? Don't they realise that people will give more if they know the mailing will be for free? Yet again it's all down to using common sense. I sent the box of supplies anyway. I simply hope that my ploy wasn't in vain and that they received it.

On 22 November I heard on the news that they called a truce on the fighting in Gaza and Israel, but for how long? All we can do is keep asking the angels and God to help bring peace and hope to the people. I hope my contribution arrived in Gaza.

"Mankind must put an end to war,

Or war will put an end to mankind." – John F. Kennedy

***

I have read many books over the last eighteen months. I bought a Kindle e-book, which made it much easier for me to choose the particular books I like to read. The Kindle provides many books to choose from. After scouring through, I became exhausted. I asked my angels to help me choose a book. I was drawn to a book by Todd Burpo called *Heaven Is for Real*.

I know now that my blessed angels led me towards this book. Its contents took my breath away! The book is about a little boy named Colton; He is almost four years old. Colton became very ill, after being misdiagnosed, he suffered a burst appendix. He became so ill that he actually left his body in the operating theatre. In other words, he was transported to heaven. He didn't have to die in order to have a divine experience, like most people do. He was very special and was sent to this world to help mankind.

This was just like a repeat of my experience at Alan Bellinger. I left my body for a little while to gain the knowledge that God had in store for me, so that I could come back and tell the world what I had experienced. Colton speaks of the angels singing to him the love he felt whilst in heaven. This also happened to me, so I knew he wasn't making it up.

Colton wasn't meant to die. God sent this special little boy to earth to tell his story. This was Colton's scenario for his reincarnation in this life. He wanted to help save the world and was one of God's evolved souls. He volunteered himself for this mission. He chose the right parents and siblings, who would serve him in the best possible way for this new life. They all agreed before they all reincarnated; that this was the way they wanted to help humanity. The timing is perfect as we are reaching 2013.

Eventually Colton makes a miraculous recovery from his traumatic ordeal. It wasn't till afterwards that Colton began to tell his parents what he had seen and heard while he was in heaven. One day he said to his mother, Sonja, "I have two sisters, Mummy, don't I?"

At first Sonja wasn't paying too much attention because she was sorting some bills at the kitchen table. Colton kept repeating what he had just said. When Sonja finally heard his words, she was dumbstruck. "No, Colton, you only have one sister, Cassie."

Colton was insistent. "No, Mummy, you had a baby die in your tummy, didn't you?" Wow.

"How do you know all this, Colton? Who told you?" It was true, that Colton had seen his sister in heaven. He told is mum she gave him lots of hugs and told him how happy she was that one of her family members had come to visit her. She couldn't wait for the day that they would all be reunited!

"Okay, then," Sonja said, "what does your other sister in heaven look like?"

"She looks a lot like Cassie, but she has brown hair."

Sonja had miscarried years before, and they had never told Colton. Over the coming weeks, months, Colton would volunteer information that he'd witnessed when he'd gone to heaven. One day Colton said to his father that Jesus had markers.

Daffodil

"Excuse me, son, what did you say?"

Colton repeated that Jesus had markers. He answered in a way that only an innocent child of four years old could. He pointed to both his hands and feet – the places where Jesus Christ was crucified to the cross.

This book has given me more validation – not that I needed it, for I know that God exists. When Colton was first rushed into the operating theatre, he shouted out, "Don't leave me, Daddy! Don't leave me!"

Colton's father, Todd Burpo, was devastated. He found a room where he could be alone. He broke down and shouted at God for letting this happen to his son. He was angry at God. "How could you do this to me, after all that I have done for you. All the help I have shown others?" After all, Todd was the church pastor in his community. Todd was losing faith rapidly.

Then he pleaded with God to save his son. Colton didn't want to come back to earth, and he told this to God. "But you have to, son. I promised your dad that I would send you back. I have to answer his prayer."

Colton later told his dad that he saw him praying in a room to God, to let his son live. This was while Colton was in heaven!

This reminded me of the day I was told I had broken my hip and would need yet another operation. When the consultant left the room and I was alone, I was devastated and angry with God, shaking my fist towards the heavens while tears streamed down my face. "Why, why? After all that I have done, helping others to heal and giving treatments to people who were suffering, and praying for others! Why?" I was and still am a very caring person. It's who I am. Little did I know that this was part of a bigger picture yet to unfold?

Colton also met his grandfather in heaven. "Are you Todd's son?"

"Yes," Colton replied.

The man replied, "I'm your dad's father. Colton told his father that he had met him, and what a nice guy he was. Todd was taken aback! He had very fond memories of his father. I strongly recommend this book for everyone, especially for people who are looking for answers or who have lost faith,

Also mentioned in a book was a girl called Akiane. She was born in 1994 underwater, in Mount Morris, Illinois, to her Lithuanian atheistic mother and her American father (a chef). At the age of four, Akiane had a life-changing spiritual transformation that brought the family to God. At the age of four, she began drawing a self-portrait; she was painting at the age of six. The inspiration for her art comes from visions, dreams, observations of people nature, and God. She paints from imagination, reference materials, and models. She wants people to find hope and God through her paintings.

At the age of seven she began writing poetry and aphorisms. She wakes at four every morning to get started on her paintings and writings. She works four to five hours every day. Her biggest wish is for everyone to love God and one another. Her life goal is to share her love for God and the people around the world. You can find out all about Akiane on the Internet. You'll be truly amazed.

You only have to see and hear her in her interviews to get a real insight into her character, personality, and philosophy on life. You can tell she is very special and truly inspirational. She is a very wise, old soul who has come down to earth to help mankind. I believe she is an Indigo child, one of God's chosen.

"Faces are more meaningful to me than anything else. You cannot live without seeing and touching them." – Akiane

***

I say this mantra every day: "I am that I am, that I am. For God is within me, and I'm within God. We are one." I use it throughout the day, whenever I remember and if ever I have any problems. Always believe and have faith; trust the process. It works! It's good for everyone to have a mantra. Remember that your mind believes in what you tell it.

When I was given the premonition in spring that I would pass over in my sixty-fifth year, I would often think, *when the time comes, what is it that I would like to do in the next world, or maybe in my next reincarnation?* I still would like to help people in some way. Health has always interested me, and how the human body works, so maybe a doctor, surgeon, or therapist.

I'm looking forward to the learning temples once again, for we never stop learning. However, I wouldn't want to go through a traumatic illness again, like I did in this life. Although I understand the reasoning behind it all, and I know that it was my choice, I believe that my soul will have progressed.

I found it very overwhelming at times, yet I know in my heart that God would never have given me a task which I could not cope with. He knows us all too well. Still, twenty-five years is a long, long time to be ill. There's no denying; It's has been very difficult.

I'm also looking forward to meeting my daughter, Ann. I was told she would be waiting for me when my time came. Also waiting are my parents, my grandparents, my great-grandparents, my work mates from C&A, and other friends. Yes, I can see that a glorious, happy time awaits us all.

In my meditations or prayer moments before I go to sleep, I always receive a connection from the spirit world. It always begins with a strong muscle tightness around my eyes, which I've mentioned before. When it reaches its peak, I usually see all the colours of the spectrum – mostly purple, indigo, emerald, and white. This has been going on for years; I've become accustomed to it.

In the last two or three weeks, I have not been seeing the colours I usually see. Instead, I experience a tremendous, strong white light that takes over me. When it reaches its peak and starts to subside, I can see a pure, brilliant white angel manifesting as if on horseback, but it soon disappears.

The next time it happened I pleaded for it not to go. Suddenly it changed into all the colours of the spectrum colours one never sees on earth; the last colour was the most magnificent, vivid yellow. Yellow means happiness and is the colour of the daffodil – my book's title, and the colour of the soul chakra. I can't help but think there's a message for me by showing me this colour.

That night I asked the spirit world if they would give more information next time. During my sleep in the early hours of the morning, I saw this clear picture, just like a photograph, of a child angel. It sat on the floor, leaning forward and looking at me intently, as if saying, "Yes, what you are seeing is not a dream – it is real."

I was aware that I was having this experience and that I was in my bed; I was aware of my surroundings.

The angel had curly hair that settled on the tips of its shoulders; the colour was like copper. Its skin had a golden glow. It was naked, though all I could see was from the waist up. It had no wings, but I could tell it was defiantly a child angel of about eight or nine years old. As I stared at the angel's face, it reminded me of my mother, but what convinced me it was an angel was that it had no nipples on its chest!

The picture was so clear that it will stay with me always. I thanked the spirit world as I turned over in my bed with a smile on my face. I truly hope now that whatever the spirit world wishes to show me will be clear so that I can pass it on to the reader.

***

Earlier in the book, I mentioned how to get in touch with your angel. One night I asked my guardian angel, "Who am I?"

In the early hours of the morning, I had a vision of a giant angel in the corner of my bedroom ceiling. I could only see him from the waist up, and he had his back to me. He was very bronze and muscular, with dark hair that fell over his ears.

At the time he reminded me of a gypsy at the fairground in the olden days. It was only later that I realised why he had shown himself to me in this way. He represented all the gypsy souls who had died in the concentration camps in World War Two.

Daffodil

I felt like a little child stood at the side of my bed. I was aware of my surroundings. He put two fingers under my chin, tilted my head back, and said to me, "You were a child from the concentration camps."

Later that same week In the early hours of the morning, I saw a picture in my mind's eye of a German soldier. It was on a bright sunny day with a clear blue sky, and I could feel the sun on my face. As I looked at the soldier, I felt annoyed, and blurted out the words, "For God's sake!" It woke me up. Next thing I was shown "B3109". This number kept repeating itself over and over, and I couldn't get it out of my head.

I laid there, thinking. Was this the number that was branded on the inside of my wrist as a child living at that time? This is what they used to do to all the prisoners in the concentration camps. The prisoners were accounted for in this way. What else could the numbers represent? Unless it was the soldier's identification number? Still the connection stood out for me: German soldier, the concentration camp, the number, and the child.

Regarding the angels, I've also felt that butterflies feature strongly when it comes to all things supernatural. Buddhists believe that the butterfly represents the spirit of a dead soul. I've always been fascinated by them, I always stop when I see one, just to glimpse its beauty and grace.

I happened to come across a book called *15 Real Life Angel Stories: Global Evidence of Angelic Assistance*. It was edited by Richard Bullivant just my thing!

On 22 May 2011 there was a tornado in the American Midwest, in the town of Joplin. It left devastating consequences. More than 160 people were killed, and thousands were injured. After the tornado receded, stories began to emerge, and most were told by children.

The same stories were told by different children from different parts of the city, and among those who had no contact with each other. The children were all telling the same story. They had seen little "butterfly angels" flitting about and hovering over people, seemingly to offer protection to the frightened people who were praying to God to help them survive.

Reporters for the local newspapers began to hear the same story over and over again, from all kinds of people. They felt that the butterfly angels were there to protect them.

One little daughter asked her mummy, "Did you see them, Mummy? Weren't they pretty?" The mother became confused and asked her daughter, "What are you talking about?"

The little girl replied, "The butterfly people!" She also told her mother that she had seen the butterfly people lift people up and carry them to safety.

Another report came from two brothers, aged three and four. They had been trapped outside along with their grandfather. The best that they could do was to jump into a ditch. The winds were so fierce it tore the shoes off the grandfather's feet, but he and the two boys survived.

Both boys told their grandfather that they knew they would not be hurt. "How did you know?" he asked the boys.

They answered in unison, "The butterfly people were above us, protecting us. Didn't you see them, Grandpa?"

It is interesting to know that the Greek word *psyche* is the same term used for both the butterfly and the human soul.

Also, historians have noted that in Nazi concentration camps in Poland, dying prisoners carved dozens of butterflies into the walls of their cells. This made me cry. I understand my affinity with the butterfly more so now.

I highly recommend this book. Obviously this story goes into greater depth, and it has other interesting stories.

Slaughter of the Innocent

It is now December 2012, ten days before Christmas. I never look forward to Christmas – never have. Perhaps it's because I know celebrating Christmas is much nicer in heaven than it is on earth; up there, it holds much more meaning. Or perhaps it's that my soul longs to go home. Then I wake up to horrendous news in Connecticut on 14 December: twenty innocent little children and six adults have been shot and killed at a school by a twenty-year-old.

What is happening to this world? Obama has to do something to change the gun laws. My heart goes out to the parents of these innocent children. How does one cope in such horrendous circumstances? It's a living nightmare. How does one carry on with life?

All we can do is send out prayers and ask Archangel Michael to give strength and courage to all who are experiencing this terrible scenario. I know it's hard to comprehend, but remember that all these innocent children put themselves forward and volunteered.

Again I remind you: we live in a world of illusion; none of this is real, but we are conditioned into thinking it so. This is what you have to remember throughout your life, as you live it. All the terrible atrocities that happen in this world are not real. We live in a world of illusion.

Something had to happen of great magnitude to shock the world – something so drastic to change the gun laws of America and around the world. There's reasons behind it all. But remember, it's all about choices that we will make. What are we going to do about it?

All atrocities that happen around the world will keep happening in order to show humanity to itself, till things start to change for the better. Their parents can rest assured that their loved ones are in heaven, looking down on their parents right now and sending love.

The parents will be even more proud of their blessed children, for these are special souls, indigo children. There are books and information on the Internet about the indigo children, who have been born especially to help with our planet. They are teaching the world that we don't need guns and that life is sacred. Humanity will eventually change. For the better.

When atrocities like this happen, if you want to help, you can read instructions from the books ;*The Secret* and *The Power*, which I will introduce you to later in the book. First, send out loads of love to all the people involved. Then ask for armies of angels to bring healing and all that is needed to help all the parents, and to bring strength and courage for a quick recovery for the community. It helps if you can visualise the people receiving love and help, visualize seeing the community come together. See any injured little ones recovering quickly; see smiles on their faces.

We all want to know why, but if you wallow in thoughts of sorrow, that is what the universe, will act upon. You will receive more sorrow. Only send your positive thoughts out to the universe. What you ask for, you will receive back. It's bound to happen, whether your thoughts are positive are negative.

The universe responds to your thoughts; it's like gravity. Remember that this applies to everything in life, good or bad. The greatest tool is to use love every time. When bad things occur, it is only because there is a lack of love. Love is the greatest tool that God gave to us. If you use love throughout your life in any situation, you're bound to have a good life.

Fill yourself every day with love. You can't go wrong. Send it to people whom you don't like, the ones who make your life hell. You will be astounded how your life will change for the better. It won't be up to you as to how it will happen – the universal law takes control every time. It has been there since the beginning of time, it always will be.

The Beatles

The Beatles were the most famous pop group in the sixties. It was the beginning of a new revolution for pop music. I once saw a documentary on TV about the famous four and the trip they took to India in 1968. They found a famous guru, a spiritual leader, Maharishi Mahesh, who taught them the meaning of life through spiritualism and meditation.

Throughout the interview with the guru, he answered every question with the word "love". "Treat everything with love," he said. "Love is the answer. Treat every bad thing with love, every good thing with love." He repeated it over and over again.

Love is the answer to everything. When the Beatles were in India, they learned that their manager, Michael Epstein had died. He had killed himself. At the time John Lennon's wife, Cynthia, said it seemed as if they were in the right place at the right time after Michael's death.

Maharishi Mahesh gave the Beatles direction. The guru helped the group by telling them that Michael's spirit was still with them, and they could help by sending good thoughts for an easy passage to his next evolution.

At the time I thought the guru was a bit of a crackpot. Now when I look back, I think about how wise this man was. He knew about the secret, the universal law.

When I was young, I knew very little about life – only that I was crazy about the Beatles. John Lennon was my favourite, and with my first week's wages at age fifteen, I bought my first record, "Please Please Me", in 1963. I knew spiritually they were going to be very famous.

Life was so exciting then, with new pop groups coming on to the scene. There were also the new fashions: Mary Quant invented the mini skirt. Twiggy was a young fashion model at the time, she was so thin – hence her name.

I remember my mum looking shocked the first time she saw me in my first mini skirt. I thought she was going to choke on her cup of tea! But later I noticed my mum's generation: skirts were becoming much shorter. It didn't take long for Mum to join them. "Well," she said, "if you can't beat them, join them I say."

Also at that time: I remember Harold Wilson winning the Labour Election, addressing the nation, and telling them, "We had never had it so good." I still believe that the young people of that era had the best times when it came to fashion and music. Life was good. One never heard of gangs stabbing and killing one another, and no man ever kicked a man once he was down. It was not like it is today. I vaguely remember the Teddy boy gangs in the early fifties.

Perhaps it was because World War II had ended in 1945. People were finding their feet, and there was a lot to do after all the bombings. We had to create a whole new world. Such was the damage that war brings. But amongst it all there was laughter and camaraderie. People were starting to feel happy once again. They were free.

Jobs were plentiful; you could walk into your new job in the morning; and if you decided by lunch time you didn't like it, you would find another job in the afternoon.

Threat to Our World

Is Kim Jong-un another despot in the making? The defiant dictator's nuke test sparked a global fury. The rogue state of North Korea set off a nuclear test explosion so powerful that it caused an earthquake.

This man has to be stopped. He is threatening our world; this is the third nuclear test that has been carried out by this despot. It is said that North Korea was trying to build a bomb to strike the United States' west coast in a bid to win more aid from Washington.

North Korea is such a poor country. A hidden famine is believed to have killed ten thousand people. In October 2012 the dictatorship claimed it could strike America after revealing what appeared to be an intercontinental ballistic missile featured in a military parade. Leaders are thought to have enough material to build up to eight nuclear bombs. North Korea said it was a response to "outrageous" US hostility.

The claim came after the United States imposed tighter sanctions when Pyongyang launched a rocket in December 2012. The latest test was in defiance of the UN orders to shut down atomic activity or face more sanctions and international isolation. A statement approved by all fifteen UN Security Council members at an emergency meeting condemned the test as a "clear threat" to international peace.

How can this stupid little dictator, with his stupid hair cut to match, be allowed to govern a country? He can't even look after his own people. He's too young and inexperienced. The people are living in poverty and starvation, with no one to stand up for them. They fear for their lives. It's all down to fear once again. The people are too frightened to stand up for themselves in case of reprisal. It's history repeating itself.

You are probably thinking, "Well, what can we do?" We can do a lot by using the collective conscious with our thought patterns. The more souls that come together with the right mind set, the more we can change. It needs all the United Nations, for souls to come together from all over the world and to pray, to wish for a better future. The more people who get involved, the more powerful we become in our quest for world peace.

By putting these thoughts out to the universal law, we are asking for world peace and for all nations coming together and working as one. We must believe and trust that this will take place, but we must do it with love. Have faith and believe it will be resolved as soon as possible.

We cannot turn a blind eye to this tyrant Kim Jong-un. We have to stop men like this who want to take control over a frightened nation, making its people live in fear every day of their lives. Some nations will say, "It's none of our business," Of *course* it's our business! They are our brothers and sisters aren't they? It's our duty to help.

Later, Kim Jong-un was to have his uncle, Jang Song-Thaek, aged sixty-seven, and all of his aids executed for treason and corruption, for following the ways of the hated West and for being a womanisers. In actual fact, Kim Jong-un felt threatened by his uncle's power.

Later there was speculation as to how theses executions were carried out. One story was that Jang Song-Thaek was thrown into a cell with a dozen starving Alsatian dogs that were purposely denied food for three days, making the dogs ravenous. It was rumored that Kim Jong-un witnessed this appalling atrocity. How can this despot be fit to run a country?

Then two weeks later, it was revealed in the national newspaper that Kim Jong-un had executed all direct family members and relatives of the uncle he had killed, including the children! A source added, "The executions of Jang's relatives mean that no traces of him should be left. The purge of Jang Song-Theak's people is under way on an extensive scale from relatives and low level officials."

Daffodil

All the remaining family members were recalled to the Pyongyang area of the country by the ministry of state troops in early December 2013, before being killed. This marks the biggest political upheaval since this heartless, despicable tyrant; Kim Jong-Un inherited power in 2011. The Kim dynasty has ruled North Korea for six decades.

I know that sometimes when we hear of such terrible crimes and atrocities being committed in this world, it's very hard to comprehend. The spirit world tells us that we must forgive, but in cases like this, even I find it very hard to forgive. However, I know that this is what it's like to live the human experience; it is natural to think in this way. We have to rise above it. This man needs spiritual help before he murders anyone else.

The book *The Secret* says the only way that we can help is to send as much love as possible out to these troubled countries, North Korea and South Korea, to bring peace to both nations. We should also send love to Kim Jung-Un and to all the people there. Only love can cure all of the problems of these two nations. We all have to put it out to the universe for these two countries to unite peacefully. Where there's a lack of love in this world, it can only be cured by giving more love.

***

Throughout this whole experience, right from the beginning and before I started to write this book, I've never felt that I was different or special in any way, or that I had been chosen – like my dear friend Barbara kept insisting that I was. I'm a down-to-earth woman and speak from the heart. Yes, I've made mistakes in my life which I very much regret. I have sinned like everybody else.

This life has taught me lessons that I needed to learn, and it is only by my actions that God gave me this opportunity to find my true self, the person I really am. It's like I've come to know myself after all these years.

Writing a book, or being famous, or trying to prove myself in any way and making lots of money isn't what I'm about. What this journey has taught me is how I could help mankind. I've done the very best that I can, and therefore this has made me happy with who I am. I like who

I am; I've achieved my goal by finding my way back home to God, my father, with the choices I have made in this life.

We all have this gift from God to find our real selves through our own actions and choices in this life. We are all God's children, and we have to be taught there's a wrong way and a right way, just like we do with bringing up our own children in this world. Eventually we get it right, and our children learn the lessons.

More Past Lives

In the early hours of the morning, I was half asleep, but then I noticed I was moving quite fast. I was aware that someone was by my side. As I looked to my right, all I could see was a pair of hands and arms. I could also see rosary beads in a man's hands and the cuff of his sleeve. I got the impression that he was a guide, a monk. I've been told that in the past I have a Benedictine monk who sometimes walks with me. Then the guide spoke to me. "You had two past lives in the fourteenth century. We didn't know much about you then."

Next I'm looking down at my inside left ankle. I can see a big open wound! I realise I'm bleeding to death. Then I have the feeling I have to get away. I'm in a small dwelling, and I'm trying to get free, dragging myself from room to room. I have the feeling that a man is chasing me; I don't know whether he is trying to help me or kill me.

My thoughts are, *I don't want to be saved. I want to go home to God, to heaven. I'm not afraid to die.* I already had the knowledge of the soul's survival in that life, just like I know in this life.

Then I find myself in a room, I quickly shut the door behind me. I know I haven't much time left. I lie on the floor and ask the angels to fetch me quickly before the man comes. All of a sudden I sense and hear a big whoosh! I sense my soul being released from my body, and I am rising up towards the ceiling. I'm going home at last! Just then the man breaks down the door. He sees this happening to me he knows I've died.

Then I feel like a little child. I am given a black box, I know what's inside: a review of the life I've just had. I'm trudging up these wooden stairs with great big gaps in between, frightened that I may fall in between them. I struggle with this black box, but someone takes it from my hands and opens it for me.

Suddenly I'm in awe! I see all these people coming to greet me. I feel so happy and overwhelmed as I look at their faces one by one, everyone is moving fast around me. It's a celebration! All the people are dressed in peasant costumes of that time; I notice how drab the colours look. Everyone is happy to see me. I see Marlene's face before me; she looks happy as she glides along with the rest of the crowd. *This is wonderful,* I tell myself. *This is how it is when we die.*

Then I see a young peasant girl walking towards me. She is the only one who hasn't acknowledged me like the rest. She has her eyes lowered to the floor she is dressed in a rough creamy calico cotton skirt, with a long-sleeved blouse buttoned to the neck. She has a matching head cap, which covers all of her hair and ties under her chin. It is only then that I recognise her. The girl is me! I feel happy.

In my next past life, I find myself in what looks like an old barn, dark and drab with straw scattered around the floor. It has a high ceiling. I climb up to the top of some wooden stairs and look to my right. I see this young man; he is tall with heavy side burns. His sleeves are rolled up; he is wearing a long black leather apron. He is a blacksmith, a Farrier It feels like were in an old tavern. He stands leaning against the end of a bar.

He looks at me and smiles with recognition and love. It feels familiar, as if he is about to say, "Hello, mum." His demeanor is familiar to someone I know in this life. I look at him as if to say, "Do I know you?" For a split second his face metamorphose slightly so that I know who he is. I feel such love for him. It is Richard, my son in this life now!

I then see a man serving behind the bar. He is dressed in a white shirt with big bell sleeves and a black leather waist coat. He is handsome with thick, curly, salt-and-pepper hair. He looks at me with the same surprise, love, and recognition. I stare but I don't recognise him straightaway. Could it be Wayne, my eldest son in this life? He seems to have the same demeanour as Wayne. Is he my husband in that life? I'm not sure. All I know is there is some recognition between us as I stare at him. I feel happy.

Daffodil

Then the guide tells me that I was a good person at that time. I am overwhelmed with emotion and relief. It's something I needed to know. I open my eyes and thank the spirit world. I am filled with love and gratitude.

I've never had anything as clear and precise as those visions; they were surreal. I wish I could draw. I'd love to draw in detail what I saw in that past life, the men's and women's faces especially the fashion and the surroundings. But then I tell myself that even if I could draw, my hands would let me down because of the RA. Still, it will stay in my memory forever.

When I was a child at school, I wasn't good at art. I was hopeless at drawing. If I tried to draw a house, it would be a square, a roof, a window in each corner, a front door, and a path leading up to it.

But when I had a paper and pen and started to doodle, I noticed that I could draw the perfect Egyptian eye – something I've drawn throughout my life, just like the ones you see on the walls of the Egyptian temples. Is it possible I used to draw theses eyes in a past life, also Mosaic tiles have always fascinated me – the ones you see in temples and old buildings in Greece. What do you keep drawing when you doodle?

Since I saw these past lives, I was shown more. It's like I'm being shown a photograph. On three separate nights; I saw a picture of a woman holding a basket of washing in her right arm, smiling sideways at a boy of about twelve. Her hair was up in a bun, the scene was a happy one.

The second night, I saw two elderly people, a man and a woman, on a road in the distance on a hill. They were both looking down the hill, surrounded by fields and trees in the countryside. They both had suitcases on either side on the ground; the picture was black-and-white. It seemed like the eighteenth century. It felt like a distant memory of another time.

The third night, I saw two naked, muscular men. Their bodies looked sculptured, more like statues made of stone, it looked like they were wrestling. They looked identical with blond, curly angel hair. I'm sure now that the two I saw are in fact my guardian angels, which I have seen together over the years in the past. You can have more than one guardian angel.

***

I am suffering more with my RA. I've lost the use of my right hand. I feel like my body has been in a bad accident. The pain is evil, and there's no let up these days; it's getting worse. I give myself a good talking to. "C'mon, Eileen, you have to be strong. You have to pull yourself together. Keep pushing forward, and you have to try harder. Be strong and try harder."

At about 3.00 in the morning, Harry shouted out in his sleep. "Try harder!" At first it didn't connect with me. I thought it was funny. Then I realised that was the last thing I'd told myself before I went to sleep.

The only difference was that it wasn't Harry's voice! A spirit had used Harry's voice box to get the message across to me. The voice sounded innocent. I felt the energy of a fourteen-year-old boy with learning difficulties.

It never ceases to amaze me how the spirit world can make things happen. They used this young boy's voice so that I could easily distinguish it from Harry's voice. How clever. Of course, Harry wouldn't know anything about it. He'd simply look at me with that familiar strange look on his face when I told him the story the next day. Still, it was comforting to know that spirit had been listening to my plea for help.

***

As my life unfolds, something's happening to me in a spiritual sense. It's usually around 3.00 AM, I don't always understand at the time, such as the photographs I'm being shown at random.

After three pictures were shown to me, I had a spiritual experience in the early hours of this morning on 23 January 2013. I laid on my right side in bed, and about three feet above my head was the door on my right.

All of a sudden I felt a man's presence. He was tall with fair hair; he wore a suit with a double-breasted jacket. I saw his arm and hand come round the door; he threw me a box of tissues that landed near my side. I immediately recognised the box: a blue and white box, still new and unopened, that I'd bought from Asda the previous Friday. When I awoke, I went in the living room. The box of tissues was still where I had put it on the table.

The next day I kept asking myself, *what does it mean? Now why does anybody hand you a box of tissues?* I must admit, it has left me concerned because I think of my family straightaway. I hope to know the answer soon.

25 January 2013

Two nights ago, I see my father in the country on a warm, sunny day. He was leaning over one of those wide country gates and resting his arms on top. I zoomed right in on the right side of his profile so I that could get a better look. He was staring at the ground below him. He wore a hat a bit like the ones he used to wear, as I stared at him, I got the impression that my father was waiting for me. That was all. I can't help thinking it will be soon.

1 February 2013

I went to bed and said my usual prayers. I also asked for more information from the spirit world, and whether it was possible to get in touch with Angel Margaret, who had written the book through Gerry Gavin, which I had mentioned earlier in the book.

Eventually I saw a figure of a woman. She seemed to be all of one colour: her hair, clothes, and skin blended into one colour, a silvery gray metallic look. She seemed to float around my bedroom, I watched her closely has she did so. She kept moving and turning so that I could get a better look at her. I looked at her hair, I noticed it was the same colour silvery gray. It was long and tied at the back in a pony tail to the right side. What was strange was that above her left ear about three inches, her head was shaved. She looked to be in her early thirties. She had a smile of wonder as she moved around, staring at me the whole time.

She appeared to me just like a hologram, all in gray. I felt neither comfortable nor uncomfortable; I simply didn't know what to think, what to make of it. Was this Angel Margaret, or was she a ghost? If I think about this moment, I still see her very clearly.

3 February 2013

At about three in the morning, Peggy put her paw on the bed near my body; this was her signal for me to allow her in bed for a cuddle. It immediately woke me, and then I was shown a brass key where she had put her paw. Does it have anything to do with the above story? Is Angel Margaret going to unlock more information to me? Is this what the key meant? We shall see. After all, I had asked Angel Margaret to help me with more information from the spirit world.

The Secret

About a month after seeing the key, I found a book called *The Secret*, by Rhonda Byrne. As I was flipping through the book's contents, I noticed some of the illustrations in the book. One was a key! It suddenly reminded me of Angel Margaret and the key that I had seen, although the key I'd seen was brass. It looked like metal or silver in the book, but it was the same shape. Too much of a coincidence, don't you think?

In the book *Messages from Margaret,* she speaks about how we can control our lives by simply changing our thoughts. As soon as a negative thought comes into our minds, we should change it straightaway to a good thought. It doesn't matter what it is, as long as it makes us feel happy and not negative.

She also said not to use the words "I want". If you use the words "I want", that is exactly what you will get – it will leave you wanting. The universe hears your thoughts and words. If it is money you are asking for, say instead, "I could do with a financial boost," or name a figure you have in mind. Visualise the check coming through the post, and you seeing the amount you asked for. The more thought you put into it, the better results. It becomes your reality. That goes for anything you ask for. It's your birthright.

The book *The Secret* goes into greater depth than Margaret's book.

The greatest teachers that have ever lived have told us that the law of attraction is the most powerful law in the universe. Great thinkers such as Socrates, Plato, and Pythagoras; da Vinci in his paintings; and Beethoven through music – they all knew about it. It has always been there, and it always will be.

You will probably say to yourself, "How can this be? I can control my life by just changing my thoughts?" All I can tell you is to try it and see for yourself. We've all been conditioned into thinking the way we do; from previous generations. Nobody said it was that simple. All this information has been lost through hundreds of years.

It's like a good old recipe that Grandma invented. Only she knew how to cook this special dish and all its secret ingredients that went into it. Her recipe got lost or destroyed, so nobody knew of this delicious dish. Nobody had any idea, so it couldn't be passed on to the next generations.

***

We all have the key to change our lives. When you wake in the morning, ask yourself, how you feel? More often than not, it will be something negative. Now think of something that makes you happy that brings a smile to your face – a picture, a funny joke, or a piece of your favorite music.

Whenever my father was feeling low or ill, my mother would put on some of his favorite music. This instantly made him feel good, he would rise from his chair and start dancing. She would joke, "A thought tha-wa badly!" He'd carry on dancing and chuckling away to himself. He instantly felt better; it always brought a smile to his face.

We all have to think in this way, if we want a better life. It's as simple as that. Change your thoughts immediately – don't give an inch to a negative thought.

I'm reminded of Paul Parker, who said, "Our life is all to do with the mind." I know what he meant now. I didn't at the time. We can take control of our lives by controlling our minds.

As a child, I would often hear in the background, "When you grow up, you can be whatever you want to be." I would think, *how?* I still hear it being said today.

At the time my dream was to be a professional dancer. How did I aspire to my dream? I had no idea. All I had to do was put the thought out to the universe, have faith, and believe that this would be granted. But I thought it was only a dream.

When you ask the universe for a wish, you have to consider that the matter has been dealt with, already granted. One hint of doubt and you ruin your chances, for the law of attraction will have heard it, too. But of course, at that time I didn't know about the secret, and nobody told me! Now I'm beginning to believe it is possible: sending the thoughts out to the universe and believing that it can happen by having faith.

I also mentioned earlier in the book how I managed to stop evil spirits coming through to me in my mind. I would feel something was about to happen in my mind, and I would know to change my thoughts immediately. It always worked! This was my soul remembering what to do at that time. My thoughts would change to something like, "What shall I cook for tea?" Or, "I must remember to feed the dog." They were simple thoughts, but I was grateful that they always worked!

My intention at this time is to be able to walk with my prosthesis. I ask the most powerful law in the universe, the law of attraction. This law has been there since the beginning of time. What a pity we were never told. It is the law that determines the complete order in the universe, every moment of your life and everything you experience.

It doesn't matter who you are or where you are – the law of attraction is forming your entire life experience. This all-powerful law is doing so through your thoughts every second. You are the one who calls the law of attraction into action, and you do it through your thoughts.

Can you imagine the outcome if everybody on this planet was to put it into action every day? The amount of good that could be achieved, all the possibilities – wow! I wouldn't know where to begin! We could all change the world to become a better one, simply by changing our thoughts.

This is what God meant, when he said that we are all capable of greater things, if only we knew it. Every man, woman, and child should know of the secret. It is our birthright. It's not just about positive thinking. It's about, having faith, trust, and belief that what you ask for will happen.

First you have to have sincere love and gratitude in your heart. Give thanks throughout the day as you go along. Send love out to the universe and be grateful for what you have

When I awake in the morning, it's usually my worst time. More often than not I ache, I'm stiff, and I dread another day. Now when I awake, I tell myself I feel much better and am getting stronger each day. "Today's going to be a good day!" What happens then? The law of attraction hears my thoughts, and it sends out more healing, more strength to my body. It's that simple.

It's been a long time since I was on my feet, almost a year. I have been visualizing myself getting up out of my wheelchair and taking my first steps. I came to put on my old prosthesis that I haven't worn for a year.

I was determined to walk with the aid of my crutches. And I did it! But I've grown out of it. It doesn't fit me anymore. I'm sure if it had, I would have been able to have taken more steps. I'm now in the process of getting a new one. I'm determined to walk again by simply changing my thoughts: "I can do this." We all can!

Have you ever noticed that some days when something goes wrong, it can be insignificant but starts to escalate all through the day? In your mind, everything starts going wrong, and you're soon having a bad day. That's because you've told yourself that everything is going wrong.

The universal law hears your thoughts and sends you more things that go wrong. You got what you asked for. It never lets you down, whether your thoughts are good or bad.
Remember that if your day starts off with something going wrong, change that thought straightaway to something like, "Everything in my life is working out just fine. This is a good day".

What pleases me most is finding out what we can all do by sending out the right thoughts to the universe, for humanity and the planet. The universe is full of abundance; no one need go hungry, there's enough for everyone. The key thought is that instead of feeling sorry for these poor and hungry people we see in the media, we send the right thoughts out to the universe.

Tell the universe that you would like to help these unfortunate souls. Ask them to send in their army of angels, and see the angels bringing food in abundance and providing shelter.

As you do this, imagine the people receiving this abundance; visualise their smiling faces as they receive this wonderful food. All the starving children are filling their hungry little bellies. Now, isn't that a wonderful sight to behold!

When people see these starving people on TV, they feel immediate sorrow for them, they shed tears, and they even send donations. I've done it myself, and it's only human. If you can help, you will. There are good people out there.

Carry on sending your donations, but also visualise these unfortunate souls being happy and receiving it. We all would like to save the world, and we all do what we can. Your positive thoughts are much more powerful when trying to help the needy. This is what God meant when he reminded us all that we don't realise how powerful we are.

If we want to help, instead of tears and sorrow, tell the law of attraction what these people need. If you continue to send out tears and sorrow, that is what they will continue to receive!

It's the same as when you feel sorry for people more unfortunate than yourself. Don't feel sorry for them; instead of seeing them that way, visualise them healthy and happy, and that is what they will receive. If your partner has been diagnosed with cancer, don't see the situation as getting worse. Use your imagination and visualise him or her improving each day.

See your partner as you always have, happy and healthy. Throw plenty of love at your partner. Use plenty of laughter; buy funny DVDs to watch, or anything that will make you both laugh. The universe has heard your thoughts, and it will all reverberate back to you. It has too because it's like gravity. It's your natural birthright.

We can all benefit by choosing the way we think. It's a matter of training your mind and having the right mindset. You can do it! Practice now. Start by telling yourself each morning when you awaken that you feel much better, much healthier. When you think about it, we can all achieve great things by learning to change our thoughts. Look at how much we could help humanity across the globe. We could prevent events from happening: famine, wars, financial decline, animal extinction, the decline in jobs – the list goes on. We could turn this world around for the better.

If I were to leave a legacy to my children and grandchildren, it would be the two books *The Secret* and *The Power*. What a wonderful life they all could aspire to and pass on to their children.

I bought the books and also the film. Although the DVD is exactly the same as the book, I would say it's more like a lecture, with all the same people in the book as on screen explaining the subject in its entirety. I've told two of my sons and two of my eldest grandsons all about the books because it was convenient at the time.

I hope that one day they will all want to read it. It's there if they want to have the best that life has to offer, and to have the simple knowledge that goes with it. But I also must remember not to force it onto my family. It's because I am a mother and want the best for all my family. What greater thing could I leave behind after I've gone home?

I remember once as a little child, my father asked me a question. "Eileen, do you love yourself?" At the time I didn't know what to say. So he put it another way. "If I was to put a big bun on a plate and a little tiny bun by the side of it, which one would you choose first if I were to offer them to you?"

I didn't want to answer in case I said the wrong thing. I didn't want to disappoint him. "Er, I guess I would choose the big one."
He laughed and said, "Well there you go, then. You do love yourself."

Daffodil

The reason I mention this is because as a little child, I thought it was wrong to love myself. How wrong I was. But how would I know, if I was never told? How would Dad know if he was never told? It's a memory I've never forgotten. I had to experience it so I could right about it, to remember how important it is that we all love ourselves first.

Why not try right now. Visualise a five-year-old child. Look at her and see the innocence in her face. Now go up the child and hold her in your arms. Feel the love pour out of you for this innocent child. Rock her backwards and forwards, giving assurance that everything is going to be all right. The child looks up at you and smiles. You smile back. It is only then you recognise -that the child is you.

How much better do you feel right now? When I first tried it, it made me cry. I love this child; I love who I am. Yes, Dad, I do love myself!

***

One Sunday night I climbed into bed and said my prayers. I started to drift off to sleep, but then I was awakened by a spirit. I felt the blanket lift off me, and then it tried to get into my bed. I felt a cold shiver run through my body. That's how I knew it was evil.

I was angry and kicked out my leg. I spoke in a stern voice, "Go to the light. Turn towards God!" I don't like it when things happen like this ... but why did I feel so angry? I'm supposed to help spirits. Perhaps it was the fact that the spirit felt evil. Afterwards, I asked my angels for protection in case of anymore negative energy that maybe hanging around my aura.

Whilst on the subject of protection and asking for help, my grandson's Jordan. He has decided to join the police force where he lives, in Manchester. He will be training for the next three years without pay, meanwhile he works part-time in a men's retail department store. He's full of enthusiasm and enjoys all the police training, "There's never a dull moment," he tells me.

Although I am very proud of Jordan for getting to this stage in his life at nineteen, I can't help but feel concerned for him. Things have changed so much for the worse when it comes to the dangers of policing.

He came to see me one day with his girlfriend, Stephanie. I hadn't seen him in almost three and half years. Jordan has now passed his driving test, so he will be able to drive over from Manchester more often. Whilst he was here, he'd brought his police uniform to show me. He looked so grown-up, like a man! It didn't seem that long ago when they were all little. How the years have flown.

I felt compelled to tell Jordan about the angels. It was like that nudge I get from time to time from the spirit world. "Jordan, if ever you are in a bad or dangerous situation where you need help, all you have to do is ask for help from Archangel Michael." He looked at me with respect and nodded his head.

This advice goes out to all of you readers who work in dangerous environments. All you have to do is call on Archangel Michael. Remember that he's the one who protects and fights our battles.

Past Life

In the early hours of the morning, I felt like I was in a small room as I looked ahead of me. I saw the profile of a woman sitting at a table. There were several other people sat at the table with her, all having a meal. I could only see the woman's profile and the dress she was wearing. It was a black plain dress with long sleeves buttoned up to the neck, and a bit of white lace showing. Her hair was tied back in a neat bun at the nape of her neck.

As the woman lifted a spoon to her mouth, she suddenly stopped. It was as if she was aware of my presence. With both hands on her knees, she lifted her dress as she slowly rose from her chair and turned towards me. She stared at me. She was small and petite with a beautiful complexion, she looked about thirty.

There was nothing in her features that I seemed to recognise, only the fact that she had a lovely, fresh complexion. Her expression was one of slight embarrassment – sort of a sheepish grin, a guilty look.

I thought, *Is this my biological grandmother on my mother's side?* Yet it felt as if I was looking at myself. Is it possible that I gave up my child, my mother, in that past life?

I have already wrote in the book earlier that there was the possibility that I was the mother of my own mother in a past life. It felt like the Victorian era. I'm sure that was the reason she looked embarrassed, like she was having to confess that she gave up my mother for adoption.

The pictures I was shown were so clear and in colour this time. I also mentioned earlier in the book that souls can return to the same family group time and time again. This time the soul could be the sister, brother, mother, or father, depending on which scenario the soul wanted.

I would imagine if I was the mother of my own mother in that past life, I would feel embarrassed and guilty. I would choose to reincarnate to be with her again in a future life by wanting to be her mother, to try to make amends. Of course, I wouldn't have any knowledge of this when I reincarnated.

***

In the early hours of the morning, I was shown a life-like picture of a baby lying on a hospital bed, dressed in what looked like a cream and pink bunny rabbit suit. The sun was streaming through the window onto the bed where the baby laid, smiling and happy. As I looked down at the baby, I noticed the little bunny suit had little pink rabbits printed on it.

It was as if the baby girl was going home with its new parents for the first time. It made me feel happy and joyful to the point where I wanted to shout out to Harry and tell him that I'd just seen the most beautiful little baby girl! But I didn't. I laid there thinking about what it meant.

Sometimes when you see a baby in your dreams, it could be symbolic. It could mean a new beginning, a new start, or being born again. The reasons for the bunny rabbit suit could mean something around Easter, when Christ was resurrected. Why had I been shown this? Was it another sign from the spirit world that the baby could be me?

When I think about seeing the baby, it's about the same time as I discovered the book *The Secret*. Could this mean that I was going to improve with my health? Was I going to cure myself by using the secret, by changing my thoughts? In other words reborn?

The Secret tells us all how we can prevent illness and retain our health. But what about the premonition that I would pass over in my sixty-fifth year? As I write, this is my sixty-fifth year now.

I must admit that since changing my thoughts, I'm feeling happier; I refuse to be sad. I fill my mind with happy thoughts and keep telling myself that my body is getting stronger each day, even if it's not! It's like the muscles in the body that have become atrophied over lack of use. The only way they can become strong again is through exercise. The only difference is that this muscle is in the brain. The only way we can reach this muscle is through our thoughts, by practicing every day.

Start with feeling love and gratitude for everything in your life. Send love out to all humanity, for they are your brothers and sisters. Send out love to your enemies – the ones you don't like, the ones who irritate you the most. It's important that you have no bad feelings, only the feeling of love. Remember that love is a powerful tool, a powerful medicine.

It's good to start with the little things and let it build up. Try to keep on the happy frequency, just like a radio. Remember that you have spent a lifetime thinking in the way you do. The change won't just happen overnight, but with perseverance and determination; it can change your life for the better.

If it's possible that I have caused my ill health myself due to the way I think, then that means I can undo all the damage that I have caused to myself by changing my thoughts. I can make myself healthy.

It's important that we pass this information on to the next generation, never to be lost again. It has always been there.

I like feeling happy and joyful. I know it's working at this present moment, and it's doing me good. Or is it that the spirit world has let me experience my health improving, to show the reader that yes, it can be achieved?

It is now April 2013. It is about three weeks since I have been practicing the new thought pattern. Every day I've said to myself that my eyesight is improving. Every day I'm seeing much clearer. After about three days, I noticed I could see the small print on the bottom of TV much better.

The improvement seems to be concentrated in my left eye. When I was in the Asda car park, I was able to test my sight with the registration numbers. I could see them much clearer. I said to Harry, "I can see this, and I can see that, whereas before I would be struggling to see." This has inspired me more to use this method all over my ailing body.

Is it possible: Can I improve my health? It's the early days yet, but I'm certainly going to try. Is this why Angel Margaret showed me the key, which led to *The Secret*? This is not just about positive thinking. I think we've all done that before. It's about training the brain to change its thought pattern.

Whenever something or someone upsets you, in your mind you can walk away from it. The point is not to give it any feeling; bring yourself out of it. Think of five or ten things that make you instantly happy, and fill yourself up with happiness. You'll be amazed at how you feel! Then send lots of love towards the things that have upset you. Always try to stay on the happy frequency.

Remember that you are changing a lifetime of thinking one way, because you didn't know about the secret, and sometimes you'll forget. However, you are adjusting to a whole new way of life that will bring you all that you desire – love, happiness, health, wealth.

It's been a month now since I've put the thought pattern into practice, and I'm pleased to say that my life has changed for the better. I find the more I give out of gratitude and love, the more my problems seem to resolve.

Today, I saw my physiotherapist, Rebecca, because I have been in my wheelchair for twelve months. I thought I was going to need at least four to six weeks of physio before I were able to walk in my new prosthesis.

Within one hour, not only did she have me walking with the aid of the bars, but she also had me climbing up and down four steps! It felt great to be able to stand on my own two feet again. I surprised myself with how much progress I had made with such little effort. This put me in a great mood for the rest of the day. I thanked the universe, and this has inspired me even more! I want you, the reader, to benefit from my experience.

Daffodil

I have been telling the universe, "If I'm to pass over in my sixty-fifth year then, I would like some quality and happiness to my life for the time I have left. That was precisely what I have had in these past few weeks.

***

Can you believe it? Three days later, as I sat at my computer desk, I suddenly became so listless and lethargic. Most of all, I became emotional. I could have burst into tears at any time, but it didn't feel it was coming from me. I was perplexed to suddenly feel this way. I had gone from one extreme to the other. Why did I feel this way? Why did this awful cloud come over me?

Then I was aware that there was a group of spirits at the back of me as I sat in my computer chair. I could feel the angels, and I saw a picture in my mind's eye of them grouped together. The angels were standing at the back of the group of spirits, watching me the whole time.

I was picking up on their energy and emotions – it wasn't my own. They were all crying for me! Afterwards, I had a strong sense of foreboding. I looked at Peggy, and she knew, too; she never left my side that day. I told Harry about it when he came home from work.

Two days later, I had the most terrific pains in my stomach. *Oh please, spirit world, not again! Just when I was starting to feel so much better!*

I ended up in the hospital once more. I was diagnosed with a perforated bowel, and they found I had developed diverticulitis! Obviously I thought that this was my time, that I was going to die. It was horrendous; all I could have were tiny sips of water for the first four or five days. They pumped me with IVs full of antibiotics. When the consultant gave me the bad news, I could see the concern in his eyes, especially with all the other health problems I had.

At last they made me stable. When I discussed the options with my consultant, he asked me if I would be prepared to have an operation. That was why I was given only tiny sips of water, so that I would be ready for theatre at any time. Because I had been in such pain, I agreed.

In the early hours of the fifth morning, I listened to my body, my heart, and my soul. I knew my weary body couldn't take an operation; I wasn't strong enough. I made my mind up to not do it. I'll leave it up to the universe handing it over to God. If it's time, then so be it. After all, it was my sixty-fifth year, and I'm supposed to pass over, aren't I?

When I told the consultant that I wasn't prepared to have the operation, he didn't try to dissuade me. infact he looked relieved. They gave me lots of antibiotics by drip; I continued to improve each day. But obviously I was wondering about the perforation. Apparently the antibiotics would have closed the hole up by this time; I was making good progress. Then I asked the consultant, "What's the probability of it coming back again?"

"It won't come back in the same place," he said, "but it could pop in another area of the bowel at any time."

So really the operation would have been pointless. It was not worth the suffering and the setback, for it could happen again at any time; but now I've become a ticking time bomb.

That day they allowed me plenty of clear liquids, then gradually introducing clear soups and porridge. Never have I appreciated food so much in all my life. I started to pick up each day. I was sent home nine days later, supposedly with another two days of oral antibiotics to take, but they never supplied them. I tried to explain to the nurse over the phone, she said that someone would get back to me, but no one did.

I'm hoping that it's totally cleared up?

When I was in hospital, I laid in my bed one night with my hands by my side. Suddenly I felt a hand over my left side where my large bowel is, but most of all I recognised the healing heat. At the same time, in my mind's eye I saw the same guide dressed in robes who had told me that I would be shown more to do with the book. Telepathically he said, "Not yet." It brought me comfort; I knew all was not lost.

Daffodil

Whilst in the hospital, I knew my spiritual work was not yet finished. But where would I find the energy? I felt so weak. Somehow the spirit world gave me the strength. I had to keep on the positive side; I had to stay happy. I had to climb on to that happy frequency no matter what, no matter how bleak the future looked. I mustn't give in.

Beryl Bressinger

On the second night in hospital, at about two in the morning, I heard the porter and a nurse bringing another patient onto our ward. A few minutes later, a doctor and his entourage gathered round Beryl Bressinger's bed. The doctor started to talk to BB and gave her information about what they were about to perform there and then in her hospital bed.

When I first saw BB, she was flat on her back, so she couldn't see me. I noticed her diaphragm and lower abdomen: she was so swollen that I couldn't see her legs. At first I thought she was a double amputee.

I couldn't help but notice how gentle and caring the doctor was. *What a lovely soul,* I thought. There are some lovely people in this world. He genuinely cared for this woman, it lifted my spirits. He knew BB must be suffering terribly. I asked the angels to help guide the doctor.

"Now Beryl, what I'm going to do is I'll be moving you, rolling you around from time to time to release the gases that have accumulated in your diaphragm and lower tummy." I'm sure there must be a medical term for this procedure. But I'll just tell it how it is.

As he gently rolled her, I could hear the gases being released. With each one she had, I was so pleased for her. I kept thinking, *Oh, she must feel better for that. Bless her.* I'd heard of trapped wind, but never to that extent.

BB had had a scan before the gas procedure. The next morning the doctor came to see her. "Beryl, I'm afraid we are going to have to operate straightaway. You have a blockage in your large intestine."

Daffodil

Oh God, how much worse could it get? This woman also had multiple sclerosis. Again the doctor talked Beryl through the operation procedure, with the same loving, caring attitude as before. This doctor hadn't even been to bed the night before. I wish I could remember his name. These people are the unsung heroes, don't you agree?

As the doctor spoke to BB, it helped make up my mind to come to a decision about what to do about my own circumstances. I certainly didn't want to be put through what Beryl was going to be put through. They were going to put a cannuler into the vein in her neck. After the operation, she would be put into an induced coma for the next twenty-four hours. Her lungs would collapse down, and she would be put on a ventilator that would breathe for her. Then she'd move to the intensive care unit for who knows how long.

When Beryl was being moved from the ward, I felt as if I knew this woman. I shouted, "Good luck, Beryl. I will think about you, love." Although she couldn't see me, she shouted a thank-you. Then the other patients joined in. I'm sure it brought comfort to her that she wasn't alone; and others were thinking of her.

The next day, I asked the sister how BB had gone on in the operation. All she could tell me that she was in intensive care. I do hope she made it. She was only sixty-two years old, and I could see she had a loving husband. Perhaps one day she will discover my book and recognises her story.

The more I thought about having an operation; I knew my body wasn't strong enough. Dad used to say before his hernia operation, "You have to be fit to withstand an operation." "It's funny how I've remembered that quote. What if infection set in? What if another hole popped during the operation? There were too many what-ifs.

Anyway, I was compromised. My hands didn't work anymore, so how could I possibly cope with a stoma bag attached to me? The hole they put on the left-hand side to empty the bag of waste had to be kept spotlessly clean in case of infection. My mind was made up. I certainly wasn't leaving it down to Harry, bless him. He's enough to cope with.

When I told the consultant, I'm sure there was a look of relief on his face. He knew that it could be a waste of time. My case was too compromising. Now I'm going to enjoy what little time I have left.

***

Once again I'm back on the happy frequency. I've never been so happy, and life is very good! Since coming home from the hospital, I'm determined not to let anything spoil my happiness. I climbed back on the happy frequency using the thought pattern every day. Everything I wish for and hope for seems to just fall into my lap. It's amazing. I have control of my life again, despite the bleak outlook.

I fear nothing. I know I'm getting all the help from the guides and angels. Using the universal law in the most positive way certainly works! It's all there, the greatest tool that God gave to all of us; to use in this troubled world.

Eileen Cooper

Whilst in hospital, I met an old lady of eighty-four. They called her Eileen, too, so at times it would get a little confusing, but we'd make a joke of it. When she first came into the room, she was accompanied by a nurse holding her arm. She shuffled her feet slowly across the floor towards her bed. As I looked at her, my first thought was, *Oh my gosh, she looks so poorly.* Her complexion was so pale and waxy. Anybody could see that this woman was very ill.

The nurse took her blood sugar levels, the reading was 2.2 – she was about to go into hypo. The nurse then gave her a high-sugar juice drink. It was apparent Eileen was a diabetic, type two. Eventually she started to come round. She looked so much better as her colour started to return.

She had come in for investigations for other problems. We soon got to know one another, and eventually we were laughing and joking. She told me her life story. She'd had a hard life bringing six children up, four boys and two girls. She'd worked all her life, and that her husband wasn't much help He died at age sixty-eight, bless her. She'd been on her own for a while.

As she began to tell me her story, I could tell there wasn't much love coming from her children. She now felt she'd become an inconvenience to the family. One daughter was complaining about having to bring her to hospital for appointments and such.

What puzzled me was that her daughter had brought her into hospital that very morning. They had been waiting for hours, since nine in the morning, to be sorted out with a bed. It was well after lunch time. Surely her daughter must have recognised Eileen's diabetic symptoms and her colour? But she did nothing about it. I could tell there wasn't much caring there.

On the morning Eileen was told she was going home, it was about nine in the morning. She was excited to be going home to her cat, Cleo. She started to pack all her things, ready for home. After quite some time, the nurse kept running in and telling Eileen they were trying to get in touch with her daughter, to bring her home. It never happened.

The next day it happened again. Eileen sat there patiently waiting all day to go home. It was worse than waiting at the airport after a long delay. And on top of that, it was her eighty-fifth birthday!

Surely her family must have known it was their mother's birthday. But she was stuck in hospital. Eventually her son-in-law walked into the ward at four in the afternoon, whilst her daughter went looking for the nurse.

He never greeted her and just mumbled about how inconvenient it was that they had been trying to get in touch with hospital. In actual fact, they had spent the day before at the Liverpool race course! When her daughter walked in to the room, she didn't even acknowledge her mother!

At last I said, "You are here. Your mother has been waiting since yesterday morning. It's been worse than being delayed at the airport. I feel so sorry for her. She's been so patient, and she's such a lovely woman. I've really enjoyed her company." I had to get my point across. "After all, it's her birthday today."

The daughter answered in a sarcastic tone, "Is it?" I could have cried for that woman. How could a fifty-year-old adult be so cruel towards her mother? There was no kiss, no "Happy birthday, Mum", no birthday card nothing to show.

When Eileen was leaving, she came over to thank me and give me a kiss. I know she was happy that I had spoken up for her.

Daffodil

Again, I was in the right place at the right time. Then I asked myself, *what do you do with a situation like this? What would the universe have me do? What thought pattern can I use to make the situation better?*

All I can do is to send Eileen loads of love. I visualise her smiling and being happy with her precious cat, Cleo. I do not let myself feel sorry for her, for that would only bring more sorrow.

There are two sides to every story, but your mother is your mother at the end of the day. She gave you life. Where situations arise like this, it means there is a lack of love in that area. All you can do is feed it with love. Visualise good things happening. Love heals and solves everything.

Christine

Another lady I met in the hospital in the same ward was Christine. Christine was the same age as me. She came into hospital with quite a few health problems. She was in for the long haul while her health issues were carried out. We got to know each other over the next three days.

We seemed to have a lot in common, due to being born in the same era. As I got to know Christine, I could feel her fear and negativity. When I asked her if my thoughts were right, she admitted, "Yes. I've been like it all of my life. I can't help it."

My thoughts, *Oh, I've got a lot of work to do here. Spirit world, you will have to give me strength.*

I gradually and slowly told Christine how she could change her life if she wanted to, just by changing her thoughts. I told her how it is still working for me as my life continues. She didn't seem convinced at first, but the more I told her about my life – especially the supernatural experiences – the more she became interested.

Christine always thought the worst things were going to happen to her. Even when she was happy, she worried that something was going to come along and spoil it. Obviously this set the foundation for all her health problems. Her mind was set from a young age. I told her as soon as she started to use the tools that God gave us, she would start to see the benefits. It wouldn't be easy – she would have to use the muscle in her brain to get there.

When you think of it, it is so easy to do, and it costs you nothing. After all, that's happened to me. I'm determined to stay happy and positive with lovely thoughts and appreciation and gratitude for all I have. Why? Because it works and continues to do so.

Everything I hope and wish for seems to fall into place; all my problems resolve. That's why you, the reader, can benefit from my discovery. You can be happy, and you can have what you desire. Why not give yourself six weeks? Keep a diary, and practice. Be happy and send out lovely thoughts. Thank the universe and God. Be eternally grateful. Then sit back and see what happens over the next six weeks.

Eventually the time came to say goodbye to Christine. She told me she'd really enjoyed my company, and she said how interesting it had all been despite her being ill. She would look out for my book one day. I hope she does, for it can only help. All I know is that I was in the right place at the right time for Christine.

On the day I was to be discharged, it was as if all the answers about the human experience on this planet came flooding towards me. We are all children of God, filled with pure love. That is how we will return to God, made pure once again. We are pure spirit, experiencing being human on this earth. That is all. It is all an illusion. We will drop our bodies, for they are no use to us anymore; they are simply vehicles in which to move around.

The world is changing, and it will change for the better. It's already happening in areas of the world right now. We rarely hear of good, positive news because we have been conditioned to fear our fellow man. It's built on a foundation of negativity across the globe. It's up to humanity to change this via our thought patterns, the collective consciousness.

Man is responsible for all the destruction in the world and the state it is in. It needs a massive injection of pure love. Mankind has to change its thoughts to positive, loving thoughts. You were meant to be happy, so stay happy and don't allow negativity into your life. Soon you will want to shout about it, because it is so simple to create.

I have been home from hospital for a week now. I'm so glad to see my little Peggy; she's been so attentive. I'm progressing each day. I had my first few steps walking with the aid of my Zimmer frame around the house.

My goal is set: to attend my son Wayne and his lovely fiancée Joanne's engagement party on 22 June. I have ten days to improve my well-being. Wayne and Joanne are made for each other. I want my family to see me up on my feet, if it's the last thing I do on this earth.

Ten days later

I made it to the party! I asked the universe to find me the right dress, shoes, and accessories. But most of all, I asked it to let me walk into that party with my crutches, upright and confident.

I believe that the spirit world allowed me to have a good time with my family as another reward for my efforts. Thank you, heavenly father. It was such a lovely night that night; there was magic in the air.

The Change

When I was in the hospital, I knew things were going to have to change big time. I was going to have to educate myself about digestive problems, diverticulitis, IBS, perforated bowel – anything that could possibly affect my health in any way. How grateful I am that I'm computer literate. I love technology, with everything at my fingertips.

I started straightaway. As I explained earlier in the book, all sickness starts with the mind first – what we think, we will become. If you've been more of a negative thinker, one who worries all the time, eventually this may turn into a disease such as an autoimmune disease, especially if you've been doing it for years. T

Then it may lead on to other problems, such as in the digestive, especially as we become older. I have had bowel problems since having my firstborn. In those days they put you on iron tablets if you were anemic and pregnant.

The down side was that the iron could make you very constipated; your stools would be hard. But even in those days, I would always check for any blood. I acquired lots of these episodes, and it made my life miserable. I would have to take laxatives to counteract the iron.

This happened on and off throughout my life. I thought, *Well, I'll just have to put up with it.* I didn't realise I could help myself with the right information. I would hear the occasional remark of, "You should try this. It's good for opening the bowel."

Eileen Veronica Richmond

Foods to avoid are: anything made from white flour. Only eat wholemeal bread or buckwheat or rye. But these foods didn't always appeal to me, and neither were they always convenient.

Eventually I discovered that to keep the right balance in our bodies, the foods that we put into ourselves should consist of 80 per cent alkaline and 20 per cent acidic. Too many acidic foods over a long period of years can be harmful to the body. That has been my case – too much acid build-up in my blood and around my joints, along with lymphatic fluids, contributed to my illness.

Refined White Sugar

Sugar is the worst. This information is not meant to scare you, but to bring it to your attention the dangers of using sugars in your daily life, so that you can make the right choices. White sugar is unnecessary, especially when there are natural sugars which we can consume that won't harm us.

In 1957 Dr William Coda Martin tried to answer the question, "When is a food a food, and when it is a poison?" His working definition of poison was "Medically: any substance applied to the body, ingested, or developed within the body which causes or may cause diseases.

Physically: any substance which inhibits the activity of a catalyst, which is a minor substance, chemical, or enzyme that activates a reaction." The dictionary gives an even broader definition for poison: "to exert a harmful influence on or to pervert".

Dr Martin classified refined sugar as a poison because it has been depleted of its life forces, vitamins, and minerals. What is left consists of pure, refined carbohydrates. The body cannot utilize this refined starch and carbohydrate unless the depleted proteins vitamins and minerals are present.

Nature supplies these elements in each plant, in quantities sufficient to metabolize the carbohydrate in that particular plant. There is no excess for other added carbohydrates. Incomplete carbohydrate metabolism results in the formation of toxic metabolites, such as pyruvic acid, which accumulates in the brain and nervous system, and the abnormal sugars in the red blood cells.

These toxic metabolites interfere with the respiration of cells. They cannot get sufficient oxygen to survive and function normally. In time some of the cells die.

This cell death interferes with the function of part of the body and is the beginning of degenerative diseases. Refined sugar is lethal when ingested by humans because it provides only that which nutritionists describe as empty or naked calories. It lacks the natural minerals that are present in the sugars from beet or cane.

Sugar taken every day produces a continuously overly acid condition. More and more minerals are required from deep in the body in the attempt to rectify the imbalance. Finally, in order to protect the blood, so much calcium is taken from the bones and teeth that they decay, and general weakening begins.

Excess sugar eventually affects every organ in the body. Initially it is stored in the liver in the form of glucose (glycogen), because the liver's capacity is limited. A daily intake of refined sugar above their required amount of natural sugar soon makes the liver expand like a balloon.

When the liver is expanded and filled to its maximum capacity, the excess glycogen is returned to the blood in the form of fatty acids. They are taken to every part of the body and stored in the most inactive areas: the belly, the buttocks, the breasts, and the thighs. Too much sugar makes one sleepy, and one's ability to calculate and remember is lost.

We can all change this by just changing to natural sugars, which taste much better anyway. Black molasses is the best natural sweetener. It is full of vitamin B complex, which is also good for the nervous system.

Here is a list of side effects for having too much acidic food in the system.

1. Weight gain or loss
2. Osteoporosis
3. Heart attack
4. Skin eruptions
5. Tendency to infection

6. Depression
7. Acne problems
8. Leg cramps and spasms
9. Low energy
10. Chronic fatigue
11. Frequent colds and bronchitis
12. All kinds of arthritis

This is a list of foods which are good for us, with the most alkaline in them.

Lemon
Olive oil
Watermelon
Broccoli
Asparagus
Garlic
Spinach
Onion
Grapefruit, mango

Look on the Internet for more options.

Do you remember earlier in the book, when I went to see the psychic surgeon Steven Turrof?

The reason was so he might be able to heal my left ankle. I didn't want to lose my left leg if it could be treated. He ended up treating my upper bowel instead of my leg. I must have been having problems then with my bowel, and I didn't realise it. I suppose it gave me an extra several years without any problems, because I wasn't having any pain or discomfort, and I was going to the toilet regularly. I thought it was a problem solved.

What I failed to realise was that I was still feeding my body with the wrong foods. Several years later this was to be the outcome: perforated bowel and diverticulitis disease. For people who suffer with bowel problems such as irritable bowel syndrome, colitis, And Crones disease, or for those who have reflux acid or heartburn every time you eat a meal, this is your body telling you there's something wrong.

I've been home now from hospital three weeks. I am now on a new diet. I can't believe how quickly my health has changed for the better. I have had porridge for the past few weeks for breakfast – five days whilst in hospital and three weeks at home. This is an alkaline food that is full of vitamin B complex, which is very good for the nervous system.

I have a banana and apple chopped up for my lunch sometimes, or a soup with a small piece of wholemeal bread. For the evening meal, I sometimes have a jacket potato, a large piece of broccoli, and a carrot with a little chicken. I've totally gone off red meat. I allow myself a knob of lurpack butter and sometimes a piece of cathedral cheese, my favourite.

Butter is packed with selenium, which our bodies needs in small amounts to stay healthy. Also, cheese is packed with calcium, which is good for bones and teeth. It is also good for the immune system because it helps prevent cancer and mood swings, and it contains antioxidants. You only have to look it up on the Internet to realise the benefits. Too little selenium in children can cause heart disease.

Recently scientist are now saying we need saturated fats to stay healthy?

There are a lot of foods you can choose from to balance your alkaline and acidic foods. At the moment I have given up red meat because I don't think it's good for the human body. If I do eat meat, it is chicken, but only small amounts. Red meat can also have an effect on our bodies, depending how the animal was slaughtered. All animals have souls and are more intuitive than man. If the animal knows it is about to be killed, the stress will be absorbed into the meat. Also it will affect us in a spiritual way. If the animal is brought up in a friendly environment, where it is exposed to fresh air, sun, and grass every day, and where it is fed on nourishing foods without antibiotics, and if the animal is killed in a humane way, then the meat will be tender and succulent.

This goes for all God's creatures. We should always give thanks to God for the food we are about to receive. We should also give thanks to the animal which provided it.

Remember that I did not start this program to lose weight; the weight simply came away without any real effort. All foods that enter my mouth are chewed slowly to a pulp before I swallow. This gives my digestive system less work to do, so that the foods I eat pass easily in my digestive track.

I always remember Paul McKenna once speaking on TV about dieting. If you chew your food slowly and take your time, odds are you will feel full and won't be able to finish your meal. This is true. Not only that, but you will enjoy your food more because you take your time and can really taste the different textures.

On the Internet you have access to lists of alkaline foods and acidic foods. Also you can learn about probiotics. In Boots Chemist they sell PROBIO 7v, which contains two types of fiber and seven types of bacteria. The pills have many benefits.

1. Maintains intestinal hygiene and balance
2. Preserves friendly bacteria levels
3. Supports good digestion and intestinal function
4. Reinforces the body's immune system and natural defenses

It's made from 100 per cent natural ingredients. You can buy five hundred capsules for £12.29. It's ideal for people who lead busy lives. It says to take two capsules daily, but I'm only starting with one to see if my body responds okay, as a precaution because of the perforation I had.

Since coming out of the hospital, I have responded so well. I have had no pain, and the bloating stopped after three weeks. I have my bowels open every morning. I look forward to my food and have had no nausea symptoms. I have more energy, and I don't feel sluggish anymore. I'm not taking naps like I used to in the afternoon, and I'm losing my cravings to foods that are harmful to my body. I never feel hungry. It's worked like magic! My eyes look brighter, and my skin glows. It can't be bad, eh?

I also think it's because the health change has happened so quickly. I was only allowed sips of water for five days, and this gave me the detox that I needed to flush out all of the impurities in my system. This would be a good idea, a kick start, if you could maybe detox for a couple of days first. It will also give your internal organs a rest, especially the liver and kidneys. It simply depends how desperate you are to improve your health.

Remember to drink lots of fluids. We are always told to drink lots of water, but we don't always feel like it. The best way I've found is to fill a 500ml bottle of water and put in the tiniest drop of barley water or rosehip syrup. Because of the added flavour, it's a lot easier to drink.

Cake Recipe

I have a special recipe for a cake that Harry made for me, for the bowels. This gets the ball rolling, if you are desperate to get started, especially if you're constipated at the moment. No scales are needed.

You will need:
One mug of mixed fruit, or two or three grated carrots, or both.
One and half mugs of wholemeal flour, or any healthy flour as long as it's not white refined flour.
One teaspoon of bicarbonate of soda, to help the cake rise.
Half a mug of vegetable oil
Three eggs
A pinch of salt
A teaspoon of mixed spices
Three or four caps of spirit such as brandy or whiskey; this will help preserve the cake
One large tablespoon of black molasses.

If you want to add extra sweetness to the cake, it's best to spread honey over the top of the cake while still warm. I've just found out that cooked honey is a no-no. Eaten from the jar, it is nectar. When cooked, it becomes poison according to Ayurvedic Indian food lore. You may want to use the Internet to look for various diets for balancing the foods we eat.

There seems to be a larger variation including meats, depending what type of body you have in Indian culture. If you can afford Manuka honey, this is more beneficial because it contains healing properties. I put a teaspoon in my porridge every day to replace sugar. It's now used in medical dressings.

1. Sift the wholemeal flour into a mixing bowl; this is just to get some air into the flour. The wholemeal will separate from the flour. If it does, simply mix it all in anyway. At the same time, keep adding the vegetable oil till it's gone.
2. Sift the bicarbonate of soda into the mixing bowl and then put in the spices. Add the pinch of sea salt. Gradually mix in the fruit; grate in the carrot. Add all of the ingredients and keep mixing and folding. Then mix in the eggs one by one. Give it a good stir to let in the air. If you think the cake mix is a little dry, pop in another egg or add a little milk.
3. Use a little butter to grease a seven-inch-deep cake tin, preferably with a removable bottom. Pour in the mixture
4. Cook in the centre of the oven on 180°C for 50 minutes.
5. Test centre of cake with a sharp knife. If it comes out clear with no mixture sticking to it, it's cooked.

Now have a small piece of this cake every day till you have a bowel movement. Once you have had a bowel movement, cut this down to a piece every other day.

Alternatively, you can add three or four small oranges without the pips, chopped up small then put in the blender including the peel together with the eggs, pour into the cake mixture gradually, and stir well.

Now start introducing alkaline foods into your diet: bananas, apples, pears, pineapple – the list goes on. Have porridge for breakfast with the old-fashioned oats. Quaker Simple oats contain hidden sugars, and so do breakfast cereals. It's not fair when people are trying to lose weight.

Keep a diary on any food you have eaten that has brought discomfort after eating. Always look out for hidden salt and sugars in your foods. It's the same with our pets: the foods we feed them contain hidden sugars, salts, and also propylene glycol – a derivative of anti-freeze! Can you believe it?

It's supposed to preserve and keep the pet food moist. It has been known to cause anemia in cats and dogs, known as Heinz body anemia. The FDA has banned using it in cat food, but is still used in dog food!

No wonder domestic cats and dogs are becoming obese! Some pet foods are not what they appear to be.

Regarding food combinations, some of it will be trial and error. You'll learn as you go along. Some foods are volatile if eaten together in the gut. Again, you can learn all about this on the Internet, or from books. Take something as simple as beans on toast. When I tried some, it wasn't the beans that gave me heartburn – it was the tomato sauce.

After about three weeks, when you are going to the toilet regularly with no problems and the bloating stops, you will feel energised. This alone will keep you motivated. Plus, the weight that drops off.

That aspect, combined with the right thought pattern, will make the foundation for a, happy healthy body. Remember that you can have the foods you desire – you don't have to starve yourself and be miserable if you want to lose some weight. Simply try to stick to 80 per cent alkaline and 20 per cent acidic. If you must eat meat, then balance it out, but give yourself a break from meat occasionally.

Diets

Have you noticed over the last twenty to thirty years how more people have become obese, and how it's affecting the children? There are more children becoming obese. The increase has risen in diabetes for young and old. This is down to the wrong foods we are putting into our bodies, and the wrong diets. We are all individuals. We have to find the right foods for our bodies.

Diets don't work: One reason is; it takes three weeks for the body's stored fat to come off before you start to lose any weight. You will reach your target weight if you are determined to lose weight. Then you have to keep the weight off. By this time, you probably feel miserable because you have tried so hard by giving up all the foods you used to enjoy.

We are just like plants: if we nurture our bodies and provide the right nutrients, water, and sunshine, then we will thrive. First, we have to check our digestive system. This is the hub, so to speak. It's like our car we have to maintain, the most important part of the body. If we continue to put in the wrong foods, along with negative thinking, it sets the foundation for disaster.

Do you have problems after eating certain foods, such as heartburn, constipation, diarrhea, stomach cramps, acid reflux, or pain when passing stools? In extreme cases, have you suffered with ulcers in your stomach? These are all signs that your stomach and digestive tract are not happy.

Sometimes other things may affect our digestive tracks, such as stress, rushing around, and not eating properly. Anxiety can be the cause; what affects your mind has an influence on your digestive tract. All the time our brains are sending messages around our bodies. When our bodies don't function properly, the mind and the body rebel, and that can have an effect on our physical bodies.

We have to change how we see food, how we eat food, and how we choose food. Strike the right balance: 80 per cent alkaline, 20 per cent acidic like I said earlier. This is the right consistency for the digestive system if you want a healthy gut. I promise you) that you can only benefit from this information. It comes straight from the spirit world. I don't consider myself an authority on diets. Neither do I have any medical background, except for anatomy and physiology, which I studied at college and acquired my certificates. Most of my knowledge comes from years of study, research, and my own personal experiences. What I have come to trust and believe in is information coming from a far higher intelligence, the spirit world. They are never wrong.

Working with the thought pattern along with a diet program works perfectly together. You can't go wrong. Enjoy your newfound energy. No more sluggishness and tiredness! You will sleep much better. Everything improves: your skin has a glow, your eyes look brighter, and all this makes you more motivated. You want to stay like this all the time, don't you? Life can be wonderful! Do you realise that with this programme, you can actually turn the clock back" That's got to keep us women motivated!

don't use weighing scales. Put them away until about six weeks after you have started to lose weight. Don't forget **it takes three weeks to lose your stored fat.** Everyone is different. It may take one person on the same program a shorter or longer time to lose weight.

First, don't look in the mirror in the morning telling yourself, "Oh God, I'm putting weight back on." Remember that the universe hears your thoughts and words; even if it's just a thought in your mind; the universe has to reciprocate. It gives you everything you ask for, and it doesn't know right from wrong. It obeys you. It's like gravity. Have you ever heard that saying "Be careful what you wish for"?

This is where you have to use imagination and visualisation, combined with the diet program. Have you a favourite dress or outfit that you would like to wear again? Think thin, and you will become thin. Set yourself this challenge: see yourself wearing the clothes, and see yourself happy and content, smiling in the mirror. Hold that look and keep doing it over and over again. Be proud of yourself and who you are.

At the same time, send out thanks and gratefulness to the universe and to God for showing you the way. By doing this, the universe will hear you and will send out more useful information to you.

The more you are grateful and give thanks to the universe, the more will fall into your lap. Be happy and stay happy. Don't let anything spoil the new found you. This is what God intended for you. Remember if a negative thought enters your head, you have the power to change it straightaway with a positive thought that makes you happy. Get used to doing this – **train your brain!**

I am living proof that this program works

When I started this program for myself, I was doing it for my digestive and intestinal problems. It wasn't to lose weight. I knew I had to change my diet it didn't suite me. I couldn't go on the way I had been, putting too many acidic foods into my body.

When I was young, I remained a steady weight of eight stone most of my life. As I grew older and was not able to exercise, I crept up to nearly nine stone, but never beyond. I have started to lose that bit of excess fat without even trying. It is not a lot for me, but I can see the difference and feel much better. My face doesn't look as bloated, which the steroids can cause as well.

Microwave Ovens

The worst product that was ever invented is the microwave oven. In short, microwaves ovens distort the molecular structure of foods. They destroy many of the nutrients and cause other problems with our immune system over a period of time. If you love your family, then take the extra couple of minutes to heat the food the proper way.

Why did the Soviet Union ban the use of microwave ovens in 1976? Radiation coming from the microwave oven causes ionization, which is what occurs when a neutral atom gains or losses electrons. In simple terms, a microwave oven decays and changes the molecule structure of the food by the process of radiation. Had the manufacturer called them radiation ovens, it's doubtful that one would have ever been sold. **Yes how shocking**!

I hear you all shouting, "How am I going to cope without my microwave oven?" We have to get back to the old ways. Our ancestors and grandparents used to cook fine without them. Besides, we still have the use of conventional ovens. It's best if our vegetables are steamed and just slightly underdone. Although some of the nutrients will be lost in cooking, it will retain more if you undercook them.

If you want the best out of life, then you have to put in the effort. Don't you want to feel the best that you can be mentally, physically, and spiritually? Don't you want to be the human being that you are meant to be, and what God intended? I'm sure you do, and you would want this for your children. It's up to you to make the changes. Throw that microwave oven in the trash bin!

If you wish to find out more about the dangers of microwave ovens, there's loads of information on the Internet. Go to the Global Healing Centre's website.

***

Breathing is another way to help the digestive track. A lot of us don't breathe properly; we tend to shallow breathe. Yoga or Pilates is the best exercise you can do, because it involves lots of stretch movements.

Take in a deep breath. As you breathe out, extend your stomach; and lower abdomen at the same time pushing outwards. This helps the digestive system; it's like an internal exercise, and it helps with a fresh flow of blood supply and oxygen to the intestines. Don't be surprised if your tummy makes a lot of noise afterwards – this is a good sign.

Find an exercise that you enjoy doing; not one where you dread going to the gym. It has to be enjoyable to get any real benefit. Personally if I could choose to exercise; I would choose dancing every time; ballet is very good also -fantastic for the posture

Heat Wave

Harry and I managed to get away for four days when the heat wave started in July 2013. We took the caravan to the coast, Skegness, where we met up with Wayne, Joanne, and her daughter Chloe. It was nice to have a break because we hadn't been away for almost two years.

There's a nice coffee shop in the centre of Skegness, near the shops that we often frequent. We all went along and sat outside the coffee shop, having a laugh passing the time of day.

All of a sudden this woman seemed to appear from nowhere. Harry and I sat facing Wayne and Joanne, so they didn't see the woman as she rested her hand on Jo's shoulder, leaning over to look straight at me, as she said, "I've been watching you, and there's such a lot of love in your family." I smiled and nodded my head in agreement.

I watched as the woman walked away. I noticed she was on her own with a small rucksack across her back. For a minute I had a strange feeling. I saw her left profile, something was familiar about her. She was in her sixties with gray hair.

Then Joanne noted looking at me, "How strange was that" You just don't get people coming up to you in the street, especially an older woman on her own, saying, 'I've been watching you.'"

I turned towards Joanne. "But what a nice thing to say."

Later that day, Jo and I kept remembering what the woman had said. When we came home from the coast, we would still talk about it weeks after. Even Harry remembered the woman.

After a couple of weeks, I was convinced the woman must have been an angel that had blended into the crowds. This is what angels do.

One night when I sat at my computer looking through my manuscript, it hit me like a bolt out of the blue. I felt emotional and wanted to laugh and cry all at the same time. I remembered the woman, her smiling at me, and what Joanne had said at the time. It was then that I recognised the woman.

"But of course! It was the lady who was in the hospital at the same time as me, Beryl Bressinger. It was Beryl's spirit who appeared that day. Beryl must have died.

If you remember, I had wished her luck and sent her healing prayers; when we were on the same ward together; in the hospital ward I could only see Beryl's left profile and her gray hair. That's why she looked familiar. How amazing! She'd come to look for me because I had sent her healing thoughts, and probably to say thank you.

By her appearing to me, I was able to write about the experience. It's possible that my mum could have introduced herself to Beryl in the spirit world, to inform her that I had been sending her prayers and healing and that I was mums daughter.

Perhaps Beryl wanted to know who I was; and was curious to know why a stranger could be so kind. I believe Beryl had been watching me for some weeks with my family around me, not just on that day outside the coffee shop. She perhaps came with my mum to the engagement party, too, where all my family gathered.

Beryl looked at me that day and said, "I've been watching you," eventually I realised she meant past tense; has if she had gotten to know me. I've never seen a spirit that clearly. Thank you Beryl. How else would she know **about all my loving family** and that we shared so much love together? We have all become closer in the last two years, especially Wayne and me. I've never known him to show so much love towards me. I feel now that our karma is resolved.

***

Daffodil

I have been given all the information from the angels and the spirit world regarding the meaning of life and the tools to make life great. Of course, it's up to you to make the right choice. All the information is there for the taking. I don't think I have anything more to learn.

It's a funny thing that right from the beginning of the book, I speak of the word love throughout. How important it is in our lives. But I didn't have all the information back then. It's as if deep inside, my soul already knew. I was finding my way back home to God.

All I can tell you now is that I have kept up the thought pattern, bringing it into my daily life and not letting anything interfere with my happiness.

I asked the spirit world to give me some quality of life, if I am to pass over sometime in my sixty-fifth year, which is now. My life has changed in so many ways. The more I give out in love and gratitude, the more I receive. Never again did I think that I'd be walking again. All problems seem to resolve by themselves. It's like being given little gifts of love that put a smile on my face and make me happy.

You realise this is how you want to stay all the time. Life is a joy, even if you suffer with your health. Of course, there will be times in your life that negativity will raise its ugly head, but now you have the power to change it. **And you can**, because you're the boss of your own destiny.

You are all equipped with the tools that God gave you. You can do what I have done, for we are all connected. **We are all one.**

Inhumane

You remember earlier in the book when I spoke of Tina Nash, the young mother of two boys who was brutally attacked by her boyfriend? She suffered devastating consequences by having her eyes gouged out. Remember how disturbed I was by this horrifying story in the national newspaper *The Mirror*?

To my horror, I read a similar story, if not worse! A six-year-old boy was found soaked in blood with his eyelids turned inside out. He was a blinded victim of the world's sickest black market trade. His eyes were discarded nearby, but the corneas were missing, revealing an organ trafficker was behind the attack!

A female kidnapper had told him, "Don't cry, and I won't gouge out your eyes." She took the child from his home in the North China province of Shanxi. He was then drugged and lost consciousness before the attacker removed his eyes.

Central TV told viewers about this on Monday. Film footage showed the heavily bandaged boy being taken from an operating theatre and placed in a hospital bed, writhing in agony as family members stood at his bedside, weeping. The victim's father said, "We didn't notice his eyes were gone when we discovered him. We thought he had fallen down from high and smashed his face."

This gruesome assault is just the latest shocking evidence of this grim trade. The illegal trafficking of organs in China is a growing problem. Seven people were jailed last year when a teenager sold a kidney for an illicit transplant operation; he used the proceeds to buy himself an I Phone and I Pad!

Daffodil

Organ trafficking was outlawed in China two years ago, but trade continues to boom, particularly with kidneys. The World Health Organisation said last year that the issue is becoming a global problem, with huge amounts of money being offered.

A spokesman said there is a growing need for transplants and big profits to be made. It's ever growing and is a constant struggle. The stakes are so big, and the profit can be so huge, that temptation is out there.

The attack has caused outrage across China. How and why could someone be so cruel? I've heard of babies in China lying dead in the gutter just because they are female, and passers-by ignore them turning a blind eye.

China has become one of the richest countries in the world, as well as being one of the biggest polluters in the world. They profit at any cost to the natural environment. They are not just content with making enormous amounts of money; human life is becoming a commodity at any price. "Tell us what you want, and we can provide it," is becoming the Chinese culture of today, whether it's human or materialistic.

Where do we draw the line in a world such as this? Where every day we hear of such atrocities in the media? Are parts of the world going crazy, turning humans into subhumans? In China the need to make money and prosper seems to be the most important aspect in life. They don't seem to be bothered about the pollution they produce, or what effect it has on wildlife, not to mention human life.

There's only one way China is heading, and that's on the road to disaster. It's all because China has become too greedy. It wants more and more, at any cost.
What sorts of generations are going to reincarnate into this country? Remember that their memory will be erased,
So if they had a previous life in China, they'll have no idea what life should be like. They will have to learn, hopefully by making the right choices, not by making the same mistakes as their ancestors made.
They will have to learn all the fundamental things that a good life can bring. That is, if it's not too late for China to recover. All I can say right now is **God help them**. We should send prayers and healing for

this country and its people, to change for the better and to reach out for God's help.

***

As I lay in bed one night, I was in such pain; thinking of what more I could do to help myself. I heard my father say, "Eileen, it is only a body. It is only a body." I had also been wondering lately, when the time comes for me to pass over, what will I die of?

I hope I don't have to suffer anymore. I heard a voice in my head say the word "flat-line". I know the word means; when one is hooked up to a heart monitor machine, and if the heart stops beating, the medical staff use the term flat-line. This would be just fine by me, if my heart was to stop at the end of my life. I think I've suffered enough.

Herbs versus Medication

I feel that I must mention here the dangers of a particular drug. For the last twenty years, I have been prescribed Diclofenac/Voltorol for my RA. This is a slow-release anti-inflammatory drug. It has come to my attention now that this drug can affect people with heart disease, and it may even cause heart problems.

This is just one of the many side effects the drug can cause. When I had my bowel perforation, I was told that this drug may have been the cause of the perforation. It's also well-known for causing stomach ulcers. If you leave one of these tablets on your tongue for a few seconds before swallowing it, you experience a burning sensation. Imagine what this drug can do over a period of years to your insides! It is important that you take it with meals.

My consultant took me straight off the drug in hospital. Because of this, they increased my steroids to try to counteract the problem. But by the time I came out of hospital and the steroids had been reduced to my normal dose, I was in agony I could barley move.

All patients have had to be notified by their GP about the drug. I discussed this with my GP. "What will happen now? You can't just take a patient off a drug that she has come to rely on for the last twenty-odd years."

By this time my body had begun to seize up, on top of the increased excruciating pain I was experiencing; how was I going to manage? My GP understood my circumstances, so I remained on the drug. She simply had to make me aware of the implications.

I thought *there's got to be a better way to treat all illness. Not just with dangerous medication.* It reminded me of the voice I'd heard all those years ago, whispering in my ear when I was so ill at the time. "**The body will heal itself.**" But how?

Deep down I truly believe that the body can heal itself. It was ironic that I came across a program on TV, on the Community Channel. This was a documentary about a Gypsy woman who had discovered a powerful natural cure for all illness. Natural herbs. Her name is…..

Juliette de Bairacli Levy

Levy was born in Manchester, England, in 1912. She died peacefully in Switzerland in 2009 at aged ninety-six. She grew up in Manchester and attended the university to study to become a veterinarian. Juliette didn't like the dissection of animals and how the life of a dead animal was simply accepted. She soon left university, somewhat disheartened, but she still wanted to pursue her love of animals and find a better way to cure animals.

She went to live with the Gypsies and nomads, the Bedouin, and the American and Mexican Indians to learn all she could about herbs and how they could be used to cure animals and humans. She was the first to discover a cure for distemper through the method of natural herbs. She has travelled the world, taking her pioneering work as far as Europe, Turkey, North Africa, Israel, and Greece. Levy is the author of many books.

She wrote:

> The human race should make a study of herbs and not be content to remain ignorant of medicine which is mans rightful inheritance; and which has only become lost to men through their ignorance and laziness and their departure from natural living.
>
> People should not be content to pay high prices for chemical medicines; which are seldom beneficial to the

human body because they are unnatural, and which are very often harmful, Their total effects being unknown.

Instead they should learn to know the wild medicinal plants – the herbs which are free for the gathering. Teeming in the countryside the world over, are medicinal herbs and edible plants. It shows disbelief in the power of God to pass them by.

Mankind cannot forsake herbs. They are promised in the Bible to the human race, and that promise is well known, for it is proudly quoted in every herbal book.

In the old and New Testaments there are over a dozen mentions of herbs or medicinal trees of value to mankind for food or medicine that our Forefathers valued.

Man can never excel nature in medicine manufacture, for she makes the best ones

There is an herb or several herbs to cure or relieve every ailment of man and animal, bird and insect and herbs applied in agricultural practice will even cure crops of their diseases.

A veterinarian who reared Newfoundland working dogs wrote to Juliette for help as a last resort. The vet had tried everything to cure one of her dogs, to no avail. The dog was dying of a kidney and liver degeneration; it couldn't have been a worse scenario, with not much hope.

First, the dog was put on a fast for five days, with lots of fluids. Then they slowly fed it with fresh dandelions. Gradually foods were introduced over a period of weeks. The dog went on to make a full recovery and lived for another four years!

This news travelled fast around the veterinarian industry. Letters of help and advice poured in seeking Levy's help for cures and advice for animals. She soon became world famous and devoted her life to writing many books. Juliette went on to publish herbal remedies for adults and children, with great success.

Is it any wonder, when you think about it? God left all this to us by creating the plant kingdom, wild flowers, and the trees. We can use them to heal naturally. After all, the simple aspirin comes from the bark of a tree.

Throughout the books, I noticed that Levy uses a lot of honey and milk as one of her main cures for animals, adults, and children. She also mentioned that we shouldn't cook with honey, so I would imagine it's best to simply warm the milk.

As I mentioned earlier, Manuka honey has many healing properties and is sold in good herbal shops, in different strengths. Avoid the ones with added sugar – it has to be pure. Levy always chose the clear shade of honey.

She devoted her life to mankind through decades of research, teaching man to learn again all about plant life, trees, herbs, and vegetation. She showed how man can benefit by using natural herbs for all types of illnesses instead of dangerous drugs. Also, herbal remedies can be used on animals. We have to get back to the old ways of our ancestors, using natural ways to heal ourselves and our animals. Medical drugs have become a regular commodity.

I've always held a strong belief that you have to get to the root cause of an illness. It's no good just treating the symptom. Before you know where you are, you could be taking the drug for years to come. Then there's the side effects of drugs. The doctor puts you on another drug to counteract the first drug, and before you know it, you're taking a cocktail of tablets. It's no good and too dangerous for your body. Your internal organs will start to suffer.

It's up to you. This is your choice; to choose an alternative solution to illnesses for you and your family. It may be too late for me now, but I've already made changes, starting with honey and warm milk solution.

Thank you, Juliette de Bairacli Levy, for your contribution to mankind. You have saved valuable information that must be passed down to further generations to come.

Daffodil

***

As of 2013, the bee population has declined by 50 per cent in the last twenty-five years in the UK and the United States. It is estimated that there are 250 species of bees, and they're all on the decline. One-third of what we eat is reliant on the bee pollination. The bee is greatly underestimated.

Manufactories of pesticides and the UK government are in denial of any serious dangers. Neonicotinoids have been banned in Italy, Germany, and France due to these fears. Now the bee is travelling more to the city centers, pollinating the flowers, when all this should be taking place in the countryside.

Why do you think that is? Yes, it's the Neonicotinoids pesticide, which is used to kill aphids. Not only does it kill the aphids, but it also affects the bees' brains. When the bee travels from the nest normally, it can memories the area within a five-hundred-meter radius. It always travels in a straight line. Therefore never getting lost – it always finds its way back to the nest in a straight line.

Scientists used an experiment, tying a tiny minute camera on top of the bee's head so that they could track the bee's journey as soon as it left the nest. Some of the bees were exposed to the pester side. All of those bees lost their way back to the nest! The bees that weren't exposed found their way back to the nest.

There's also the theory of the Varroa mite, which also carries a deadly virus. It attaches itself to the bee's underbelly, sucking all the life out of it and causing deformities. Eventually the bee dies.

Whatever the reason, the bee is on the decline. We have to put a stop to this, or the farming industries are going to find themselves in trouble not just in this country, but all over the globe. There was a quote in one of Levy's books that haunts me.

"When man stops seeing the 'Bee' he must take it as a warning." –

Juliette de Bairacli Levy

Sir Bob Geldof

Bob Geldof is another great man honored with a knighthood and many other honorary awards. In 2006–2008 he was nominated for the Nobel Peace prize. In 1984 Bob responded to a news report from BBC correspondent Michael Buerk about the famine in Ethiopia.

He mobilized the pop world to do something about the images he had seen. Together with Midge Ure, another singer-songwriter with the group Ultravox, they wrote the song "Do They Know It's Christmas". In order to raise funds, the song was recorded by various artists under the name of Band Aid. In its first week it became the UK biggest fastest-selling single in history, and it eventually went on to raise eight million pound for the Ethiopians.

Following this massive successes, preparations were started for the biggest rock concert the world had ever seen. On 13 July 1985, Live Aid was created at Wembly Stadium in London, and also John F. Kennedy Stadium in Philadelphia.

I always remember that special day. Harry was replacing new windows in our home; we had just bought our first council house. It was a lovely, sunny day, and we were watching Live Aid on TV with the music turned up loud. The atmosphere was fantastic.

All nations all around the world came together for a much-needed cause: helping the people of Ethiopia. The TV would show film footage of harrowing scenes from this country it was unbelievable that men women and children were starving to death. Things had to change.

Thank you to Michael Buerk, the news reporter from the BBC, for bringing it to the attention of the British people. It lifted my spirits to know that the whole world was coming together to do something about this awful catastrophe.

Live Aid was a huge success. Not only that, but it brought attention to the world to see what's really going on in these unfortunate countries. Hundreds were dying every day of starvation through no fault of their own. It was the African governments.

Bob found out later why African countries were in such turmoil. It was due to bank loans from Western banks and Africa's failure to repay the banks. For every pound donated in aid, ten times as much would have to leave the country in loan repayments. This had to happen in order to bring humanity together to take a look at itself yet again. We had to make a choice. We had to do something about this. We had to find ways of raising money to help the people of Africa. We couldn't allow this to happen to our brothers and sisters.

I believe this set precedence for all the charity work and organizations across the world to carry on with Bob Geldof's good work to leave a legacy. It's also a reminder to the world that we have to help – we cannot turn a blind eye. Thank you, Sir Bob Geldof, for your contribution to humanity.

Malala Yousafzi

Malala Yousafzi came down to earth on a special mission: to help all young women live in peace and to be treated with dignity, as well as the right to equal opportunity and the right to be educated.

Malala was shot by the Taliban in 2012 on her way to school. She was only fourteen years old. She was flown to Birmingham, England to have major surgery to rebuild her skull. Her crime was daring to go to school, standing up against the Taliban and fighting for the rights for every child to have an education.

She attended the United Nations two years later on her sixteenth birthday, 12 July 2013. She urged every nation to give every child an education. She was backed by a petition signed by three million people, which was presented to UN Secretary Ban Ki-Moon.

Pakistani Malala now lives in Birmingham. Malala said she was speaking as one girl among many. Those present included hundreds of young people from more than eighty countries. She said, "I speak not for myself, but so those without voice can be heard. Those who have fought for their rights to be educated."

She said the attack not only inspired her to work harder for women's rights but had taught her compassion.

> I am the same Malala. My ambitions are the same. My hopes are the same. My dreams are the same.
> My dear sisters and brothers, I'm not against anyone.
> Nor am I here to speak in terms of personal revenge against the Taliban nor any other terrorist group.

> I 'am here to speak up for the right of education of every child.
>
> I want education for the sons and daughters of the Taliban and all those terrorist and extremists.
>
> I do not even hate the Taliban who shot me; even if there is a gun in my hand and he is in front of me.
>
> I would not shoot him.
>
> This is the legacy of change: I have inherited from Martin Luther King. And Nelson Mandela.

Ban Ki-Moon added that; far too many places students like Malala and their teachers are threatened, assaulted, and even killed through hate-filled actions. Extremists have shown what frightens them the most: a girl with a book. Malala's landmark speech came as British charity Save the Children warned that almost fifty million children are without schooling in war-torn countries.

Let us pick up our books and pens; they are our most powerful weapons. One child, one teacher, one pen, and one book can change the world. Education is the only solution. Education first. Malala has become a powerful symbol not for just girls' right to education, but for the demand we do something about it immediately.

Here is a perfect example of the human soul. Malala came to this world to change it for the better, to fight for equal rights for education. It was not just for her own country of Pakistan but for everyone who has been denied an education because of religion, culture, and gender.

Something bad had to happen before the world would take notice. An innocent, fourteen-year-old girl was shot twice, once in the head and once in the neck. After two years Malala has made a full recovery. She wasn't meant to die. God had a plan for her, and Malala bravely accepted.

Malala did not fear the Taliban, the terrorists, and the extremists. She believed in equal rights for everyone, and this became her passion. This has also inspired her to fight for the rights of women. I believe that Malala will bring an end to all women's suffering all around the world, where men and women will become equal.

Eileen Veronica Richmond

There will be no more Shari law against women. This is one of the great changes that are taking place already. She will become an icon just like Nelson Mandela and Martin Luther King, who inspired her. Mandela fought for the rights for black men and women of South Africa to ban Apartheid. Martin Luther King fought for black men and women of America in the fifties and sixties.

Scenarios like this will keep happening all over the world; till peace and love reign. It will be a golden age. I know in my heart, Malala, that you will continue in your fight to bring about a better world. You will fight for peace, justice, and equal rights for women. Thank you, Malala Yousafiza, for your contribution to humanity.

Nelson Mandela

Nelson Mandela is another great icon who brought peace and broke Apartheid with the help of the ANC in South Africa. He won the Nobel Peace prize in 1993.

Mandela was a very educated man, a supreme lawyer in his own right. He was also a very brave man who stood up to the powers that be by risking his own life on many occasions. He was willing to die for his people for what he believed in. He fought for equal rights for everyone no matter what colour or race. He wanted equal opportunity for everyone.

I remember reading Mandela's biography *Long Walk to Freedom*. At the beginning of Mandela's career as a lawyer in the early 1930s. He was defending one of his clients in court at the time. The judge, in summarising, asked the defendant to turn his back towards the jury. The man was convicted of the crime on the assumption of the way this man's shoulders were positioned. In other words, because his shoulders slouched, he must be guilty! I found this outrageous. Who could believe such a thing? How primitive, how stupid!

In those days Black men and women were second-class citizens in their own country. Mandela helped form the first black government of South Africa. He served twenty-seven and a half years in prison for being against Apartheid, which kept black and white people separated. He was released in 1990 and went on to become president of South Africa.

He was a great man who witnessed an injustice on his own people, and he fought for justice despite serving twenty-seven years in prison. He succeeded in his mission because it was God's plan.

18 July 2013
Nelson celebrated his ninety-fifth birthday in the hospital today. He is still stable after five weeks in the hospital.

September 2013
Nelson was sent home from hospital to die in his own bed.

5 December 2013
Finally Nelson Mandela departed from this world. I bet there's one big party going off in heaven today! Thank you, Nelson Mandela, for your contribution to humanity.

> "No shackles or cells can match the strength of the human spirit."– Barack Obama

The Syrian Conflict

It is now two and a half years since the uprising in Syria. More than 100,000 people have been killed since it began. Many people in Syria want to see an end to all this violence. Two and half years ago, President Bashar al Assad could have stepped down from office. He could have walked away and prevented this from escalating. Now it could possibly turn into another world war.

Now we have the Syrian conflict, with chemical weapons. It is stated that President Bashar al Assad ordered the bombing of chemical weapons on the Syrian people on 21 August 2013. The true number of people who have been killed is unknown, but it is estimated that over a thousand people died, mostly children.

What has happened to the Syrian people is abhorrent. How could President Assed order his military forces to bomb his own people with chemical weapons? These were unarmed innocent men, women, and children. Does he not know the meaning of "**Democracy**"?

If we are killing innocent children, then what hope is there for future generations to come? How such evilness can exist on this planet is beyond me. How can there ever be peace? Children are being born today in war-torn countries that have never known peace.

The children don't know what a normal life should be like. All they've ever experienced is fear, bombs, bloodshed, and parents being killed. They aren't growing up in a normal environment. What effect is this going to have on their lives as they grow into adults – if they should survive the war at all?

I can understand the majority of people want revenge on President Assad and believe that this man and his armed forces should be brought to justice. But is this the answer? Do we want more bloodshed and more killing, sending our British soldiers to war again and causing heartbreak for the mothers and young wives? Do we want more children growing up without their fathers? Another war is not the answer!

Ban Ki-Moon, the general secretary of the United Nations, is looking for proof of evidence of chemical weapons being used. He's also working on how the issue could be resolved. When Ban-Ki Moon was being interviewed, he quoted the lyrics from a song written by John Lennon in 1969, which inspired John to write about how he felt about the anti-war movement in Vietnam and all wars in general. "All we are saying is give peace a chance."

This is the only way that war can be resolved: by giving peace a chance. It's the only answer. The United Nations has to come together for peace talks with President Bashar Assad. I believe that the president should be made to surrender all his chemical weapons, which should all be destroyed. Another war is not the answer! We can all do our bit for humanity by sending peace and love to this country—including President Bashar—in hope that he will come to his senses to resolve the problems.

Weapons of mass destruction shouldn't even exist. The same goes for nuclear weapons and all dangerous weapons stored across the world. They are far too dangerous too store on such a fragile planet. With earthquakes, the weapons could explode at anytime, anywhere.

I know there are procedures in place for a nuclear weapons attack. Even so, this hardly makes it a 100 per cent safe. It only takes a maniac like the North Korean leader Kim Jung-Un to press the button.

Therefore how do we resolve this? With love and peace, or with more bloodshed? War is not what the British people want. Neither can we stand by and watch Assad commit these atrocious crimes on his people. There has to be another way to end this war – all wars! Peace talks should be continuous. **"All we are saying is give peace a chance."**

We can help these war-torn countries by asking God to send down his army of angels in droves, especially Archangel Michael, to help with this situation.

***

22 July 2013

On a happier note, let's congratulate Kate and William. How lovely that a baby boy was born to the Duke and Duchess of Cambridge. He was named George Alexander Louis. He is the young prince of Cambridge.

I believe this baby to be the reincarnation of the late Princess Diana of Wales. This child will help humanity and he will bring great spiritual changes to our world, to create a better world.

The Trauma of Life

Once I was a healthy woman; once I was fit.
Then along came a demon, an illness that stole all of it.

Twenty-five years, it tried to destroy me,
But I would never give in.

It stripped me of my beauty, my joy, my humour, too.
It even tried to break my spirit, but that it could never do.

My body weak and twisted, what was I to do?
Left alone with all this pain,

How would I cope with all the strain?
Deep inside I searched my soul and found the path which led me home.

Then in the midst of life's confusion, I finally found my resolution.
My angels, guides, taught me how to survive

So that just like the phoenix, I'd rise every time.
We are never alone in our hour of despair.

That's why God and the angels will always be there.
Illness taught me we're not just a body. We all have a soul, a spirit body.

At last when death relieves me from this trauma,
It will not mean that my life is over. It's just a new beginning,

For I will be home in heaven at last with my heavenly father,
So happy the trauma of life is over.

Daffodil

People say that God punishes us, giving God a bad name. Now, I ask you, if we are all God's children and are all a spark from God, then we are a part of God. That makes us God, too, with all God's powers. Therefore why would God want to punish us? God would be punishing himself! What would be the purpose?

No, the only person who punishes us- is ourselves.

I will know who I am when I pass over, as will all of you. We will have the answers at that point. I know that my life had a purpose. It's been a great honour to have served mankind in this way. I wish you all peace, love, light, and much soul progression. 'God bless you all, my brothers and sisters.

Life can be wonderful! We can all make it so. All it needs is for nations to come together, to live in peace and harmony, to love one another, and to have respect for one another. We can make it a heaven upon the earth and no nation need starve. God provided everything in abundance enough for everyone on this Earth. The universe is full of abundance – all we have to do is ask. This is what God intended for all his children.

Love is always the answer.

Devastation

As it neared my birthday, I became more anxious at the fact that it wasn't going to happen – that I wasn't going to pass over into the next world in my sixty-fifth year.

On the morning of my sixty-fith birthday, I laid in bed. Harry had just left for work. As I sat up in bed, I began to cry: I have never cried so much in all my days. I felt all kinds of emotions running through me. I was utterly devastated; I felt crushed, abandoned. My whole world had collapsed around me. Why hadn't it happened? My heart felt broken in two, like a big hole in my chest. It hurt so much.

You're probably wondering why I felt like this. Most people would be relieved that they didn't pass over. It was the fact that I was told by a spirit guide that this would happen. I had accepted this; it was part of my mission. It was supposed to happen – wasn't it? I totally believed him. I put all my faith and trust in him.

For days I walked around in a thick black cloud, asking myself the same questions over and over again. I couldn't stop crying.

I turned to Harry in despair. "Harry, my heart is broken. I don't know what to do. I feel in pieces." No answers came to me from the heavens. I felt utterly alone.

Days passed. I had to do something. All I could do is keep moving forward. What else was there to do? Therefore I went back to my book, right from the beginning. *Maybe I'll find the answers. Maybe there are mistakes that have to be rectified. Perhaps the book's not good enough. Or is it just wishful thinking, trying to find a logical reason?*

Daffodil

I must admit a few weeks prior, I heard a voice in my head say, "There's always room for improvement." I chose to ignore it! Why did I? The voice was loud and clear. Was it because I knew deep down my book might not be finished, as it was getting closer to my birthday?

The year prior to my sixty-fifth birthday, I had accepted that I was going to pass over. I stopped myself from doing things. If I was shopping, I would remind myself that I wouldn't be here. On many occasions I would say to myself, *that's a waste of time, a waste of money. I won't be here, anyway.*

But the worst thing for me was that I began to question the whole project, the book. Was it all lies? As I began to read my book, I did very little editing. I couldn't seem to find anything misleading. Deep in my heart and soul, I know I have written only the truth and what the spirit world has taught me. I couldn't work in any other way.

In the manuscript I came across the chapter about Wombwell Church and the medium Julia Winfield. I felt the urge to go back. I had to do something. Also, I wanted to go back to my Reiki healing. Maybe I could get some answers. I made plans with Joanne, Wayne's fiancée, for us to go together.

Joanne hadn't been feeling too well for quite some time. I had this gut feeling that there was an urgency to take her, and she was showing a real interest in spiritualism. We both had hands-on healing prior to the open circle. It had been four years and nine months since I'd gone to church and had any healing. One of the healers, Peter, remembered me.

Joanne had a young girl attend her who was training to become a healer. When we both came out of the healing room, I looked at Joanne, who was all flushed. "Well then, how did it go?" I asked. I could see she was in awe!

She couldn't believe how intense the heat was, coming from that young girl. It reminded me of when I went to see Steven Turof, the psychic surgeon. It was the same intense heat I had experienced.

The young girl, Julia, told Joanne that she needed to come back for more healing. Therefore my concern for Joanne wasn't without reason. Joanne has improved since the healing took place. I feel like I've planted the seed in Joanne. I hope that this experience inspires her to find out more, and that it eventually leads her to her spiritual path.

As we sat in church waiting for the session to begin, I noticed how full it was with people. I'd never seen it so packed. I didn't know whether this was a good sign. Somehow it didn't feel the same; it felt oppressive. In an open circle, people can come and develop their psychic ability. As we sat there concentrating and waiting for someone to volunteer, no one did, including me, but I wasn't in the right frame of mind to do so.

Eventually the medium Julia Winfield rose from her seat. She gave a couple of readings to some people in the audience, which were inspiring. She's always so accurate. Finally Julia turned towards me to give me a reading. I couldn't believe my luck, with the church being so full. I so needed help that night because I felt so low.

Julia began. "I've got a woman here. She says she's your mother. She says you're so upset, you are absolutely devastated, heartbroken." As Julia said these words, she rubbed her chest as if it hurt. "You have been so down, and it's not over yet, love, is it?"

"No," I wispherd- *Gosh, how true is that?*

"You go through so much pain every, day, and it's never ending. It never stops, does it? She's telling me you've been through the mill a lot times. You take too much on. Your load is heavy, but she says you are a fighter. You are wearing her wedding ring, which always draws her nearer. She's never more than a foot away from you."

This was so true. I always felt Mom near me, especially when I went into the hospital.

Then Julia told me, "Your mother says you have a decision to make. And it will be hard. Only you can do it." Then Julia turned to look at Joanne. "I don't know who this is at the side of you, but your mum absolutely loves her and the things she does for you."

Julia tells me the spirit world is listening. "They hear you. There's lots of spirits around you. I see smiles. They are putting you in healing waters; just like the colour of your dress you're wearing now, turquoise. They are bringing you lots of light. Look forward and be positive. Mum says you spend hours on your own. She sees you looking at some results?"

Prior to going to the church that night. I had spoken to my mother, telling her I was going to the spiritual church and I needed her to be there for me. I needed help answers.

While coming home in the car, Joanne and I discussed what had happened at church. It was Joanne's first time at a spiritual church with mediums and healers. I could tell she was impressed by it all, especially the fact that she had witnessed the reading from Julia on my behalf. Joanne knew too well how this had devastated me; there was no consoling me at the time.

I have to try and help myself with Reiki treatments. The pain is becoming more intense. That's the other thing: by passing over in my sixty-fifth year, I wouldn't have much longer to go before I would suffer no longer. I would be free from all the pain at last.

But it didn't happen. Why? This would have had such a big impact on the book. I was willing to pass over to validate it more to the reader. I was willing to lay down my life for what I believed in, to help humanity.

Did the spirit world change their mind? Nothing is set in stone, remember. Could this be karma? Did I let someone down in a past life, and it caused great sorrow? Have I more work to do on this planet?

I know somehow the spirit world had to get Joanne to the spiritual church for healing, and to be inspired by the medium. Was this the reason I didn't pass over? Was there a health issue with Joanne, an urgency which I had already suspected?

It reminded me of the times I had to go into hospital with life-threatening illnesses, which would keep me in hospital for up to two weeks at a time. Was it all arranged by the spirit world, so that I could reach as many people as possible with my philosophy on life why we are all here? Was I meant to convince people that our existence on this earth has meaning, and we are all here for a reason?

When I look back at that scene ; where this spirit guide who told me that I would pass over in my sixty-fifth year, we both stood in front of my house several meters away, facing an iron gate. I remembered clearly standing at the side of him, my head level with his chest. He seemed huge but not threatening; his voice was clear and calm as he spoke to me.

If this spirit guide had been evil, from the dark side, I would have known it. I would have felt it in my very being. I would have felt that dread and fear prior to him speaking to me. But I didn't, so I feel I must have faith and trust in the spirit world, especially my angels. They know best, the reasons will show themselves eventually. Is the spirit world testing me further?

No matter what happens to me, this book was written with truth and sincerity, coming from the spirit world. I know that there is a dark side to this world that can be extremely clever, leading us all into falsehood. I know I was given the truth from the spirit world because I felt it deep in my heart and soul, not in my mind.

This is how God reaches us: through feelings, our sixth sense, images, pictures, and a knowing. God and the angels speak to us through our souls.

The dark side will never break my spirit; neither will it stop me from believing in my angels and the spirit world. My belief in God will stay even stronger within me. If I must suffer, then so be it. Bring it on, as they say! I know one day my suffering will be over, and I will go home to my heavenly father.

I've been talking to the spirit world a lot, especially since the medium Julia said the spirits were listening to me. One night I sat on the edge of my bed, sending out healing prayers to all my family and friends. When I had finished, I decided to do some straight talking to the spirit world.

I asked the spirit world why this was happening to me. Why didn't I pass over when I was told I would? I also asked to be shown more, to see my spirit guides' names and faces. I asked for new guides to come into my life to teach me more. After I got into bed, I asked for protection in case I astral travelled.

I had only been in bed for a little while when I heard the name George. Straightaway I thought, *No good to me, if I can't see him*, trying to sound respectful.

Within a couple of minutes, I saw a man in my mind's eye. He was over six feet tall with a firm posture; he wore a maroon smoking jacket. His hair was gray and long, worn over his collar. He had a gray-streaked beard combed to a point, with not a hair out of place. He was well spoken. He smiled at me with a friendly nod as if to say, "How can I help, Madame? Anything to oblige, my dear." He had impeccable manners. It was as if he was speaking to me in a department store. Then he vanished. I was left wondering who he might be.

Two or three minutes later, I saw the word "Maggie" written in black ink. I still had the same attitude: *No good to me if I can't see her*. All of a sudden I was aware that Harry and I were cuddled up in bed together. But it wasn't in my bedroom – and it wasn't my home, either. It was another lifetime. The room was small with a tiny dresser and an oil lamp on it. I jumped as someone touched my ankle "Harry, let me deal with this; leave it to me."

As I pulled back the blankets, I saw a woman standing at the side of the tiny dresser. She looked like she was from the eighteenth century. She was dressed in a long skirt with a checked apron in yellow; her sleeves had frills at the elbows. She had a low neckline, and a frilly cap covered her hair.

I pointed my finger at her. "Look, I'm not frightened of you."
She gave me a curious look as if to say, "Why would you be?" It was as if I had taken her out of her comfort zone. She had a plea in her eyes, as if to say, "Well, what can I do?" She didn't look at all pleased.

We were so near one another, and I remember looking at her skin on her chest. Then I asked her, "What happened to you then? How did you pass over?"

Harry interrupted. "Yeah, what happened?" As I turned towards Harry, he looked so different. He wore a long nightshirt just past his knees, and he had mousy long straggly hair.

Then Maggie vanished.

I was left there thinking, *that was so vivid, with such detail. Are these my new guides?* As I have said before, I have heard the name George before. Maybe he is my guide. All I can do is wait and see.

The next night nothing happened. Was it because I was waiting for something to happen? It seems that things like this only happen when I least expect it.

The following night it happened again. I saw a handsome man facing a door. The door had white paint peeling off it because of the hot sun. It felt like I was in the Caribbean. It felt warm, and I could see clear blue sky. The man wore a mint green vest with a pair of old worn white jeans. He had long, black curly hair. He faced the door, as if he was about to open it. I noticed he was holding up twenty-pound notes in both hands. It felt like it was me behind that door.

My first instinct was *is this payback time for what's happened? Or am I going to come into some money?* Paul Parker, the medium, once told me that I would be given fifty thousand pounds, and he could even see the signature on the cheque. Paul didn't know whether it was about some compensation for me or my husband at the time.

That was about six years ago. When I look back on this prediction, I can't help but feel that it's what I may have received if I had pursued my claim for medical negligence. Although Paul is a very good psychic medium, mediums don't always get it in the right order.

I feel that Maggie is from a past life. I'm not sure about George. The handsome man in the Caribbean could have been a past life, but what was he doing at my door? The thought did cross my mind: Was I a prostitute in that life? We have experienced the all, remember. If not then, it's possible that we will in the future. All I can do is wait and see

Daffodil

what transpires. I'm grateful for what the spirit realm gave me … but I would like more.

At the moment I don't feel too bad, health wise. I feel better mentally, which is more important to me. It helps me to cope with the pain. I still have this insatiable appetite to read as many books as I can on spirituality – all nonfiction books about people's own experience and revelations. They are such wonderful stories. Lots of stories are similar to my own, which always encourages me.

Perhaps I've not read enough yet and need to learn more. Who knows? That's one thing we all have in common. We never stop learning, even when we pass over. The great halls of learning will always be there for us, giving us more opportunity to make progress with our soul as we try to reach for perfection in order to be in God's own image.

As the days and the weeks passed by, I'm reminded yet again why I didn't pass over. Is it possible that I misheard? **No.**
I was told that I wouldn't be around when the book was published. I would be ill for three months from May, June, and July – which came true. I was told I would pass in my sixty-fifth year.

Did I misinterpret the word "pass over", thinking that it meant I would die? When the guide said I would pass in my sixty-fifth year, did he mean the tests and the lessons that I've been put through over the years will be over?
If I'm honest, I don't remember hearing the word "over" only the words "pass in my sixty-fifth year". I took it for granted that the guide intended "pass" to mean that I would die.

But then, why not simply say, "You will die in your sixty-fifth year"? I know that what I have been put through all my life have been tests and lessons. Perhaps the guide meant I would pass my exams, so to speak, in my sixty-fifth year?

But I still believe that I had to go through that heartache and devastating experience. It could have been a past karma. There was no mistake; it was meant to happen. Or was it the last lesson, to see how far I would take the experience? If it was, then I have certainly passed my test! Besides, the spirit world doesn't make mistakes. As I have said, I had never felt such grief at the time. I now believe it was my last lesson and that I passed it. No matter what happens, nothing will break my spirit or my belief in God, my heavenly father.

When I was a child, I was brought up in a strict Catholic environment. Most Catholic families had a picture of Jesus Christ hung on the walls in their homes, as well as a crucifix. The picture was called the Sacred Heart. This was a picture of Jesus Christ from the waist up with his heart exposed. I remember staring at this picture many times when I was a child.

Just last night when I was in bed, I had a flash of a picture in my mind's eye, and it woke me up instantly. It was in such colour and detail, and it only lasted for two minutes, but that was enough for me to absorb and remember every detail. I was gazing up at this beautiful ceiling. It had such intricate detail with gems and pearls studded into its surface.

It was as if I was in a great cathedral. Then as I looked straight ahead, I saw this great giant marble staircase in the centre of the cathedral. There in the centre of the stairs stood Jesus Christ! He was in full view and stood very tall. He looked at me; his hair was long wavy and smooth.

At the same time I noticed another man standing at the side of Jesus and dressed in robes. Although he appeared tall, he was much smaller than Jesus. He had long gray hair with a pointed beard that almost touched his belly. He had a darker patch of hair just below his chin. He stared at me, and it was hard to read his mind. Who was this man?

At first I thought it might be St Peter, but later that day, I thought he might be a guide I hadn't seen before. Or was he one of God's ascended masters? I felt I had been brought to this scene as a reward, to show me that it was all true and to reassure me. I should never doubt and should always have faith that I'm on the right track to finding my way home. I felt honored.

Just before Christmas, there was a miniseries on Channel Five called *The Bible*. I thought, *I wouldn't mind watching this film.* I assumed that

Daffodil

Harry wouldn't be interested in viewing the film, but to my surprise, he agreed. It was a series shown on four successive Saturdays.

The reason I had become interested in watching the film was because I had never read the Bible, only little snippets now and then. I found it complicated and sometimes confusing. I thought the film would somehow explain it better.

Then I remembered that there were also untruths written in the Bible, to suit the upper religious hierarchy. For example, the Ten Commandments should have been called the Ten Commitments, for who would God be commanding? If we are a part of God, and God is a part of us, then we become one. Therefore God would be commanding himself.

A lot that was written in the Bible was to put fear into people's souls. We are all God's innocent children, and we belong to God. Another untruth in the Bible would be that God would turn away innocent children at the end of life, simply because they were never baptized. I find this hard to believe. God would never turn away an innocent child!

Also, lambs were used in sacrificial ceremonies. I find it hard to believe that God would wish this. God created the animal kingdom with the same love as he created us in the beginning. A lot that was written in the Bible at the time: These people weren't even around when Jesus Christ was alive, so how could they possibly know?

I would recommend all people to watch the film *The Bible* and read the book, so that you can gather your own conclusions as to what you think is true. Our God is not a God that one should fear. He is our heavenly father, our creator. He loves us all so very much and has our best interest at heart just like a real father would. God never turns anyone away.

Shame

Shame on you, Sweden, for allowing this to happen.

At the Copenhagen Zoo, a beautiful, healthy, two-year-old giraffe called Marius was put down. Despite an international outcry campaign to save him, and the offer of a new state-of-the-art giraffe house built just two years ago in South Yorkshire, at Doncaster Zoo. Why?

Poor Marius was shot dead with a bolt gun. The Danish zoo claimed Marius had to be killed to avoid inbreeding. Also, he was surplus to their requirements! Twenty thousand people signed a petition to save this precious animal. Not only did they put down this beautiful healthy animal, but they turned it into a show, a spectacle, by allowing young children to watch the autopsy! Why? Marius's remains were photographed being fed to the lions in front of children.

What were these parents thinking? You can't call this education. This will do more harm than good to these children. All this does is desensitise them. **It's wrong**!

This is what I meant about animals living in captivity, which I wrote about earlier in the book. Children are becoming desensitised to such horror. Some of these children will never forget what they witnessed that day; it will stay with them forever. What good can come from this? None whatsoever.

All this was totally unnecessary. Zoos around the world had offered to give Marius a home! One woman added, "Why not give the giraffe contraception for the rest of his life? They don't have to kill him. Why can't they send him to the zoos that have offered to take him, where he could live out the rest of his life?"

Robert Krijuff, boss of the Netherlands wildlife park, whose last-minute offer was rejected, said, "I can't believe it! We offered to save this giraffe's life. Zoos need to change the way they do business."

I find this so upsetting. What can we do? One thought comes to mind. Why not make a tribute to Marius? Why not make a soft toy of Marius the Giraffe and sell it for charity? All proceeds could go to animals around the world that are in need of help. At least then, Marius's death will not have been in vain.

I feel strongly that something should be done as a reminder to all, especially to the children, that it is not all right to kill a beautiful, healthy animal! After all, it is man's mistake in the first place for putting the giraffe in this predicament.

More Animal Slaughter

The same week, I was horrified to see the cover of a newspaper about a poacher in Kenya who was killing elephants for their tusks, for the ivory. What was sickening was how this man boasted that he had killed more than seventy elephants. He took pleasure as the elephants screamed as they died. To him, it was just business.

Central Africa as lost 64 per cent of its elephants in the last decade. The ivory trade is worth £6 billion a year in Africa. That is not only funding terrorism, but it also endangers a species. Elephants are another one of God's beautiful creations that will become extinct in the next decade.

Elephant tusks and rhino horns have no medicinal purpose whatsoever, other than serving the Asian market for making trinkets. Overall, there isn't much evidence to support the plethora of claims about the healing properties of rhino horns. In 1990 researchers in Hong Kong found that large doses of rhino horn extract could slightly lower fever in rats, as could extracts from Saga Antelope water buffalo horns.

But the concentration of horn in traditional Chinese medicine specialists is many times lower than those used in the experiment. In short, the scientists say, "You'd do as well chewing on your own fingernails."

This needless slaughter needs to be stopped before it's too late. Only the most heartless could fail to be moved by this terrible ordeal that slaughtered elephants have to go through every day. Man has to stop cruelty to all animals. All the world's leaders should be hanging

Daffodil

their heads in shame that they are doing very little to help this horrific situation.

Don't they realise its funding terrorism – that in itself should give the United Nations the impetus to do something about it. If they were to condemn China and other Asian countries, along with Western people who also deal in ivory, then perhaps this would help stop a lot of the poaching.

We should make it a priority to bring a stop to all this unnecessary cruelty and suffering to our beautiful animals. This is not what God intended. With the way this world is allowing cruelty and turning a blind eye, there will be nothing left for our grandchildren to inherit. Our animals don't have a voice. We have to be their voice!

Earlier in the book, I spoke of young children being exposed to TV and video game violence. I mentioned how it can desensitize a child's mind. It seems like this problem is becoming worse. Some parents do not care what mental damage this can cause to a young child.

A teacher in Wales felt it was his duty to do something about it. He was concerned about his young pupils, and so Mr Morgan wrote to each of the parents. He begged parents not to let their children be exposed to the new Xbox video game *Grand Theft Auto*, which is rated for those over eighteen. The game has sold thirty-two million copies worldwide and charts the dark underworld of America's cities. It holds the Guinness world record for the most controversial video game of all time.

Mr Morgan wanted to explain the issue by sending letters to parents, in a bid to stop shocking behaviour on the playground. These children were acting out the scenes in the video game. Some of the children initiated games that involve simulating rape, and sexual intercourse, using the strongest of swear words. Children were heard having conversations about prostitution and drugs. Children play-acted extremely violent games that sometimes resulted in actual injury!

He told the parents that social care teams may have to be called in, if they did not heed his warnings. He added that some of the parents had destroyed some of the copies of the game. These parents were as shocked and horrified as he was. Some of the comments from parents so for were supportive.

What is happening to our world? Where has all the innocence gone? There isn't any. Analysis editor, speaking on behalf of the *Daily Mirror*, it states that *Grand Theft Auto* has an over eighteen rating for a reason. Sex, drugs, and violence are central to criminal themes in video games. Characters can be beaten up, shaken down, or run over. Women are degraded on a routine basis. The language is almost universally post-watershed. But these games aren't intended for children!

The developer Rockstar has made an eighteen-rated entertainment experience intended for adults, in much the same way that the films of Quentin Tarantino are. No right-thinking parent would let a six-year-old watch the likes of *Reservoir Dogs* or *Pulp Fiction,* and the same should go for *GTA*.

I'm so pleased that Mr. Morgan had the courage to speak out. This exposure is happening all around the world, all too often. Why are these directors who make this kind of entertainment obsessed with making films and video games full of sex, violence, rape, and pornography? Obviously it's because there's money to be made in this sort of thing. It sends all the wrong messages, not just to children but adults as well.

While speaking of such terrible entertainment, it was a privilege to watch such films as *Captain Philips, The Butler, Twelve Years a Slave,* and *Philomena*. All four films were based on true stories, and they are not just entertaining but also educational, teaching morals, ethics, principles, and integrity. These films explain past history to our children so that it is never forgotten.

Amanda Holden

How courageous of Amanda Holden to speak out. She is well-known for her appearance on *Britain's Got Talent*. I couldn't contain my shock and horror when I opened my daily newspaper. There was a story about fetuses being disposed of in hospital incinerators, along with other human medical waste. How insensitive.

Figures reveal that 15,500 fetal remains under twenty-four weeks old have been incinerated by twenty-seven NHS trusts during the last two years. Ten trusts admitted to burning more than one thousands sets of remains as clinical waste, and two others used waste as energy for the furnaces that powered the hospitals.

Amanda herself suffered a miscarriage. As a young mother, she was devastated after she had the miscarriage in the hospital. She was told her baby would be incinerated with the rest of the day's waste. This was really difficult for her to bear. She replied, "It wasn't waste, it was my baby." Unfortunately Amanda had already given birth to a stillborn in 2011.

Amanda's approach worked. The MP, Dr Dan Poulter, promised to investigate. It has led to the practice being banned throughout the NHS! Well done, Amanda.

A spokesman for the Cambridge University NHS foundation trust said, "Trained health professionals discuss the options with the patients and families respectfully and sensitively; both verbally and in writing. Parents are given exactly the same choice; on the disposal of fetal remains as for a stillborn child; and their personal wishes are respected." That's how it should be. The choice should be left to the grieving parents, knowing that their babies were treated with the upmost respect and dignity at the end of their lives.

I explained early in the book that as soon as a baby is conceived in the womb, whether the mother miscarries or the baby is aborted, that baby will continue growing up in heaven. They are special places for these babies. Every baby is taken care of, and every facility exists for the baby, such as hospitals and nurseries. They are taken care of by older spirits. Then they go on to nursery and continue to grow and learn in the great halls in heaven, till the time is right to reincarnate.

You cannot kill the spirit of a fetus once it's conceived. I hope this brings comfort to all mothers who have miscarried. You will see your baby again in heaven, when your time comes. There is no death. I hope to bring comfort to Amanda, knowing that one day she will be reunited with her two babies.

Barbara Thompson

Earlier in the book, I mentioned my dearest friend Barbara. We have been writing to each now for twenty-one years. Since 1993 we never see each other, but we have the odd phone call now and then. We both retired from work through illness.

When we both worked together at the C&A in Sheffield, I would follow Barbara around the store like a little lamb. I knew she was spiritual, I wanted to know her views on life after death. This was just after losing my father in 1989. We would always get together if we could, talk about the same subject.

Barbara came across as a down-to-earth person, a genuine trustworthy friend. I'd trust her with my life. She wasn't like the rest of the other girls. She was her own person she was not frightened to speak her mind, especially if she saw injustice.

She loves nature and animals, and she loves to be out in the country, where she feels at home. She is not one bit materialistic. Barbara came out of an abusive marriage and has one son. She devoted her life to animal rescue, collecting funds. She lives alone at home with Bronte, her dog, and Casper, a one-legged cat she rescued.

Barbara has lived on her own now some twenty years. As we have exchanged letters over the years, we've come to know each other very well. We share our inner secrets and thoughts, especially on spiritual matters, and we talk about Jesus Christ and whether God really exists.

Over the years, one of Barbara's problems has been fear. It still is to this day. No matter how I have tried to help her with this problem, I can't get through to her, even though I know she has followed my advice regarding different methods on how to do so.

Her problem is that she is frightened of what will happen to her after she dies. She fears what will be waiting for her. She puts this down to the continuous nightmares she has. Although she'll go to bed contented, she will have a nightmare more often than not. It will awaken her, and then she is frightened to go back to sleep.

It occurred to me that she can't be the only one who suffers with fear. There must be thousands like her all over the globe, suffering from the same thing. I sent Barbara a five-page letter, cramming all the information I could, including the emotion of fear. Although parts of this letter are mentioned earlier in the book. I thought I'd enter the letter I wrote to Barbara to help others who may have found what I wrote in the book a little confusing.

Letter to Barbara

Hello my dearest friend Barbara.

First let me put your mind at rest, to try and soothe all your troubles and fears away.
(This includes you the reader.)
Sit in a chair, relax your shoulders, take three deep breaths, close your eyes and relax if you can for a few minutes.

Now, I'm going to reveal to you the secret of life. Revealed to me by the spirit world (The real reason for my book.)

We live in a world of illusion. This world is not our true reality. When I say illusion, I don't mean everything around us is an illusion. For instance, a table or a chair, of course they're real. A world of illusion is mentioned throughout the bible and in loads of books I've read over the years,

I mean the terrible things that go on in this world; the trauma, the devastation, wars, atrocities, cruelty, every conceivable thing that points to the greatest up-evil that you can imagine in this world. **None of it is real.**

It's like when you go the theater to watch one of Shakespeare's plays. The audience sits there watching and listening to the play; weighing up all the characters good, and bad, waiting for the outcome.

The play ends the curtains close. Everyone goes home. None of it was real. It was just a play that Shakespeare wrote, that's just how your life is.

We only act out these scenarios, for a greater purpose: for our soul's progression.

This world is full of trauma.

What you have to remember is: You chose to be born, you wrote your own blueprint; for this particular life you are living now. And this is just one life, out of so many lives you have lived. They will be many more lives to come.

You will live forever Barbara, your soul is eternal. It's only our bodies, our gender, that will change; and that's only if we want it too. We can stay the same if we choose to.

Everything that has happened to you in your life was meant to happen and will continue. The people you meet along the way. No such thing as chance meetings, no such thing as a coincidence, also accidents, (your arm for instance!) Barbara broke her arm.

All accidents happen for a reason. This does not mean that you are being punished. It could have happened to change your life for the better; the real reason why you are here? It all depends on the choices you make. Will you become a victim? Are will you turn it around to maybe helping others less fortunate; has many have done.

Look at the late Christopher Reeves known for the film Superman) he was made a quadriplegic by being thrown from his horse in 1995; he required breathing apparatus, and a wheelchair for the rest of his life. But instead of becoming a victim.

Daffodil

He changed his life around by lobbing; for people with spinal cord injuries; and for human embryonic stem cell research, founding the Christopher Reeve foundation and co founding the Reeve-Irvine research center.

Before we came to earth we have all the help from the masters. What our personal scenario is going to be. We are given all the help and advice needed for a new life. We will never be given anything that we can't deal with or that is beyond our capability.

When this question was put to Mother Teresa on how she copes with such extremes, she replied) "Yes it's hard, I wish God wouldn't trust me so much". That's why you and I are kindred spirits. We made a promise to each other: to help one another through this traumatic life.

Believe me, compared with our real home this earth is hell! And we are all brave souls to come here in the first place!

I wouldn't have survived without you B. I am so grateful for your true friendship. I feel that close to you sometimes: that we become one in the spiritual sense; on this spiritual journey. I can't imagine life without you, my lovely beautiful friend.

The only thing that is real on this planet Barbara is us- as spiritual souls. The choices that we will make, how we treat others- will we choose love or hate or fear in your case? Word fear meaning (false evidence appearing real) just let these' words sink in for a moment, fear is not real-it only what you make it, what we think the most we create in all matters.

Isn't it a good job our memory is erased when we are born; no one would be able to face life if they knew what lay ahead. I would have been hysterical!

They will always be suffering on this earth B. There has to be; it's all part of the learning process. Take the starving children in Africa' Heidi Baker' comes to mind.

This is all arranged to make humanity look at itself. Pointing a finger at humanity saying', "Well then, are you going to help us: or turn a blind eye." It's just another scenario, a reminder for humanity, a test for the human soul—giving man a chance to hopefully make the right choice; and help the suffering of this world.

Harsh I know: but these children are far more advanced spiritually. It's their way of volunteering to help mankind. This will always be, till man puts a stop to end it all.

Man had to learn: that we are all one and the same. We come from the same source GOD. We have to learn to love our neighbour, to treat each other with love and respect.

So all the soldiers that have been killed in wars over the centuries: none of it was real; the world is a stage and we are the actors remember. The soul's came down to help humanity because at sometime, at some point, man will have to stop killing one other: and until this is learned, history will keep repeating itself.

So all the mothers out there: can rest assured. That their son's, are all alive and kicking! Probably looking down on their grieving parents: wishing "If only you knew mum, and dad", "I'm very much alive: please don't grieve for me- when I'm so happy!" "I came down to help humanity, and now that life is over. I' am home where I belong; where I'm at my best"; "Till my next venture into reincarnation".

It's the same with people who murder: The victim gives permission to the perpetrator before they come down: they write their story together. For whatever lessons they want to learn—what they alone have chosen.

Some souls work in groups, like the family, or pairs, like you and me, or on their own. My mum once said that I and Harry made a good team, after she had died! And we do after been married almost fifty-one years together! I know I have shared many lives with Harry.

Let's face it: when we are born, we are all innocent babies: come straight from God's pure love, all here to experience what it's like to be human. Quote from Buddha) "**Life equals suffering.**"

They will always be advanced souls willing to help us out: to help humanity to help to bring peace, and harmony, to this troubled planet. It's what makes the world go around. We are all here to make a difference: to progress with our souls; and to try and make this planet a heaven on earth by bringing peace and harmony.

The thing is: we don't realize the strengths, and power, we posses. Because we come from God; that makes us part of God. So why do you have to suffer with fear? You don't— not when you posses all the power within you to overcome it, with God's help.

Honestly B. can you think of a better reason why we are all given a life?
If everything was perfect in life; we'd have nothing to do, think for a, moment, we would all be like zombies, all the same wondering aimlessly. But we are not, we are all unique. Have you noticed the; billions of people on this planet; all have different faces, different voices. No two are the same, not even identical twins. All different nationalities.

We are all souls on this troubled planet; trying to be the best that we can be all connected from the same source. God has a plan for all of us.

It's the same when we choose to be born. We can also choose our death and how we die; that's if we want to know?

Take the plane crash for instance. Souls volunteer to end their life this way to help humanity.

What happens: there's an intensive investigation to how the plane crash happened in the first place. They find the fault; and its put right: saving lots of lives in the future.

So the souls who volunteered to leave the world in this way didn't die in vain. Everything that happens in this way has a significant meaning.

Are you becoming a little confused? Heavy stuff- I know; it's a lot to take in?

What I'm trying to explain is: the world is a stage. Where we come down of our own accord we choose our scenario, parents, siblings, pets, how we look even our flaws etc.

But this is not real life as we know it, that only happens after death, when we all go home. It's all a learning process. We are all at school. All learning all at different levels, some lives, and scenario's are easier, some are very harsh lives indeed.

I think one of your lessons in this life, is to overcome fear? And I desperately want to help you my dearest friend.

The best day of your life, is the last day of your life!! Because it's over! Schools out, we can all go home: to our real home at last: lessons learned, or unlearned. It doesn't matter; we have the rest of eternity to learn again. And it will always be our choice.

God and the Angels will not interfere with our blueprint: the scenario we have chosen for ourselves, even if it meant saving our life, we wouldn't appreciate it.

It has to be for your highest good and intention. That's why some people are healed and some are not. God only interferes, if it is not your time to die.

That's why God does not always interfere when things go wrong; if it's for your highest good. If you chose a life of strife, and struggle, illness etc, because they were things that you wanted to know, and learn about and the chance for your soul to progress, which is the most important reason you are here in the first place: then God and the Angels will not interfere.

If God and the Angels interfered and took all that you wanted to learn in this life, even your suffering, and you found out after you had passed over; you would be more than annoyed! Because you would want to come back and do it all again. So that your soul continues to progress.

I don't know about you, but I never felt like I belonged here: that this is not all there is. I wasn't sure if God existed, but I do now.

My only question would be, is God and Jesus Christ one and the same? Then sometimes I think, God is too great to be human, he comes across as pure white light. I just know deep within my heart; that something exist so powerful, so great, that words cannot describe the magnitude of its vastness; that something of great divinity watches over us.

I believe in the kingdom, the power, and the glory of Gods existence.

Don't you think that this makes a lot of sense out of this crazy world we live in? And nothing at all to do with religion?

The reason we are given a life? why would God not help his children? God gets the blame for everything; when he has our best interest at heart just like a real father would??

So all the crazy things we hear in the news and media. Don't get downhearted. The world is un-folding just has it should. Man is crazy to think he can control this earth, and nature. RE badger culling!! The badgers won in the end!!ha ha ha.

I can't forget that picture in my mind's eye: where I saw Jesus Christ in an O.B.E, standing before me; on a marble staircase staring at me. What did it mean? What was he saying? – (Yes I' am here I do exist?)

And I ask myself why did I choose a hard life? But yet, I've been blessed in so many ways- Harry, family, pets, friends, so many wonderful memories, and a friend like you. I truly believe we made a pack together

So how can I help you with this fear you carry??

I'm at a loss, that's why I have written all this information for you to hopefully give you a greater understanding why we are here and **there's absolutely nothing to fear.**

This is why you feel so tired drained etc, depression causes this, I'm sure you know. But like I've said before you have to learn to change your thoughts.

Would you consider going to see a hypnotherapist-past life regression? This FEAR, needs to be brought to the surface. It's something you have brought back with you from another life.

Barbara I will gladly pay for it, probably be around £20 to £35 please don't say no! Give it great consideration,

Daffodil

I want you to be free from this, it must be awful for you. Besides there could be a story for me from the outcome,

I think it would be very interesting and may help others? Perhaps this is meant to be? I could arrange it for you. She could come to the house at your convenience? Don't you think it would be very interesting!!
Your kindred spirit love. Eileen xxx

***

Sadly Barbara declined; I hope she finds one day' a way to conquer this fear once and for all Meanwhile I will continue to pray for my dear old friend.

Reader, if you are one of the many who suffer with fear or any other emotions that are no good for your soul, remember that you have a choice. It's probably why you have returned to earth, to overcome this emotion. Don't forget that you have the power to overcome anything; with the tools that God gave you, so why not use them with confidence.

It seems such a waste of time and energy. Fear drains your energies and brings depression, lethargy, and all sorts of things. The dark side will feed of this fear; they love to find vulnerable souls.

You have to be strong. You can face anything with God and the angels at your side. You can do this! If all fails, I strongly recommend hypnotherapy regression to bring it out of you. I believe that fear is past lives that you have brought back into this life. Nightmares show you this, especially when your dreams are vivid. You can conquer this. Believe in yourself, have faith, and trust always.

Past Memory

In the early hours of the morning, I suddenly remembered an old dream I had in 1997, the same year I met Alan Bellinger. At the time, I thought it was a dream. Years later, I now realise it was an out-of-body experience.

In this experience. I found myself travelling fast on an old train built in the 1930s. It was rattling and bumpy as it flew down the track far too fast, making the journey most uncomfortable. I was wearing a long, flowing skirt with a long-sleeved blouse buttoned to the neck. I wore my hair up, the colour of my hair was chestnut brown.

I stood, trying my best not to fall. Then I remembered trying to get up off the floor and raising my head to look across the other side of the train. I was looking at the window right in front of me.

Then I saw this being wearing pure white robes start to manifest slowly, rising from the ground and raising his arms at the same time. It was male, with a long white beard and moustache, and long, white shoulder-length hair. He appeared to be all that was pure, heavenly, and wise.

But why was I remembering this experience now, after seventeen years? What was the significance? After a while it came to me. It was easy to interpret the OBE. This was my guide presenting himself to me in the OBE and telling me I was about to begin my spiritual journey – hence the train. I will learn the reason why I'm here, my mission. The journey on which I was about to embark was going to be a bumpy ride, a very difficult journey.

Daffodil

This is exactly how my life turned out to be. He was warning me of the consequences that lay ahead: the illnesses, the lows, the highs, the horrendous difficulties I endured over the coming years. The worst has been the constant pain every day during the last ten years. It's too much for any one person to bear. Is it possible now that my life is coming to an end? I am so tired, so weary. I can do no more. I've done all that was asked of me.

I know for certain that heaven is my real home, and I miss it so much. In a way, I guess I'm lucky to have all this knowledge. Perhaps that's what has given me the strength and courage to carry on with my life, no matter how bad the suffering could be at times. Sometimes I'd say to God, "Enough is enough, I'm sure I've done all I can. If there isn't going to be a miracle for me; whilst still living on earth, then isn't it time you brought me home?"

But after saying all that, there's still that tiny spark inside me that wants to live, so I still keep looking for a way to make myself better – anything that will ease the pain and give me some quality of life.

The tendons that control my fingers have snapped altogether. I have two tendons left on my left hand, enabling me to type with one finger. My right hand lays across the mouse, making it easy to click with my index finger. It's really hard to help around the house or resume any hobbies I might have had. Still, I make sure I try to put my make-up on and do my hair in a fashion,

What I've found throughout the years, no matter how disabled I became because of; the R.A. I would always find away to adapt. It's surprising what ones capable of if you find yourself in compromising situations,-there's always away.

Heidi Baker

Who is Heidi Baker? Everyone seems to be talking about her, even Oprah Winfrey? Heidi Baker was born in 1959. She is a Christian missionary, she and her husband, Rolland, are founders of the IRIS Global Ministries and the authors of several books. They founded IRIS ministries in 1980; it is a non-profit Christian ministry dedicated to Jesus and service, especially among the poor.

After twelve years ministering in Asia, they left in 1992 to do their doctorates at Kings Collage, London. In 1995 they started a new ministry for the poor and homeless children in Mozambique. They began with nothing, but within a matter of months they were given a dilapidated orphanage in Maputo with eighty children to look after.

From there the ministry has expanded to include building wells and free health clinics that service the poor and sick, as well as feeding programs for, primary and secondary schools, and cottage industries. And now they have over five thousand churches in Mozambique and a total of ten thousand churches in over twenty nations.

There are multiple bases with Bible schools, as well as community outreaches and top-ranked public schools. In September 2008, IRIS ministries started a well-digging project in northern Mozambique. Their ministry is known for reports of miracles, and in September 2010 the *Southern Medical Journal* published an article presenting evidence of significant improvements in auditory and visual function among subjects who had exhibited impairment before receiving prayers from the ministry of Heidi Baker. The miracles keep happening!

Daffodil

Originally Heidi and Rolland are from southern California. They gave away everything they had. Heidi and Rolland have learned to depend on God for everything. "If God does not show up, we are dead!" says Heidi. "When we walk as Jesus walked, we will be blessed."

Heidi remembers one of the times God showed up right on time. It was a 110 degrees on Christmas day. There were hundreds of children awaiting a Christmas party at their centre, theses children included girls that had sold their bodies, bandits, rascals, and children from the village. All had been invited.

The challenge was that they were so many children. But only a limited amount of toy bags available. So I began to give the presents out, first to those children who had never received a present before, Finally, it came down to the older girls. But all that was left was bags of stuffed animals in them.

Heidi asked one of the older girls, "What would you like, sweetheart?"

The girl replied, "Beads."

Heidi's friend and co-worker said, "There is nothing in the bags but old stuffed dogs." Heidi asked her friend to check the bags again, and when the lady reached her hand into the bag of stuffed animals, she started screaming. "Beads! There are beads in the bag!"

All of the girls got beautiful beads for Christmas. God really is God, and he's better than Santa Claus!

Heidi received a prophetic word from a man named Randy Clark. She was told, "The blind will see. The crippled will walk. The dead will be raised from the dead. And the poor will hear the good news of Jesus Christ." This was what happened. People were being healed!

Heidi's belief in God is strong. She believed in miracles and knew that God would show up every time. She only had to ask God for more food for the hungry, or help with the poor and the sick, and a miracle would happen each time. One time, 180 pieces of chicken was not enough to feed all the hungry children. Heidi asked for God's help once again. The chicken multiplied into two thousand pieces of chicken, just like the loaves and fishes that God provided for Jesus to feed the hungry. God provided for Heidi every time.

I ask myself, "Why wasn't this information splashed across our newspapers on our TVs and talked about in the media? Why wasn't it made big news across the world? This woman is creating miracles in front of thousands of witnesses, just like Jesus Christ!"

Wouldn't you think people would want to know? Wouldn't this bring comfort and peace to many millions around the world who suffer, restoring their faith in God? Heidi was interviewed on TV by Oprah Winfrey. You can find it on YouTube, but it didn't get the coverage it greatly deserved. People need to know who Heidi Baker is. They need to find GOD our heavenly father.

After she returned to the mission field in Mozambique, she began praying for the blind. She did not get good results until about a year later. A blind beggar lady came to the church. Heidi was thrilled to pray for her because she wasn't going to give up on the word she'd received from the Lord.

As she prayed for the lady, her eyes began to turn from white to gray, and then to brown. She could see! The next day she prayed for another lady who had been blind since the age of eight; this lady also received her sight. On the third day another lady received her sight despite being born blind.

All three of these women were named Mama Aida. In Mozambique, Heidi's name is also named Mama Aida. Through these healings God opened up Heidi's eyes to see how the bride in the West is blind, poor, and thirsty for God's word. Although she has worked with the poorest of the poor, she says, "I could not understand, and I could not see that people in the Western world were poor and starving, too. They were starving for the things of God. And then God opened my eyes."

What impresses me about this woman is how she turns to every man, woman, and child, telling them all that she loves them. She holds each individual in her arms, hugging them and making them feel loved and very special. After researching the life of Heidi Baker, I couldn't help but wonder, "Is Heidi Baker the second coming and God's special daughter, just like Jesus Christ was?"

When I see Heidi on the screen being interviewed in documentaries, I notice there's something very special about her. She radiates love, and it pours out of her. She beams, she glows, and her eyes are filled with the passion of God. She's not ordinary woman.

Read her book *Compelled by Love,* which is now a film? See what you think and make up your own mind.

I believe Heidi has been sent to our world by God, to save the world and to teach people about love and Jesus Christ. She shows that with the love of God, all things are possible. God is all there is.

I started writing this book in April 2006. It is now May 2014. It was just over eight years in the making. In all that time I have been searching for God, my holy father, and at last I have found him! This is also the reason that our memories are taken away at birth. We have to find God all over again. We all have to find our own spiritual paths.

Believe, and always have faith. Faith is of great significance in the spirit world.

Stephen Sutton

I have to mention Stephen Sutton. What a guy, what a scenario, what a blueprint/contract his life turned out to be. He didn't beat around the bush when deciding how he wanted to help humanity.

Stephen struggled with bowel cancer for four years. He was only nineteen years of age when he died, whilst holding his mother's hand.

Up to now, Stephen has raised five million pounds for cancer charities, and it is still ongoing. Stephen decided to do something with his life, while death was staring him in the face. He became a campaigner raising money for cancer patients.

How courageous despite being in horrendous pain at times; he was never fazed. His story touched people all over the world, not just in this country but everywhere. Donation after donation poured in, bringing out the best in people who were willing to help humanity!

When I see his picture in the media, he pulls at my heart strings. He was so young! Nevertheless, it was what Stephen planned to do before he was born. Mission accomplished Stephen! His mother, Jane, and his family must be so proud of him. The family can be rest assured that Stephen is in no more pain. He is happy and more alive than he's ever been.

Well done, Stephen Sutton, you beautiful soul. What a legacy to leave behind for all humanity!

Introducing the Violet Flame

Many years ago I came across the violet flame by chance. For those of you that don't know of the violet flame; read on as I explain further in the book. It was at a healing centre near where I lived. I found it very interesting as the group in the healing class revealed what they were experiencing at the same time. Some actually saw the violet flame in the centre of the room as they were meditating.

Although I felt impressed by it all, at the time I was busy studying reflexology, angels, and Reiki, so I really didn't have time to study the violet flame. When I look back now, I wasn't supposed to study it then; it wasn't the right time. Now, the violet flame has come to find me. Like I have mentioned before, only when the timing is right will things start to happen.

One day I was thinking everything was lost; my illness was getting worse – so much so that I would pray to God to bring me home, hoping that I wouldn't wake up the next morning. Week after week day after day, some days I would keep falling asleep. In my desperation, I spoke out to God yet again. "What's the point, God? Why am I still here? I've done all I can. I can't even help myself anymore. I need help with everything. I need a miracle Please help me."!

A couple of days later, whilst sat at the computer, I typed in "violet flame" for no particular reason, the search results took me to YouTube. I listened to a few meditations about the violet flame; after trying these sessions, I would feel very relaxed. After about a week very slowly I started to pick up; mostly I felt mentally and spiritually uplifted. Although my body still hurt with the slightest movement; somehow I felt happy.

Something in me was beginning to change. It was that strong feeling that I've experienced before in my soul, simply to feel happy was a bonus. I feel as if I'm finding myself and gaining control of my life. Is it possible that I'm creating my own miracle with the help of God and Saint Germaine of the Violet Flame?

It's early days yet, but I'm going to continue with the meditations every day, I'm seeing such wonderful colours: violet, deep shades of purple, flashes of light gold. They become more and more intense during the meditations, it all feel positive!

By the way, it is all free. It costs you nothing to learn from YouTube. I have chosen Anthony Citro and Da Vid Raphael to assist me with the violet flame. They both have such gentle, relaxing voices as they take you through the meditations and explain the violet flame. I seem to sit comfortably with these two meditation teachers. Although there are many teachers to choose from, Doreen Virtue, the angel lady, also teaches about the violet flame.

I would like to explain to you about the violet flame and how it works. It's not at all complicated, and although it mentions physics, I found it very easy to understand.

The violet flame changes negative energy into positive energy, darkness into light, fate into opportunity. The flame also erases the resultant mistakes of bad karma. Our past actions, both good and bad, do come back to us; this is the law of karma. This impersonal cosmic law decrees that whatever we do comes full circle to our doorsteps for resolution.

In general, most people pay their debts to life and balance their karma by selflessly reaching out and helping others, or by working through misfortunes that come their way, or by passing through diseases or other forms of personal suffering.

But it need not be so with the violet flame! The violet flame is able to transmute or mitigate our negative karma before it comes back to us. On the physical level, the violet flame can help heal our bodies by removing the karma that makes us vulnerable to illness and disease. The real cause of disease is rooted in our mental, emotional, and spiritual state.

How to Use the Violet Flame

The violet flame is practical and easy to use. Find a place where you won't be disturbed. Sit comfortably in a straight chair, with your spine and your head erect, your legs and arms uncrossed, and your feet flat on the floor. Rest your hands on your upper legs with palms facing upwards.

The violet flame is invoked through the decreeing. It is a unique form of spoken prayer, utilizing visualization and meditation. One of the simplest decrees to the violet flame is, "I am a being of violet fire. I am the purity that God desires." Take a few deep, slow breaths at the centre of your heart. Start out slowly, giving the decree with love, devotion, and feeling. Repeat three to nine times to begin with. The more you repeat it, the more it strengthens the power and draws down light.

Once you are familiar with the decree, you can close your eyes while giving it and concentrate on visualising the violet flame. See yourself before a large bonfire about nine feet high and six feet wide. Colour it violet in your imagination and see the flames pulsating and undulating in endless shades of violet, with gradations of purple and pink. Then see yourself stepping into the flame so that the violet flame is where you physically are. See your body as transparent, with the flames curling up from beneath your feet and passing through and around your body.

Often the words of the violet flame decree invokes ideas for other violet flame visualisations. Decreeing is meant to be fun, so be creative and use your imagination. To those who have developed their spiritual sight, the violet flame appears as a physical fire. You may be able to see the violet flame at work with your inner eye by concentrating on the spiritual centre between your eyebrows.

You can also use the violet flame to help family and friends. Visualise the violet flame around them while you give the decree, and add a prayer before you start. The violet flame can also help others of whom you might not be aware. After you have finished decreeing, you can say, "In the name of Christ within me, I ask that this violet flame be multiplied and used to assist all souls on this planet who are in need. I thank you and accept it done, according to the will of God."

Even a few minutes of the violet flame will produce results, but persistence is needed to penetrate age-old habits you would like to change. You can start out with just a few minutes of the violet flame in the morning to help you through the day. You can add the violet flame to whatever your prayers or meditation you currently practice.

One student claimed,

> The violet flame is amazing. It's opened up so many creative areas of my life. It's a science and a great gift from God. It has revolutionized my life in so many ways it as allowed me to realize the real potential of my soul, by bringing me closer to God and my personal mission. On more than one occasion the violet flame as healed me from illnesses, that have afflicted my body especially chronic back pain.
>
> As a surgeon for ten years. I am humbled about learning this science. Practicing this as brought amazing results in my life and my medical practice.
> You can use the violet flame and experience the healing transformation and spiritual up-liftment that alchemist of the spirit have sought for centaury's. But if you want the violet flame to help, you have to work with it, try it.

Remember that whenever you invoke the violet flame with the "I am that I am", the possibilities are endless. The "I am" is a primordial name of God, written in our innermost parts. It was the name God gave to Moses in the burning bush, and it corresponds to the Eastern "Om Tat Sat Om". You can always begin with this beautiful invocation: "In the name of the Christ self and in the name of the living God, I call forth the energies from the sacred fire, from the alter within my heart."

People have no concept of what they photograph into their own bodies and into their worlds by discussing the mistakes and failures of

Daffodil

others. Try to govern that, and demand a picture of that which you want. See the violet flame covering over what you do not want.

Like I mentioned above, there are lots to choose from by going to the Internet, YouTube, books, and CD. Meanwhile, I'm going to carry on with the meditations daily.

Results

It's been two weeks now, since practicing the violet flame; but there has been a big change within me. How will you know if you never try?

I have had more improvements after three weeks: not as tired and lethargic, a feeling of optimism. I notice myself laughing more. I have vivid dreams, I feel connected, and I see more colours and shades of deep purple.

Although I still experience pain in my body, I have managed to halve my pain killers from six a day to three. I expected some discomfort because they are an opiate drug, a derivative from heroin, which my doctor never told me about. I would have taken them for a shorter term if I had known at the time.

I believe the drug was interfering with my heart and slowing me down – hence the tiredness, weakness, and lethargy. I was sleeping all the time. That has all gone now. I'm more alert. Although the withdrawal symptoms are uncomfortable, I must persevere.

I asked for a sign from the spirit world. One morning I suddenly woke up after I was shown a picture of the violet flame burning in my mind's eye, and this gave me great comfort that I was on the right path. I must continue.

June 2014

Two months later, I was in a situation where I missed my V. flame meditation for three days.

I feel so ill, and I look ill. I'm having sweats, as if I'm fighting an infection. There is terrific pain in my back, near my kidneys. Sometimes I feel spaced out, with pains in the top of my head. Is it high blood pressure?

I went to the doctor. I'm not a hypochondriac – honest!

I also took a water sample and told the doctor how I was feeling. The water sample was clear. My blood pressure however was high, at 176/96 when a nurse or doctor takes your blood pressure; if it's high they are supposed to take the best out of three. He didn't. It's not like I was anxious; to be honest, I've gone past caring.

The next morning there was blood in my urine. I had passed a kidney stone during the night. The pain was gone instantly. This has been an ongoing issue with me that still hasn't been resolved for the past three years. I've gotten used to the symptoms. I know my own body and when something isn't right.

The first time it happened, I was brought to A&E. I'd been rolling in agony on the bed for about an hour. I reached out to my mother for help, I also asked the angels. After a while it happened again, the pain went instantly. My mum whispered in my ear, "Go on, get off home. You're okay, it's gone."

Looking at Harry - "Come on, we're going. I'm okay, it's gone. Let's go home." He was furious. I told him what my mum had whispered in my ear, but he wasn't amused. The doctor still hadn't arrived, but we eventually left. L was all right after that.

I have to take large amounts of calcium tablets to counteract the steroids. I am sure this is the cause of the kidney stones. What does one do? My bones are so fragile. There were talks about an operation, if I wanted it. They use laser treatment to blast the kidney stones. This is done through keyhole surgery. The only drawback, the doctor warned me, was that by blasting the stones to smithereens, the bits could scatter and imbed in the rest of my kidneys. *No*, I thought, *I'll give that one a miss*.

I make sure I do my violet flame meditation every day now. It really does work. I still suffer the pain of the RA, but I have lots more energy. The tiredness and lethargy has gone, that alone lifts my spirits. With constant meditation, things can only get better!

***

One day Harry and I went shopping to Barnsley open market one Friday afternoon. I was looking for some nice underwear. A lady behind the counter offered to help me; she looked to be in her late fifties. She kept reaching up to show me some items. I noticed she kept wincing every time she reached up, as if she was in severe pain. "You'll have to excuse me. I pulled something in my back a couple of days ago."

As I made my purchase, I turned to look at her. "What's your name?"
"Yvonne," she replied.
I smiled at her and said, "I'll send you some healing."
"Oh, thank you," she said frowning as she patted me on the back.
I turned to look at Harry he gave me one of those dreaded looks, as if to say, "What a total stranger!"
But do you know, I don't care if people look at me funny and think I'm strange. It's what I'm supposed to do. What I do care about is helping people, and if I can, I will.

I concentrated on Yvonne for two or three nights using the power of the violet flame. It's seems that the violet flame works like an extra power booster, when using it along with absent healing.

Several weeks later we returned to the stall. "Hi. Did you get those items for me?" I asked.
"Err, don't I know you?
Before she could say anymore, I asked, "How's your back?"
Oh, it got better."
I asked, "Was it gradual, or –"
Before I could finish my sentence, she said, "No, it had gone the very next day!" She looked grateful and bewildered.

I was pleased for her. I love it when I get feedback; it encourages and inspires me more. You see, I don't know Yvonne. I don't know whether she is a spiritual woman or believes in the hereafter. Who knows? But that one experience may make her think, *how could that be? How can a person send another person healing just by thoughts?* Like I've said before, thoughts can be very powerful. With the healing guides and angels, and with God's instruction, anything is possible. It may inspire Yvonne to find out more. It's all out there, waiting for us to make a choice.

***

The latest book I read confirmed it all.

Spirit World Wisdom, compiled by "Peter Watson Jenkins and channeled by Toni Ann Winniger. Toni is an amazingly clear channel who is internationally acclaimed for her psychic skills and accuracy.

Every time I choose a book, I always ask the spirit world and my angels for guidance at the time. The author has straight, direct communication with the spirit world. 'You see the information I receive from the spirit world; it's not just for me. It also happens to many other authors. Also through mediums, clairvoyants, etc.

As I began to read the book, all the questions asked by people and all the answers that were given were more or less exactly what I had always thought and had already written in my own book. But I had nothing to confirm it with; all I had was my faith that the information being given from the spirit world was the truth.

I believed in what I was writing 99 per cent of the time, but that 1 per cent of doubt bugged me a bit. *Could I be wrong?*

Can you imagine my excitement as I started reading Toni's book? All way through, page after page, it confirmed that I was right all along. As you know by now, my book was never aimed at ego, financial gain, or fame. All I ever wanted was to complete my mission, get it right, and go home! That is all the reward I need.

I believe that whatever our mission is in this life, if we have chosen a life to help mankind, then once completed, there's no reason for us to stay. This is not where we belong. Like I stated earlier, if there isn't to be a miraculous healing from this devastating RA, then I don't want to remain suffering for the rest of my life. I know my family would agree.

God Help Us

What is happening to our world? The conflict in the Middle East is escalating day by day. I put on my TV and I am heartbroken as I watch the latest update. I cannot believe what I'm seeing. Dreadful scenes of women, children, and babies terrified for their lives going without food and water, with no shelter from the searing heat of the day. Babies are being born in such horrendous conditions. God help them!

God only knows how many innocent human beings on both sides have been slaughtered, because they refuse to change to Sunni or Shia religion. These people are Muslims, yet they are killing one another. No one believes in democracy or freedom. I despair. All I can do is pray to God for this all to end. This world has to change drastically if there is to be any future for humanity.

I came across an appropriate book while all this was going on. I know the angels guided me to this book. It's called *'Face to Face with Jesus'*, authors are Samaa Habib and Bodie Thoene.

Samaa grew up in a strict Islamic family in the Middle East. From an early age, she had a desire to know God. She became a dedicated Muslim as a child. Her life was radically transformed when she encountered the love of Jesus through a dream and a vision in her teenage years.

After her baptism as a Christian believer, she faced persecution on a regular basis, culminating in a terrifying bomb attack on her church fellowship, where she had a near death experience.

She experienced a heavenly face-to-face encounter she had with Jesus. During her experience it left an indelible mark on her life. It ended with

Jesus commissioning her to come back and tell the world he was real and would be coming again soon.

Since that time, Samaa has travelled the world, sharing her incredible testimony of converting from Islam to Christianity. Her inspirational story of God's love, radical forgiveness, reconciliation, and the power of the Holy Spirit is a powerful reminder that we do not serve the God of hatred. **We serve the God of love!** Her life calling is to encourage the church to be an ambassador of Christ's love, to prepare the bride of Christ for the return of the Lord, and to remind us all to live for eternity with heaven's view.

God put Samaa on his earth for a reason. Her mission is to help the poor, repressed people of the Middle East who have been misled for hundreds of thousands of years. They have never known peace, freedom, or harmony. But worst of all, they have never experienced the pure love from our heavenly father, God.

They are not even aware of the story of Jesus Christ and how he suffered on the cross for our sins. All they had been taught; is to fear a God who would condone murder and torture if they didn't comply with Islam.

Today there are 1.6 billion Muslims living on this earth. I don't believe for one instant that a God of love would permit such atrocities to occur, and that he thinks women should have very little rights. There is information on the Internet about Sharia law. Unfortunately, I'm not permitted to enter it into my book from the websites.

What a terrifying regime to live under.

You have no rights – either adhere to Islamic rules or be killed. I feel sorry for these people. I believe the majority live in fear and have no alternative but to obey. Of course they have to protect their families by applying to the Islamic rule.

I can't imagine living in such fear. I'd be traumatised by the rules and regulations for myself, let alone worrying about my family should one of my family members rebel against Islamic rule. I suspect this has happened thousands of times. No human being on earth would want to live under such terrifying circumstances. If you don't have freedom, what's the point of life?

Samma was very brave, knowing the risk to herself and her family. At first her family disowned her. Yet over the coming years, they turned to our loving, heavenly father, and they realised that Samaa was speaking the truth when miracles started to happen.

Samma said that all her young life, she had called out to her faith, wanting to know Allah. Every time she did, no answers came. "Papa, why does Allah not answer me when I call out for help? Why does he not answer my prayers?" she asked. Her father could not answer her.

Then one day she had an opportunity to watch a film about the story of Jesus Christ, which the missionaries had smuggled into the country. After watching the film with some of her friends – risking punishment if they were found out – they were all in tears. That's when Samaa called out to God, and God answered Samaa. This changed her life forever.

Samaa travelled the world, preaching about the real God, Jesus Christ, and all that she had experienced. I believe that every Muslim has the right to read this book and form his or her own opinion.

***

19 August 2014

I wake up to hear about the terrible news of the journalist James Foley. He was beheaded by the Islamic State. In shock, I ask myself how can any human being do this to his fellow man. It was a brutal murder of an innocent man unable to defend himself. He was a journalist doing the best he could.

I ask myself what must have been running through this man's mind as he faced this horrendous consequence.

God bless this man. God bless his soul. My heart goes out to the parents, John and Diana Foley. They said their son has become a martyr for freedom. Yes, he was. It was John's mission to expose what really is going on in these's Islamic countries. It is thought to believe that the man who beheaded John Foley was a British Muslim.

What's wrong with this world? Doesn't anyone want to live in peace anymore? Why can't we all live in peace and harmony?

At the end of the day, we are all human beings we are all the same, with families to raise. Why are we bent on killing one another for the sake of our religious beliefs? There has to be a solution. We can't go on living this way. The First and Second World Wars taught us nothing.

***

In Arizona on 27 August 2014, on a firing range, a nine-year-old girl has accidently shot a gun instructor in the head after he was teaching her how to shoot with a submachine gun. **She is nine years old! I'm outraged to say the least**! This is not the way forward, teaching little children to use deadly weapons.

***

In October 2014 I received my consultation results. My spine is crumbling in the lumber region, I've lost three centimeters in height, and my bone density has deteriorated even more so. "So what happens now?" I asked the consultant.

"Increase the pain killers. Nothing can improve your condition," I already know this; they've done all they can.

I turn to God, my heavenly father. Surely it's time, Lord. Please bring me home. I don't want to suffer anymore.

My Payer Each Night

First I ask for love, healing, peace, joy, happiness, protection, strength, and courage for every man, woman, and child upon this earth, especially the ones who go through adversity and persecution every day. I focus on the Middle East and all the war-torn areas of the world. I ask for peace and harmony and for all of humanity to turn this world around for the better in order to bring about a new beginning.

I offer a prayer to God and the spirit world. I ask for healing and protection for my family and friends. Heavenly father, spirit guides, and angels, can I please have love, peace, healing, joy happiness, protection, strength, and courage for my four sons, Wayne, Darren, Richard, and Michael? Also my seven grandchildren, Emily, Katie, Jason, Christopher, Jordan, Ryan, and Kieran, and my new adopted family Chloe, Lewis, and Henry.

I wish for love, peace, healing, joy, happiness, protection, strength, and courage for my husband, Harry, and my sister, Mary. Also Joanne one and Joanne two, Maria, and Victoria, my future daughters-in-law. For all my relations and friends. To all the names written in my healing book, never to be forgotten.

I offer the same prayers to the animal kingdom, and to stop man's cruelty to all God's creations. Replenish, replenish, replenish. I offer the same prayers for the plant kingdom. Protect the rainforest, the trees, vegetation, and the plants. Replenish, replenish, replenish.

I ask for continues wisdom, guidance, understanding for myself, and as much healing for my body as possible, but only for my highest good.

When I have finished, I feel pressure on my forehead near my third eye. It builds up, getting stronger and stronger, till it seems to explode like a kaleidoscope of pure white healing light, filling my head.

Then I see a white figure start to manifest as an angel, who seems to be on horseback. He reminds me of a warrior. Then he gradually fades away and is gone. I feel that this is me in spirit. This is when I know that God, the angels, and the spirit guides have heard my prayers. All is well.

When I first started to pray every night fourteen years ago, it took a while before I saw anything. The first time I did, I saw lots of colours. Be patient and your prayers will be answered. God bless you all, my brothers and sisters.

The following is a poem I wrote for all the children in the Middle East. It's for all the children worldwide who face adversity and fear every day, and who have never known peace and harmony, only war and conflict and horrendous suffering. But most of all, it's for those who have never experienced love.

Come, Little Children

Come, little children, come unto me.
Place yourself upon my knee;
Let me rock you in my arms
To take away all of life's harms.

Let me wipe away your tears, your fears,
For this was never God's intention,
For his little ones to suffer.
Be rest assured that one day you will be free to know

What it's like to live in peace and harmony,
Where only love and kindness exist.
Once again, safe and warm in your mother's arms,
Where you belong,

One day you will be free to choose whoever you wish to be.
The choices will be yours alone,
For God has a plan for
Each and every one.

So do not despair, my little ones,
For this was God's true intention.
He did ask me to mention
You will be free!

Author Eileen V. Richmond.

O.B.E

When I came to the end of my book, two days later I experienced an OBE. In this experience, it was as if I had left my home and family for a short while. I found myself walking through a large building with high ceilings, like some kind of university. It was enormous. The feeling I had was of great freedom and movement. I felt so light as I moved around. All the heavy feelings that I had experienced in a human body had vanished. I felt so happy and so alive. I couldn't stop smiling as I looked around me.

I saw hundreds of other people of every nationality, all moving around with such ease. Everyone was smiling and friendly towards one another. As I smiled and greeted others, I looked up towards the ceilings and the walls. The shelves were crammed with huge stacks of information all sorts of different books. It was as if I could be whoever I wanted to be, as if I could study any subject I wanted. Everything was available for everyone. I had never felt so happy.

Then in the distance, I saw a group of people heading towards me. There was a girl about twelve year's old running ahead of the group. She wore a double-breasted coat and a woolly winter hat. She was so excited to see me, and her face beamed all the time. She shouted, "We've found you! We've found you!" with such excitement in her voice.

As I looked at her, I reach towards her hat. Pulling her towards me holding her. "Oh! What are you doing here?" I felt a bit disappointed, but it soon disappeared. Everyone couldn't help but feel happy. I said to her, "I'm not coming home just yet. I'm enjoying myself. I've things to do first."

As I lifted my head to look at the rest of the group. It was as if there were two older siblings behind her. I didn't see their faces, but I was aware that one was female and one was male. Then I saw the profile of a young, attractive man with dark hair. My gut feeling straightaway was that it was Harry's soul yet again, in another body!

Then the OBE came to an end. I immediately sat up in bed and noticed it was 3.15 AM. I kept repeating thank-you over and over, as I raised my head. I was so happy; I knew the spirit world were rewarding me for my efforts.

Then I asked myself, "Was the group of people I saw, my family in a past life?" Remember that nothing is ever lost, and our loved ones come to greet us when we pass over. All I can say is that I had a glimpse into a world that awaits us all. You have so much to look forward to.

God bless you all.
Eileen Veronica Richmond.

Nothing exists outside the mind of God.
God is all there is.

The End

Afterword

September 2014

To all the readers who have read this book, you were led by your angels and spirit guides. There was no mistake in you finding this book, no matter how you came across it. In other words, you were meant to read it. It's what you need in your life right now. Your angels and guides are always leading you in the right direction, but it is up to you which course you take.

At last I finally bring my book to a close. It all began in April 2006. What a journey, what a roller coaster. I've learnt so much in the past eight years, especially about myself. I had to experience most of what I wrote before I could write about it – hence the length of time it's taken me. There were times when I laughed, doubted myself, and cried with pure frustration.

However, I always knew I must never give in. I've always had faith, which has kept me going. Faith is a very significant word in the world of spirit.

God had a plan for me, a mission, and now my mission is completed. I did the best I could with all the evidence given to me by the angels and the spirit world. Not only did I write a book, but I found God and the path towards my spiritual journey, which will lead me home one day – sooner rather than later, might I add.

I still have many health problems; the physical side is the worst and can be exhausting on a daily basis. This old body can't take anymore, but my soul is forever young.

Eileen Veronica Richmond

I'm looking forward to being around thirty-ish and having a healthy body. And of course, my amputated leg will be returned to me! I can look forward to visiting the learning temples once again, where we never stop learning.

I have a feeling that I won't be coming back. I feel that this is my last reincarnation on Earth, and this is my reward. My next assignment will be helping others, perhaps in other realms.

I would just like to announce the wedding of my son Wayne, and Joanne. They were both married on 18th July 2014. What a wonderful day it was. Joanne looked stunning in her wedding dress and Wayne looked rather smart too. At least I have seen them married before I leave this earth.

I wish them both a happy healthy contented long life together. I look at my son Wayne sometimes I've never known him look so happy and contented. Joanne has certainly brought out the best in him.

I must also mention my ex daughter in-law Joan whom I have known for thirty years; may we always remain friends. Joan married her partner Mark Britton 4th June 2011. I wish them too; a happy healthy contented long life together.

God bless you all, my brothers and sisters. It's been an absolute pleasure.

Peace and light,
Eileen V. Richmond.

Recommended Books

Alexsander, Eben. *Proof of Heaven.*
Baker, Heidi. *Compelled by Love.*
Brown, Sylvia. *Life on the Other Side.*
Brown, Sylvia. *The Other Side and Back.*
Bullivant, Richard. *Fifteen Real Life Angels Stories.*
Burpo, Todd. *Heaven Is for Real.*
Byrne, Rhonda. *The Power.*
Byrne, Rhonda. *The Secret.*
Cannon, Dolores. *Between Death and Life.*
Davies, Brenda. *Journey of the Soul.*
Dempsy, Marcus. *Alkaline Diet Lose Weight.*
Gavin, Gerry. *Messages from Margaret.*
Habib, Samaa, Bodie Thoene. *Face to Face with God.*
Henrique, Risha. *The Lighted Path.*
Hetland, Leif. *Heaven's Eyes.*
Jones, Helen Parry. *Hands of an Angel.*
Kagen, Annie. *The Afterlife of Billy Fingers.*
Leaf, Caroline. *The Gift in You.*
Levy, Juliette de Bairacli. *Common Herbs for Natural Health.*
Levy, Juliette de Bairacli. *The Complete Herbal Handbook for Cats and Dogs.*
Myss, Caroline. *Sacred Contracts.*
Neale, Mary. *To Heaven and Back.*
Piper, Don. *90 Minutes in Heaven.*
Virtue, Doreen. *Archangels and Ascended Masters.*
Walker, Spiri. *The Divine Source Within.*
Walsch, Neale Donald. *Conversations with God, Book One.*
———. *Conversations with God, Book Two.*
———. *Conversations with God, Book Three.*

Wambach, Helen. *Life before Life.*
Watson, Casey. *Little Prisoners.*
Weiss, Brian. *Many Lives, Many Masters.*
Winninger, Toni Ann, Peter Watson Jenkins. *Spirit World Wisdom.*